how to help your child in

reading, writing and arithmetic

featuring
the
NEW MATH

how to help your child in

READING, WRITING
and ARITHMETIC

By FRIEDA E. VAN ATTA

A Handbook for Parents, Designed to Help Them
Help the Teacher Help Their Children.

LEXICON PUBLICATIONS, INC. • CHICAGO

This book is dedicated to the parents and teachers of America, who share what must be life's most precious responsibility—the education of boys and girls.

FRIEDA E. VAN ATTA

Letter chart, courtesy of the Zane-Bloser Company, Handwriting Publishers, Columbus, Ohio

"Little Finny" from *Happy Times with Sounds* by Lola Merle Thompson, reprinted courtesy of Allyn and Bacon, Inc. Boston, and Lola Merle Thompson

Manufactured in the United States of America

Library of Congress Catalog Card Number: 66–21472

The reading word lists on pp. 9–11 based on the reading lists of READING FOR MEANING SERIES by Paul McKee for Grades 2 and 3 published by Houghton Mifflin Company.

contents

how this book came to be written

WHEN our older daughter was eleven, she went to her father for help in arithmetic. Daddy, pleased that she should come to him rather than to Mother, who is a teacher, took a simple problem in fractions and turned it into a major mathematical production. Using principles of geometry, algebra, finger counting, and a system of numbers worked out for himself in business, he finally arrived at the correct answer. Our daughter listened to his detailed explanations, thanked him for his help, then came to Mother almost in tears. "Miss Bradford doesn't do it Daddy's way," she said. "Mommy, I just don't understand a thing Daddy was talking about."

A short time after this incident, the mother of one of my seventh-graders came to me to ask how she might help her Jimmy, who was having trouble with grammar. When I suggested that she might want to work with him at home in this subject, she hesitated, blushed, then said, "To be perfectly honest, Mrs. Van Atta, I've forgotten every rule of grammar I ever knew. Isn't there a book I could buy to use as a guide?"

Jimmy's mother is one of the many who have approached me in recent years to ask me to recommend a book that might be used as a guide to help their children with school work. Finally, I deliberately set out to find a book that I could honestly recommend to parents. Much to my surprise, I could not find such a book in print. There were many titles that sounded as though they might be exactly what was needed, but after looking them over, I soon learned that most of them were books which dealt with problems of emotional and social development or parent-child relationships. There didn't seem to be a book written specifically to help parents help their children in reading, writing, and arithmetic.

The need for such a book seemed obvious. So many parents today feel inadequate to work with their children when they come for help with school subjects. It is not anything about which to feel ashamed. As one who returned to teaching after many years away from it, I know only too well how much teaching methods and concepts have changed since most parents were in school. The average person, regardless of how much formal education he himself may have had, just isn't equipped to help his child with school work as his teacher would help him. For this reason, many modern educators believe that parents should not attempt to help their children with homework. I have never subscribed to this theory. It is true that a child can become confused if a subject is not explained clearly or if a problem in arithmetic is worked by a method different from that used at school, but I believe with all my heart that any damage done in this way is more than offset by the assurance a child receives when his parents show an active interest in what he is doing and learning at school.

After some encouragement from my husband and a few teacher friends, I finally decided to prepare the sort of book I had in mind. I outlined the project to my publisher, pointing out the need for such a book. He was enthusiastic about the idea and invited me to go ahead with it.

After almost three years of work, the book is finally completed. I must explain that it contains little that originates with me. Compiling the information and putting it into this form has been a challenging, exciting, and frequently frustrating experience. There is not just one approach but many correct approaches to almost any problem in teaching. In those sections of the book where I take a stand on subjects that are highly controversial, even among top educators, I can only say that the opinions expressed are my own, based on my experiences as a parent and upon seventeen years of classroom work.

In checking the curricula followed in the various state and city school systems across the nation, I found many differences in the subject matter taught at the various grade levels, but I also found that there is a great similarity between all modern school systems. The material presented in this book is based upon a composite of many school systems and curricula. The book does not propose to answer every problem in elementary education. It does, I believe, give a good general coverage of kindergarten and the eight grades as they are taught today, with emphasis placed on those basic subjects usually referred to as the three R's.

For help and guidance in the preparation of this book I owe great thanks to the state educational departments of New York, Michigan, Illinois, California, Texas, New Jersey, Pennsylvania and Minnesota; to the city school systems of Chicago, New York, Grand Rapids, Los Angeles, St. Paul, Philadelphia, Atlanta, Houston, Cleveland and Nyack.

how to use this book

As a parent you can have but one purpose in purchasing this book: You are interested in your child's progress in school and you want to help him. The best way to do this, of course, is through intelligent co-operation with his teachers.

This book is never to be used as a check against a teacher or her teaching methods.

Teaching is more an art than a science. While the goal is always the same, each teacher develops her art in an individual and personal way, depending very much upon her own personality and background. One teacher may so completely indulge her students with love and affection that they will strive mightily to please her. Another teacher, completely different in personality and manner, may appear to be a cold and stern taskmaster, yet so obvious is her sense of justice, her eagerness to re-

ward effort, that students perform equally well for her. You can be absolutely certain of one thing: Your child's teacher is interested in him as an individual; she cares deeply about the kind of adult he is to become. If there were not rewards of fulfillment and satisfaction beyond her salary, your child's teacher most likely would be engaged in some other kind of work, because we live in an era when day laborers and students on summer vacations are frequently paid more for a day's work than the average teacher, who must spend years preparing for her profession.

It may come as a surprise to some parents, but there are many areas where the teacher knows a child better than his parents know him. She knows how he reacts when he is on his own, away from home and the critical eyes of father and mother. She knows how he reacts to emergencies, how much he depends upon others to solve his problems; his ability to exercise manners and the social graces as he lives with other boys and girls five days a week. Long before a child's parents may become aware of it, the teacher will recognize emotional disturbances that originate at home. Because his teacher is interested in your child as an individual, she will welcome your interest in his school activities, will tell you honestly where he is strong and where he may need additional help from you at home.

This book is planned to help you help your child in his change from home life to school life. It goes on to help you assist him through kindergarten and the next eight grades of schools. It does this by (a) giving you a picture of what he is doing and what is happening to him in the schoolroom as he faces each new challenge, and (b) pointing out ways in which you, at home, can help him with his school work and with his adjustments at home and school.

Throughout your child's years in school, and this is especially true of the early elementary grades, he will learn according to a set educational plan. Information or ideas new to him are constantly being introduced. Each will be studied briefly, passed over, then returned to again and again. A subject that may be covered in a few paragraphs in this book will take weeks of classroom work to complete. To attempt to use this book on any subject that has not been completely covered in class can only confuse and frustrate your child. The teacher will gladly tell you when your child is presumed to have mastered a given subject and when your help at home can be of most value.

You will see that this book has been prepared by grades, and that each grade has two sections. The first section is directed at the parent, to refresh his memory of school subjects and to offer explanations as a modern teacher would give them before her class. The second section is a workbook to be used by the child, under a parent's guidance, to gain proficiency in those subjects where he may need help. The workbooks, you will note, are generally arranged with the easy problems first. Start with the easy ones, then work through the more difficult problems as your child's confidence grows.

Perhaps an actual example will illustrate how this book can best be used to your child's advantage. At a certain point in the sixth grade your child, we will presume, was taught how to divide fractions. He has now passed on to more complex work which requires him to put to practical use the things he has learned about dividing fractions. His work papers in school show that he regularly gets these problems wrong. When you question him about it, he probably becomes evasive. He will say that he never did understand what the teacher meant when she explained this subject. Perhaps you will use the book to review the subject with him, but you know that he still does not understand division of fractions. Finally, you go to his busy teacher who, you can be quite sure, is well aware of his special problem. She explains to you that your child continually forgets the rule: "To divide fractions, first invert the divisor, then change the division sign to a multiplication sign and continue as in a multiplication problem." She tells you that with careful practice, under your watchful eye, he can soon overcome this difficulty. *Now is the best time to use this book.*

In the Table of Contents, Sixth Grade,

look up and then turn to FRACTIONS—DIVISION OF. Read the entire section, study the examples to refresh your own memory of this subject, then go over it step by step with your child. Be sure that he understands clearly what is meant by the terms "invert" and "divisor." Have him do the examples for you until he can complete them accurately without help. Now turn to the Sixth Grade Workbook, where you will find similar problems to be solved. Give him no more than a few examples to do at any one time. Check them carefully. If he has made mistakes, work those problems with him and show him where he has made his basic mistake. On another day, without previous review, give him another set of examples to do. After he has repeated this routine only a few times, you will, I believe, be rewarded by one of the nicest feelings a teacher can experience: You will find that with just a little of your time and effort, your "student" has mastered a problem that had previously seemed insurmountable to him. He will appreciate your help and interest, because you will have helped him regain his confidence and, possibly, his standing among his classmates. I strongly suspect that your child's teacher will also place you among her "parents I especially respect and admire," because you have made her job easier and shared with her a problem that was of vital interest to one of her students.

If your fourth-grade child is having difficulty keeping up with his class in reading, a special interest on your part is sure to be helpful. You should review the sections on READING in the second and third grades, which he has presumably mastered. You may find that a review of this material will reveal areas in which he still needs help. You can then use the workbooks for these earlier grades to build his readiness for fourth-grade reading. If you can help your child develop proficiency in reading in these early years, he will benefit throughout his life; it is a known fact that once the child learns to read, he will soon read to learn.

Book lists are included at the end of each grade's section on READING. These are books that appeal to *most* children at this particular grade level, but your child will also enjoy many books on the lists for the grade previous and the grade beyond. Always keep in mind that no two children develop at the same rate. If your fourth-grader seems to get greater enjoyment out of books recommended for younger children, do not be alarmed and *do not try to change him*. Just encourage him to read.

There are many systems of grading and preparing report cards throughout the United States, but most of them have one thing in common: They show a child's proficiency in each subject studied. If your child brings home a report card that shows a "less-than-satisfactory" mark in any subject, then is a good time to contact his teacher to determine where he most needs help in that subject.

The best time to help your child in any subject is, of course, when he comes to you and asks for help. Find out his specific problem, or problems, first, then use this book to give him the help he needs.

you and your child in school

Your child is unique, quite unlike any other human being on earth. While he has many things in common with other children his age, he should *never* be compared to them. No two children develop at the same rate;

even children with identical backgrounds develop differently, have different potentials for learning. All children, however, possess special aptitudes and qualities which permit them to excel at something. The secret of successful parenthood, and good teaching, is to find these aptitudes and encourage them. Who is to say that a good mechanic, successful with his hands, fulfilling himself in his work and in his family, is any less successful than a scientist who, with different aptitudes and skills, is exploring the unknown? Both are important. If each is fulfilling his destiny to the very best of his ability, he is a successful human being and a worthy product of our educational system. He is also a tribute to the parents who have let him develop normally, without warping or twisting him into something he was not intended to be.

On the day your child enters kindergarten, he begins an adventure in learning that, under the most favorable circumstances, will continue uninterrupted for at least seventeen years, or the time it usually takes to complete four years of college. Today, when classrooms are filled to overflowing, when teachers are burdened with such heavy teaching loads that individual tutoring is next to impossible, you can be of real help in those early years when the foundation for all his later efforts is being laid.

Aside from helping with specific school problems, here are five important ways in which you can help him generally in those beginning years of study:

See that he gets plenty of nourishing food.

See that he gets plenty of rest. (Between ages 6 and 9, he needs 10 to 12 hours' sleep each night. Between ages 9 and 11, he needs 10 to 11 hours' sleep each night.)

Give your child a feeling of security. He needs your love, confidence, and understanding at home.

Do not overload his workday with too many other activities, such as piano lessons, dancing lessons, clubs, etc. Balance his day with recreation and play.

Show an interest in his school and in all his school activities. Be quick to praise, slow to censure. Remember that our place as parents is to guide and give help and encouragement when it is needed; to help our children fully realize the potential with which they were born.

This book is dedicated to the parents and teachers of America, who share what must be life's most precious responsibility—the education of boys and girls.

FRIEDA E. VAN ATTA

contents | kindergarten

helping your child in kindergarten

YOUR CHILD is about five years old. Take a minute to think what this means. A big change is about to occur in his way of life—and in yours. From now on you'll be sharing him. Others will have an important part in his upbringing.

Until now the rest of the world existed for him only as an extension of this wonderfully secure place he calls home. He went on trips with you to the supermarket, the library, the neighborhood playground, perhaps once or twice to the place where Daddy works, maybe to Grandmother's for Christmas or Thanksgiving, and for short visits to the nearby houses or yards of his little friends.

But most of the time he was close to Mother or Daddy.

Now he is making his first break away from home. He's going to spend half his day, five days a week, in a place different in every way from the place he has known. A place with different walls and floors and furniture. A new place among strangers—one strange adult and a lot of strange children.

For a while the strange adult is going to become the most important person in his life next to Mother and Daddy. The strange children are going to be his closest companions. Here, away from all the people he has known since the day he was born, he is going to start learning to depend on strangers—and on himself.

It is a sober responsibility for your child—and for you.

Actually, in kindergarten there isn't much you can do about "teaching" your child at home. He isn't "taught" even in school, not in the old-fashioned sense of the word. It is the experience he gets at school which is of value to him at this time, "learning by experiencing" how to get along with other people—how to prepare for the "studying grades" which will follow.

His teacher will lead him, gently but surely, in this understanding. Get to know his teacher. She will like to talk with you about your child.

preparing your child for school

Some children start school eagerly. Most start with a great deal of doubt and uncertainty, even if they don't show it! Try to understand the way your child feels about starting school. In the end, the way you feel about it is the way he is going to feel about it. Let him know you sympathize with him. Give him the support he needs at this time.

And *prepare* him.

Start a long time ahead and prepare him for what school is going to be like. Talk with him about it. Make school sound exciting and interesting. In kindergarten your child "learns by playing." So talk about the things he will be doing at school that will be fun.

What are the things *you* liked about school? Tell your child about them. He will enjoy hearing stories about when you were little and went to school. When the moment you leave him there alone comes, he will feel less forlorn, knowing that this is something that happened to you too. The chances are he won't feel forlorn at all, but proud, knowing he is sharing something that happened to you.

Every time you pass by the place where

he will be going to school, point out the building to him. Say something like, "Here's where my big boy (or big girl) is going to school."

Before you know it, *he* will be pointing out the building to you and telling you, "There's *my* schoolhouse."

Make an effort to have him become acquainted with one or more children who will be in his kindergarten class. There shouldn't be too much difficulty about this. If all other ways fail, simply start calling up neighborhood mothers at random. They'll be as glad as you to know that their child will enter his first classroom with the certainty of seeing at least one familiar face among all those new ones. To the child himself it will be more important than you can imagine. Having a friend from the very first day may make all the difference between an early and a late classroom adjustment.

Another helpful thing would be for you and your child to get to know his teacher beforehand. This may not, of course, be feasible. If not, then at least take him to visit the school, and if possible, the particular schoolroom where he will be. Show him where the water fountain is in the hall. If it is running, let him drink out of it. Let him drink six times if he wants to. If he can cling to some little oasis of familiarity, it will help him a lot in his early adjustment.

Make your visit a pleasure. It's a lark; you two together (no reason why Daddy can't get in on this too) having a peek ahead of time at the place where this big little boy or big little girl of yours is going to stay all alone later.

the first day of school

When you arrive with your child at the schoolhouse on that momentous first day, go all the way to his room with him. Let him see you saying a word or two to his teacher.

If he insists on taking something from home with him, let him. A favorite book, teddy bear, doll, fire engine—anything. These first days are special in many ways, and practically anything is all right if it helps him bridge the gap between home and school.

When you have settled him in his own classroom, say good-by, and leave immediately. Don't hesitate, don't linger, just leave. You are more apt not to have trouble if you are firm and matter-of-fact in your attitude. Do not expect trouble and you will be less likely to have it.

In addition to taking him to school, it will add to your child's well-being and keep him from feeling deserted if you let him know that you will be back to get him. And be there on time! *Be there ahead of time.* No matter that there are buses. He can ride home on the bus tomorrow. The first day at school can be very confusing for everybody concerned, including bus drivers. Tensions are bound to build up within your child on his first day in this new place, and when it is over he will want to see somebody he loves *right now*. (You will want to see him too, won't you?)

This is about all there is to it.

The teacher will take over and do the things she knows will make your child feel at home. You might as well be prepared for the fact that occasionally a child does cry at being left alone at school on the first day. But in almost every case this is because he has not been prepared for the experience ahead of time. That is why this book emphasizes the things you can do to make your child's first day at school a pleasurable experience instead of a frightening one. Please go back and review these things if you haven't read them carefully. Your child *can* be prepared to *like* school. But it's something you need to work on.

Now let us have a look at your child's various activities in kindergarten. Let us look first at what he is going to be doing about learning to read.

SUCH READING as your child learns this year is a result of the experiences he is having. He learns to recognize his name on his locker or coat hook, on his chair, or on his handiwork. He will also recognize some street signs, such as

STOP . . . BUS . . . SCHOOL.

He is not yet ready for reading in books. It has been shown again and again that he will learn faster and better in the long run if he is not pushed into it before he is ready. Kindergarten is the period in which your child is *made ready to read*. His interest in reading is whetted. By the end of this year he *wants* to read—and next year in first grade he will make gratifying progress.

Since he can read with understanding only about things he has experienced, this is the age for your child to have many experiences to prepare him for the reading program. His teacher contrives many of these experiences in school. You can help by planning more of these for him at home.

getting your child ready for reading

Here are some of the ways your child's teacher encourages *readiness for reading:*

His teacher, your child, and his classmates all look at many attractive pictures. The names of the objects in the pictures are printed in large letters below, as HORSE . . . DOG . . . Your child's teacher asks the children to identify objects in the pictures. These may be pictures in books, magazines—anything. Your child names colors, shapes, and sizes of things.

His teacher asks the children to "tell the story" they see in a picture.

She also asks them to think of words that sound the same. Your child's natural response to this is with words that rhyme: cat-bat-hat-rat . . . play-hay-stay. . .

Your child may be asked to hear sounds at the beginning of words (tent, turtle, toad, toy, teeth, telephone . . .). From a page full of pictured objects, he may be asked to name those beginning with the same sound.

To prepare your child for the exercise on hearing sounds that are not alike, the teacher starts with animal sounds. (Of course, your child knows that a chicken does not sound like a cow.) There are some good records available to help children identify these sounds, such as "Bozo on the Farm" (Capitol); "Fun on the Farm" (Columbia); "Sounds Around Us" (Scott Foresman).

When he is studying sounds with the other children, your child plays many singing games. In this way he gradually becomes aware of sounds that rhyme, and his memory span increases. These games also give him a good experience in group play, and he loves to do them. Take this old favorite, for example:

"Rock-a-bye baby on the treetop,
When the wind blows, the cradle will rock,
When the bough breaks, the cradle will fall,
Down will come cradle, baby and all "

Before beginning the game, the teacher asks, "Does anyone here have a baby brother or sister at home?" The discussion goes on to how Mother rocks the baby and sings to it. Then the teacher sings a lullaby. She and the children together will notice that *fall* and *all* sound alike, or rhyme. She will sing it again. Those who want to, try it with her. Then all try it. After several trials most of the children will know the song and can sing it while rocking a doll.

The teacher also asks the children to find pages in a book, identifying them by the pictures on the page.

By the end of a year in kindergarten,

where reading readiness is stressed, your child will be able to do an exercise like this:

Teacher's explanation: "From the letter that stands alone, draw a line to the words that start with the same letter."

EXAMPLE:

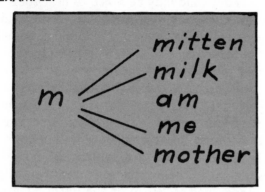

Your child learns the arrangement of things. He learns they have a beginning, a middle, and an end (a book); or a front, a middle, and a back (the piano); or a top, middle, and a bottom (a paint brush); or a first, middle, and last (three children lined up to play train).

The teacher acquaints your child with the left-to-right movement in reading by showing him pictures in a series. She asks him to tell a story from the pictures. (This left-to-right, top-to-bottom business is hard for some children to grasp. By mastering it now, your child is better prepared for reading in the first grade.)

Another way she develops the left-to-right movement of the eyes is by asking him to follow the line the ball makes from the boy's hand,

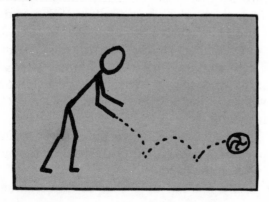

or follow the line of the kite,

or follow the string from the hand to the balloon.

She asks him to find letters that are just "alike" from groups like this:

The meaning of the word *alike* is developed by pictures.

Teacher's directions: Use a red crayon and make both apples look alike. (Mother, the teacher has first colored one apple red. You do it too.)

Which two bananas look alike? (Mother, color two of the bananas yellow before you show the picture to your child.)

▶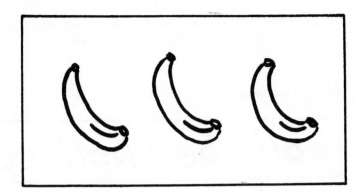

At the same time the meaning of the word *different* is taught.

Find the leaf that is not the same—the different one.

◀

The teacher and children study together the formation of capital letters, picking out the likenesses and differences.

Pick out the letter that is different.

M M N M

In some schools kindergarten children learn to see the differences in small letters.

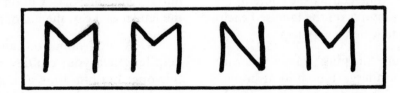

Are these alike?	*a*	*a*
Are these alike?	*d*	*b*
Are these alike?	*c*	*c*

It is not commonly done, but your child may attend a kindergarten where the children go so far as to find likenesses and differences in words.

Pick out the words that look different.

ball · be · ball · call · ball · bad

By the end of the year the teacher has trained your child to hear differences in sounds around him, and in sounds of letters and words; to see differences in shapes and sizes, and colors of objects, and to see differences in printed capital letters; and to move the eyes from left to right, whether it is looking at pictures, reading numbers, or reading a story. He is *made ready for reading.*

how you can help your child get ready to read

These same exercises and many more you can do at home with your child *after* the teacher has begun the work in school. Look at magazines with your child. Watch the billboards when you are on a leisurely drive. Don't miss a chance to take your child with you to the grocery store. Let him identify the contents of the cans by the pictures on the labels. Teach him at least one new item every trip.

Here are some "helping" games you can play with your kindergarten child at home. Perhaps they don't seem to you to have much to do with reading. They do, though. Be patient. *Your child is only five years old! His job* at this age is to *play.* If he can *learn* while playing, fine. The games suggested below help him develop an eye for shapes and sizes and colors. They give him practice in the use of his hands. They develop his judgment. They are an important part of his "readiness-for-reading" program.

1. Give him an assortment of pieces of construction paper cut into squares, stars, circles, rectangles, etc. Ask him to group them according to shape. Afterward he can group them according to color.

2. Give your child pictures you have cut from magazines of foods, heating equipment, clothes, etc. Ask him to tell you in which room of the house each is kept.

3. Again, use pictures from old magazines. Cut off part of each and let your child find the missing parts. Cut off the leg of a cow, the fender of a car, the tail of a horse, etc.

4. A good game you can play at home to help lengthen your child's attention span is this one: Let him look at a group of objects you have placed on a table (for example, a book, a pencil, a flower, a cup, a top, and a lollipop). Let him name them as he looks at them. Now cover them all with a cloth and remove one object. Don't let him see which one you take away. Ask him to name the missing object after you uncover them again.

The next time you play the game use more objects. You can use your own ingenuity to think up other games of this sort. Ask your child to help you think of some.

using a flannel board

An excellent "helping" toy for your child is a flannel board. It can be used to show objects that are "alike" or "different," or to tell stories. It is also useful for arithmetic problems in later grades.

Here is how to make one: Simply cover a breadboard or easel-board with a piece of flannel or felt. Stretch it so it is flat and un-wrinkled, and fasten it securely with thumbtacks or glue. Next, cut squares, circles, strips, rectangles, and triangles in various sizes from other colored pieces of felt or flannel (or pieces of paper with a small piece of flannel pasted to the back). These pieces can be arranged on the flannel board and will stay where they are placed.

or build a man.

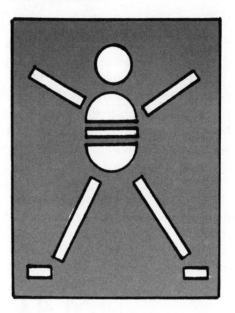

EXAMPLE:

Ask your child to build a wagon

books your kindergarten child may enjoy

Time for Poetry —*Arbuthnot, May Hill*
Sung Under the Silver Umbrella
Told Under the Blue Umbrella
Told Under the Green Umbrella
Told Under the Magic Umbrella
  Association for Childhood Education International
Benjamin Busybody —*Beim, Lorraine and Jerrold*
Pelle's New Suit —*Beskow, Elsa*
Country Noisy Book
Noisy Book
The Seashore Noisy Book
  Brown, Margaret Wise
Read Me Another Story
Read Me More Stories
Read-to-Me Storybook
  Child Study Association of America, Inc.
The Poppy Seed Cakes —*Clark, Margery*
A Tale of Whoa —*Cooke, Muriel and Sherman*
Angus and the Ducks
Ask Mr. Bear
The Story About Ping
  Flack, Marjorie
Seven Diving Ducks —*Friskey, Margaret*

Farmer in the Dell —*Hader, Berta and Elmer*
Bear Twins
Elephant Twins
Giraffe Twins
Kangaroo Twins
  Hogan, Inez
Chimney Corner Stories —*Hutchinson, Veronica*
The Little Auto
The Little Sailboat
The Little Train
Let's Play House
  Lenski, Lois
The Little French Farm —*Lida*
Snipp, Snapp, Snurr and the Red Shoes
  Lindman, Maj. Jan
When We Were Very Young —*Milne, A.A.*
April's Kittens
Mittens —*Newberry, Clare*
Katy No-Pocket —*Payne, Emmy*
The Little Engine That Could —*Piper, Watty*
The Tale of Jemima Puddle-Duck —*Potter, Beatrix*
Billy's Picture —*Rey, Margaret and H.A.*
Chicken World —*Smith, E. Boyd*
Littlest Angel —*Tazewell, Charles*
Saturday Walk —*Wright, Ethel*

IN KINDERGARTEN your child learns to print his own name. This is his first real need for writing. You may already have taught him to do this, using capital letters. But today's schools teach "manuscript" writing from the very beginning because this form of writing (*a*) requires a minimum amount of muscular coördination, (*b*) more nearly resembles the print he will learn to read in books, (*c*) is useful throughout his life, and (*d*) the change to what is called "cursive" writing in the third grade (after his small finger muscles have developed) can be made easily.

EXAMPLES:

printing with capitals— *MARY*

manuscript— *Mary*

cursive— *Mary*

Even copying letters, your kindergarten child may write them backward. He will often make ꓭ for B; ᗡ for D; Ɔ for C. This is a common occurrence, and most children overcome it naturally as eye and finger muscles develop.

ENGLISH

In kindergarten your child is not taught English under that name. Attention *is* given to the way he *talks.* He is helped to use his words in ways that are most easily understood by others. This means the use of the right words, spoken clearly. Every child has trouble with some words. Listen for your child's particular bugaboos and correct him at home. Smile when you do it! At this time you and the teacher can develop good habits, such as "Please" and "Thank you," and you can prevent bad habits such as "ain't" or "huh!"

When you speak to your child, speak slowly and clearly. Be careful not to use words and expressions you would rather he did not use, because he is sure to imitate you. You may not even be aware of those listening ears in the house.

SPELLING

There is no need yet for teaching—or even mentioning—spelling to your child.

EVEN BEFORE he starts kindgarten your child is conscious of numbers. He can tell his age, how many brothers or sisters he has, perhaps his house number and his telephone number. He is sure of one, two, three, or four numbers. Beyond that, if he is like most children, he will probably mention eight, ten, or a million, with no idea of relative size. In kindergarten the meaning of numbers becomes real to him. He learns to count to ten or more and he learns to make the symbols for those numbers which from now on he will call numerals.

concepts

Ideas in general are called **concepts.** They are among the most important parts of kindergarten training.

The idea of **more or less than, thick or thin, narrow or wide, long or short, heavy, faster than, as much as, part of** paves the way to later arithmetic learning.

Your child's teacher stresses the meaning of the concepts *larger* and *smaller*. These concepts are important in paving the way to later arithmetic learning and the words *larger* and *smaller* are taught in association with the ideas. Your child will discover that to make a group larger something must be added to it. To make the group smaller, he must take something away.

Your child is taught the idea of a week's time by answering such questions as:

▶ **What day is today?**
▶ **What day comes after Sunday?**
▶ **What day do you like best?**
▶ **What days does Daddy stay home?**

Your child learns what a **line** is by playing "follow the leader," or being told to stand in a line with the class, or being the first in line or the last. He learns concepts when he hears the teacher say, "Keep in line . . ." "Stand next to . . ." "Stand in front of . . ." "Get behind . . ." The first few times the teacher uses these words she demonstrates what is meant.

He learns what a **row** is by the arrangement of chairs in the room. The teacher asks him to sit in the front row, then the back row, or the middle row.

He learns what **steps** are, what it means to step forward, backward, to one side, to take giant steps, and baby steps. The teacher demonstrates this.

In the field of vertical lines he gets the idea of **up, down, above,** and **below.** He learns about **high** and **low.** This can be taught with reference to the floors in a building. He learns the concept of **top, middle,** and **bottom.**

In flat shapes, he learns that circles are round, squares have corners and sides, triangles have a point on top, sides, and a bottom. He learns the difference between squares and rectangles.

In numbers of things he becomes aware of **many** or **few, as many as, more than, not as many as, some, none, all, everyone, less,** or **more.**

In size, he learns **big** or **little, large** or **small, long** or **short.**

In colors, he learns to recognize red, yellow, blue, black, and brown. He may even learn to recognize green, orange, and purple.

the new math

New and different things are constantly being introduced in schools in order to keep up with today's rapidly changing world. That does not mean that the facts we parents learned are no longer true or useful. Your child will learn what we did. In addition, he will be given an opportunity to discover many new things.

More ideas and topics are being included now than were necessary a few years ago.

"New mathematics," as the term is popularly used, is a way of teaching the old established facts, as well as the new ones, to your child so that he will understand *why* they are true. If he understands the basic principles of mathematics, he will be able to apply them to situations he encounters in his future life.

Your child today is learning by active participation in classroom activities rather than by memorization of facts as presented by the teacher. He is learning through discovery. He may be asked to place any 2 objects on his desk, and then place 2 more objects on the desk. He will *discover* that there are 4 objects on his desk or that $2 + 2 = 4$.

In the same way he may remove 2 objects and *discover* that by taking 2 objects away from 4 objects he has 2 objects or $4 - 2 = 2$.

This modern method of teaching and learning is meaningful, dynamic, and exciting. To your child it is like playing a game. To play the game with other children, he must call things by their correct names. The new terminology used in mathematics today makes it sound different and strange to us, but remember that the basic facts remain unchanged.

Because of the new approach to much that your child is taught today, he can learn more mathematical concepts than a kindergarten child did a few years ago. Children are anxious to learn and move forward quickly and with eager anticipation if they are having fun during the learning process. The modern mathematics has proven to be fun for most children.

sets

Your child is introduced to the meaning of the word **set,** a term which will be used very often through all of his work in elementary and high school mathematics.

A set is a number of objects. One object can make up a set. A set can be said to be a family of things. They may be all alike, or they may not be. After all, the members of a family of people are not all alike but they are a group that have something in common—they all live in the same house. A set might be composed of objects in the sky (bird, plane, balloon) or objects that a person wears (hat, shoes, coat, gloves).

EXAMPLE: Draw a picture of all the men and boys in your family.

Answer:

This is Daddy and Billy.

Draw a circle around our two men.
Now draw a picture of all the girls and ladies in your family.

Answer:

This is Mommy and me.

Draw a circle around these two girls. Now can you tell me how many people there are in your family?

Answer:

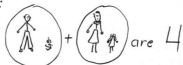

The set of men and the set of women together makes 4 people.

It soon becomes natural for your child to call a related group of objects a set. You can help him by using the term at home. The dishes on the table are a set, the things that grow in the garden are a set, the objects in a drawer are a set.

When there are an equal number of objects in each set, they are called **equivalent sets.** Accept your child's use of this new word easily and it won't bother him a bit. He added equivalent sets when he showed his teacher how many people there are in his family. There is one boy for each girl, with none left over. When one-to-one matching is possible, the sets are equivalent.

When your child is faced with sets that are not equivalent, he will be asked to think of ways in which to make them equivalent. A flannel board is an excellent tool to use in teaching this concept.

EXAMPLE: Place objects on the flannel board.

Are these sets equivalent?   *Answer:* No.

How can you make them equivalent?

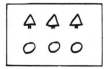

Answer 1: I can put up another ball.

Answer 2: I can take off one tree.

Both answers are correct. Your child has been encouraged to think for himself.

numbers and numerals

Your child will learn the difference between the meaning of the words **number** and **numeral.**

Number means how many objects there are in the set.

EXAMPLE:

There are three objects in this set.

EXAMPLE:

There is one object in this set.

Numeral is the sign or symbol used to name the number.

EXAMPLE:

When there are three objects, we write the numeral 3.

EXAMPLE:

When there is one object, we write the numeral 1.

number line

Your child extends the meaning of the word *line* by actually making and working with a **number line.** It is simply a straight line connecting two points. He will draw it himself or use a ruler to represent his number line. The number line must be divided into equal spaces which are named by numerals. It starts with 0, which means "not any."

EXAMPLE:

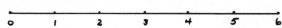

By starting at point 0 and moving to the right, your child learns the meaning of addition.

EXAMPLE: Problem: Add 2 and 2.

Method: Your child places a marker, such as a block, at point 0 and moves it as far as the first numeral tells him (2 spaces). The second numeral in the problem tells him to move his marker over 2 more spaces. This brings his block to the point named 4 and tells your child that 2 spaces and 2 spaces are 4 spaces. He has actually done the work of solving the problem himself and has discovered the answer.

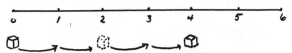

In the same way your child uses a number line to learn subtraction or how to make a number smaller than it was. He places his block at the point called 4 and marked by the numeral 4. Then by moving the block backward 2 spaces, he discovers that there are only 2 spaces left or that 2 from 4 are 2.

EXAMPLE:

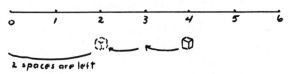

2 spaces are left

Your child's teacher will use many games to give him practice in using modern mathematics. You can join him in using the work book section of this chapter. Use it for practice after the new concepts have been taught in school. Your child will show you how much fun new math can be and how easy it really is.

23

workbook   kindergarten

reading exercises

Exercises for ear training.   Read these poems to your child until he (1) is aware of the sounds, and (2) can make the sounds himself. Let him find pictures of the things mentioned in the poems.

THE FARMYARD

The cock is crowing,
The cow is lowing,
The ducks are quacking,
The dogs are barking,
The donkey's braying,
The horse is neighing—
Was there ever such a noise?

The birds are singing,
The bell is ringing,
The pigs are squealing,
The barn door's creaking,
The brook is babbling,
The geese are gabbling—
Mercy on us, what a noise!

BOW WOW, SAYS THE DOG

Bow wow, says the dog;
Mew, mew, says the cat;
Grunt, grunt, goes the hog;
And squeak, says the rat.
To-whu, says the owl;
Caw, caw, goes the crow;
Quack, quack, goes the duck;
And moo, says the cow.

I SAW A SHIP A-SAILING

I saw a ship a-sailing,
A-sailing on the sea;
And, oh! it was all laden
With pretty things for thee!

There were comfits in the cabin,
And apples in the hold;
The sails were made of silk,
And the masts were made of gold.

THE MUFFIN MAN

O do you know the muffin man,
The muffin man, the muffin man,
O do you know the muffin man,
That lives in Drury Lane?

O yes, I know the muffin man,
The muffin man, the muffin man,
O yes, I know the muffin man,
That lives in Drury Lane.

BETTY BOTTER

Betty Botter bought some butter,
But she said, "This butter's bitter.
If I put the bitter butter in my batter,
It will make my batter bitter."

PETER, PETER

Peter, Peter, pumpkin eater
Had a wife and couldn't keep her;
He put her in a pumpkin shell,
And there he kept her very well.

LITTLE FINNY

A farmer found a funny fat fish in the lake. The funny fat fish had four little fine fins. Now this was the first funny fat fish the farmer had ever found in this lake.

"What shall I do with my find?" said the farmer. "I have it," said he. "I'll take it home to my five fine children, Fanny, Felicia, Faith, Fernando, and Fidelia."

And so to this very day, Fanny, Felicia, Faith, Fernando, and Fidelia watch Finny, the funny fat fish, with the four little fine fins, swimming around in its fancy bowl.

I. **Make these pictures look alike.**

II. Which is the different one?

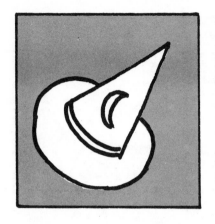  

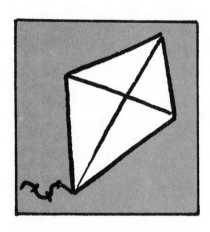 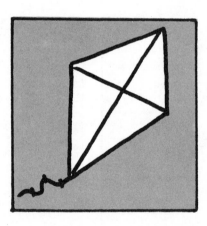 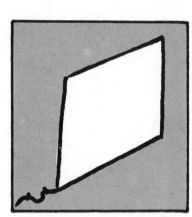

III. Which is the larger one?

IV. Color the circles red.
Color the squares green.
Color the triangles blue.
Color the rectangles yellow.

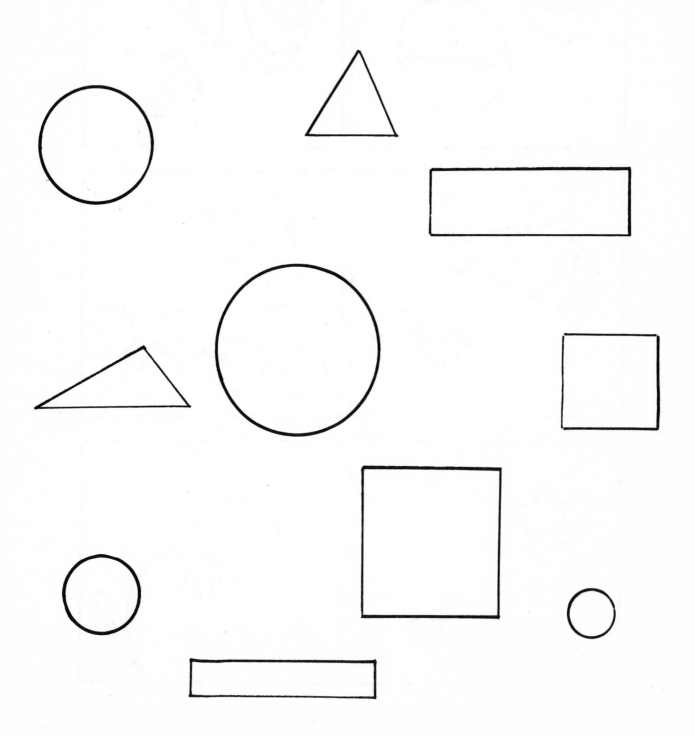

V. Color the circular shapes red.
Color the square shapes green.

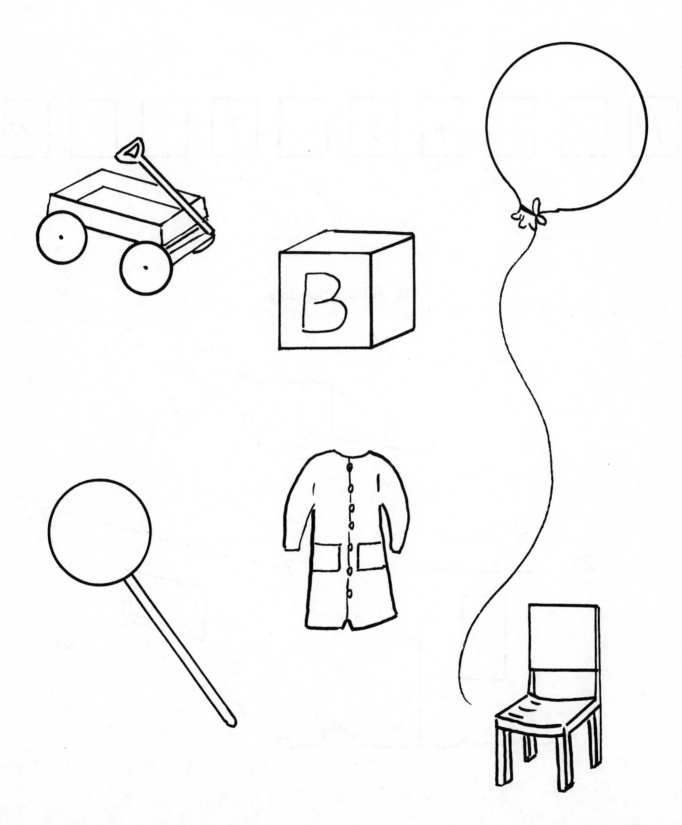

VI. Fill in the missing numbers so they are in their natural order.

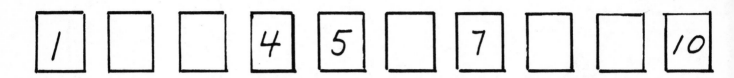

| 1 | | | 4 | 5 | | 7 | | | 10 |

VII. Follow the dots.

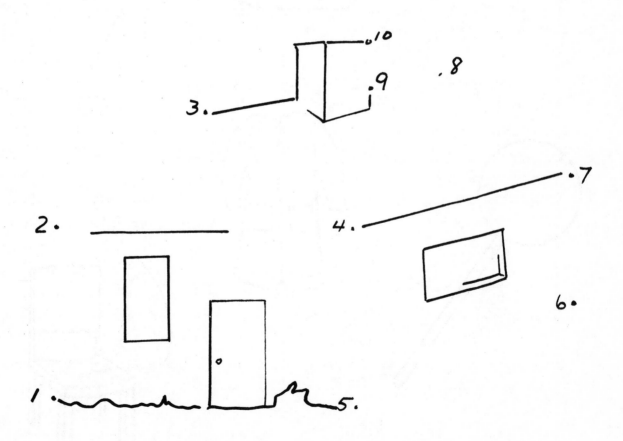

VIII. Write the numeral that shows the number in each set.

IX. Make these sets equivalent.

By adding   *By subtracting*

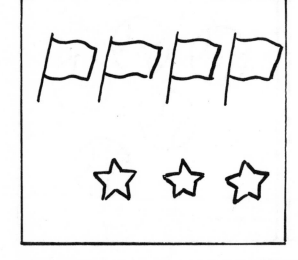

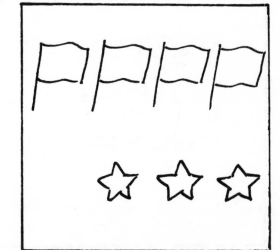

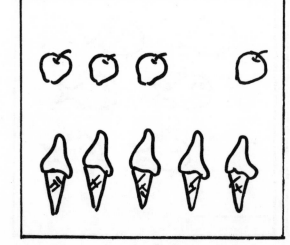

X. Change the sets to match the number named by the numeral.

XI. Put an X on the set that is larger.

XII. Put an X on the object that is

in the middle

the small one

the short one

on the bottom

on the top

35

contents | first grade

helping your child in first grade

YOUR CHILD is now about six years old. First grade is a big, big step for your child, and you will need to continue the same kind of understanding and sympathetic help at home that you gave him when he was in kindergarten. One word of caution: Don't expect your child of six to be simply a bigger five-year-old. He is more than this. Though he still depends on you for support and understanding at home, his experiences in kindergarten have changed him in more ways than you might believe. Watch him closely. Think about how he was last year at this time. You will realize how much he has changed.

a world away from mother

This change is good. It is the whole reason for kindergarten, where he was given his first real look at the world outside his home; a world away from Mother and Daddy, his pets and his toys, the familiar walls and floors; a strange and sometimes frightening world in which he must learn to depend upon other people—and upon himself.

During his kindergarten year his teacher worked constantly to help him become adjusted to the school environment. It was a time of *learning to live away from home;* of getting ready for the workaday school world of reading, writing, and arithmetic—and science, health and safety, arts and crafts and music.

All this is the world he faces in first grade. As my own Gretchen expressed it, earnestly, importantly, after a week or so in first grade, "Kindergarten was a *playing* school, Mommy. First grade is a *working* school. We *study* things, just like the big kids do."

And perhaps that sums it up. When your child enters first grade, his eyes are open, however slightly, to the complexity of the grown-up world. Kindergarten has done this for him. It has advanced him a step in maturity. It has taught him things about sharing, about taking turns, about being fair. Your child feels easier now in the natural give and take with other people—both children and grownups.

At the same time he will feel very uncertain. He will have many fears. He may not tell you what they are—in fact, he is almost certain not to. They are too awesome, some of them, for him even to mention. These fears and anxieties will continue in some degree throughout his first-grade year, and perhaps even into his second. They will generally have to do with four things:

    a) his relations with his teacher,
    b) his relations with the other children,
    c) his "studies,"
    d) his physical surroundings—all the "things" about his schoolroom, his school, the schoolyard, and his trips between school and home.

Here is how you can help your child most at this time: Be patient. In spite of all your housework and everything else, you have more time with him at home than his teacher can possibly have, what with her fifteen other little youngsters—or is it thirty in your school!

Be patient. In that way you will find out most of the little things that trouble him— little things for you, perhaps, but *big* things for him. His teacher will be glad to talk with you about them in his interest. Keep remembering this is a very important year for your child. You can see how important it is because the adjustment he makes to first grade is likely to set the pattern for his behavior in all his school years to come.

Here is a list of things that will be expected of your child when he starts first grade. You can help him to be prepared. He is expected to:

- ► **Give his name, his parents' name, address, and phone number.**
- ► **Put on and take off his boots and outdoor clothing.**
- ► **Hang his things up carefully.**
- ► **Go to the bathroom alone.**
- ► **Lace his shoes and tie a bow.**
- ► **Speak distinctly.**
- ► **Listen to stories and look at pictures.**
- ► **Be polite and courteous (within reason).**
- ► **Follow as well as lead.**
- ► **Do things for himself.**
- ► **Use a telephone.**

learning is started slowly

Your first-grader is not pressed to "start learning." His attention span is still short. Remember, six years old is still pretty young! So it is important—both at school and at home—not to push him beyond his capacity, or even beyond his interest. (He is not *pushed* into learning at any time; he is guided.) If you push him, if you make him anxious, you will set him back more than you could possibly advance him.

Be content that the learning in school will start slowly. At first it may not seem too different—to you or to him—from kindergarten. But in this grade habits of "wanting to know" are being seeded all the time. His interest in new things is being stimulated.

His teacher is trained to sound out his *readiness for learning* in any particular area, and you may be sure that before the year is out your child will have made a secure beginning with reading, with writing, and with arithmetic. Some children move faster in one subject and some in another. Often the one who starts slowly will finish fast. But that isn't the important thing. How well he learns and the pleasure he gets from learning will count more in the long run than the speed with which he learns.

The moment of greatest pride in your six-year-old's life is when he brings home his primer and reads to you. We hope that you will not criticize any errors at this moment of triumph. Don't expect too much too soon. Considering that he starts with so little knowledge, the amount your child learns in first grade is really remarkable. It will seem that only too suddenly this eager-faced youngster of yours who was kicking his feet in his crib such a short time ago will be pressing against your side, reading words in your book. He will add numbers and subtract numbers and count almost as fast as you can. This is only the beginning. You will find yourself marveling at how much new knowledge he can absorb.

how you can help your child

Actually at this stage there isn't too much you can do at home to help your child meet the new challenges of school. This is the teacher's job. She is skilled at it, and what she does with your child at school could not be accomplished at home. There are things you *can* do though. First, you can help your child greatly by insuring the kind of home atmosphere that puts him in the frame of mind to benefit from his school experience.

Show an interest in what he is doing there—not just once in a while, but every day as soon as he comes home. Listen when he talks to you, really listen. It takes only a minute or two of your time, if that's all you should have to spend. Give him these moments of feeling important.

Review things with him. This book is designed in great detail to help you do just that—to review things with your child *after* he has been introduced to them in school. You will soon discover where he needs special help, and then you can use the sections in this book which will aid him.

A child has such bright and wonderful imagination and curiosity. Don't let them die. Keep them alive with new suggestions that spring from what he is doing in school. It will help you to share many precious moments of discovery with your child. There will be heartfelt times when you are very proud of him. When you are, tell him!

IN MOST school systems your child will have covered at least three books before he has finished the first grade: a pre-primer, a primer, and a first reader. Remember, before your child learned to walk, he crawled; and before he learns to read, he will spend a lot of time in "play-work" activities such as matching letters and words, and listening to good reading. Every day his class hears new stories and reviews old ones. Very quickly he will want to start telling you his favorite stories. He will start to originate stories, and to report happenings in their proper order, and to memorize some of the poems he likes. Listen to him and encourage him in these activities. Such attention from you will add to his self-assurance. Try not to give up the bedtime story hour until he reaches the stage where he would rather read a story for himself.

Here are some of the things you might watch for in your child. They indicate a readiness to begin to read.

▶ **Can he follow the development of a story?**
▶ **Can he find words with the same beginning sounds?**
▶ **Is he alert and interested in his surroundings?**
▶ **Can he interpret (tell about) pictures?**
▶ **Is he eager to learn about things?**
▶ **Is he developing *some* control over his emotions?**
▶ **Does he like to express himself in imaginative ways?**
▶ **Can he follow directions well?**
▶ **Does he like to dramatize stories?**
▶ **Does he like to tell about experiences at school?**
▶ **Can he recognize some printed names and picture book titles?**

matching letters and words

After enough of the "play-work" activities, when your child is nearly ready to read, he begins to handle and appreciate books, and turns pages carefully; he looks at words and sentences and picture stories from left to right, and from the top of the page to the bottom; he realizes that reading can be fun.

Before he can be expected to recognize many words, however, he must be helped to see the difference in the shapes of letters. He does a good deal of this *letter-recognition* work at school, and you can help him do some of it at home if he would like to, or if you think it would help him gain skill or confidence in himself.

EXAMPLE: **Draw letters as illustrated.**

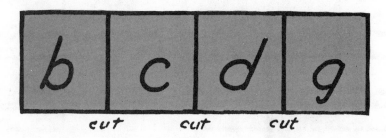

Ask your child to cut them apart and paste each one beside another letter that looks just like it.

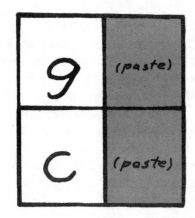

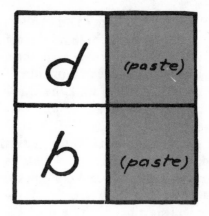

His teacher always calls the letter by name. Your child probably remembers most of them from kindergarten days.

It isn't long before you can ask him to match words that look alike:

Next he can match pictures to words.

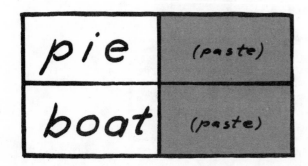

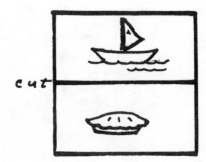

When he automatically recognizes these words, give him simple directions to follow, such as:

Make 3 pies
Make 2 boats

He will enjoy working on these exercises. They give him an outlet for doing things with his hands, so necessary at this age—and he is learning at the same time.

While he matches and identifies letters, words and pictures, he should name them with your help. It soon becomes natural for him to say "buh" for the letter *b,* whether it is at the beginning of the word "boat," or "baby," or "bead."

Here is a typical reading exercise in "matching" that may be given your school child at about the second month of the first grade. Of course, directions are given carefully by the teacher, and she works closely with him. Ask your child about these "matching" exercises. He is almost certain to find it enjoyable and helpful to do similar exercises with you at home. Daddy can get in on this too! In fact, nearly everything that is said in this book about ways you can help your child at home is directed to both parents. A child needs two parents! He needs them to spend *time* with him. And neither can quite make up for the other.

A sample exercise follows. You can make a similar list of words that are familiar—or should be familiar—to your child. Then make simple unpretentious drawings, and let him match words to the pictures. If you can't remember how to make—well, say a cow—let your child show you!

pail	cake	coat	cut
plate	toad	Joe	cut
pole	Jane	stone	

cut   cut

paste words under pictures

(paste)	(paste)	(paste)

(paste)	(paste)	(paste)

(paste)	(paste)	(paste)

All this time the teacher is introducing your child to the meanings of many of the words he will meet later when he starts to read. He has the kind of practice every day that helps him to see likenesses and differences in pictures and in sounds of words.

His teacher does many special things to increase his desire to read. For instance, she may take the children on a trip to the home of a classmate who lives on a farm. When they return to the classroom, they talk about the trip.

The teacher writes on a blackboard or puts on a chart the story of the trip as dictated by your child and his classmates.

EXAMPLE:

I saw a cow.

The cow eats corn.

The cow gives milk.

With these sentences before them, the children find pictures of cows feeding and of cows being milked. Their pictures illustrate their sentences.

They will match sentences and words in their books with those on the "experience chart" the teacher has made. They will find new words that tell about cows, such as "The cow says 'moo'" or "The cow is black and white."

When your child begins these matching exercises at school, let him continue them at home. When he makes a mistake, don't hesitate to correct him. Tell him what a word says if he asks you.

An ideal gift for a midyear first-grader would be an empty scrapbook, an envelope full of pictures of familiar objects (preferably those he has already seen in school), and another envelope full of the printed names of these objects. Let him assemble them. He will love it.

phonics

Phonics is the system of learning letters and combinations of letters by the sounds they make. By first finding individual sounds, and then putting those sounds together, the child can read words.

EXAMPLE: Read **cow.**
First think, c sounds like *k;*
Then think, ow is the sound I make when I hurt myself.
Then cow must be *kow.*

By the time he is ready for the first primer, your child can recognize at least twenty-five words by sight. These words are constantly repeated in his class, with a new word introduced every two or three days. Your child can also recognize most of the letters by sound. Learning to read must of necessity be a combination of phonics and the sight system. All systems are good if presented intelligently. The end result is the same.

Phonics is the key to pronunciation, but seldom the key to meaning. Simply saying the names of words is not reading. The main goal is reading with understanding.

The majority of public, private, and parochial schools recognize the importance and necessity of phonics in the teaching of reading. It is an aid in developing better speech, and in learning to spell. However, phonics alone will not do the job—much of our English spelling is not phonetic. There are so many rules and contradictions which make a purely phonetic system impractical! For example, there are *seven* different sounds represented by *o-u-g-h*—bough, cough, hiccough, rough, though, thought, through.

However, remember that your child's first introduction to printed words and letters was the sound of them. This gave him a tool with which to work and which he will use the rest of his life. Whether it is taught by sight or by sound, he will learn that *ph* is always pronounced *f.*

To help him at home as he tries to read, don't let him forget his first exercises in sound differences. Ask him to "sound out" his words before you tell him what they are.

Encourage him to do a lot of reading at home. It takes much practice to become a good reader, just as learning to play the piano requires much time and patience and practice.

Above all, in helping him at home don't forget *why* your child is learning to read. Discuss the subject matter with him. Ask him about it. This is what the teacher does in school. Being able to talk about it stimulates his imagination, helps to clear up any questions, and makes him want to read more and more.

different teaching methods

From the beginning classes are divided into reading groups to meet the needs of each child. Those who need more "readiness" exercises are grouped together. Those who have not yet reached the point where they want to read are kept together. They are constantly encouraged, but actual reading is deferred until such time as the teacher feels they are ready to begin. This group, incidentally, often overtakes the group that started first.

There are a few school systems where reading in the first two grades is limited to what is picked up through the children's experiences; formal reading classes are not actually begun until the third grade. It has been proved that by the time children reach the fifth grade it is difficult to determine under which system their reading was begun. It can be determined, however, whether your child was well taught or not and whether he has been encouraged to develop good reading habits by his brothers and sisters and his parents at home.

your child's first reading book

The first books your child will read are based on familiar experiences. They are about the people, animals, and objects he knows— father, mother, teacher, brother, sister, dog, cat, ball. . . . When he brings his books home to read to you, be a good listener. Help him promptly with words that trip him. Praise him highly. And pay attention—even if he's only reading, "Look, Tom, look. See me go. See me go, Tom." You want to help him learn, so don't discourage him by trying to watch TV or read your magazine while he is reading. *You* wouldn't like it if he did that to you!

On the other hand, don't watch him with an intent stare, waiting to pounce on any trifling mistake he might make. It's enough to make anybody stumble if people are listening critically to every word and syllable being read. But if your child can get the idea that you are listening to find out what happens in the story, he'll be relaxed about it. He will feel good about being the one to bring you this reading pleasure. Most important of all, he will get the idea that this is the way people find out lots of interesting things—by reading. And then he will have a good reason for *wanting* to read.

Remember that *all the rest of your child's learning is based on his ability to read,* and that the foundation for this is built in the first grade. Help him discover the wonders in the world of books. Constantly encourage him and give him a feeling of confidence in his ability to read. Work closely with his teacher —know her; let her know you. This teamwork will have its rewards in his better adjustment to all his schoolwork.

After he has begun to read sentences from a book, a good home reading exercise is this: Print (in manuscript) on a card, a simple complete sentence from his book. After he reads it, cut it into words, and let him put it together again.

To develop the idea of a complete sentence, let him identify the "who" (cow) and the "what" (barn) each time.

how your child's reading develops

After your child has mastered his primers and first reader, these are some of the things you may expect from him. He will:

▶ Read without pointing.
▶ Read the conversation in a story as though he were the person speaking.
▶ Sum up short units in his own words.
▶ Distinguish between "telling" and "asking" sentences.
▶ Work independently.
▶ Have a reading vocabulary of 400 words or more.
▶ Know well the sounds of all single consonants.
▶ Know these five vowels and the changes they make:

a	as in	ate	a	as in	at
e	as in	eat	e	as in	bed
i	as in	hide	i	as in	hid
o	as in	oak	o	as in	on
u	as in	use	u	as in	us

▶ Know the sounds of most of the following combinations:

ay	al	ou	igh	sw
ar	all	ew	old	sh
or, ore	aw	ind	st	ch
er	au	ild	str	th
ur	ow	ing	sl	wh

Encourage your child's feeling of sureness in reading by giving him books within his reading range. Some appropriate titles are listed at the end of this section.

home reading games

When you help your child at home, help him as his teacher does in school. If you do it differently, you will only confuse him and very probably set him back more than you will advance him. Here are eight different suggestions for helping your child with his reading, all in harmony with modern teaching methods:

EXAMPLE:

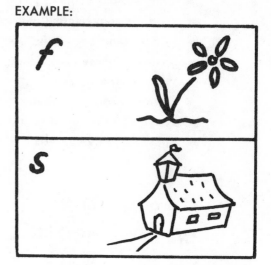

1. Help him keep a scrapbook of pictures of objects that start with the letter being studied at the time.

2. Make a similar book of all new words learned. Use pictures to illustrate.

EXAMPLE:

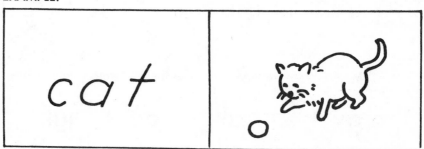

3. There is a game called "Finders" which is played like Bingo. Guide your child in his efforts to make such a game. Then play it with the whole family. It is simple to construct and easy to play. Your child will enjoy both the making and the playing. He will profit from it too.

You remember how Bingo goes. It's the same with "Finders":

    Each player has a different master card marked off into twenty-five squares. A word is printed in each square—one of the words your child is learning in school. Each word is printed again on a small card.

    To play the game, mix up the small cards and put them in a pile, face down. Each person, in turn, draws a card and shows it. The child—or the adult—with that word on his master card, raises his hand, pronounces the word, points to it on his master card, and covers it with the card that he has just drawn. The person who has five words covered in any direction wins.

Write the words in pencil so they can be changed from time to time as new words are learned in school.

EXAMPLE:

cow	car	pole	egg	mother
sing	for	tail	coat	eagle
boat	lamb	wood	carrot	pencil
turtle	head	green	shell	write
bark	meat	bee	night	milk

(Make at least four different large cards.)   (Make from 35 to 50 small cards.)

4. *Rhyming game.* Play it while you are doing the dishes together. It goes this way:

Here is Bill.

He lives on a _____ (hill)

He likes to sit on the _____

(window sill)

You and your child can make up your own rhymes, silly or not—sometimes the sillier, the better!

5. All our reading is done from left to right. Your child's eyes must be trained to do this. To develop the left-to-right pattern, add features one at a time until the man (or animal, or object) is completed.

EXAMPLE:

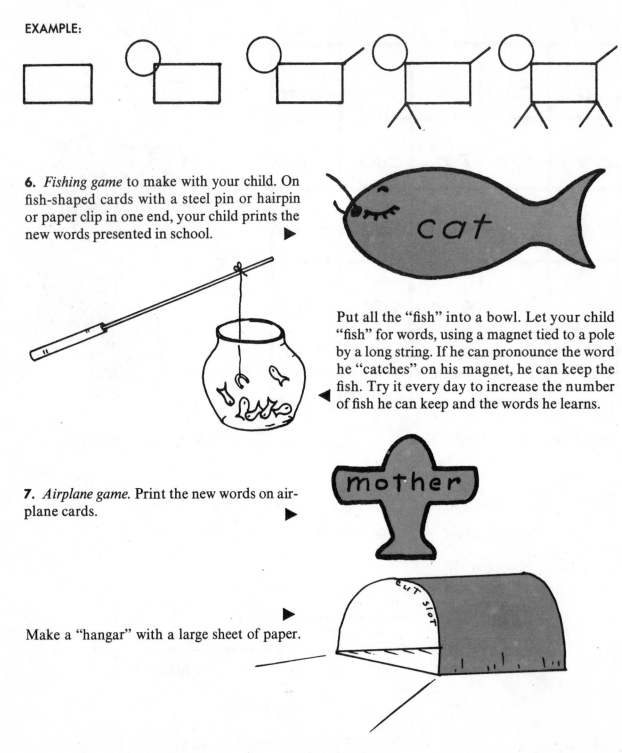

6. *Fishing game* to make with your child. On fish-shaped cards with a steel pin or hairpin or paper clip in one end, your child prints the new words presented in school. ▶

Put all the "fish" into a bowl. Let your child "fish" for words, using a magnet tied to a pole by a long string. If he can pronounce the word he "catches" on his magnet, he can keep the fish. Try it every day to increase the number of fish he can keep and the words he learns.

7. *Airplane game.* Print the new words on airplane cards. ▶

Make a "hangar" with a large sheet of paper. ▶

If your child can pronounce the word, he may put it into the hangar. If more than one child is playing, the child who gets all his cards into the hangar is "the best" safe pilot.

50

8. If your child has trouble identifying sounds, these ideas may help you:

wh	What sound do you make when you blow out a candle?
r	What sound does the lion make when he roars?
sh	What sound does Mother make when she doesn't want you to wake Daddy?
ch	What sound do you make when you sneeze?
ow	What sound do you make when you hurt yourself?
oo	What sound does the wind make when it blows around the house?
gr	What sound does a dog make when he growls?
m	What sound do you make when you eat something very good?

These are just a few of the ways in which you can help your child at home with his reading. You—or you and your child together—will think of other ways. Never hesitate to talk over with his teacher any problem that bothers you.

An excellent, attractive monthly magazine your child will enjoy very much is *Highlights,* published by Highlights for Children, Inc., P. O. Box 269, Columbus, Ohio. It contains stories and features, and many "Things to Do," all with much educational value. The *Children's Digest,* published by *Parents' Magazine,* is good, and there are others. Your child will look forward with pleasure to receiving his own mail each month. In using the magazine he will be developing basic skills and knowledge, and he will be learning to think. His interest in other people and other things will be stimulated. His desire to read more will grow.

BEFORE YOUR child has finished first grade, he will be able to print his own name; he will use capitals at the beginning of proper names, at the beginning of a sentence, and in writing the word *I;* he will print simple sentences and print his own tags: "To Mother . . . To Daddy."

But please don't be impatient with him about his writing or try to force his progress. As in reading, progress comes slowly at first. Before he can write words and sentences he must learn to form the letters.

He will first learn printing, or, as it is called, *manuscript* writing. It will look something like this:

> All letters are made from circular
> and straight lines.

Later, when the small muscles of his fingers and hands have developed, he will learn what is called *cursive* writing, in which his letters are connected.

He will not use all capital letters, so there is little use in your teaching him to print his name at home in this way.

how your child is taught to write

Many teachers use the following system to teach the formation of letters. You should be familiar with it too.

HOW TO MAKE LITTLE LETTERS

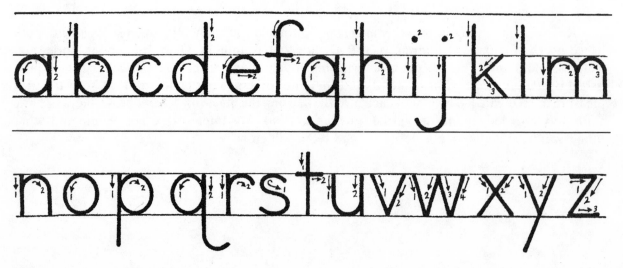

HOW TO MAKE BIG LETTERS

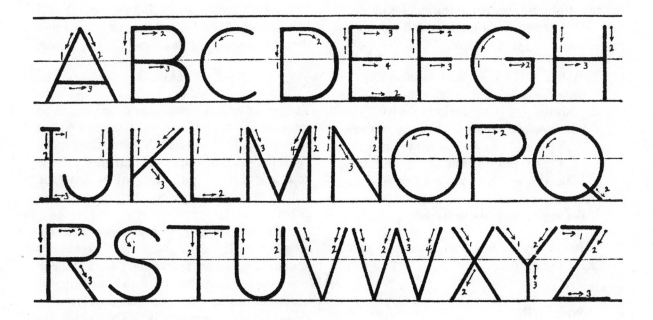

Your child knows that capitals and tall letters are made twice as high as small letters. The letters extending below the line go about as far as those that extend above it.

Vertical and slanting lines are made from the top down. Circles start at the top.

is made counter-clockwise. Make each part of a letter as you come to it.

EXAMPLE:

In *d*

first make *O*   then */*

and you have *d*

Your child learns all the straight line letters together:

f h i j k l t v w x y z

and all the circular letters together:

a b c d e g m n o p q r s u

His teacher encourages him to write large because his small muscles are not yet ready to work together. He uses a thick pencil with a soft lead. At school, as he should at home, he uses lined paper. It helps him to learn to write his letters in a uniform size.

He learns that letters in a word must not touch each other, and that words are one finger-space apart on paper.

If your child is left-handed he should be taught to hold the pencil at least one-half inch above the sharpened part. This will allow him to see what he is doing and will prevent him from developing a hooked position of his hand.

53

the differences between letters

At first your child will have trouble recognizing the slight differences in the shapes of letters. Here are some home helps: If he confuses *b* and *d*, you can say:

> "This is *b*. *b* is tall like a building. *b*
> looks to the right.
> "This is *d*. *d* looks to the left."
> If he confuses *m* and *n*, you can say:
> "This is *m*. *m* is on the line.
>   *m* has two little hills.
> "This is *n*. *n* has one little hill."
> For the letter *p*: "*p* is down below
> the line. *p* looks to the right."

After study of this sort, then you can originate some riddles.

EXAMPLES:

> Who am I?
> I am tall like a building.
> I look to the right.
> Who am I?   (answer, *b*)

ENGLISH

As in kindergarten, English is not taught formally. However, your child learns much about the use of the English language this year. The teacher, and you, can help him to avoid forming bad or lazy speech habits and can help him create good speech habits.

If he hears clear well-spoken English around him in all his activities, he will learn to speak clearly and well without being aware of any teaching.

Try not to let him say, "I seen her," or, "This ain't mine," or "Uh-huh!" or "Yea." It is harder to break a habit once it is formed than to develop it right from the beginning.

SPELLING

Your child will not be taught to spell until he can make all the letters from memory and has begun to read. In some schools formal spelling is not taught at all in the first grade, and if your school is one of these, it will be better for him if you do not stress spelling at home either.

Talking, spelling, and writing are closely interwoven. These are the tools of expression or communication. Your child's teacher helps him to apply these tools through meaningful situations throughout the school day. He talks about his home, his family, his activities, his pets. He imitates what he learns from adults. So watch your own diction, and your use of words and voice tone! The first words he writes will be the ones that mean the most to him, the ones he uses the most in his speech, such as mother, daddy, see, baby, run.

He learns to spell a new word (1) if he gets the proper pronunciation and understands the meaning of it first, (2) if he makes a picture of the word in his mind, and (3) if he can recognize differences in words: *hat . . . cat.*

At home let him copy familiar words from his pre-primer and let him use his finger to trace over the words in the book.

SPELLING AIDS

▶ List a few familiar words, then list them again, omitting letters. Ask him to fill in the missing letter.

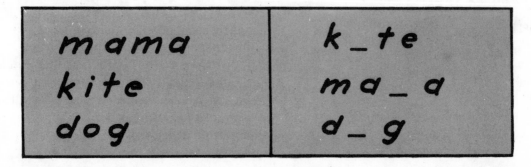

54

▶ **Reassemble jumbled letters to make words.**

▶ **Use the words as picture titles.**

(paste)
_____

(paste)
_____

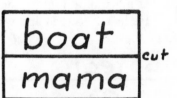

boat

mama   cut

▶ **Write the missing word in the sentence**

I   see   _____

mama

These exercises are easy to do at home. Be sure to use only familiar words and sentences already learned at school (if spelling is taught in the first grade). Use large clear printing. Work with your child until you are sure he understands what he is to do. Do not continue beyond the point of having fun.

Your child's arithmetic continues to be taught with many concrete aids to allow him to discover for himself the ideas the teacher is developing. You can be helpful by supplying similar aids for his practice at home. Keep your empty spools, beads, blocks, bottle caps, etc. Make an inexpensive flannel board on a box cover (see page 9 of the kindergarten section of this book).

numbers

In the first grade your child learns to count to 100. The counting numbers, 1, 2, 3, 4 . . . are called **cardinal** numbers. He also learns the **ordinal** idea of numbers up to 10. An ordinal indicates the proper place of a number, such as first, second, third, fourth . . .

He learns to read and write the number words for the numerals up to 10. Examples:

object	number word	numeral
🌳	one	1
🍦🍦	two	2

An exercise like the one that follows gives your child excellent practice in recognizing numbers in a group, and in naming and writing the numeral and the word that names the number. Ask him to fill in the blank spaces to finish the table.

number word	objects	numeral
five		
six		
seven		
four		
three		
four		
six		
five		
three		

sets and subsets

Because in Kindergarten he learned to work with things in groups called sets, your child now works with numbers in sets of 10s and 1s. This helps him to understand our number system. It shows him the importance of 10; that two 10s are 20, that three 10s are 30, etc.
Examples:

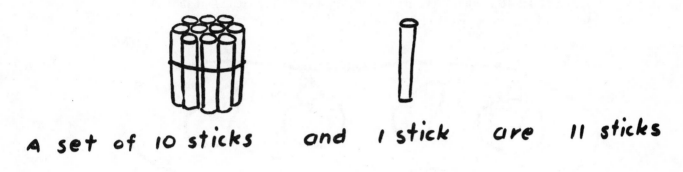

A set of 10 sticks   and 1 stick   are   11 sticks

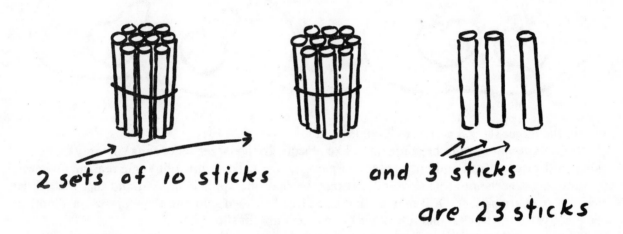

2 sets of 10 sticks   and 3 sticks

are 23 sticks

After your child learns to make sets with actual objects he will discover that his work can be made easier by letting one object stand for ten, if it is used in the right place. This teaches him to use a **place-value** box.
Example:

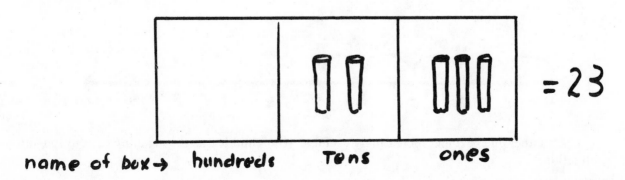

name of box → hundreds   Tens   ones

= 23

Each marker in the tens box stands for 10, so the 2 markers represent 20. Together with the 3 markers in the ones box, this picture represents 23 objects.

After he does exercises like this with pictures and symbols, he will go on to do them with numbers only.

Example: 20 + 3 = 23

Your child will learn that there are sets within a set. They are called **sub-sets.**
Example: In this set are 4 pieces of fruit—2 apples and 2 pears.

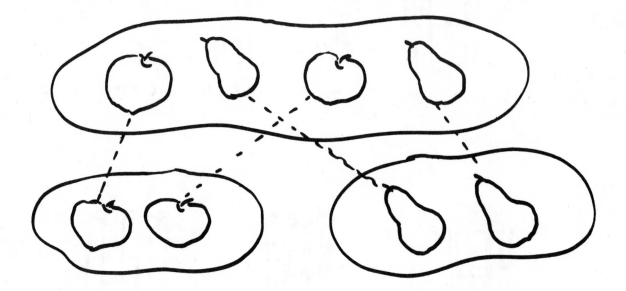

Within the larger set is a subset of 2 apples and a subset of 2 pears.

Subsets do not need to be made up of like objects. In the larger set of four you may make one subset of 1 piece of fruit and one subset of 3 pieces of fruit. There must be some reason, however, for grouping objects into sets as you do. It may be that one apple is bruised and the other three pieces of fruit are perfect. Or it may be that one piece has been sold and three pieces have not, or one piece is for the teacher, and the other three pieces are for the children.

Let your child practice picking subsets from sets made with real objects that you provide for him at home—spoons, forks, crayons, spools, etc.

number line

Your child continues to use his number line. He will use it as he learns to count to 100 by ones, and then to count by twos.

Example:

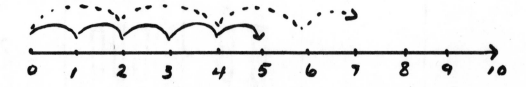

The number line becomes increasingly useful as your child learns the meaning of addition and subtraction.

addition and subtraction

Your child will name and use the signs +, −, and =, or plus, minus, and equals. He will write his problems of addition and subtraction in various ways. They are all intended to help him understand the concepts of adding and subtracting.

He will first think of addition as the joining of sets.
Example:

He will discover that the order of the numbers he adds, called addends, makes no difference.
Example:
$$3 + 2 = 5$$
$$2 + 3 = 5$$
$$2 + 3 = 3 + 2$$

He will think of subtraction as a separation of sets.
Example:

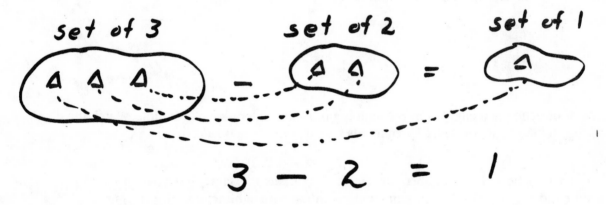

Your child will make and use an *addition–subtraction table*.
Example:

+	0	1	2	3	4	5
0	0	1	2	3	4	5
1	1	2	3	4	5	
2	2	3	4	5		
3	3	4	5			
4	4	5				
5	5					

The + in the first square indicates that the table is to be used for addition. The first column on the left names the first number to be added. The top row names the second number to be added.

Problem: 1 + 2.

Method: Draw a line into the table from the 1 in the left-hand column.

Draw a line down from the 2 in the top row.

These two lines intersect at 3, which is the correct answer.

Your thoughts make this triangular pattern:

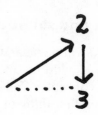

as you say, "One and two are three."

Example:

−	0	1	2	3	4	5
0	0	1	2	3	4	5
1	1	2	3	4	5	
2	2	3	4	5		
3	3	4	5			
4	4	5				
5	5					

The − sign in the first square indicates that the table is to be used for subtraction.

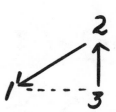

Subtraction is thought of as the undoing or **inverse operation** of addition. Watch the direction of your thinking, as you say, "Three minus two are one." Follow the arrows:

The position of the numbers on the table remains the same, but your thinking is reversed. Your child may tell you that he can "undo addition with subtraction." He is right.

Example: Problem: 5 − 3 = □

Method: Use the subtraction table. Think inversely:

Start with the 5 that is directly under the 3·in the top row. The answer is the figure in the left-hand column which is in the same row as the 5 you started with.

The table shows that 5 − 3 = 2.

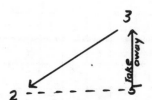

Your child will learn to add three numbers together. He will begin to use the *associative* property of addition. This is a way of adding in steps and helps him to speed up his work.

Example: Problem: Add $4 + 3 + 2$

Method 1: In his earlier work in addition your child learned to combine two numbers. He readily sees now that $4 + 3$ are 7 and he shows that thought process by putting brackets around the numbers he is combining:

$$(4 + 3) + 2 =$$
$$7 + 2 =$$

This done, there remains only one step to the solution of the problem:

$$7 + 2 = 9$$

Method 2: Your child may more readily see the sum of $3 + 2$. Then he writes:

$$4 + (3 + 2) =$$
$$4 + 5 = 9$$

equations

Number stories written so that the part to the left of the $=$ sign is worth the same as the part to the right of the sign are called **equations.** Your child will be asked to find the correct number for a blank space in order to complete an equation.

    Example: $3 + \square = 5$

He may use the number line to find the missing number.

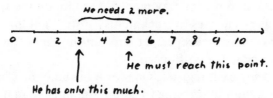

He may use his experience of one-to-one matching of objects in sets to find the missing number. Example:

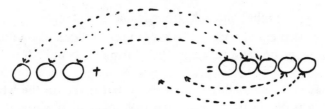

He needs two rings to complete his equation.

concepts

Your child learns the concept of time.

    He uses a play clock, and learns that the numbers are there to show the hours in a day. They are placed in a circle with the 12 at the top, the 6 at the bottom, the 3 between the 12 and 6 on the right side of the circle, and the 9 between the 12 and 6 on the left side of the circle. He learns that the hands move to the right; that the longer, or minute, hand moves faster than the shorter, or hour, hand. He learns that each number marks an hour's time by the hour hand; that each little black mark shows a minute by the minute hand—and that it takes 60 minutes to make an hour. Don't force your child to "learn to tell time." Telling time by a clock is a difficult thing for any child to grasp. But clocks fascinate most children, and suddenly one day your child will master the principle of "telling time." You can help prepare him for this important moment in his life by holding yourself ready to answer his questions, and spending a little time with him now and then, talking about the clocks you have at home and examining them. He may like to have a play wrist watch, or may like to keep an alarm clock by his bed.

    He continues to work with the concept of size. He learns **larger than** and **smaller than** by comparing objects in the room.

He learns to understand and use:

behind	Stand *behind* me.
before	3 is *before* 4.
ahead	Stand *ahead* of everyone and be the leader.
after	*After* 1 is 2.
next	When I am through, you will be *next*.
over	Put your hand *over* mine.
under	Then my hand will be *under* yours.
above	The fourth floor of the building is *above* the third floor.
below	The basement is *below* the level of the ground.

Your child puts these concepts to use in his classroom by acting them out with the other children. You can engage in this kind of instructive play with him at home.

using money

He distinguishes between a penny, a nickel (five pennies), and a dime (ten pennies or two nickels).

He plays store in the classroom with play money. Let him do the same thing at home. You be the customer. Buy the things he chooses to stock in his "store." Let him set the price, however fantastic it may be at first. He is the storekeeper; let him run the show. You can have your turn when you are the storekeeper and he is the customer.

Sound him out about a toy cash register. One for a birthday or Christmas present might be a good idea. It will be an aid to him in learning to count and later to make change.

shapes

He continues to work with circles, squares, triangles, and rectangles.

Cut some circles in two equal parts—this gives him the idea of one half. He also learns one half by dividing the apple he brought to school, by sharing his cookie exactly, by folding his paper. He learns to write ½.

He also learns that ⅓ is one of three equal parts that make up the whole apple or the whole cookie. He learns that ¼ is one of four equal parts that make up a whole.

problems

Your child will use his knowledge of sets and the number line to solve simple problems.

Example: Problem: Tom has three pennies and Sue has five pennies.
Question: How many pennies do they have together?
Answer:

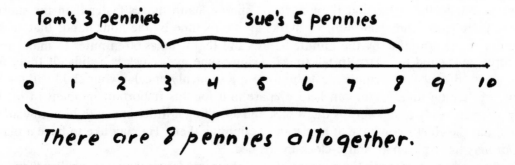

Question: How many more pennies has Sue than Tom?
Answer:

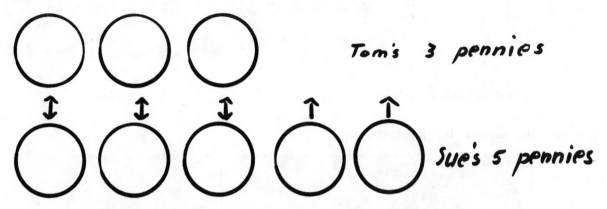

Tom's 3 pennies

Sue's 5 pennies

By one-to-one matching, your child sees that Sue has two more pennies than Tom. He will write it this way: $5 - 3 = 2$.

It is essential that your first-grade child become thoroughly familiar with numbers and numerals through ten—their meaning, how to read and write them, and to understand the meaning of adding and subtracting them. The teacher uses many devices to make her lessons meaningful and to keep the children actively engaged in discovering answers for themselves. By doing this she is stimulating them to think.

Experiments have proven that children enjoy the new system of teaching mathematics, that most of them find it easy, and that it does give them a strong foundation for future work in arithmetic.

workbook | first grade

reading exercises

I. Draw a line between things that are alike.

b	d	F	L	r	r
p	p	E	E	n	n
d	b	L	F	h	h
k	x	j	f	c	e
x	t	i	i	o	c
t	k	f	j	e	o
p	q	m	w	s	c
q	p	w	n	o	s
d	d	n	m	c	o

II. Which one is different? Cross it out.

a	a	a	a
c	o	c	c
b	b	b	d
g	g	g	a
A	A	A	A
D	O	D	D
O	O	O	C

64

III. Which is different? Cross it out.

boat	boat	~~oat~~	boat
pie	pie	die	pie
coat	coat	boat	coat
pipe	pipe	pip	pipe
nose	nos	nose	nose
ear	ear	eer	ear
e	e	e	o
three	tree	three	three
rat	rat	rate	rat
hide	hide	hid	hide

IV. Draw a line between words that are alike.

green	orange	red	yellow	two	three
white	green	blue	blue	one	two
orange	white	yellow	red	three	one
dog	doll	ball	duck	cat	baby
all	ball	kite	doll	doll	ball
fog	dog	duck	fall	dog	cat
tree	ball	blue	red	tree	dog
red	tree	orange	yellow	ball	doll
two	dog	white	blue	dog	three

V. Draw a line between things that are alike.

2	four	1	one	4	five
3	two	6	four	2	four
4	three	4	six	5	two
2	ten	9	one	7	five
5	five	3	nine	2	seven
10	two	1	three	5	two
2	two	9	six	3	seven
8	seven	6	nine	5	three
7	eight	1	one	7	five

VI. Do what it says.

Make two boats.

Make a big ball and a little ball.

Draw four  and color them red.

Draw five cats.

VII. Draw a line between the picture and the right word.

cake   Jane

flag   coat

pail   stone

VIII. Match the words.

tree	here
Alice	came
come	lake
see	the
and	jack
look	not
came	Alice
the	and
lake	come
no	look
jack	see
here	tree
not	no

with	hand
down	one
me	three
up	pole
one	sell
draw	with
ten	dog
hand	me
pole	draw
dog	down
three	tin
sell	ten
tin	up

IX. Write the correct word on the blank line.

1. The man worked hard at his ___Job___ .   job rob Bob

2. The boy has a fishing _____ .   nod pod rod

3. Jane has a little _____ .   doll dollar

4. The man called his _____ .   fog dog log

5. The boy climbed to the _____ .   pop hop top

6. The goat has a little _____ .   kid did hid

7. The girl cut her _____ .   lip dip tip

number exercises

X. Use your crayons.

red	green	orange
blue	black	yellow
blue and yellow	red	green and brown
green	red and blue	yellow and red

I. Practice writing your numerals in natural order.

0	1	2	3	4	5	6	7	8	9

II. Write the numeral that comes after

5 __6__   4 ____   8 ____   2 ____
2 ____   7 ____   6 ____   9 ____
1 ____   2 ____   5 ____   1 ____
3 ____   4 ____   9 ____   3 ____
9 ____   1 ____   3 ____   8 ____

III. Write the numeral that comes before

5 ____   4 ____   10 ____
3 ____   9 ____   3 ____
2 ____   2 ____   5 ____
4 ____   8 ____   8 ____
7 ____   6 ____   4 ____

IV. Put all the numerals on the clocks.

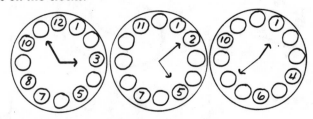

V. Match each number word with a set and with a numeral.

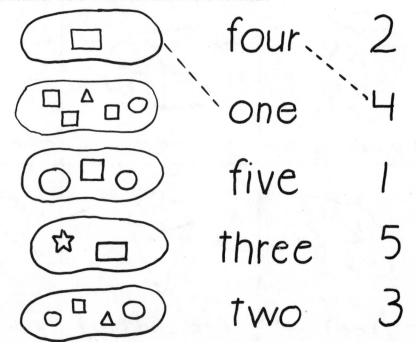

70

VI. How many?

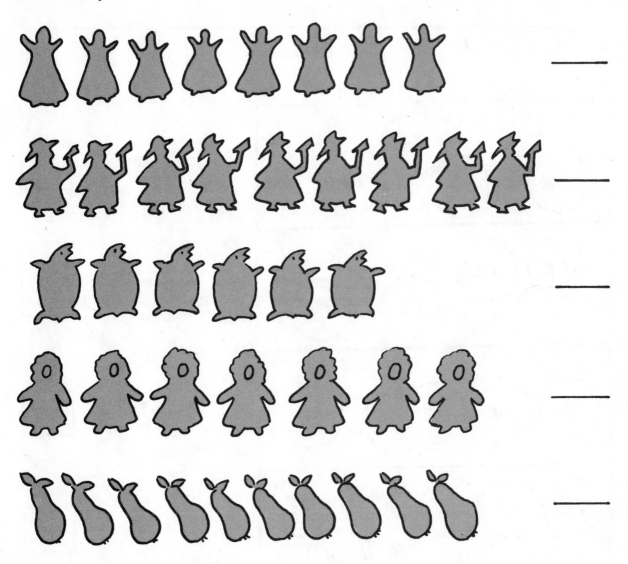

VII. Add by joining the sets of dots on the dominoes.

4 + 2 = ☐   4 + 1 = ☐

3 + 2 = ☐   2 + 2 = ☐

1 + 4 = ☐   3 + 1 = ☐

1 + 3 = ☐   2 + 3 = ☐

VIII. Add the pennies by using the number line.

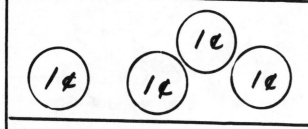

1¢ 1¢ 1¢ 1¢	1 + 3 = ☐
1¢ 1¢ 1¢ 1¢	2 + 2 = ☐
1¢ 1¢ 1¢ 1¢	3 + 1 = ☐
1¢ 1¢ 1¢ 1¢ 1¢ 1¢	3 + 3 = ☐
1¢ 1¢ 1¢ 1¢ 1¢	2 + 3 = ☐
1¢ 1¢ 1¢ 1¢ 1¢	4 + 1 = ☐

IX. Draw sets of shapes for each problem.
Show the answer with a numeral and a set.
Example:

$2 + 3 = \boxed{5}$

$(\triangle \triangle) + (\circ \circ \circ) = (\triangle \triangle \circ \circ \circ)$

$3 + 3 = \square$

$4 + 2 = \square$

$5 + 1 = \square$

$2 + 4 = \square$

$3 + 1 = \square$

X. Draw sets of shapes for each problem.
Show the answer with a numeral and a set.
Example:

$5 - 3 = \boxed{2}$

$(\triangle \triangle \triangle \circ \circ) - (\triangle \triangle \triangle) = \boxed{\circ \circ}$

$5 - 1 = \square$

$4 - \square = 2$

$5 - \square = 4$

$3 - 1 = \square$

$6 - 2 = \square$

XI. Name the dark part of each figure.

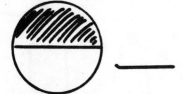 _____

 _____

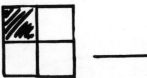 _____

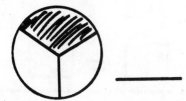 _____

 _____

  _____

XII. Write an equation for each picture.
   Example:

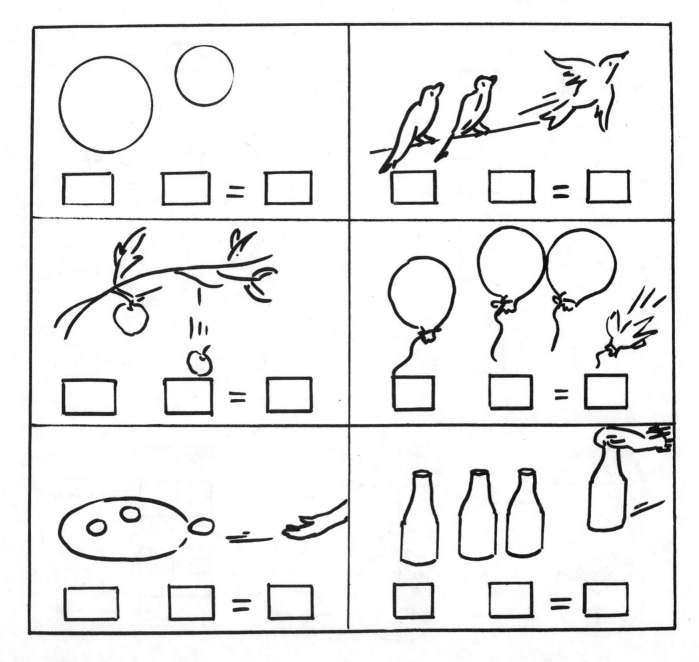

XIII. Solve these equations.

7 + 2 + 1 = ☐   4 + 4 + 1 = ☐

5 + 3 + 2 = ☐   2 + 2 + 2 = ☐

1 + 5 + 1 = ☐   3 + 1 + 2 = ☐

4 + 2 + 2 = ☐   6 + 1 + 2 = ☐

8 + 2 + 1 = ☐   5 + 1 + 2 = ☐

XIV. Use the associative property of addition.

3 − 3 = ☐   5 − ☐ = 2

8 − 5 = ☐   7 + 3 = ☐

4 + 4 = ☐   5 + 4 = ☐

8 − 7 = ☐   2 + ☐ = 6

2 + 6 = ☐   ☐ + 8 = 8

7 + 1 = ☐   2 + ☐ = 5

☐ + 3 = 7   5 + 5 = ☐

9 − 0 = ☐   10 − 2 = ☐

XV. Use one place holder for each set of 10 in the 10s house.
   Example:

$$2\;3 = \boxed{\begin{array}{c|c} || & ||| \\ \text{Tens} & \text{ones} \end{array}}$$

Two Tens

$$2\;4 = \boxed{\begin{array}{c|c} & \\ \text{Tens} & \text{ones} \end{array}}$$

$$3\;1 = \boxed{\begin{array}{c|c} & \\ \text{Tens} & \text{ones} \end{array}}$$

$$1\;0 = \boxed{\begin{array}{c|c} & \\ \text{Tens} & \text{ones} \end{array}}$$

$$1\;2 = \boxed{\begin{array}{c|c} & \\ \text{Tens} & \text{ones} \end{array}}$$

$$3\;5 = \boxed{\begin{array}{c|c} & \\ \text{Tens} & \text{ones} \end{array}}$$

contents | second grade

helping your child in second grade

YOUR CHILD is now about seven years old.

He will not find as much difference between first and second grade as he did between kindergarten and first. With the aid of this book you will be able to help him at home in much the same way as you did in previous grades. In fact, from time to time during the earlier months of this school year you may find it of value to turn back to material covered in the first-grade book. Much of it will apply equally well now for review or home tutoring purposes.

No two children move at the same speed in all subjects, or become interested in the same things at the same time. Your child's "moment of readiness"—whether it is for reading or for telling time—cannot be forced. But with sympathetic attention it can be discerned and nurtured. You will quickly sense when he needs a little home help on any particular subject. If you cannot tell just where he needs help, consult his teacher. When you have determined his need, then use this book. Dip back and forth between the first-grade book and this second-year book as it suits your purpose.

learning in second grade

In second grade your child "rounds out" the knowledge he acquired in first grade. In first grade he was made aware of a lot of new things. He didn't fully understand some of them then—he wasn't supposed to. He was merely "exposed" to them so that he could learn them more readily in second grade.

Telling time is an example. In first grade your child *almost* learned to tell time, but probably not quite. Before his second-grade learning is over he will tell time as well as you do. Reading the calendar is another example. In first grade he learned a bit about it; this year he learns the rest. In first-grade arithmetic he made just a beginning at adding and subtracting. Watch him with numbers this year! All these things—and many more— will be covered in this second-grade book under appropriate headings.

reading for understanding

It was only last year that your child began to read. It was such a new and difficult experience that about all he could be expected to do was to get out the words. He didn't particularly try to understand what he was reading. The act of reading itself was the accomplishment. He read, "I see Joe." And, "Joe can see me." His concentration was terrific. The words came out one at a time. He seemed to be putting his whole quivering body into the effort. To you, watching him proudly, it was painful and laughable and pathetic and wonderful all at the same time. He didn't always know what he was reading, but he *was* reading.

Now in the second grade he will start out the same way, but sometime during the year he will become "easier" in his reading. He will begin to master this medium of expression. The act of reading will become, in a sense, second nature to him, and he will start to get information.

In school he will have daily exercises to develop this "reading for comprehension." He will become quick and eager to answer his teacher's questions on what he has read silently. And because of this it is going to be easy for you to help him at home.

When he brings his reading book home, ask him to read a story to himself, by himself. Then ask him to close the book and answer your questions about the story. Make your questions short, clear, and definite. Ask things like, "What was the boy's name?" "What color was his wagon?" "Why did he go to Grandmother's house?"

how your child advances

As the year progresses you will observe that he learns to read more signs in public places such as theaters, street crossings, and high-

ways. Encourage him in this. Make a game of it when you're riding or walking along. Let him tell you how many words he can recognize on billboards or in windows. Or let him keep an eye out for certain words or phrases.

Here are some other ways he advances in his reading ability, and in nearly every one of them you can help him:

▶ He learns to recognize the difference between a line and a sentence.
▶ He begins to use a table of contents to locate page numbers.
▶ He has exercises in finding words that end alike, such as:

singing, jumping

▶ He is able to find different words that begin with the same consonant, or blend, as:

spell, spill

▶ He finds little words in big words, as:

sing, another

▶ He can add s, ing, er, ed, and est to make new words.

EXAMPLES:

farm	farms
farm	farming
farm	farmer
farm	farmed
warm	warmest

▶ He learns that some words can be used in several ways. For instance,

spring

A *spring* of cold water came from the hillside.
Be careful! That dog may *spring* at you.
Spring will soon be here.
One *spring* on our car is broken.

Or,

sound

We heard a loud *sound*.
We got home safe and *sound*.

Some other words that can be used in more than one way: face, catch, stop, store, time, story, let, second, hard, course, rest, gobble, place, feel, cross, show, rich, foot.

▶ **Additional sounds he masters as the year goes on are:**

st	c plus e equals *s*	sm
sw	augh	sn
br	eigh	sl
cl	ould	sp
		oy, oi

▶ **He learns that *q* always has a *u* with it; that *g* with *e* or *i* sounds like a *j*, and that this is why *u* is put in to separate a *g* and an *e* or a *g* and an *i* when the *g* is hard as in "go."**

EXAMPLES:

guest, guess, guide

▶ **He learns that *kn* is *n*, as in *knife*; that *wr* is *r*, as in *wrong*; that *ph* is *f*, as in *paragraph*.**
▶ **He realizes that stories are divided into separate thoughts called paragraphs.**
▶ **He learns that words that name things are called nouns, and words that tell about nouns are called *adjectives*.**
▶ **He learns to rhyme words.**

EXAMPLES:

fill, hill, will, mill

in, win, thin, grin, spin

wet, get, pet, set, met

▶ **He is able to find the quotation marks and the exact words someone says.**

help your child get good
reading habits

While habits are being set at this age, encourage your child to read with his eyes, not his lips or his fingers. A first step in discouraging the practice of following words with fingers is to use a pencil or marker instead. To stop lip reading, let him hold his fingers over his lips.

when your child cannot
read a word

What about the word in the sentence that your child cannot read? Well, when reading is new to him, it is better to tell him. If he stops too long to figure it out, his reading becomes choppy and loses its natural flow.

But after you have told him the same word a dozen times or so, that is enough. Then it is time for him to learn the word for himself. There are several ways he can do this. If there is a picture on the page, he can sometimes figure out the puzzling word by looking at the picture.

Sometimes he finds out the word for himself by reading the rest of the sentence. Suppose the sentence is, "The bird sings in the tree," and your child doesn't recognize the word *sing*. If he reads the rest of the sentence, the word *sing* may seem logical to him. The bird wouldn't walk in the tree, or fly, or swim, or run. He might sit there. But perhaps your child can recognize the word *sit*. This obviously isn't *sit*. *Sing* is about the only other thing it could be.

The words that are likely to be the most difficult are the ones which cannot be pictured. He can learn *cat, dog, horse, airplane, doll*, almost without trying. But words like *those, who, come, did, were* will take more time. He gets a lot of practice on these at school, but usually he will find one or more of them particularly bothersome. These will be the ones on which to concentrate at home. There are a lot of good "word" games you can play to help him recognize these offenders. The fish game explained on page 12 is a good one.

the word wheel

Here is another game you can make at home to give your child general word practice. He will find it helpful and lots of fun. It is called the Word Wheel.

Cut out two cardboard circles, one smaller than the other. Fasten them in the center so they rotate easily. Print single-letter consonants on the rim of the circle, and sound combinations on the edge of the smaller one. Different words can be formed by rotating the circles.

EXAMPLE:

Rotate the circles. Your child will see that some combinations of letters do not make words.

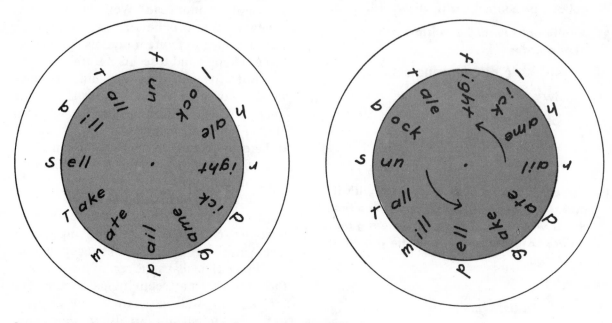

how to help your child read for understanding

To give your child practice in reading for understanding, make a chart which asks him to draw things according to directions. The construction takes only a minute or two.

It might be something like this:

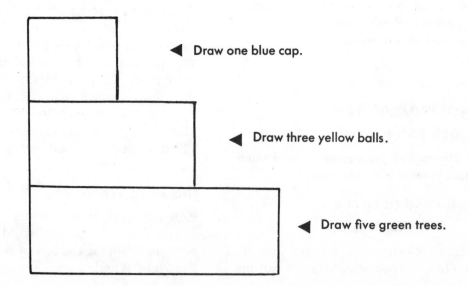

◀ Draw one blue cap.

◀ Draw three yellow balls.

◀ Draw five green trees.

reading word list

If your child is able to read all of these words easily by the end of the second grade, he is a good reader. He should not be expected to spell them. Before he starts to read them for you, review the phonics he had in the first grade—the vowels, the consonants, and especially the common combinations of letters. Some of these combinations are *sh, st, wh, gr, ow, oo, ch, sw, th, igh, aw* and *ay*.

above	Bob	corn	faster
across	bone	cost	feed
add	Boston	couldn't	feel
afraid	both	covered	fell
age	bottom	cow	fence
Agnes	bounce	crocodile	field
ah	bow	cup	fifth
air	break	curious	fill
almost	breakfast	cut	fine
also	bridge	dance	finger
always	bring	dear	finish
angry	broke	deep	five
animal	brother	didn't	flew
Ann	build	different	flies
answered	bunch	dig	flowers
any	burn	dinner	follow
apart	butter	dirty	food
apples	buy	doesn't	footman
apron	car	dollar	found
arm	card	door	fox
babies	care	dragon	Freddy
bakery	careful	drank	fresh
balloon	carpet	dress	friend
bank	carry	drink	frightened
barn	catch	drown	front
batter	caught	dry	full
beard	cent	each	game
bed	chair	earn	garden
been	chief	earth	gay
begin	children	egg	George
believe	Chinese	else	gingerbread
beside	chop	end	giraffe
best	city	enough	glad
Betty	clever	even	glass
between	climb	every	goat
bigger	cloth	everybody	goes
bird	clown	everything	golden
bit	coach	eye	goldfish
blow	cocoa	face	ground
board	cookies	fairy	grow

hair	light	open	robe
hand	line	oven	rode
handle	listen	owl	Roger
happen	little	pair	roll
harbor	live	pan	room
hard	loaf	paper	round
harder	lock	park	ruffle
hasn't	longer	part	sailor
hat	loud	pass	sale
hello	lucky	patient	Sally
help	magic	patter	Sam
hen	mail	pen	same
higher	make	people	sandwich
hill	man	pet	Saturday
himself	matches	picnic	school
hint	mayor	piece	scissors
hit	men	pipe	scooter
hole	merry	place	sea
hope	middle	plain	second
hose	might	please	seen
hungry	mind	plow	sell
hurt	miss	police	send
I'd	Monday	politely	sense
I'll	monkey	poor	sent
I'm	morning	pop	seven
Indian	most	post	sew
island	mouth	pretty	shall
isn't	mud	princess	shape
I've	mumps	promise	sheep
jar	music	puff	ship
joke	name	puppy	short
judge	narrow	purple	should
juggle	neat	push	shout
keep	neck	queer	shut
kitchen	need	question	side
knew	nest	quickly	sign
knock	new	quiet	silent
laid	next	ragged	silly
lamb	nickel	railroad	sit
land	noise	rang	six
large	none	read	size
last	nose	ready	slept
late	nothing	really	slow
laugh	oatmeal	remember	small
learn	office	report	smell
leave	often	rest	smile
left	oh	return	snow
leg	old	right	somersault
lemonade	once	ring	son
letter	only	road	spring

stairs	ten	trouble	window
stand	tent	truck	wings
start	test	trunk	wire
station	their	try	wise
stay	think	Tuesday	women
step	third	turn	won't
stopped	thought	twelve	world
store	through	twice	wrong
stories	Thursday	twin	year
story	tidy	uncle	you'll
strange	tie	under	young
stretch	tired	unhappy	zoo
such	toast	until	
sugar	together	wag	
suit	told	wash	
summer	too	wave	
sure	took	wear	
surprise	top	Wednesday	
table	touch	well	
tail	town	while	
taken	tractor	whisper	
talk	traffic	whistle	
tapped	tree	whole	
teacher	tried	wide	
telephone	trotted	wife	

reading games

Here are two suggestions for using this word list and for learning other difficult words from his reader.

1. Check the words your child frequently stumbles over. Print each of these difficult words on a piece of cardboard that measures about 3 by 5 inches. These are your reading flash cards.

Now make a "fishing" game. Put a paper clip on the corner of each card. Make a "fishing pole" by tying a small magnet by a string about 12 inches long to the end of a stick. Your child and a group of his friends can now go "fishing." Put the cards, printed side down, in a heap in the center of the table. Let each child in turn catch a "fish." If he can pronounce correctly the word on the card he has attracted with the magnet, he may keep the card. If he cannot pronounce it, tell him what it is, but he must throw the "fish" back into the "water." When all the "fish" have been caught, each child counts his "catch." The one with the most "fish" is the winner.

2. Select *one* column of words from the preceding list. Ask your child to find or draw pictures for as many words as possible. (For *while,* it would be impossible to find a picture, but for *large* he may find something that illustrates the meaning of the word.) If he does not find a picture of a goldfish, for example, it may be that he cannot read the word. Find out. If he has trouble, help him. Then, together, find or draw a picture of a goldfish. Color it, talk about it, discuss the care of goldfish, etc. It is likely that he will remember the word when he meets it the next time, wherever it is.

books your second-grade child may enjoy

Brownies—Hush —*Adshead, Gladys L.*
Billy and Blaze
Blaze and the Forest Fire
     Anderson, Clarence W.
Country Fireman —*Beim, Jerrold*
This Is the Bread that Betsy Ate —*Black, Irma*
Beachcomber Bobbie —*Bourgeois, Florence*
Schoolhouse in the Woods —*Caudill, Rebecca*
A Yard for John —*Clymer, Eleanor*
Nils —*d'Aulaire, Ingri and Edgar P.*
Ted and Nina Go to the Grocery Store
     De Angeli, Marguerite
Boats on the River —*Flack, Marjorie*
A Home for Sandy —*Gay, Romney*
Little Toot
Loopy
     Gramatky, Hardie
Penn Goes to Camp —*Haywood, Carolyn*

Down-along Apple Market Street
Jack O'Lantern for Judy Jo
     Hill, Mabel B.
Rusty Wants a Dog—*Huber, Miriam, and others*
People Who Come to Our House—*Judson, Clara I.*
Who Goes There?—*Lathrop, Dorothy P.*
Little Airplane
Little Farm
     Lenski, Lois
Diggers and Builders —*Lent, Henry B.*
Make Way for Ducklings —*McCloskey, Robert*
Jimmy the Groceryman —*Miller, Jane*
Here Comes the Postman —*Park, Dorothea*
The Little House on Stilts —*Patton, Lucia*
At the Zoo —*Robinson, William W.*
Little Wiener —*Scott, Sally*
Cowboy Tommy —*Tousey, Sanford*
The First Christmas —*Trent, Robbie*
Elephants —*Zim, Herbert*

writing | second grade

IN THE second grade your child's handwriting improves, though he still uses the manuscript form that was taught him in the first grade.

This is a good time to go back and review the section on WRITING in the first grade, because writing in the second grade is essentially a continuation and deepening of habits introduced there.

This year your child:

▶ Begins to write the alphabet in order. (The main reason for knowing the alphabetical order of the letters is to help him use a dictionary.)

▶ Learns to write his first and last names, address, grade, school, city, state, and date.

▶ Writes answers to questions. This is an exercise you can help him with at home. Ask him simple questions. Let him write down the answers. Get a blackboard or make one. (There is a blackboard paint which you can buy. It comes in several tints and can be painted on any surface and used by your child as he would a slate blackboard.) This will be helpful to him because his finer muscles are still not completely developed, and it is easier for him to write large than small.

Observe your child when he writes at home. This is the time to prevent bad writing habits. See that his posture is good, that he is not cramping his fingers, that he uses proper lighting. Point out to him his mistakes in letter formation. (*See* the first-grade WRITING section for this.)

ENGLISH

Your child doesn't call it English. He studies it only in connection with his study of words. Correct speech becomes a natural part of his reading and spelling. He gets practice telling stories to his class. He learns to give simple directions clearly enough for the rest of the class to follow.

Help him at home with his speaking English. For instance, sometimes when you have friends in, let your child join in the conversation. It will help him to overcome awkwardness and develop the poise you have at times admired in certain children. It doesn't appear like magic; it must be developed, with practice. Even in his everyday living, you can help him practice.

SPELLING

Your child may or may not make important advances in spelling this year. It is quite common for spelling ability to lag behind reading ability, so don't worry if your child is not a "good speller" at this stage.

how spelling is taught in school

Schools differ on the time to begin teaching spelling. Some start it in an easy way in the first grade, some begin in the second, and some do not start until the third grade.

In general, the words your child will learn to spell in any of the beginning grades will be those he uses frequently in his daily writing. He will pick up the spelling of many of these by himself.

Whenever the formal teaching of spelling is begun in your child's school, it is sure to follow a prescribed pattern. It is a way that has been thoroughly tested and found effective. It is, fortunately, a simple method that can be used in the home as well as in the school. It will be outlined here, step by step, so that if your child is weak in spelling, you can work with him at home in the manner with which he has become familiar at school.

This is the way it goes. When your child's teacher is ready to introduce new words, she doesn't give them to your child in a dull list, as they may have been given to you when you went to school! First his teacher reads a short story to the class. Then she takes several additional steps.

Here are the steps that follow the reading of the story:

▶ She guides the children in picking out the words in the story that are new to them.

▶ The children look at the words carefully and name the letters in each word.

▶ They make other sentences with each of the new words.

▶ They play games with the new words—such as finding other words that rhyme with them. (Ask your child what other word games they play —it is a good way to stimulate his enthusiasm for study at home.)

▶ They write the words several times—with the teacher's help if necessary, or referring to the words in a book or on the blackboard.

▶ By this time they are familiar with the words, and they try to write them from memory—"without looking."

▶ If they are not able to write them all correctly by this time, they go back for more games and exercises.

spelling list

Even if the formal teaching of spelling it not part of the second-grade work in your school, your child will learn many words from his reading and writing. Wait until close to the end of the school year before you drill on them at home. Do not give him more than 10 words at one time. Carefully check the spelling of the words but also check the formation of letters, neatness, size of his writing. It is easier to prevent bad habits than it is to break them.

Following is a basic New York State list for the second grade:

a	four	made	some
after	from	make	store
all	fun	man	
am		me	take
an	gave	milk	that
and	get	morning	the
are	girl	mother	them
at	give	my	then
away	glad		there
	go	name	they
baby	going	new	this
back	good	night	three
ball	got	no	time
balls		not	to
be	had		today
bed	happy	of	two
big	has	on	
black	have	one	under
book	he	our	up
box	help	out	us
boy	her	over	
but	here		very
	him	pat	
came	his	pets	want
can	home	play	was
car	house	pretty	water
cat	how	put	we
come			went
	I	ran	were
day	if	rat	what
dear	in	read	when
did	is	red	white
do	it	run	who
dog			will
doll	know	said	with
down		Santa	work
	last	saw	
eat	like	say	yes
	little	school	you
find	live	see	your
five	long	she	
for	look	so	zoo

spelling game—"Lock Him Up"

Select a word with not more than five letters, with which your child is familiar. Do not tell him the word you have chosen. Draw a dash for each letter in the word. (See example.) Put the first letter in place. Now the game begins. Ask your child to guess the correct letters to complete the word you have in mind. Each time he makes a wrong guess he receives a penalty, which is one line toward the construction of a box in which to "Lock Him Up."

EXAMPLE: Think of the word **house.** Draw 5 dashes.
Write **h** on the first dash.

h _ _ _ _

To one side draw a figure to represent your child. Ask your child to start guessing, telling you one letter that he thinks might fit into the word.

He guesses **a.**
It is wrong, so you begin to draw the box. One wrong guess—one line of the box.

He guesses again. He says **l.**
Wrong again. You draw one more line of the box.

He guesses **s** this time.
Right. Do not make another line of the box but put the **s** on the dash where it belongs in the word. (Note: If a letter appears twice in the word, put it in both places.)

h _ _ s _

He guesses **e.**
Right again. Write the **e** on the last dash.

h _ _ $s e$

He studies the word and gets a clue. He guesses **o.**
Right again.

$h o$ _ $s e$

Now he feels sure that he knows the word so he guesses **r.** Wrong! Add another line of the box. He is almost locked up. All you need is the cover and the lock!

He studies the word again and sees another possibility. He guesses **u** and is saved!

$h o u s e$

Now it is your child's turn to lock you up—if he can! Too many wrong guesses and not enough thinking could make a picture like this!

practicing spelling at home

Each week your child will bring home work-papers from school. Let him show them to you and talk about them. Encourage him by showing interest.

The kind of work he has done on these papers will show you if there are words on which he needs some extra help. Be sure he knows the meaning of the words and how to use them. Most children these days love to spell—if too many new words are not forced down their throats at one time! Use those dull moments in the car or while doing the dishes together to practice on the hard words.

To give your child a reason for putting letters together to form words, always use the words in sentences. If you select simple sentences, he will be able to write the whole thought. This gives him practice on his handwriting, teaches that the reason we learn to spell is to be able to communicate with others in writing, and gives him practice in beginning sentences with capitals and ending them with periods.

help your child write a story

By the end of the year your child can write this story as you read it to him slowly. He can put the capital letters and periods where they belong. Read the story through to him first so that he gets a general idea of what it is about. Then read it again as slowly as necessary while he listens and writes it down. He may not have had all these words in school. If he asks how to spell a word, tell him.

This is enough mental effort for him at one time. On another occasion encourage him to make up a story of his own and write it down. It does not need to be elaborate. Even a few simple sentences developing a thought or incident will be a challenge to his imagination, and to his skill in spelling and writing. Some children like to do this. If your child does, it may well become an agreeable everyday habit for a while.

Here is the story:

A BAT

Most people are afraid of me. I am ugly but I fly in a lovely way. My wings have a nice shape.

I am not blind. I do not see as well as some animals. I will not bump into you if you stay out of my path.

Like the owl, I sleep in the daytime. I sleep with my head down. I hang by my heels. Do you think that is a funny way to sleep?

I eat insects. I can twist and turn as I fly.

arithmetic second grade

An important part of modern mathematics is the correct use of the language of "sets" and number "properties." It must, however, be kept at a minimum. The *discovery* and *understanding* of ideas is continually emphasized before the mastery of specific facts.

numbers and numerals

Your child learns to count by ones through 500. He counts by twos, fives, and tens to 100. The number line will make it easy for him.

EXAMPLES:

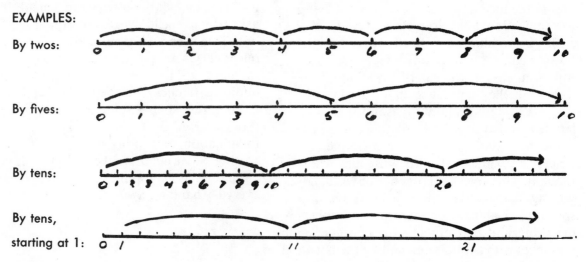

By twos:

By fives:

By tens:

By tens, starting at 1:

The place-value concept in numbers is stressed. Help your child understand it with questions like the following. Let him use actual objects as he explains his answer to you.

This year your child is made aware of number **patterns.** Being able to discover them will be a "trick" that will aid him throughout his lifetime.

A pattern is a design of the number arrangement. It is made by the regular repetition of certain numerals or by a special sequence of numerals. Can you discover the pattern in the following sets of numerals?

EXAMPLES:

41, 21, 51, 71, 31   (The digit in the ones place in each is the numeral 1.)

64, 37, 28, 19, 55   (The sum of the digits in each numeral is 10.)

1, 2, 3, 5, 6, 7, 9, 10, 11   (Every fourth number is omitted.)

Your child learns the Roman numerals through XII: I, II, III, IV, V, VI, VII, VIII, IX, X, XI, XII. They are used often enough to make it practical for your child to know them.

sets and subsets

Here is a project you and your child can work on together. Use it to help him recognize and name quickly the number of objects in sets.

DIRECTIONS:

Make many cards of sets. They should not be smaller than 3″ by 5″. Make some of the sets of simple objects, such as Xs or dots. Make some from pictures of objects cut from magazines and pasted on the cards, and draw some yourself. Be sure to have your child help you.

Make just as many cards on which you put the number words related to the cards of sets.

Make a third set of related cards on which you put the numerals related to the cards of sets.

The exercise is to match the cards correctly:

 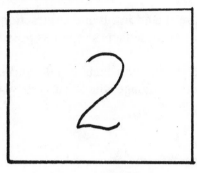 

These cards may be used for a variety of activities, such as recognition of equal or equivalent sets, and in adding (combining) or subtracting (separating) sets.

Your child learns the meaning and uses of the symbols to express "greater than" (>) and "less than" (<). He will use them first with sets of objects and then with numbers, as he learns to write his arithmetic thoughts in sentence form:

EXAMPLE:

  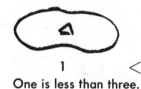 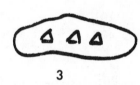

2	>	1	

Two is greater than one.

1	<	3

One is less than three.

addition and subtraction

Your child develops the concept of adding and subtracting by combining and separating sets:

EXAMPLES:

Make an equation to show:

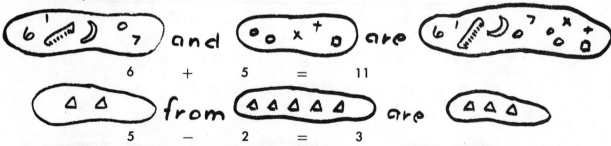

6 + 5 = 11

5 − 2 = 3

An incomplete equation, or one in which a □ is used as a place holder for the number to be found, is called an **open sentence.**

EXAMPLE: 3 − 1 = □   (open sentence)
3 − 1 = 2   (closed sentence)
3 + □ = 5   (open sentence)
3 + 2 = 5   (closed sentence)

Your child learns that parentheses which enclose the sign + or − in an arithmetic sentence mean "do this first."

EXAMPLE: $4 + (3 + 1) + 1 = \square$
             $4 + 4 + 1 = 9$

Your child will continue to use the addition and subtraction tables he made in the first grade (pages 61–64), but help him to master these facts as soon as possible. It will speed up his later work in arithmetic.

He will use the addition and subtraction facts to add and subtract two-digit and three-digit numerals. Use the correct arithmetic language when you work with your child at home. It will help him understand what he is doing.

EXAMPLES:

	As you work together say:
302	2 ones plus 6 ones equal 8 ones
	0 tens plus 7 tens equal 7 tens
+ 76	3 hundreds plus no hundreds equal 3 hundreds
378	The sum is three hundred seventy-eight.

	As you work together say:
603	3 minus one equals 2 ones
	0 tens minus 0 tens equals 0 tens
− 201	6 hundreds minus 2 hundreds equals 4 hundreds
402	The difference is four hundred two.

multiplication and division

Your child learns the meaning and use of multiplication by counting by twos and by repeating addition.

EXAMPLES:

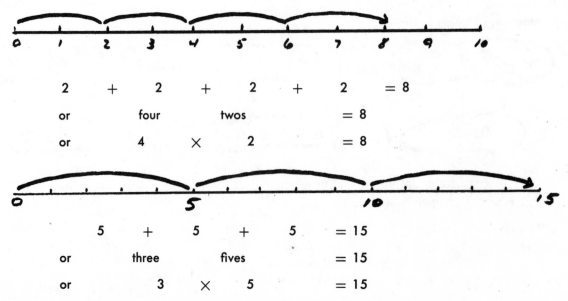

2	+	2	+	2	+	2	= 8
or		four		twos			= 8
or		4	×	2			= 8

5	+	5	+	5		= 15
or		three		fives		= 15
or		3	×	5		= 15

Your child will make a table to help him memorize simple multiplication facts. He is not expected to learn all the facts this year but he does learn to use the table.

X	0	1	2	3	4	5	6	7	8	9
0	0	0	0	0	0	0	0	0	0	0
1	0	1	2	3	4	5	6	7	8	9
2	0	2	4	6	8	10	12	14	16	18
3	0	3	6	9	12	15	18	21	24	27
4	0	4	8	12	16	20	24	28	32	36
5	0	5	10	15	20	25	30	35	40	45
6	0	6	12	18	24	30	36	42	48	54
7	0	7	14	21	28	35	42	49	56	63
8	0	8	16	24	32	40	48	56	64	72
9	0	9	18	27	36	45	54	63	72	81

He calls the answer of a multiplication problem the **product.** Each multiplication problem has two **factors.** One of the numerals in the column on the left of the table above becomes one factor. One of the numerals in the first row across the top becomes the second factor. If the problem is 3 × 2, the product is 6 because that is where the three-row and the two-column intersect.

EXAMPLE:

X	0	1	2	3
0	0	0	0	0
1	0	1	2	3
2	0	2	4	
3	0	3	6	

Division is introduced only through the teaching of multiplication and fractions. It can be understood when actual objects are used:

EXAMPLE:

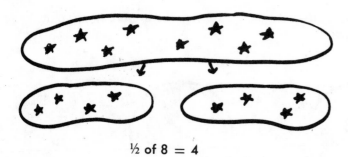

A set of 8 stars.

Half of them form a subset of 4.

½ of 8 = 4

The equation.

Eight divided into two equal subsets puts 4 in each subset.
Putting the two subsets together again equals 8.

4 + 4 = 8 or 2 × 4 = 8

fractions

Strengthen your child's understanding of fractional parts. The flannel board is an excellent device to use for this work. Make colored squares, circles, triangles, and rectangles to show ½, ⅓, ⅔, ¼, ²⁄₄, ¾, and ⅙. Use sets of objects, also, to show the same fractions.

EXAMPLES:

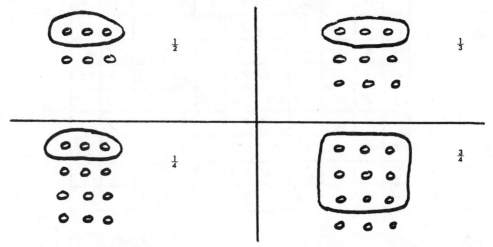

shapes and measurements

Your child becomes more familiar with shapes as he uses them in learning measurements. He learns that a square is a flat surface with two measurements—length and width. A cube has three measurements—length and width and depth.

The measurement or telling of time is developed this year. Minutes can be shown as intervals of time in a number line.

EXAMPLES:

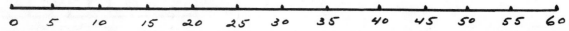

Each space is 1 minute.
60 spaces is 1 hour.
How many minutes in half an hour? (A. 30.)

A clock face can be thought of as a circular number line for the minute (long) hand.
Bend the number line to form a circle.

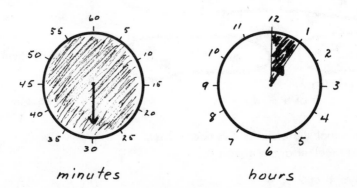

It takes the minute hand as long to move once around the clock face as it takes the hour (short) hand to move from one number to the next.

Telling time is really quite a complicated business. So don't expect your child to be a master at reading the clock until late in this second year. Do not begin "ten minutes after" or "fifteen minutes to" until the hour and half hour are easy reading for him.

Remember:

▶ **The short hand tells the hours.**
▶ **At every hour the long hand points to 12.**
▶ **The long hand shows minutes and moves all the way around the clock every hour.**
▶ **There are 5 minutes between every number.**
▶ **Half past is the same as 30 minutes after.**
▶ **At half past every hour the long hand is at 6 and the short hand is halfway between the number of the hour and the number of the next hour.**
▶ **At lunchtime, or at noon, the clock folds its hands. It puts one hand over the other.**

thought problems

The skills and concepts your child learns this year are used in solving simple word problems. Be sure he knows
    a) what facts are given;
    b) what he is asked to find;
    c) what operation he should use in solving it.

Do:

Either: $82 + 80 = \square$
$(80 + 80) + 2 = \square$
           $160 + 2 = 162$ miles in all.

or: 82 miles to the lake
    $+$ 80   miles back home
      162   miles in all

EXAMPLES:

1. Bob's father drove 82 miles to go fishing. He came home by another road, driving 80 miles. How many miles did he drive in all?

Think:
    a) Two factors are given.
    b) I am asked to find the total distance Bob's father drove.
    c) By adding the two factors, I will arrive at the answer.

2. There are 426 pupils in the school. If 225 pupils are girls, how many boys are there?

Think:
    a) 426 pupils means boys and girls together.
    b) If 225 are girls, the rest must be boys.
    c) I'll subtract.

Do:

Either: $426 - 225 = \square$
$(400 - 200)$ and $(20 - 20)$ and $(6 - 5) = \square$
200   and   0   and   1 $= 201$ are boys

or: 426   all the pupils
   $-$ 225   girls
       201   boys

Your child is not held to one method of solving his problems. The important thing is that he understands what he is doing.

reading exercises

I. Write in the missing word from the list.

1. Mary and Beth are _friends_.   village
2. The grass is nice and _____ .   friends
3. I am _____ , I want to sleep.   garden
4. The sun is so _____ .   apple
5. The man works in the _____ .   green
6. There are no weeds in our _____ .   sleepy
7. I eat an _____ every day.   light
8. It's late, I am _____ .   tired
9. What a _____ new dress you have!   eight
10. Turn out the _____ , please.   bright
11. The wet road is _____ .   speak
12. Comb your _____ .   well
13. Let us plant a _____ tree.   pretty
14. Don't you feel _____ ?   eggs
15. We bought a dozen _____ .   crows
16. My, how you have _____ .   grown
17. Can you hear the _____ ?   thunder
18. _____ clearly.   hair
19. The cock _____ .   pine
20. There are _____ baby chicks.   slippery

II. Write in the missing word from the list.

1. He is _standing_ in line.   mule
2. He _____ for me to come home.   waited
3. Write a good _____ .   standing
4. It is not fair to _____ .   splash
5. Please don't _____ on me.   sentence
6. She is as stubborn as a _____ .   picture
7. Draw a pretty _____ .   cheat
8. Let's take a _____ .   trip
9. The ocean is very _____ .   deep
10. I smell a _____ .   skunk

III. It is fun to use words in more than one way. See how many ways you can use these words. Write them in the sentences below.

flat   **foot**   **shell**   **bark**   **blanket**

1. Some people live in a _____*flat*_____ .
2. Daddy opened the clam _____ .
3. The black puppy began to _____ .
4. The dog hurt his _____ .
5. I sleep under a _____ .
6. This is a _____ stone.
7. I broke the _____ of the egg.
8. This is the _____ of the hill.
9. There is _____ on trees.
10. The _____ of snow on the ground is white.
11. This stick is a _____ long.
12. She cracked the _____ of the nut.
13. My house has a _____ roof.

IV. Write these words after the word or words below that mean nearly the same thing.

pair   suddenly   ranch   overhead

skinny   discover   follow   tied

twirled   trail

1. not fat _____*skinny*_____   2. a big western farm _____
3. turned round and round _____   4. fastened _____
5. a mountain path _____   6. go after _____
7. two of a kind _____   8. all at once _____
9. find out something new _____   10. in the sky _____

V. More words to use in more than one way. Write them in the sentences.

| ring | pays | feet | cross | tap |

1. I will ___ring___ the bell.
2. It _____ to know how to do many things well.
3. Alice has a gold _____ .
4. A puppy has four _____ .
5. There is a _____ on top of the church.
6. The little dwarf's hammer went _____ , _____ , _____ .
7. Put a _____ around the right word.
8. Mrs. Brown _____ me for the work I do for her.
9. We _____ the road.
10. We _____ on the windowpane.
11. Can you jump three _____ ?
12. Mother was very _____ with me.

VI. Write each word in the proper column.

elm	mouse	sheep	lettuce	cabbage
cow	maple	potatoes	oak	horse
pine	wood	beans	apple	coal
dog	carrots	gas	lion	corn

fuel	animals	vegetables	trees

VII. Cross out the word that does not belong.

1. run   jump   hop   ~~train~~

(<u>Run</u>, <u>jump</u>, and <u>hop</u> are things we do. They belong together. The word train does <u>not</u> belong. Cross it out.)

2. coat	hat	mittens	night
3. one	fly	four	three
4. turtle	frog	dish	fish
5. table	chair	bed	horse
6. house	sled	barn	church
7. tree	ducks	geese	hens
8. snow	sled	summer	cold
9. two	jump	six	five
10. flower	spring	garden	sit
11. farmer	oar	river	boat
12. cabin	woods	streets	mountains
13. boy	lady	man	coast
14. party	birthday	catch	cake
15. circus	clowns	house	balloons
16. cake	ice cream	bone	apples
17. hen	rooster	chicken	money
18. frog	pool	chair	turtle
19. cowboys	cattle	ranch	supper
20. ticket	fish	ride	train
21. ten	twenty	pig	five
22. draw	cry	paint	color
23. bread	meat	grass	milk
24. three	boys	nine	two

VIII. Can you guess what these stories are about?

1. Mother has a brown one.
   It is made of leather.
   She has nickels inside of it.
   Mary has a black one.
   It is made of silk.
   She has some nickels inside of it.
   I have a little red leather one.
   There are some pennies in my red one.

   What have we? _____

2. It looks like a box.
   It is not a box.
   It is a square.
   It is black.
   It is not a toy.
   On the top there is a little glass eye.
   The eye is round.
   I look into the eye.
   I see a little girl.
   She is looking at me.

   I take her picture with my _____

3. It has four legs.
   They are very short.
   They move very slowly.
   Its back is made of shell.
   Its back is very heavy.
   It is so heavy, it cannot move fast.
   It likes the mud.
   It moves about in the mud.
   It is not very big.

   What is it? _____

4. I made it in school.

It is made of paper.

It opens like a book.

On the outside there is a picture.

The picture is about Cupid.

Cupid has a bow and arrow.

On the inside is a message.

It is a message of love.

The message is, "I love you."

                    What did I make in school? _____

5. It is very, very busy.

It looks like a big fly.

It has little wings.

It works very fast.

We get honey from it.

It likes the pretty flowers.

It likes to fly from flower to flower.

I am afraid of it.

It might sting me.

                               What is it? _____

6. They are taller than houses.

They are larger than flowers.

Some have pretty seeds.

Some have pretty flowers.

They give us shade in the summer.

Squirrels like them.

                           What are they? _____

IX. Underline three other words named by the first word.

1. animal	<u>cow</u>	<u>pig</u>	house	<u>monkey</u>
2. building	barn	fire	school	house
3. girls	men	Mary	Polly	Sue
4. colors	blue	round	red	brown
5. letters	G	B		A
6. toys	jolly	airplane	doll	ball
7. boys	George	Fred	Joe	City
8. animals	kitty	light	horse	dog
9. people	father	mother	wagon	sister
10. dishes	cup	plate	red	glass
11. words	paper	toy	lmno	boy
12. children	Freddie	Susie	Mr. Smith	Tommy

X. Tell *who* and *what*.

who / what

1. Tom / walked down to the river.
2. Betty ran after Tom.
3. Betty and Tom played in an old boat.
4. Tom filled the boat with leaves.
5. The children climbed into the boat.
6. Their mother called them to come home.
7. They ran to the house.
8. Their father had come home from work.
9. They had fish for supper.
10. The children like to go fishing.
11. Their mother is a good cook.
12. After supper, the children played again.

XI. Pick out the right word. Write it in the space in the sentence.

1. sun   cut   next   1. If you <u>*cut*</u> your hand, put something on it right away.

2. round   found   own   2. Never eat candy you have _____ on the floor.

3. well   milk   tell   3. If you are not _____, go to bed as soon as your mother tells you.

4. game   same   place   4. In playing a _____, always play fair.

5. Can't   Ball   Call   5. _____ the fireman as soon as you see a house on fire.

6. oak   block   rock   6. Stay a _____ away from a big fire so you will not get hurt.

7. black   block   blue   7. Thank you for the _____.

8. game   gas   grow   8. The block is part of my _____.

XII. Sometimes two words together have one meaning. Draw a line under the right word.

1. Near the shore of the lake is a house with a bright light. It is a

    schoolhouse   <u>lighthouse</u>   flashlight

2. Tom saw a man who put out a fire. He was a

    snowman   handbag   fireman

3. Mother knows a place to build a fire. It is a

    fireboat   fireplace   housework

4. Fred's father works every day. He is a

    workman   handbag   barnyard

5. When it rains, you need a

    snowman   doorstop   raincoat

6. John has a new boat with a white sail. It is a

       sailboat   bluebird   sailfish

7. The farmer keeps his animals in the

       fireplace   barnyard   lighthouse

8. Mother keeps her money in a

       fireboat   handbag   sailboat

9. After dark I use a

       policeman   flashlight   bluebird

10. In the tree I saw a

       redbird   housework   doorstop

XIII. Write "yes" or "no" to answer these "think" questions.

1. Will a policeman help you if you are lost?   *yes*

2. Do you get a present every day?   _____

3. Is a minute round?   _____

4. Do you fish for sheep?   _____

5. Do you buy smoke?   _____

6. Can you eat a vowel?   _____

7. Do you feel better when you smile?   _____

8. Does a baby chew milk?   _____

9. Will water burn?   _____

10. Is a sheep older than a lamb?   _____

11. Do we use a knife to peel a banana?   _____

12. Is a day longer than an hour?   _____

13. Does Jack write on bark?   _____

14. Can you see a horse in a big city?   _____

15. Can you make a snowman in the summer?   _____

XIV. Draw lines under the parts of two words that sound alike.

1. <u>how</u>   roof   <u>cow</u>
2. gray   way   met
3. clown   pull   down
4. walk   talk   round
5. fall   that   sat
6. see   tree   sail
7. light   house   night
8. light   hen   then
9. seed   need   same
10. warm   harm   arm
11. dark   park   tall
12. fly   sky   honey
13. wait   boat   paint
14. book   hot   cook
15. where   hen   white
16. key   honey   play
17. Betty   some   story
18. sit   stone   stay
19. grow   one   green
20. church   sick   such
21. school   spool   doll
22. lots   box   ox
23. new   never   few
24. hens   guess   dress
25. long   desk   song
26. night   fight   few

XV. Read the story. Write the answers to the questions below the story.

A VISIT TO THE PARK

One day Betty took her baby sister to the park. She wanted to rest in the sun and read her book while the baby played.

Soon two boys started to play ball near them. One time the ball hit the baby's foot. The baby cried but the boys only laughed. Betty had to take the baby home.

She told her mother about the boys. Her mother said the boys should have played ball on the ball field.

The baby was not hurt, but Betty did not get a chance to rest in the sun or to read her book.

1. What is the name of the baby's sister? _____
2. Where did she take the baby? _____
3. How many boys played near them? _____
4. What did the boys play? _____
5. Were they nice boys? _____
6. Where should the boys have played? _____
7. Is it a story with a happy ending for Betty? _____

XVI. Read this story and answer the questions below it.

MY PET

My dog is a wonderful friend. His name is Spot. He likes to be told that he is a good dog.

I trained my dog when he was a puppy. Now he obeys me when I say, "stop," "come," "stay," "down," and "no."

My dog does not need much care. He has his own bed. I clean it every morning. I brush him on Saturday. I give him fresh water and good food every day.

1. What is my dog's name? _____
2. What does he like to hear? _____
3. When did I train him? _____
4. Does he obey me? _____
5. When do I clean his bed? _____
6. When do I brush him? _____
7. What do I give him every day? _____

writing exercises

I. Write the missing letters in the alphabets.

a	b		d			g
		j		l		n
	p			s		
v		x		z	

A		C		E	
	H				L
M			P		
S		U		W	
		Z			

II. Write the name of each one.

fish   _____   _____

_____   _____   _____

_____   _____   _____

III. Write another word that sounds like

1. house	_mouse_	16. silk	_____
2. and	_____	17. dish	_____
3. red	_____	18. far	_____
4. cat	_____	19. thump	_____
5. lock	_____	20. eat	_____
6. fun	_____	21. gold	_____
7. my	_____	22. spool	_____
8. toy	_____	23. bat	_____
9. me	_____	24. stand	_____
10. clown	_____	25. took	_____
11. sing	_____	26. make	_____
12. all	_____	27. coat	_____
13. ride	_____	28. mail	_____
14. can	_____	29. kitten	_____
15. night	_____	30. ringing	_____

IV. Write a sentence about each picture. Remember that each sentence that tells something should begin with a capital letter and end with a period.

1. _____

2. _____

_____

_____

3. _____

4. _____

_____

_____

V. More sentences. Tell what the wind does.

1. _____

_____

2. _____

_____

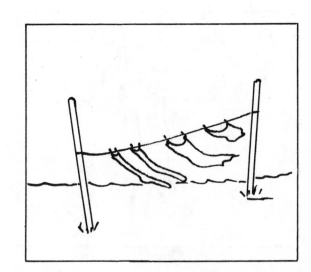

3. _____

_____

4. _____

_____

114

VI. More sentences. Write a sentence that asks a question about each picture.

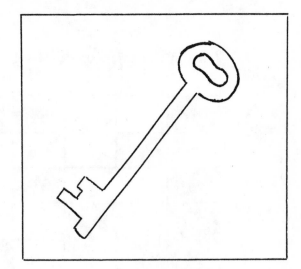

1. _____

2. _____

_____

_____

3. _____

4. _____

_____

_____

arithmetic exercises

I. Write in the missing numbers.

1			4	5			8	9	10
	12				16				20
21			24			27			
31		33			36				40
41	42			45		47	48		
	52		54				58		60
61		63		65		67			70
	72				76			79	
		83		85		87			90
91			94				98		
101		103			106			109	110
111			114			117		119	
	122			125			128		130
		133			136			139	
141			144			147			150
	152				156		158		160
		163				167		169	
171			174	175			178		180
	182			185				189	
191	192		194			197			200

II. How many are there in each group?

_____

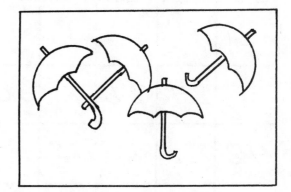

_____

_____

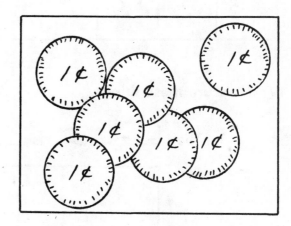

_____

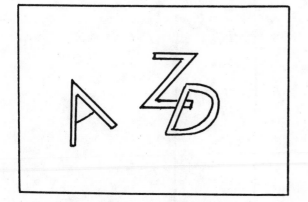

_____

_____

III. Write in the missing numbers. Count by 2's.

2	4		8		12		16	18	
	24	26		30					40
42			48		52	54		58	
	64			70		74	76		80
82		86			92			98	

IV. Measure these things.

1. The 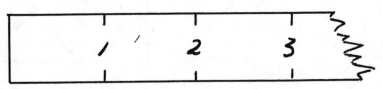 is _____ inches long.

2. The is _____ inches long.

3. The box is _____ inches tall.

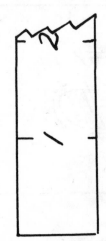

118

V. Find the pattern and write the missing number on each line.

10 _____ 30 _____ _____ 60 _____ _____ 90 _____

6 16 26 _____ _____ 56 _____ _____ _____ 96

5 10 _____ _____ _____ 30 _____ _____ _____ 50

55 _____ _____ 70 _____ _____ _____ 90 _____ 100

VI. Add.

2	3	4	5	6	7	8	2	1	2	2	3
1	1	1	1	1	1	1	2	2	4	3	2

2	4	6	5	2	1	6	5	2	3	6	4
6	5	3	4	7	8	2	5	8	3	4	4

8	5	2	4	3	7	1	3	4	2	2	3
2	3	5	3	6	3	6	5	4	3	8	7

VII. Add.

11	37	63	46	37	28	31	27	25
13	52	12	21	51	41	64	71	43

73	82	64	28	28	62	25	62	41
15	16	25	11	61	34	44	25	67

32	82	27	72	73	54
75	17	11	16	15	24

VIII. Add.

4	2	3	3	5	2	5	6	3	2
2	5	3	4	2	4	3	1	2	5
4	3	3	1	2	1	1	3	4	1

3	2	3	4	3	5	2	1	7	6
2	4	1	3	5	1	3	5	1	1
3	4	3	2	1	1	2	1	1	2

5	8	6	5	2	2	1	3	1	7
4	1	3	3	2	1	2	5	1	2
1	1	1	1	2	3	1	1	4	1

IX. Subtract.

5	6	6	5	5	6	4	2	7
− 3	− 4	− 1	− 1	− 4	− 2	− 3	− 1	− 1

6	4	3	4	3	7	8	7	9
− 5	− 1	− 2	− 3	− 1	− 4	− 2	− 5	− 5

6	8	9	8	7	9	8	7	8
− 3	− 4	− 3	− 1	− 3	− 2	− 3	− 2	− 7

2	9	8	10	7	9	9	10	10
− 2	− 7	− 6	− 1	− 6	− 4	− 6	− 8	− 7

X. Subtract.

63	87	96	86	49	29	57	86	77
−32	−33	−44	−43	−26	−14	−35	−52	−12

87	69	89	95	49	77	56	68	89
−64	−48	−17	−43	−25	−11	−34	−51	−71

73	45	45	55	75	45	63	38	29
−21	−32	−23	−41	−25	−31	−41	−15	−16

XI. Subtract.

12	13	13	13	13	12	12	12	11
−6	−6	−7	−8	−9	−7	−8	−9	−6

14	14	14	14	14	13	13	13	14
−7	−8	−9	−6	−5	−7	−6	−8	−10

13	13	13	13	13	13	12	12	12
−4	−5	−6	−7	−8	−9	−4	−5	−6

11	11	12	13	13
−5	−4	−4	−4	−3

XII. Quick problems. Draw a line to the right answer.

7 + 3	6	6 + 2	9	6 + 3	7
4 + 2	10	2 + 5	7	3 + 4	8
5 + 4	8	1 + 8	8	6 + 2	9
2 + 6	9	4 + 6	10	1 + 9	10

8 + 2	10	2 + 3	7	1 + 2	8
6 + 1	5	5 + 5	5	9 + 1	9
3 + 2	7	4 + 3	10	4 + 5	10
2 + 7	9	3 + 6	9	5 + 3	3

10 − 7	1	7 − 6	2	9 − 4	6
8 − 6	2	7 − 3	1	7 − 5	2
5 − 4	3	9 − 7	4	10 − 4	5
9 − 5	4	8 − 5	3	6 − 3	3

10 − 6	2	9 − 3	5	10 − 3	4
7 − 4	4	10 − 2	6	6 − 5	7
5 − 3	3	8 − 3	7	8 − 4	1
10 − 3	7	9 − 2	8	9 − 6	3

8 − 4	10	3 + 3	10	9 − 6	6
5 + 3	8	6 − 3	6	1 + 2	3
7 − 1	4	8 − 1	3	10 − 7	3
6 + 4	6	9 + 1	7	1 + 5	3

SECOND GRADE

XIII. Finish the set pictures.
Examples:

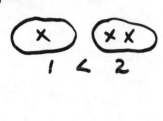 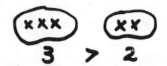

1 < 2   3 > 2

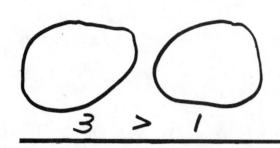 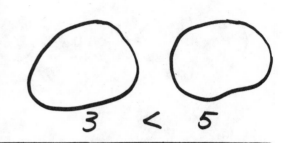

3 > 1   3 < 5

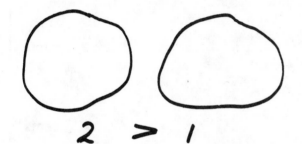 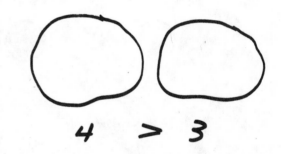

2 > 1   4 > 3

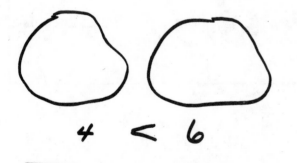 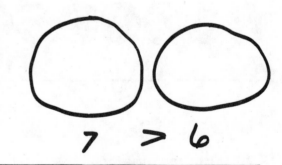

4 < 6   7 > 6

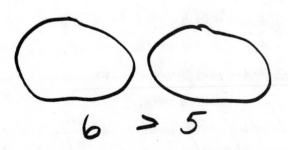 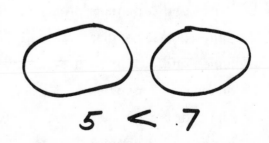

6 > 5   5 < 7

123

XIV. How much money?

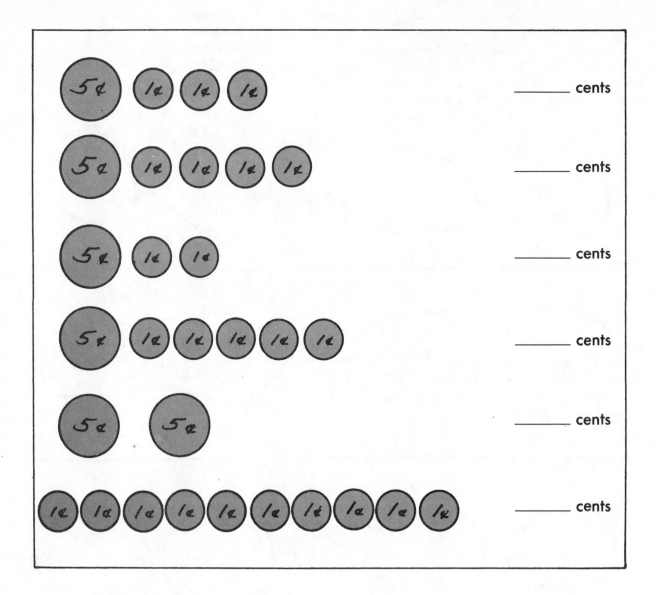

_____ cents

_____ cents

_____ cents

_____ cents

_____ cents

_____ cents

XV. Write the answers.

5 dimes and 6 pennies are _____ ¢.   3 dimes and 5 pennies are _____ ¢.

6 dimes and 2 pennies are _____ ¢.   8 dimes and 9 pennies are _____ ¢.

4 dimes and 3 pennies are _____ ¢.   2 dimes and 5 pennies are _____ ¢.

9 dimes and 9 pennies are _____ ¢.   5 dimes and 1 penny are _____ ¢.

7 dimes and 3 pennies are _____ ¢.   6 dimes and 7 pennies are _____ ¢.

5 dimes and 5 pennies are _____ ¢.   2 dimes and 8 pennies are _____ ¢.

124

3 dimes and 4 pennies are _____ ¢.   2 nickels are _____ ¢.

1 nickel and 1 penny are _____ ¢.   1 nickel and 4 pennies are _____ ¢.

2 nickels and 6 pennies are ___ ¢.   2 dimes and 1 nickel are _____ ¢.

10 dimes are _____ ¢ or $ _____ .   3 nickels are _____ ¢.

1 dime and 1 nickel are _____ ¢.   3 dimes and 1 nickel are _____ ¢.

1 dozen is _____things.   1 foot is _____ inches.

1 quart is _____ pints.

XVI. What time is it?

XVII. Follow directions.

Color ½ of the ball red
Color ½ of the ball green

Color ¼ of the ball red
Color ¼ of the ball blue
Color ¼ of the ball green
Color ¼ of the ball yellow

Color ⅓ of the ball yellow

Color ¾ of the ball orange

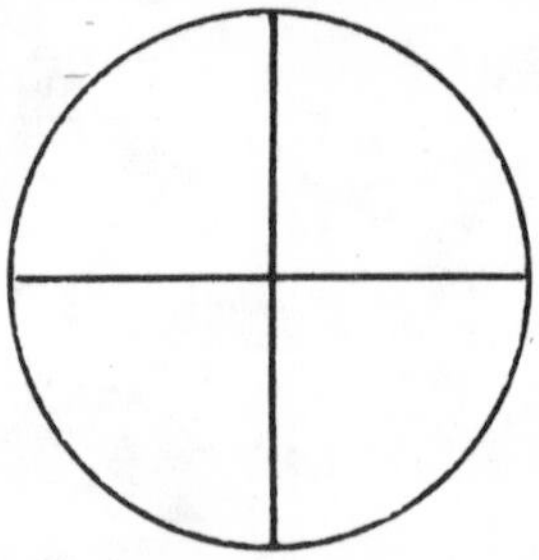

XVIII. Write a fraction to name the shaded part.

_____ _____ _____

 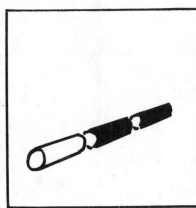 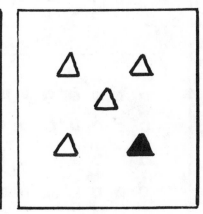

_____ _____ _____

 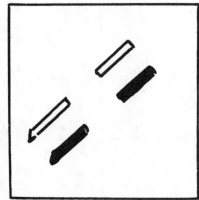 

_____ _____ _____

XIX. Put a ring around each set of ten and write the numeral for the number of objects in each frame.

Example:

1	2
tens	ones

XX. Mark an X on

the second object

the fifth object

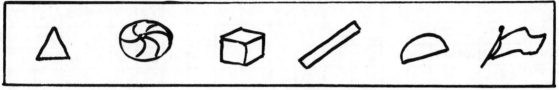

the third object

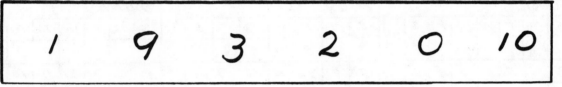

| 1 | 9 | 3 | 2 | 0 | 10 |

the sixth object

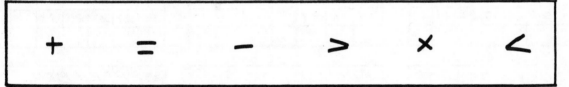

| + | = | − | > | × | < |

XXI. Quarts, pints, and half pints.

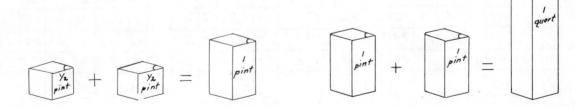

½ pint and ½ pint are 1 whole pint.   1 pint and 1 pint are 1 quart.

1. Kitty drinks ½ pint of milk every day.
   One whole pint will last _____ days.

2. There are _____ pints in one quart.

3. Kitty will drink a whole quart of milk
   in _____ days.

XXII. Measuring time. Read the name of each month, then finish the sentences on the next page.

JANUARY
S	M	T	W	T	F	S
					1	2
3	4	5	6	7	8	9
10	11	12	13	14	15	16
17	18	19	20	21	22	23
24	25	26	27	28	29	30
31						

FEBRUARY
S	M	T	W	T	F	S
	1	2	3	4	5	6
7	8	9	10	11	12	13
♡	15	16	17	18	19	20
21	22	23	24	25	26	27
28	29					

MARCH
S	M	T	W	T	F	S
	1	2	3	4	5	
6	7	8	9	10	11	12
13	14	15	16	17	18	19
20	21	22	23	24	25	26
27	28	29	30	31		

APRIL
S	M	T	W	T	F	S
					1	2
3	4	5	6	7	8	9
10	11	12	13	14	15	16
17	18	19	20	21	22	23
24	25	26	27	28	29	30

MAY
S	M	T	W	T	F	S
1	2	3	4	5	6	7
8	9	10	11	12	13	14
15	16	17	18	19	20	21
22	23	24	25	26	27	28
29	30	31				

JUNE
S	M	T	W	T	F	S
			1	2	3	4
5	6	7	8	9	10	11
12	13	14	15	16	17	18
19	20	21	22	23	24	25
26	27	28	29	30		

JULY
S	M	T	W	T	F	S
					1	2
3	4	5	6	7	8	9
10	11	12	13	14	15	16
17	18	19	20	21	22	23
24	25	26	27	28	29	30
31						

AUGUST
S	M	T	W	T	F	S
	1	2	3	4	5	6
7	8	9	10	11	12	13
14	15	16	17	18	19	20
21	22	23	24	25	26	27
28	29	30	31			

SEPTEMBER
S	M	T	W	T	F	S
				1	2	3
4	5	6	7	8	9	10
11	12	13	14	15	16	17
18	19	20	21	22	23	24
25	26	27	28	29	30	

OCTOBER
S	M	T	W	T	F	S
						1
2	3	4	5	6	7	8
9	10	11	12	13	14	15
16	17	18	19	20	21	22
23	24	25	26	27	28	29
30	31					

NOVEMBER
S	M	T	W	T	F	S
		1	2	3	4	5
6	7	8	9	10	11	12
13	14	15	16	17	18	19
20	21	22	23	24	25	26
27	28	29	30			

DECEMBER
S	M	T	W	T	F	S
				1	2	3
4	5	6	7	8	9	10
11	12	13	14	15	16	17
18	19	20	21	22	23	24
25	26	27	28	29	30	31

Sentences about the calendars.

A. *Months*

1. Put a circle around your birthday. It is in _____ .

2. There are _____ months in the year.

3. Christmas is in _____ .

4. Halloween is in _____ .

5. _____ , _____ , and _____ are hot, summer months.

6. The first month of the year is _____ .

7. Thanksgiving Day is in _____ .

B. *Days*

1. There are _____ days in July.

2. There are _____ days in June.

3. There are _____ days in a week.

4. You go to school _____ days a week.

5. On _____ and _____ you do not go to school.

6. If today is Monday, tomorrow will be _____ .

7. If the date yesterday was May 3, today is _____ ____ .

8. A heart on Valentine's Day shows you that the date is _____ ____ .

9. The first of July 1960, is on a _____ .

10. The fourth day of every week is called _____ .

11. You learned to play ''Here We Go Round the Mulberry Bush'' in school. The song tells us that we go to church on _____ .

12. The day in the July calendar where you see a flag is called _____ _____ ____ _____ .

13. The date of the first Wednesday in November is _____ _____ .

XXIII. Problems to make you think. Do your work in the box. Then write the answer on the blank line in the problem.

1. Tom has 5 calves. He is going to keep 3 and sell the others. He has _____ calves to sell.

2. Jane had 10 tickets to sell for the school circus. She has 3 left. She sold the other _____ tickets.

3. Mary has 8 tickets to sell. Bob wants to buy 10 tickets. She must get _____ more tickets.

4. Ann sold 9 tickets. Larry sold 3. Ann sold _____ tickets more than Larry.

5. Bob has 13¢. He has a dime in one pocket and _____ cents in the other pocket.

6. Ted has a quarter. On Saturday he is going to earn 14¢. Then he will have _____ ¢.

7. Tom had 88¢. He spent 65¢ for a plant. He has _____ ¢ left.

8. Bill caught a fish 13 inches long. Pete had one 9 inches long. Bill's fish was _____ inches longer than Pete's.

By the time your child has reached the end of the second grade, he should be able to complete the following tests satisfactorily, without any help from you. Do not ask him to do more than one test a day. Grade him "Very good," "Good," "Fair," or "Better go back and review some more!" except in Part III in Arithmetic.

reading

I. Read this story. Then follow the directions in Column II.

Would you like to know more about birds? Books will tell you many things about them. Watching birds will tell you many more things.

The best times to go bird watching are in the morning and in the evening.

There are some things you must not do when you watch birds. Never make a noise. Birds are afraid of noise. Never wear bright-colored things, or the birds may see you moving about.

A small bird book will help you to know a bird by its colors.

Listening for bird calls is a lot of fun. You will soon know a bird by its song even if you cannot see it. "Pretty, pretty!" tells you a redbird is near.

II. Cross out the sentences that do not tell about the story.

1. You can find out about cows in books.
2. There are two good ways of finding out about birds.
3. You must know the best times to go bird watching.
4. To be a good bird watcher, you must know how to whistle.
5. If you wear something red and shining, the birds will fly near you.
6. Take a cage with you so you can catch a bird.
7. Bird books have colored pictures of birds in them.
8. You can tell a bird by its call.
9. Take a flashlight so you will not get lost.
10. A bluebird calls, "Pretty, pretty!"

writing

I. Write as well as you can.

1. My name is _____ _____ .

2. My friends call Daddy _____ . _____ .

3. My friends call Mother _____ . _____ .

4. I live in a town called _____ .

5. My telephone number is _____ .

6. _____ _____ and _____ _____ are my friends.

7. We go to church on _____ .

8. If I get lost, I will ask a _____ to help me.

9. I say "_____ _____" to my teacher when I come to school in the morning.

10. I shall always _____ before I cross a street.

II. Write a story about the sun. These pictures will help you.

good morning

good night

flowers and trees

_____

_____

_____

_____

_____

arithmetic test

Part I. Use your crayons.

1. Color the largest ball.

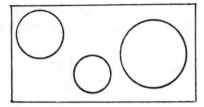

2. Color the shortest pencil.

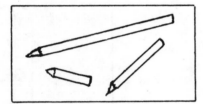

3. Color the tallest candle.

4. Color the smallest block.

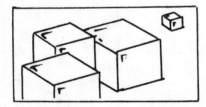

5. Color the big house.

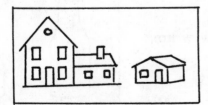

6. Color the first balloon.

7. Color the cake that has more than one candle on it.

8. Color the narrow road.

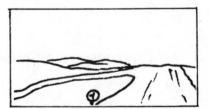

9. Color both balls.

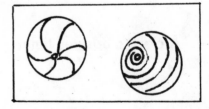

10. Color the wide book.

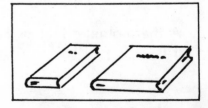

Part II. Draw a line from each sentence to the correct picture.

1. A ruler measures inches.

2. A scale measures pounds.

3. Milk is measured by quarts and pints.

4. A clock measures time.

5. A thermometer tells us how cold or how warm it is.

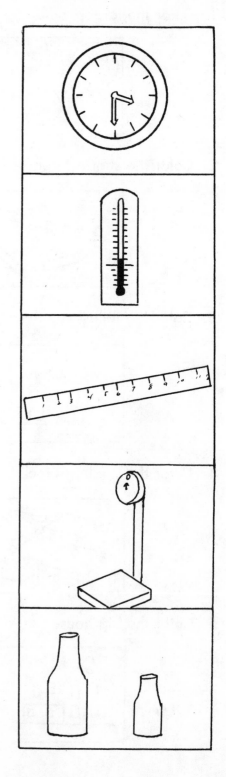

Part III. Write the answers. (Mother, grade this page, allowing 1 point per answer.)

1. 10¢ and 5¢ and 2¢ are _____ cents.

2. There are _____ days in a week.

3. There are _____ months in a year.

4. 6 and 6 are _____ dozen.

5. 7 boys and 5 girls went swimming. To find how many children are in the water, you must _____ 7 and 5. The answer is _____ .

6. Watch the signs.

10	3	5	4	4	6	3	8	7	2	7	5
− 4	+2	−1	+6	−2	−4	+7	−5	+2	+6	+4	+3

15	20	72	70	66	25	45	14	62	54
+24	+30	+13	+12	−33	−10	−32	+10	+24	+24

3	4	7	7	3	6	3	5	2	3	4	1
3	2	1	4	5	3	5	2	2	2	3	9
+3	+4	+2	+1	+2	+1	+1	+2	+2	+1	+2	+1

87	73	47	69	32	68	47	29	39	55
−24	−21	−12	−48	−10	−51	−13	−21	−12	−33

(Rest, and take the end of the test at another time.)

7. Find the patterns and fill in the missing numbers.

    1 2 _ 4 5 _ 7 8 _ 10 11 __ 13 14 __ 16 17 __ .

    3 2 1 6 5 4 _ _ _ 12 11 10 _ _ _ 18 17 16.

    2 _ 6 _ 10 14 __ 18 __ 20 __ .

    1 11 21 31 __ __ __ __ 81.

    22 __ 44 __ 66 __ 88.

8. Write the correct symbol, $<$ or $>$.

4 5	9 7	4 1
1 3	5 3	3 7
3 6	8 7	10 11
	2 4	

9. Write the correct symbol, $<$ or $>$.

$\frac{1}{2}$ $\frac{1}{4}$

$\frac{1}{3}$ $\frac{2}{3}$

$\frac{2}{5}$ $\frac{4}{5}$

$\frac{1}{6}$ $\frac{1}{3}$

$\frac{2}{2}$ $\frac{2}{4}$

10. Write the answers. You may use your multiplication square for help.

$2 \times 1 = \square$	$3 \times 1 = \square$
$2 \times 4 = \square$	$4 \times 2 = \square$
$3 \times 2 = \square$	$4 \times 3 = \square$
$3 \times 3 = \square$	$2 \times 1 = \square$
$1 \times 4 = \square$	$2 \times 2 = \square$

contents | third grade

helping your child in third grade

YOUR CHILD is now about eight years old. He is growing up! Kindergarten, first grade, second grade—he has had the experience of all these, and is quite "settled-in" to the school environment. His teacher is no longer a substitute for Mother and Daddy as she may have been in the "preparation" grades. He doesn't need his teacher so much now. He is mature enough to know that she is there only to help him learn.

And he wants to learn!

With help from you and from his teacher, your child will gain an astonishing amount of knowledge this year in addition to the bare bones of reading, writing, spelling, and arithmetic. This book has been planned to help you help the teacher help him. In working with your third-grade child at home you'll need to use an approach somewhat different from the one you used when he was in the first and second grades. Now you'll need to treat him in a more grown-up way. He is growing up in his attitude toward school and his studies. He is not so inclined to consider them as something imposed upon him by adults. He is beginning to understand the reasons for them.

reading | third grade

IN THE first grade your child read to master the skill of reading. In the second grade he developed enough assurance to read for the meaning of sentences. In the third grade he has advanced to a point where he actually uses his reading ability in his daily living. He reads newspaper headlines. He can use a table of contents. He "looks up" things.

the child who is not interested in reading

You should understand that some children take to reading much more enthusiastically than others. However, by the time a child has reached the third grade, he can be expected to show some interest in reading. If he doesn't, it is time to find out why.

Start with a physical examination. Consult with his teacher and the school physician.

If he appears to be all right physically, then consider whether he is emotionally ready to read. This is the time to do any retracing, or to give special help before going ahead with the class on more complex assignments. You can be of real help to your child and his teacher with this problem. Remember that his teacher is overloaded with teaching responsibilities today. Use the earlier books of this series to work with your child in reading. By following the exercises outlined, you can bring his "readiness to read" nearer. By all means consult your child's teacher. She will probably tell you exactly where he most needs help.

reading for understanding

In school your child now has daily drills on comprehension—on understanding what he is reading—because, starting with this grade, all schoolwork begins to depend on his ability to read and understand what he is reading.

There are many ways that you can help your child improve his facility to read.

reading games

Here are some games you can play at home with your child to improve his reading ability.

▶ Give your child a card containing several sentences, each of which has a missing word, and an envelope containing an assortment of words. Each word should be represented in several forms, both singular and plural for nouns, comparative and superlative for adjectives and adverbs. Let your child find the correct word and form for each sentence. You can get sentences from his reader.

EXAMPLE: Select the right word from:

big, bigger, biggest, plays, played, walking, walk.

My doll can ＿＿＿＿＿＿ .
My doll is ＿＿＿＿＿ than Peggy's.
The dog ＿＿＿＿＿ with the ball.

▶ Assemble black-and-white pictures in a scrapbook from magazines and old coloring books. Print simple directions under each picture for your child to follow. Let him read the directions to find out what to do.

EXAMPLE:

Color the girl's dress red. Color the pumpkin orange. Draw a box in the wagon, etc.

▶ Collect a group of simple pictures. Then write simple sentences on cards. Let your child match the sentences to the pictures. Later he may want to write his own sentences.

EXAMPLE:

This bird is flying.

▶ After reading a story with your child from one of his own magazines, such as *Humpty-Dumpty* or *Highlights Magazine*, discuss it with him. Ask him to list the main events in the order in which they happened. Ask him to name the main characters. He should recall such details as the kind of clothes somebody is wearing, or places mentioned in the story.

▶ Occasionally ask your child to read one of his magazine stories for a specific reason, such as, "Read it so you can tell me what the story is about," or, "Find out the color of Susan's dress," or "How many people are in the story?"

▶ Draw a house. (See following page.) Put a family name over the door, that is: a combination of letters that will be the basis for many new words. As your child finds what consonants or sounds can be used to make new words, he can add windows, then shingles, to the house.

EXAMPLE:

Words made so far with the consonants in the window:

lame name game

Other words that can be made: **same, came, dame, fame, tame.**

Other family names that can be used: **ern, ouse, ime, ack, ate, ail, ill, ile.**

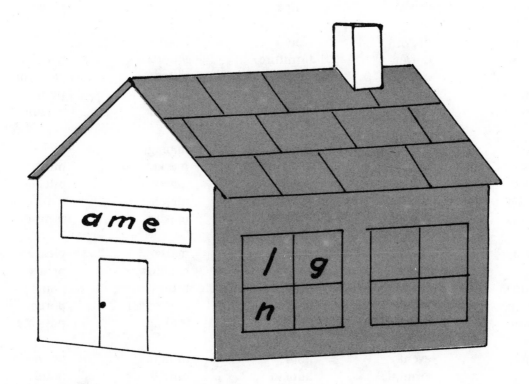

reading word list

Word lists vary with different reading systems. Following is a very short, basic, third-grade list. Practice the words with your child but do not study more than 25 at one time. Let him add new words as he learns them from his reading.

able	anxious	beyond	built	charge
account	appear	bicycle	bundle	charming
accuse	army	biscuit	buried	chase
actor	arrive	blame	business	cheerful
admit	ashamed	blanket	busy	cherry
against	attack	blossom	butcher	chicken
agree	attention	borrow	buttons	chimpanzee
alarm	attract	bother	caboose	chuckled
aiiow	audience	bought	California	clang
already	autumn	bowl	canaries	clear
amazed	barbecue	branch	cause	clipper
among	basket	bravery	certain	close
amount	battery	break	chain	cloud
amusement	beautiful	breath	chance	coffee
announcer	behave	bright	change	comfortable

company	doctor	force	lazy	partner
compare	double	forth	lead	passenger
compete	doubt	forward	lean	pasture
complain	dreary	freight	leap	patch
concern	drive	fringe	leather	pause
confess	drove	fruit	length	peach
confused	during	furniture	lettuce	peddler
contented	eager	gather	lizard	performance
continue	earth	gentlemen	lose	perhaps
contrary	early	glitter	lumber	person
copper	easy	grapes	manage	pick
correct	edge	great	market	pinch
cottage	either	groceries	marry	pitcher
country	empty	habit	marsh	platform
courage	enemy	happiness	master	pleasant
course	engineer	harbor	matter	pleasure
court	enjoy	heart	meadow	plenty
cousin	enter	heavy	meant	point
cowslip	escape	herd	messenger	porch
creature	especially	hitch	midnight	possible
crept	event	hour	minute	potato
crowd	example	human	mirror	pour
curtain	except	hundred	mischief	power
customer	excited	husband	mistake	practice
dairy	exclaim	idea	motorman	praise
dandy	expect	imagine	mountain	prepare
danger	experiment	immediately	mustache	pretend
Daniel	explain	impatient	mystery	probably
daughter	express	important	nail	problem
decide	fair	impossible	necessary	property
declare	family	inquire	needle	protect
delicious	famous	insist	neighbor	proud
delight	farther	instead	neither	puzzle
desire	fault	interest	nibble	quarrel
difference	favorite	invisible	notice	quite
direct	feather	jacket	ocean	raise
direction	figure	jelly	order	rapidly
disappear	finally	jungle	ought	raspberries
discover	flour	knitting	ourselves	reach
distance	foolish	language	palace	realize

reason	season	slipped	stocking	train
receive	selfish	smoke	stolen	trait
recognize	sentence	snails	straight	travel
refuse	servant	soldier	streak	treat
remain	several	sorry	stripe	tremble
remarkable	shadow	speak	struggle	trousers
repeat	shelf	special	stupid	trust
reply	shook	spice	sturdy	umbrella
reward	shore	spoil	success	usually
river	shoulder	spoke	sudden	vacation
safety	shovel	spread	suggest	vegetable
scamper	shower	square	suppose	village
scatter	sight	squawk	suspect	voice
scene	signal	squeal	switch	wander
scissors	silver	squirrel	syllable	weak
scold	simple	stall	thick	weather
scowl	since	statement	thief	week
scratch	single	steal	though	wheel
scream	sixteen	steel	threw	whimper
search	sleeves	stockade	ticket	wrinkle

books your third-grade child may enjoy

Helpful Helicopters —*Allison, Dorothy K.*
Thumbelina —*Andersen, Hans C.*
Mr. Popper's Penguins
    Atwater, Richard and Florence
The House Beyond the Meadow —*Behn, Harry*
Madeline —*Bemelmans, Ludwig*
Shoemaker of Kish —*Bernardin, C. A. J.*
Pete the Parakeet —*Black, Irma*
The Fast Sooner Hound
    Bontemps, Arna and Conroy, J.
Chris Turner Magician —*Brady, James T.*
Dick Whittington and His Cat —*Brown, Marcia*
Cowboy Sam and the Indians
    Chandler, Edna W.
In My Mother's House —*Clark, Ann Nolan*
My Pet Peepelo —*Credle, Ellis*
Once upon a Time: Twenty Cheerful Tales
    Dobbs, Rose
Story of a Baby —*Ets, Marie Hall*
Big Book of Cowboys —*Fletcher, Sydney E.*
The Sun, the Moon, and the Stars
Your Wonderful World of Science
    Freeman, Mae and Ira

Tell Me About God —*Jones, Mary Alice*
Miss Posy Longlegs —*Mason, M. E.*
Picture Book of the Weather —*Meyer, Jerome S.*
Winnie-the-Pooh —*Milne, A. A.*
The Snake That Went to School —*Moore, Lilian*
The Secret River —*Rawlings, M. K.*
Market Day for Ti Andre —*Rodman, Maia*
Elephant Herd —*Schlein, Miriam*
How Big Is Big?
Let's Look Under the City
    Schneider, Herman and Nina
And to Think That I Saw It on Mulberry Street
Horton Hatches the Egg
The 500 Hats of Bartholomew Cubbins
    Dr. Seuss
Caps for Sale —*Slobodkina, Esphyr*
A Child's Garden of Verses
    Stevenson, Robert L.
First Book of Automobiles —*Tatham, Campbell*
The First Christmas —*Trent, Robbie*
The Happy Prince —*Wilde, Oscar*
First Book of Birds —*Williamson, Margaret*

THE THIRD grade is an important grade for your child in writing because it is the year in which he usually changes from the *manuscript* style of writing to the one educators call *cursive*. Cursive is simply the old-fashioned kind of writing that you yourself were probably taught from the beginning. It is the kind in which the letters flow along and are connected. The reason your child was not taught it in first grade is that it has been found that until the small muscles of his hand and fingers are developed, he does better with the manuscript style of writing.

But now he is ready to make the change. Don't expect too much writing perfection from him this year because he must learn new ways of making some of the letters, and because he has to develop a new style of writing. In some schools the manuscript style of writing is continued through all grades. In all schools it is retained as a useful form, with occasional practice periods given.

Your child will not have too much trouble in adjusting to the new writing style. He will have regular short supervised class periods when the different way of writing is taught and practiced. He is first shown how much alike the two styles are and then shown the differences (if there are any) in each letter.

Here are the differences in the two styles:

Manuscript:

a b c d e f g h i j k l m n o p q r s t u v w x y z

Cursive:

abcdefghijklmnopqrstuvwxyz

The cursive style varies slightly in different systems, but some generalizations can be made about forming the letters so that they are easy to read.

To write clearly, your child must first see for himself that a closed *o* is easier to read than one which is left open:

EXAMPLE:

bux (poor)

box (good)

that *g, q,* and *d,* should be closed:

EXAMPLE:

doy (poor)

dog (good)

that *l, f, h, k,* and *b* must have a loop big enough to see through:

EXAMPLE:

pull (poor)

pull (good)

that the tall letters should be about twice as high as the short letters.

EXAMPLE:

eittee (poor)

little (good)

In school your child learns to write simple letters, to address envelopes. At home encourage him to write his own invitations when he has a party and to address his own Christmas greetings. Encourage him to make lists in cursive handwriting—almost any kind of list: shopping lists, lists of his toys, books, playmates. Encourage him to write about anything that interests him—but at this stage never criticize his awkward letters or his neatness. This is a year of practice and development.

Here is a check list of writing rules. Review them often with your child.

- ▶ Sit in a comfortable position for writing. Hold the pencil easily; fingers should not be cramped.
- ▶ Make the letters correctly.
- ▶ Make all letters slant in the same direction.
- ▶ Make connecting strokes and ending strokes short.
- ▶ Leave the width of the letter o between words.
- ▶ Make loops correctly, so that there will be a "path of light" between the lines of writing.
- ▶ Make capital letters and tall letters twice the height of small letters.
- ▶ You should be able to see through each e.
- ▶ The letter t is not quite as tall as the letter l.
- ▶ The lines that connect the letters b e or w e do not come down to the line.
- ▶ Numbers are the same height as t.
- ▶ The downward stroke of f is straight.
- ▶ A period is on the line.
- ▶ Be sure to dot i above the i, and to cross the t.
- ▶ Point the small handwritten s.
- ▶ There is no loop in a small d or p or t.
- ▶ Do not use unnecessary beginning and ending strokes and flourishes.
- ▶ Rounded-letter forms are more easily read than angular ones. Watch your m's and n's.
- ▶ The o and a should always be closed.

ENGLISH

The best way you can help your child with his English in the third grade is simply to listen when he talks, then correct any bad speech habits you may detect. If he likes to tell stories, either about what actually has happened to him or others or stories made up out of thin air, encourage him to do so. It will give him good practice in putting words together effectively. It will also give him the confidence to talk before groups.

Many of the things your child does in English at school can be repeated at home if you and the teacher feel that he needs special help. Here is how the teacher works with him at school:

Almost every day a period is given to oral and written English. Your child tells and writes simple stories. He makes announcements to his class. He learns to leave out or take out useless material and to organize new material. He is reminded to speak clearly at all times. He has practice in using periods, question marks, and capital letters. He learns that some ways of saying things are more acceptable than others. It is correct, for example, to say, "He is not here." It is incorrect to say, "He ain't here."

SPELLING

Your child makes important progress in spelling this year. He is doing more writing now, and begins to realize the need for correct spelling. The words in his spelling lessons are those in everyday use. The greatest emphasis in third grade, however, is placed on how to study and learn new words. He can do this at home as well as at school if you and his teacher feel that he needs the extra study. Here is the procedure that he follows at school:

▶ **First, he must be able to pronounce the word correctly.**

▶ **Then he must know the meaning of the word and be able to use it in a sentence.**

▶ **If it is easy to see, the teacher helps him to pick out the *root* from which the word is made. For example, in the word *going*, the root is *go*.**

▶ **He next studies the arrangement of letters, first by looking at the word and saying the letters, then by writing the word several times.**

▶ **He now tries to write the word without help, then checks the word himself to see if he has written it correctly. If he has made a mistake, he then repeats the entire procedure. Once he knows his words, he should, of course, be able to spell them orally, write them and use them correctly in sentences.**

spelling word list

Following is a list of about 250 words commonly used by third-graders that your child should be able to spell by the time he finishes the third grade. If he has begun to read stories on his own, he will be familiar with the spelling of many more. In using the list at home, be sure not to give him more than 20 words at a time.

about	anything	because	broke	catch
afternoon	apple	been	brother	caught
again	arithmetic	before	brought	chair
airplane	around	behind	buffalo	chicken
almost	asked	better	built	children
along	asleep	birthday	busy	Christmas
already	assembly	blue	buy	church
always	aunt	both	by	clean
another	babies	bread	cannot	close
answer	beautiful	bright	carry	clothes

color	forget	learn	please	teacher
coming	found	leave	poor	teeth
cool	Friday	light	puppy	Thanksgiving
couldn't	friend	lives	quite	their
country	front	loving	rabbit	things
cousin	funny	low	radio	thinking
cowboy	garden	lunch	rain	those
cried	glass	mail	ready	thought
cry	goes	marbles	real	through
daddy	gold	March	remember	throw
dance	gone	mean	riding	tie
December	grandmother	meat	right	together
didn't	grass	meet	rode	tomorrow
different	great	merry	roses	tonight
dinner	green	might	round	too
does	ground	money	Santa Claus	town
doing	guess	monkey	Saturday	tried
done	hair	mouse	says	truly
don't	half	mouth	seen	uncle
each	Halloween	move	sheep	until
early	haven't	near	shoes	use
Easter	having	news	should	vacation
eight	heard	next	since	valentine
enough	high	nights	sister	watch
everything	hope	nothing	something	wear
eyes	horse	o'clock	sometime	weather
face	houses	off	spring	where
fairies	hundred	once	stamps	which
farmer	ice	only	stick	while
farther	I'll	other	stockings	why
fell	I'm	paint	street	window
few	Indian	pair	string	winter
fifth	inside	pencil	study	wish
fight	isn't	people	summer	won't
finished	it's	piano	Sunday	would
fishing	its	pick	suppose	writing
flew	kitten	picture	sure	wrote
floor	knew	pie	table	year
flower	large	piece	tail	yellow
fly	later	place	talk	yesterday

IN THE third grade your child first reviews everything he has learned about numbers in the beginning grades. He uses the basic facts he has learned earlier to help him solve the new work, which is becoming more difficult. He is constantly encouraged to think for himself and to attempt solutions without help. You can help his teacher help him grow in arithmetic. Don't just thrust facts and answers at him for him to memorize. Be sure he understands what he is doing and give him a chance to do it. Be a good listener. Let him explain some of the ideas in New Math to you. The further he advances, the more important it becomes that he understand the reasons for what he is doing.

A word of caution: When you undertake to help your child at home with his arithmetic, keep an open mind about the way he arrives at his answers. Arithmetic is taught differently than it was when you went to school. Your child learns more than one way to do his work

and he is free to use the method he prefers.

To familiarize you with methods he may use, attention will be given throughout this section to explaining some of them. Arithmetic is much more interesting than it used to be. Today's teaching methods assure that your child will learn more arithmetic more easily and quickly, and will understand it better than in any previous generation.

As far as possible arithmetic is taught to your child in terms of his daily experiences and with the aid of real objects. He can understand it more quickly and easily if you show him that two marbles and two marbles are four marbles than if you simply say, "Two and two are four."

Your child develops multiplication and begins division this year, and he becomes proficient at adding and subtracting whole numbers and simple fractions. He learns to call the parts of his problems by their correct names and he uses more of the new language of "sets."

numbers and numerals

Your child uses a number line to count

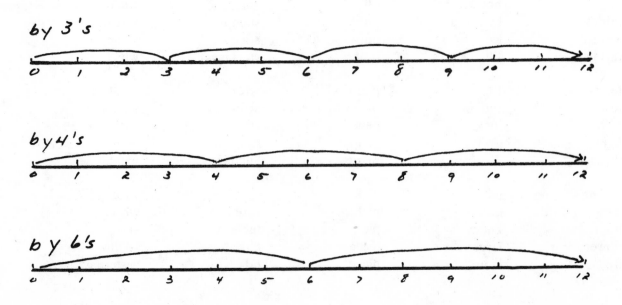

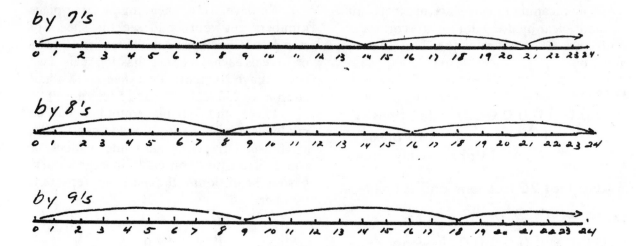

by 7's

by 8's

by 9's

Your child continues to work with place values of digits in larger numbers. He understands that the value of a digit depends on the column in which it is placed. Each column is called a "house." If it is in the first house on the right, the "ones house," it has a value of less than 10. If it is in the "tens house," it has a value of how-many-tens-there-are. The numeral 20 shows a 2 in the "tens house" and a 0 in the "ones house." This means there are 2 tens and no ones in this numeral, or 20. A digit in the "hundreds house" is equal to that many hundreds. 500 shows a 5 in the "hundreds house" and no tens and no ones.

Develop place value by tying toothpicks into bundles of ten. Draw squares for the houses and name them. Your third-grader will become familiar with the names of four or more of the houses in our number system. By knowing the names of four houses, your child can read a number that has four figures. He puts each digit into its proper house and gives it the house name.

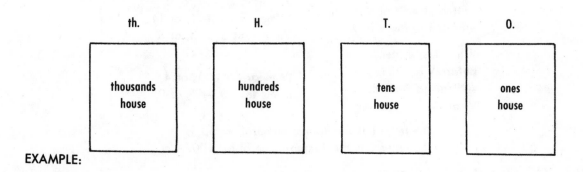

th.	H.	T.	O.
thousands house	hundreds house	tens house	ones house

EXAMPLE:

Read 1,524

Use the houses above. Put the 4 into the ones house, the 2 in the tens house, the 5 in the hundreds house, the 1 in the thousands house. The number is read: One thousand five hundred twenty-four.

He learns the use of zero as a "place holder." Zero means *not any*. In 203, for instance, we have 3 ones, not any tens, and 2 hundreds. But if we did not use the *0* in the "tens house," we could not show that the 2 is in the third house, or the "hundreds house."

The meaning of two-place numbers can be made clear by using dot pictures or beads on frames. They can show that 12 is 10 ones and 2 ones;

EXAMPLE:

0 0 0 0 0 0 0 0 0 0   ten ones
0 0   two ones
          Total   twelve ones

and that 25 is 2 tens and 5 ones.

EXAMPLE:

0 0 0 0 0 0 0 0 0 0 ⎰ twenty ones
0 0 0 0 0 0 0 0 0 0 ⎱ (two tens)
0 0 0 0 0   five ones
          Total   twenty-five

To develop the meaning of three-place numbers, let your child see the sheets of stamps of Christmas seals. There are 10 rows of 10 seals each. One sheet has 100 seals. Two sheets have 200 seals. Two sheets and a half sheet have 250 seals (200 and 5 tens more).

Three- and four-place numbers can be made clear with a simply made peg board, as shown. Drive long nails into a block of wood. Name the "houses." Slip large kindergarten beads onto the nails to represent numbers.

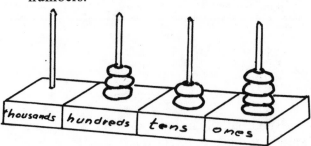

The positions of these beads shows that the number is 324.

Long ago the Roman people used numerals instead of figures. Roman numerals are still used sometimes on clock faces, as chapter headings, and in giving dates.

Your child learned to read Roman numerals to XII last year. This year he learns to read and write them through 100.

When I or II or III is written **after** V or X it is **added** to the V or X.

When I is written **before** V or X it is **subtracted** from the V or X

The letter I is the Roman numeral for 1.
The letter V is the Roman numeral for 5.
The letter X is the Roman numeral for 10.

⎰ VI means 5 + 1, or 6
⎨ XI means 10 + 1, or 11
⎱ VIII means 5 + 3, or 8

⎰ IV means 5 — 1, or 4
⎱ IX means 10 — 1, or 9

The letter L is the Roman numeral for 50.
The letter C is the Roman numeral for 100.

When X is written after another X, or L, or C, it is added.

⎛ XX means 10 + 10, or 20
⎜ XXX means 10 + 10 + 10, or 30
⎜ LX means 50 + 10, or 60
⎨ LXX means 50 + 10 + 10, or 70
⎜ LXXX means 50 + 10 + 10 + 10 or 80

When X is written before L or C, it is subtracted.

⎛ XL is 50 — 10, or 40
⎝ XC is 100 — 10, or 90

Following these patterns, write:

35 (three tens and five) _____

36 (three tens and five and one) _____

75 (fifty and ten and ten and five) _____

99 (one hundred minus ten, and nine) _____

27 (two tens and five and two) _____

(ANSWERS: XXXV, XXXVI, LXXV, XCIX, XXVII)

sets and subsets

Without using the terms, be sure your child understands associativity and commutativity.

Illustrate these properties with sets of actual objects and with number lines if possible, then with pictured representations.

EXAMPLES:

Associativity (grouping) in addition:

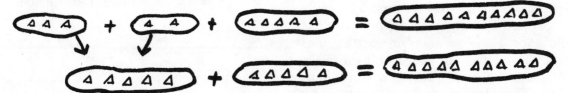

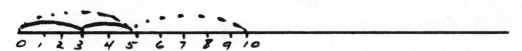

$$3 + 2 + 5 = 10$$
$$5 + 5 = 10$$

2. $7 + 4 =$
$(7 + 3) + 1 =$
$10 + 1 = 11$

Look for combinations of 10 as the easiest number to work with.

Commutativity in addition:

1.
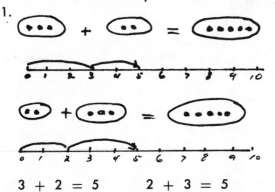

$$3 + 2 = 5 \qquad 2 + 3 = 5$$

Commutativity in multiplication:

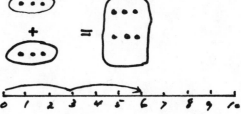

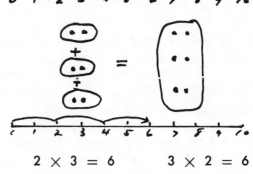

$$2 \times 3 = 6 \qquad 3 \times 2 = 6$$

addition and subtraction

Third-graders must learn the basic facts of addition and subtraction which are all the two-number combinations in our number system. The teacher will spend much time reviewing them with the class. Should your child reveal a need for additional help at home, you should take all the time necessary to see that he completely understands them. Use number lines, the addition-subtraction table, and flash cards.

Playing games is one of the best ways for your child to learn the facts of addition and subtraction. Learning is easier when work seems like fun.

Together you and your child can print the number combinations on small cards, called "flash cards." Omit the answers. The cards can be used in many ways to improve your child's speed and accuracy in recalling answers. If you use tag board or lightweight cardboard, the cards will stand many handlings. The kind of cardboard that some laundries put inside freshly laundered shirts is excellent for the purpose.

One suggestion is to make each card in the shape of a fish.

Turn all the cards face down. Now have your child and his young friends test their "fishing" skill. Decide first if it is to be a game of addition or subtraction and use only the appropriate cards. As each child draws or "catches" a fish, he must call out the sum or difference of the two numbers on his fish.

If the answer is correct, the child keeps the fish. If not, he must turn it face down and mix it with the other fish waiting to be caught. After all the fish have been "caught," the child with the biggest catch is the winner.

Another teaching game can be made with 20 snap clothes pins and a wire coat hanger. Paint 10 of the clothes pins a gay color and leave 10 of them natural. Snap 3 colored clothes pins on the hanger, then add 1 plain one. $3 + 1 = 4$

Then show that subtraction is an inverse operation or the "undoing" of addition by removing the plain one again.

$$4 - 1 = 3$$

Number lines are valuable aids for addition.

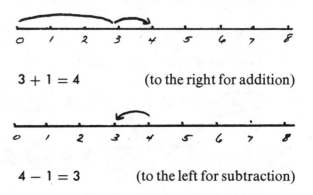

$3 + 1 = 4$ (to the right for addition)

$4 - 1 = 3$ (to the left for subtraction)

Your child adds columns of single digits by associating pairs of numerals. He knows that 10 is an easy number to work with and he tries to find combinations of 10 when it is possible.

EXAMPLE:

$$\left.\begin{array}{r} 5 \\ 5 \end{array}\right\} 10$$
$$\frac{4}{14}$$

He also combines numerals as he discovers addition facts he has learned from the addition-subtraction table.

EXAMPLE:

$$\left.\begin{array}{r} 5 \\ 3 \end{array}\right\} 8$$
$$\left.\begin{array}{r} 6 \\ 3 \end{array}\right\} 9$$
$$\overline{17} \quad (8 + 9)$$

To make it meaningful, use actual dimes and pennies to illustrate addition.

EXAMPLE:

63 cents (6 dimes and 3 pennies)
+ 22 cents (+ 2 dimes and + 2 pennies)
85 cents (8 dimes and 5 pennies)

	8	5
H	T	O

When he adds larger numbers, totaling 10 or more in the ones column, your child learns to "carry" to the tens column. Your child actually renames the houses when he transfers a set of ten from one house to the next house.

EXAMPLE:

27
+ 35
12

(7 ones + 5 ones = 12 ones, which means 1 ten and 2 ones)

50
62

(2 tens + 3 tens = 5 tens, which means 50)

(2 ones are left in the ones column. The 1 ten is written in the tens column and added to the 5 already there.)

1
27
+ 35
62

It can be written like this:

(The one is "carried" and added immediately with the other digits in the tens column.)

Your child will add three-digit numbers with "carrying" from the ones column to the tens column, and carrying from the tens column to the hundreds column when the tens column totals 10 or more tens.

EXAMPLE:

172
+ 238
010 (2 ones + 8 ones = 10 ones or 1 ten)

100
300 (7 tens + 3 tens = 10 tens or 1 hundred)

410 (1 hundred + 2 hundred = 3 hundred) (total) or

172
+ 238
410

Understanding any one step in arithmetic depends on understanding what has gone before. You can see the importance, then, of reviewing with your child any arithmetic lessons he may have missed on days when he was absent. You will need to help him catch up.

Your child learns that subtraction is necessary:

▶ **To find the number left.**

EXAMPLE:

Tom has 10 bottle caps on his desk. He takes 2 away. How many are left? We say 10 take away 2 are 8, or 2 from 10 are 8, or 10 minus 2 are 8. We think "subtract." We write: $10 - 2 = \square$.

▶ **To find how many more you need.**

EXAMPLE:

I have 2 bottle caps, but I need 10 of them to put around the brim of my hat. How many more do I need? THINK: How many more do I have to add to 2 to make 10? WRITE: $2 + \square = 10$.

▶ **To find how much larger or smaller one number is than another. This is called comparing numbers.**

EXAMPLE:

Jack has $10 in the bank. Jane has $2. How much bigger is Jack's savings account than Jane's? THINK: What is the difference between 2 and 10? WRITE: $10 - 2 = \square$.

155

After he has mastered the basic subtraction facts your child will be ready to subtract two-digit numbers. He writes these in column form.

Some schools teach the "additive" form. In the example you think, "What will I have to add to 1 to make 2?"

$$\begin{array}{r} 32 \\ -21 \\ \hline 11 \end{array}$$ ("I need 1, write 1 in the answer.) Then think, "What do I have to add to 2 to make 3?" ("I need 1," write 1. The answer is 11.)

If your child understands what subtraction is, other methods will not confuse him. More than one way to find a missing number will, in fact, increase his understanding.

After he has mastered the subtraction of two-digit numbers, he will be ready to subtract three-digit numbers from three-digit numbers.

EXAMPLE:

$$\begin{array}{r} \$8.88 \\ -\ 3.62 \\ \hline \$5.26 \end{array}$$

Then he uses zero:

EXAMPLE:

$$\begin{array}{r} \$8.88 \\ -\ 3.60 \\ \hline \$5.28 \end{array}$$

Then he has problems which have zero in the answer:

EXAMPLE:

$$\begin{array}{r} \$8.88 \\ -\ 3.68 \\ \hline \$5.20 \end{array}$$

Then he uses 2 zeros in the answer:

EXAMPLE:

$$\begin{array}{r} \$8.88 \\ -\ 3.88 \\ \hline \$5.00 \end{array}$$

Next come problems with borrowing the ones column. Introduce the subject of borrowing by using sets of actual objects. In the following example use coins.

EXAMPLE:

$$\begin{array}{r} \$.32 \\ -\ .16 \\ \hline .16 \end{array}$$

Write it as you think it:

$$\begin{array}{r} {}^{2\ 12} \\ \$.\cancel{3}\cancel{2} \\ -.16 \\ \hline .16 \end{array}$$

Explain borrowing this way:

In the example you have 3 dimes and 2 pennies and you are subtracting 1 dime and 6 pennies. You can see that you cannot take 6 pennies away from 2 pennies. Borrow 1 dime (10 pennies) from the 3 dimes and give it to the pennies column. Then the problem will be:

2 dimes	12 pennies
−1 dime	6 pennies
1 dime	6 pennies

If your school teaches the additive form, explain borrowing by asking your child to think this way: Since the 6 is already larger than 2, I cannot add anything to it to make 2. But I can add a number to 6 to make 12, so I think of 12 instead of 2. Then I think 6 and 6 are 12 and I write 6. I carry the 1 of the 12 to the next column and add it to the 1 that is there. That makes it 2. Now what can I add to 2 to make 3? 2 and 1 are 3 and I write 1. To check it, add the subtrahend and the difference. The answer should be the top number. Think 6 and 6 are 12. 1 and 1 and the 1 from the 12 which I carried are 3. My problem is right.

$$
\begin{array}{r}
.32 \\
-\,{}^2\!\!\!\not{1}6 \\
\hline
.16
\end{array}
$$

The next step in subtraction is borrowing in the tens column. These problems are always presented in "story" form, never just as numbers.

EXAMPLE:

The class had a candy sale and sold $1.72 worth of candy to buy scenery for their play; they needed $3.15. How much more did they have to earn?

$$
\begin{array}{r}
\$3.15 \\
-\,1.72 \\
\hline
\$1.43
\end{array}
$$
Think (unless you are using the additive method): "5 pennies take away 2 pennies is 3 pennies." Write 3. "I cannot take 7 dimes away from 1 dime, so I will borrow from the next row, which is the dollar row. I will borrow 1 dollar (10 dimes in a dollar) and give it to the 1 dime."

Now the problem says:

2 dollars	11 dimes	5 pennies
— 1 dollar	7 dimes	2 pennies
1 dollar	4 dimes	3 pennies

This is the way to write it:

$$
\begin{array}{r}
{}^{2\ 11} \\
\$3.15 \\
-\,1.72 \\
\hline
\$1.43
\end{array}
$$

Example of the additive form with borrowing in the tens column:

$$
\begin{array}{r}
{}^2 \\
\$\not{3}.15 \\
-\,1.72 \\
\hline
\$1.43
\end{array}
$$
Think: "2 and 3 are 5, write 3." Think: "7 and what are 11?—7 and 4 are 11." Write 4 and carry the 1 of the 11 to the next column, and add it to the 1 that is already there, making it 2. Then think, "2 and what are 3? —2 and 1 are three." Write 1. The answer is $1.43.

Now onto borrowing in the tens and hundreds columns.

EXAMPLE:

$$
\begin{array}{r}
{}^{5\ 4\ 13} \\
\$\not{6}\not{5}.35 \\
-\,37.62 \\
\hline
\$27.73
\end{array}
$$

Then, with zero in the minuend

EXAMPLE:

$$
\begin{array}{r}
{}^5 \\
\$3.60 \\
-\,1.25 \\
\hline
\$2.35
\end{array}
$$

with zero in the tens column

EXAMPLE:

$$
\begin{array}{r}
{}^2 \\
\$3.07 \\
-\,1.25 \\
\hline
\$1.82
\end{array}
$$

Zeros in both the ones and tens columns—

EXAMPLE:

$$
\begin{array}{r}
{}^{2\ 9\ 10} \\
\$\not{3}.\not{0}\not{0} \\
-\,1.25 \\
\hline
\$1.75
\end{array}
$$
Think: I'll borrow a dollar (10 dimes) and give it to the dimes place. Then I'll borrow a dime and give it to the pennies. Then I will have 2 dollars, 9 dimes, 10 pennies.

multiplication and division

Your child continues to use multiplying as a short way to find the total of sets of equal size. (See Multiplication, Grade 2) By using real objects, such as coins, he sees that 2 nickels are a dime, or 2 fives are 10, or $2 \times 5 = 10$. He learns the commutative property of multiplication: $2 \times 5 = 5 \times 2$.

He uses the multiplication table he made in the second grade but now he is expected to memorize the basic facts, so he will have less and less need for the chart.

Your child uses the basic facts to multiply a two-digit number.

Without carrying:

EXAMPLE:

$$\begin{array}{r} 12 \\ \times\ 2 \\ \hline 24 \end{array}$$

And with carrying:

EXAMPLE:

$$\begin{array}{r} \overset{1}{15} \\ \times\ 2 \\ \hline 30 \end{array}$$

Think: "2 fives are 10," write the 0 and carry the 1 to the tens column. "2 ones are 2," then add the 1 that was carried and write 3.

To divide means to separate a number into more parts. Your child begins by separating a set of objects into several smaller sets of equal size.

EXAMPLES:

1. How many twos in 10?

$\underset{..}{1}\qquad \underset{..}{1}\qquad \underset{..}{1}\qquad \underset{..}{1}\qquad \underset{..}{1}\qquad$ sets

A set of 10 dots is separated into five smaller sets of two.

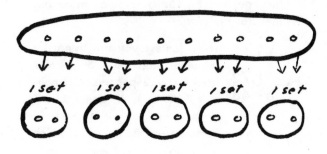

2. How many nickels in 15 cents?

There are 3 nickels in 15 cents.

5 pennies is 1 nickel
5 more pennies is 1 nickel
5 more pennies is 1 nickel

Your child learns that division is an inverse (opposite) operation to multiplication.

EXAMPLE:

$$2 \times 5 = 10 \qquad 10 \div 5 = 2$$
$$\text{and } 10 \div 2 = 5$$

There are two signs for division. In the arithmetic sentence use $\div$, but another way is $2\overline{)10}$ with quotient 5. As your child uses larger numbers, he will use the second, or long form, for division.
Your child learns the basic division facts of 1s, 2s, 3s, and 5s. Use the multiplication table when working with him, but use it inversely.

EXAMPLE:

$$6 \div 3 = \square$$

Find the 6 under the 3 in the top row. Find the number in the first column on the left, which is 2.

This table tells you that $6 \div 3 = 2$.

Before your child goes very far in division he will need to know about remainders, the numbers "left over" if the division is not even.

$\div$	0	1	2	3
0	0	0	0	0
1	0	1	2	3
2	0	2	4	6
3	0	3	6	

158

EXAMPLE:

Jim has a dime and buys pencils that cost 3 cents each.
How many pencils can he get?

Each set of 3 pennies will buy one pencil. One penny is left over.

$$\begin{array}{r} 3 \text{ R } 1 \\ 3\overline{)10} \end{array}$$

He writes:

He learns to use two-digit dividends (the number inside the box) with no carrying and no remainder.

EXAMPLE:

$$\begin{array}{r} 23 \\ 2\overline{)46} \end{array}$$

He uses a divisor (the number in front of the box) that doesn't go into the first figure of the dividend.

$$\begin{array}{r} 64 \\ 2\overline{)128} \end{array}$$

(He must use the first two dividend numbers as a numeral; in this problem it is 12.)

Next, he works with a three-place dividend with no carrying and no remainder.

EXAMPLE:

$$\begin{array}{r} 123 \\ 2\overline{)246} \end{array}$$

He divides with a zero in the tens place or units place with no carrying or remainder.

EXAMPLE:

$$\begin{array}{r} 304 \\ 2\overline{)608} \end{array}$$

If your child has difficulty with division as he begins to work with larger numbers, review the place value of the digits of two- and three-place numbers. Use 0 as a place holder.

EXAMPLE:

$$\left.\begin{array}{r} 3 \\ 20 \\ 100 \end{array}\right\} 123$$
$$2\overline{)246}$$

THINK:

246 is 2 hundreds, 4 tens or 40, 6 ones. The first step: "How many 2s are there in 200"? There are 100. Write 1 in the hundreds column, zeros in the tens and ones columns.

The second step: "How many 2s are there in 40?" There are 20. Write 2 in the tens column and 0 in the ones column.

The third step: "How many 2s in 6?" There are 3. Write 3 in the ones column.

The last step: Add (mentally) the 100 and 20 and 3. The quotient is 123.

The example above illustrates the distributive property in division, or the dividing a number by parts. This property will help your child do simple "division" in his head.

EXAMPLE: $63 \div 3 = \square$

THINK: $60 \div 3 = 20$

                  $3 \div 3 = 1$

                $20 + 1 = 21$

Therefore $63 \div 3 = 21$.

He understands the relationship of multiplication and division and their properties.

2 sets of 4 equals a set of 8 $2 \times 4 = 8$

4 sets of 2 equal a set of 8 $4 \times 2 = 8$

A set of 8 divided by 4 puts 2 in each $8 \div 4 = 2$
set.

A set of 8 divided by 2 puts 4 in each $8 \div 2 = 4$
set.

Prove these facts on the multiplication-division table.

fractions

Your child develops the meaning of fractions by dividing real objects and sets of objects into parts, and he learns to write fractions. He calls the number below the line the **denominator.** It is the name of the fraction. When a pie is cut into four parts, the pieces are called fourths. When you eat one piece of the pie, you eat ¼. If you should eat three pieces, you would eat ¾ of the pie. The number above the line tells us how many of the parts are being used. It is called the **numerator.**

Measures of length, time, weight, and money will be divided into fractions or parts of a whole. Find reasons at home to have your child use fractions. For example: he can divide an apple between you and himself. Be sure he tells you that you are each getting one half and that your pieces are (or should be) exactly the same size.

Your child learns that:

▶ **To find ½ of a number, he divides it by 2.**

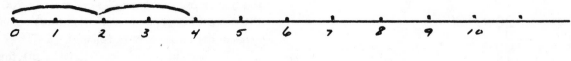

½ of 4 = $\square$
$4 \div 2 = 2$

160

▶ **To find ⅓ of a number, he divides it by 3.**

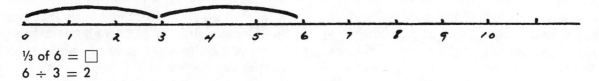

⅓ of 6 = □
6 ÷ 3 = 2

▶ **To find ¼ of a number, he divides it by 4.**

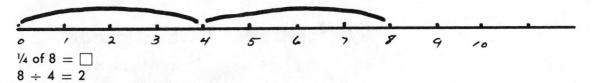

¼ of 8 = □
8 ÷ 4 = 2

▶ **To find ⅕ of a number, he divides, it by 5.**

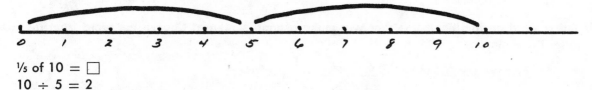

⅕ of 10 = □
10 ÷ 5 = 2

▶ **To find ⅙ of a number, he divides it by 6.**

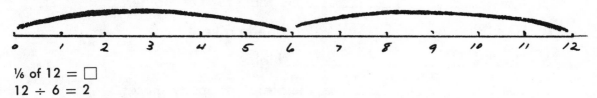

⅙ of 12 = □
12 ÷ 6 = 2

shapes and measures

Your child learns how to measure, and begins to add some common ones.

▶ **A ruler is used to measure inches, feet, and yards.**

▶ **Containers are used to measure pints, quarts, gallons.**

▶ **Scales are used to measure ounces and pounds.**

▶ **Clocks are used to tell hours, half hours, quarter hours, minutes.**

▶ **A calendar tells days, weeks, months, and years.**

▶ **A thermometer measures heat and cold.**

Your child uses pennies, nickels, dimes, quarters, half dollars, and dollars. He learns to make change from a dollar. He learns to write money in decimal form.

Your child easily recognizes the more common shapes—squares, rectangles, circles,

and triangles.

Thought problems give your child a practical use for his arithmetic.

Before beginning a problem be sure he knows:

▶ **What facts the problem tells.**

▶ **What the problem asks.**

▶ **What operation is necessary to solve it.**

If your child has trouble with a problem, give him a similar situation with very easy numbers. In working the easy one, he will grasp the principle involved and be able to apply it successfully to the more difficult one. Always let him judge the reasonableness of his answers, based on his everyday experiences. For instance, if he sells lemonade from a table in his front yard, he knows that it is not fair to charge 50 cents a glass—it is out of proportion to what he or his mother had to spend to make it.

If your child has trouble with a problem, give him a similar situation with very easy numbers. In working the easy one, he will grasp the principle involved and be able to apply it successfully to the more difficult one. Always let him judge the reasonableness of his answers, based on his everyday experiences. For instance, if he sells lemonade from a table in his front yard, he knows that it is not fair to charge 50 cents a glass—it is out of proportion to what he or his mother had to spend to make it.

workbook | third grade

reading exercises

I. Put a word on the blank line that will make a good sentence. Choose the word from the list after the sentences.

1. Frank _painted_ a picture.
2. Pull the _____ up to the table.
3. Mary _____ the table for her mother.
4. He _____ the rope in a knot.
5. The kite _____ high.
6. Joe _____ the plate into many pieces.
7. The queen bee lays the _____ .
8. Did Santa Claus fill your _____ ?
9. Daddy bought _____ to a show.
10. Let's _____ we are grownups.
11. Pile the wood in the _____ .
12. The kitten _____ with fright.
13. Let us all go in _____ .
14. I have a cat named _____ .
15. There are four _____ in every year.

broke	together	chair	set	eggs
woodshed	painted	Whiskers	pretend	flies
seasons	trembled	tickets	stocking	tied

162

II. Add as many endings as you can to make new words out of root words. Sometimes the spelling changes before adding an ending.

EXAMPLE: paint *(painted, painting, paints, painter)*

1. jump _____ _____ _____ _____

2. cry _____ _____ _____ _____

3. farm _____ _____ _____ _____

4. skate _____ _____ _____ _____

5. find _____ _____ _____ _____

6. throw _____ _____ _____ _____

7. like _____ _____ _____ _____

8. wind _____ _____ _____ _____

9. empty _____ _____ _____ _____

10. give _____ _____ _____ _____

11. watch _____ _____ _____ _____

12. order _____ _____ _____ _____

13. play _____ _____ _____ _____

14. hurt _____ _____ _____ _____

15. carry _____ _____ _____ _____

16. knit _____ _____ _____ _____

17. grin _____ _____ _____ _____

18. spot _____ _____ _____ _____

19. wipe _____ _____ _____ _____

20. snow _____ _____ _____ _____

21. dry _____ _____ _____ _____

III. Write the root word of each of the following.

EXAMPLE: shaking (*shake*)

1. smiled _____
2. whipping _____
3. noiseless _____
4. sweeter _____
5. tripped _____
6. maddest _____
7. gazing _____
8. candies _____
9. supplies _____
10. louder _____

11. shady _____
12. swimming _____
13. skating _____
14. boiling _____
15. dishes _____
16. calves _____
17. frozen _____
18. hammers _____
19. wives _____
20. tried _____

IV. Underline the word or expression that means almost the same thing as the first one.
(Mother—you may use the word in a sentence first.) Don't do them all at one time.

1. **calm**	louder	<u>still</u>	very cold
2. **pretend**	explain	show	make believe
3. **trembled**	screamed	was killed	shook
4. **escaped**	got inside	got away	was excited
5. **messenger**	letter	present	someone with news
6. **foolish**	exciting	scary	stupid
7. **wiped**	dried	cleaned	spread
8. **snapped**	wore out	broke quickly	pulled out slowly
9. **realized**	talked about	cared about	knew about
10. **settled**	sank to the bottom	looked down	left honey
11. **fellow**	boy	girl	colt
12. **protect**	feed	attack	keep from harm
13. **attack**	run from	hide from	rush out to hurt
14. **trapped**	caught	killed	scared
15. **cabin**	palace	boathouse	small house
16. **signals**	rules	lessons	signs

17. courage	luck	rage	bravery
18. scatters	puts in a box	puts away	throws about
19. shady	not sunny	muddy	shiny
20. village	a big city	a small town	a farm
21. elbow	part of a foot	part of an arm	part of an airplane
22. die	grow weak	stop living	break in two
23. roam	a sheep	part of a house	wander
24. search	hunt for	a light	marsh
25. feasts	clever tricks	goes hungry	eats a big meal
26. roar	a waterfall	not well cooked	a loud noise
27. fear	a long way off	clear weather	be afraid
28. sneak	a mean person	a creature	try to move without being seen
29. limb	trunk	fruit	branch
30. kneel	look down	bend down	get down on your knees
31. wren	big bird	eagle	little bird
32. switch	blossom	long stick	trunk
33. inquire	ask	subtract	explain
34. grand	fine	fire	unhappy
35. dreary	dark	sunny	windy
36. admit	allow to enter	see	attract
37. streak	line	spot	light
38. hopeful	afraid	trusting	sure
39. tearful	laughing	hungry	crying
40. delightful	very enjoyable	tiresome	dreary
41. forgetful	careful	unselfish	unable to remember
42. thoughtful	kind	unthinking	wicked
43. helpless	brave	strong	weak
44. senseless	foolish	wise	fair

V. Read the sentences in each group. Then write the sentences in the right order to make a story.

A.

1. I ate a great big piece.
2. I put in some eggs.
3. I frosted the cool cake.
4. I got out a bowl.
5. I mixed the flour and the sugar.
6. I put it into the hot oven.
7. I poured the batter into the pan.

1. _____
2. _____
3. _____
4. _____
5. _____
6. _____
7. _____

B.

1. Mother made blueberry pies.
2. Some day I want to learn how to make them.
3. We packed a picnic lunch.
4. Blueberry pie is my favorite kind of pie.
5. We filled three quart pails full.
6. We hiked to the woods to pick berries.
7. We brought them home.

1. _____
2. _____
3. _____
4. _____
5. _____
6. _____
7. _____

C.

1. We rowed out onto the lake.
2. We planned another fishing trip.
3. We drove out to the lake last night.
4. We caught seven fish.
5. We pitched our tent.
6. We fried them for breakfast.
7. We got up early this morning.

1. _____
2. _____
3. _____
4. _____
5. _____
6. _____
7. _____

VI. **Find three words that start with . . .** (Check answers in your dictionary.)

1. qu _____ _____ _____
2. sc _____ _____ _____
3. sn _____ _____ _____
4. tw _____ _____ _____
5. bl _____ _____ _____
6. br _____ _____ _____
7. sp _____ _____ _____
8. sw _____ _____ _____
9. sl _____ _____ _____
10. sm _____ _____ _____
11. cl _____ _____ _____
12. str _____ _____ _____

VII. **Make a picture dictionary. Use both capital and small letters. Cut pictures from old magazines. Start with the word** *automobile.*

Paste the picture on the Aa page.

EXAMPLE:

Continue your dictionary with the following words. Include new ones as you learn them.

acorn	book	doctor	family	hose
adult	castle	entrance	garment	island
bank	cave	eyebrow	gem	jar
basket	drum	factory	hem	market

VIII. **Unscramble these sentences. Begin them with a capital letter.**

1. more splashing and a loud grunt then she heard.

2. Baby down from seat her slid.

3. a puppy with Tracks was black and white spots.

4. cold is the turning weather.

5. out of Tripper he led the barn.

6. milk didn't give a cow of the drop.

7. different stamps likes Jim to collect kinds of.

8. a collar wears Spot around his neck.

IX. **Cross out the word that does not belong.**

1. bus   fare   go   stop   conductor
2. paint   brush   paper   jam   picture
3. book   word   fly   read   story
4. milk   food   pure   black   drink
5. farm   field   silo   barn   store
6. end   feathers   wing   bird   fly
7. cry   smile   soft   baby   stone
8. warm   wool   sheep   baa   board
9. peep   nest   crawl   bird   fly
10. red   dark   green   yellow   pink
11. long   sweet   sour   bitter   good
12. kind   happy   gay   joyous   sick
13. wind   eat   rain   snow   sleet
14. scream   talk   shout   yell   smile
15. mole   hole   ground   blind   tall
16. bill   lost   pay   change   money
17. sleep   clown   nose   funny   gay
18. bark   arm   leaf   trunk   limb
19. lake   flat   float   swim   ripple
20. legs   flat   top   sit   table
21. class   children   pencil   books   wash
22. subtract   hole   add   divide   multiply
23. game   board   fun   work   win
24. teacher   servant   doctor   hour   merchant
25. church   number   house   store   bank

Homes Made of Mud

There is a kind of wasp that builds its home of mud. It makes its nest by mixing clay or mud with a kind of glue from its mouth.

This kind of wasp, called a mud dauber, lives alone. The nest is made by the mother wasp for the babies to live in until they grow up. Then the nest is not used any more.

The nest is built like a little tube about as high and as large as a small thimble. This is the cell in which the baby wasp will live.

When the cell is finished, the mother wasp flies away to find a spider. When she finds one she stings it. The sting does not kill the spider, but it keeps it from moving. She brings the spider to her nest and places it at the bottom of the cell.

She brings other spiders until the cell is filled with spiders. Then she lays an egg among the spiders. After that, she closes the top of the cell with mud.

When one cell has been made, filled with spiders, and covered over, the mud dauber builds several other cells right beside the first cell. She fills each cell with spiders and lays an egg in each cell.

When each baby mud dauber hatches, it finds fresh food to eat. The spiders remain alive until they are eaten, even though they cannot move. It may take several weeks for the young wasps to eat the spiders and be big enough to break out of the cell.

Questions on "Homes Made of Mud"

1. What kind of wasp builds its home of mud? _____
2. How many eggs does the mother wasp lay at one time? _____
3. How large is a cell in the nest of a mud dauber? _____
4. How is the new baby mud dauber fed? _____
5. About how long does it take for the baby to be old enough to break out of its cell? _____

XI. Reading for information.

Find the answers to these questions by looking in other books. Your school science book will be very helpful. (Mother, your child may need some help to get started. If you have the *First Books,* published by Franklin Watts in New York, the work will be easy and fun.)

1. What kind of door keeps flies out of the house?
2. What does the farmer keep in a silo?
3. How many stomachs does a cow have?
4. What is a baby frog called?
5. How does a baby frog look different from a full-grown frog?
6. How many teeth does a toad have?
7. What are the leaves of an evergreen tree called?
8. How does a bluejay help a farmer?
9. What funny little gray animal lives in the ground and cannot see you?
10. What is a spider's house called?

XII. Draw a line through the whole sentence that does not belong in each paragraph.

1. All the boys and girls like Mr. Gray's store. He sells goldfish, kittens, puppies, and rabbits. Mr. Gray likes to eat candy, too.

2. Baby Tommy sat in his high chair playing with his toy dog. The floor was dirty. Suddenly the toy dog fell to the floor. Tommy cried because he could not reach it.

3. The lady wore a new blue dress. The man looked up into the sky and saw many airplanes. He watched them come nearer and nearer. The roar became louder and louder.

4. Dick went to the store for his mother. She gave him an allowance of ten cents every week. She asked him to get bread, apples, breakfast food, and butter. She knew that Dick enjoyed going to the store.

5. I like both winter and summer. I like to play in the snow and to skate, but I also like to play ball and to go on picnics. Mother lets me go to the movies once a month.

english exercises

I. Write *is* or *are* after each of the following (remember that *is* is used for "one," and *are* is used for "more than one").

1. two acorns_____
2. Daddy's car _____
3. maple tree seeds _____
4. a needle _____
5. an egg _____
6. two bees _____
7. tumbleweeds _____
8. elm leaves _____
9. dragonfly _____
10. dragonfly wings _____
11. tiny black seeds _____
12. a wasp's nest _____

13. ice-cream cones _____
14. dandelion seeds _____
15. burrs _____
16. a violet _____
17. pine needles _____
18. a butterfly _____
19. milkweed pods _____
20. sea shells _____
21. a caterpillar _____
22. a long snake _____
23. a pin _____
24. a sunflower _____

II. Put a period or a question mark at the end of each sentence.

1. Is the boy's name Larry
2. The girl's name is Carol
3. My birthday is in June
4. When is your birthday
5. When did you open your package
6. Did it rain last night
7. I lost my little black bear
8. We carved a lantern from the pumpkin
9. Did the dog frighten you
10. We made pictures of black cats
11. Do you like pumpkin pie

12. Our lantern had great big eyes
13. Did you see our jack-o'-lantern
14. Is this group of words a sentence
15. You are doing good work
16. Keep on until you finish the page
17. Have you finished it yet
18. I like Indian stories   Do you
19. That class planned a good program
20. Linda said she didn't feel well
21. Mother made doughnuts for us
22. We sold lemonade
23. Do you like lemonade
24. Would you rather have orangeade

III. With a colored pencil write the capital letters where they belong.

        M   C

1. my brother's name is charles.
2. my dog fido came to school with me.
3. last monday was a holiday.
4. we are going to new york on saturday.
5. did you think i was lost?
6. may i help you, edith?
7. susan's mother is very nice.
8. our committee will meet on tuesday.
9. father and i went to lake como.
10. did mary tell you the news?
11. gretchen and peter brought their skates.
12. what did miss hall say?
13. tommy's mother sent him home.
14. david, this is my mother, mrs. lane.
15. did you send for the doctor?
16. yes, dr. smith is coming.
17. it is almost christmas time.
18. i like thanksgiving, too.
19. our cat's name is mittens.
20. our class went to the brookfield zoo.
21. i am an american.
22. the family moved from velva, north dakota.
23. they moved to houston, texas.
24. mimi is in michigan now.
25. carl flew to chicago.

IV. Write these sentences over, and make them sound correct.

    1. No, he ain't here. _____

    2. I seen three puppies. _____

    3. There is six of us ready to go. _____

    4. These pictures is pretty. _____

    5. Oh, yes, I have saw many bears. _____

    6. Why have the children came here? _____

    7. The boys have came with their sleds. _____

    8. I and Jack will help you. _____

    9. We was just leaving. _____

    10. Have they went home yet? _____

V. Write the word that means more than one.

1. man *men*	11. letter _____
2. foot _____	12. coat _____
3. house _____	13. box _____
4. dress _____	14. meeting _____
5. book _____	15. banana _____
6. friend _____	16. baseball _____
7. stick _____	17. rope _____
8. child _____	18. name _____
9. bell _____	19. holiday _____
10. farm _____	20. teacher _____

VI. Cross out the consonants you do not sound.

1. tight	6. knee
2. comb	7. listen
3. wrong	8. chalk
4. sign	9. autumn
5. thumb	10. calf

VII. In the box write the vowel you hear when you name the object in the picture.

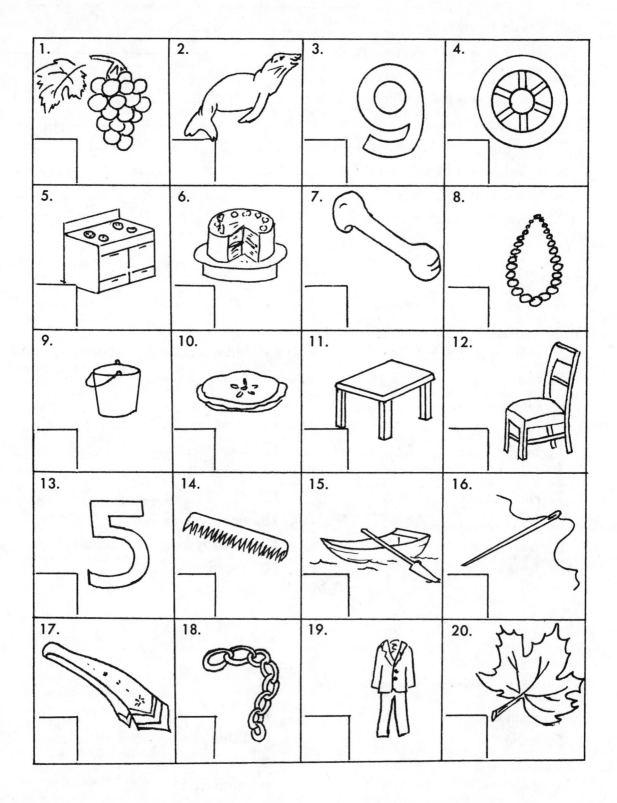

VIII. Write the short form (contraction) for:

1. would not   *wouldn't*
2. is not   _____
3. did not   _____
4. cannot   _____
5. do not   _____
6. I am   _____
7. could not   _____
8. will not   _____
9. it is   _____
10. are not   _____

IX. Write the word from the list that fits the meaning.

1. sixty minutes   *hour*
2. not strong _____
3. flying machine _____
4. young cow _____
5. young horse _____
6. two pints _____
7. day after Monday _____
8. change into ice _____
9. ten plus one _____
10. flat piece of wood _____

board	race
colt	storm
hour	poem
airplane	freeze
gallon	weak
eleven	Wednesday
calf	mare
weak	trunk
Tuesday	lamb
quart	minute

X. Correct all the mistakes in these sentences.

1. you is a good cook
2. my sister's name are gretchen
3. cindy and penny is at our house
4. their dog's name are mr dickens
5. they is the daughters of mr and mrs hall.
6. they go to lincoln school
7. they live in nyack, new york
8. they was here yesterday, too.
9. does joe play on your team
10. I have got a puppy.
11. I bought a new pensil.
12. my teacher's name is miss crawford

XI. In each of these paragraphs there are 5 misspelled words. Find them and write them correctly.

1. We played owtside today. The boys plaiyed basball and the girls jumped rope. I like sumer games better then winter games.
2. On ranny days I like to work on my scrapebook. Mother gives me her old magazins from which to cut pitchers. I have mostly animal pichers in my book.

XII. Here is a story without periods or capital letters. You write it again correctly.

my uncle is a shoemaker on saturdays he locks his store and goes fishing with us he catches many big fish he gives them to aunt mary to cook for us

XIII. Put the capital letters and periods in this story too, and then see how much easier it is to read.

martha came over to play we made mud pies we pretended they were cherry pies because it was washington's birthday we didn't really eat the pies

XIV. Make up stories of your own for Mother and Daddy. Here are some ideas for you.

The funniest animal in the zoo.   A skating party.

My new skating sweater.   My Halloween costume.

The deer in our woods.   The Girl Scout cook-out.

The airplane pilot.   My funny pussycat.

The circus.   Rules for the hike.

XV. Write these addresses on envelopes you make, or on envelopes your mother gives you.

Mrs. R. O. Allen   Mrs. J. L. Smith
25 Grand Street   29 Lowry Street
Sunnybrook   Springfield
Illinois   New Jersey

Dr. Arthur Gordon   Miss Elsie Hall
38 Linden Road   325 West Alice Street
Milford   Orangetown
Connecticut   Ohio

arithmetic exercises

I. Find the pattern and fill the blanks.

a) 3, 6, _____, 12, 15, _____, 21, 24, _____.

b) 4, 8, _____, 16, 20, _____, 28, 32, _____.

c) 6, 12, _____, 24, 30, _____, 42, 48, _____.

d) 7, 14, _____, 28, 35, _____, 49, 56, _____.

e) 8, 16, _____, 32, 40, _____, 56, 64, _____.

f) 9, 18, _____, 36, 45, _____, 63, 72, _____.

II. Write these numbers.

Five hundred ten   _____

One thousand two hundred six   _____

Six thousand one hundred fifteen   _____

Four thousand two hundred fifty-four   _____

Eight hundred ninety-three   _____

Five thousand   _____

Nine hundred eleven   _____

Two thousand three   _____

Seventy-five   _____

Four hundred thirty-six   _____

III. Write the Roman numerals for:

8 _____	15 _____	70 _____	110 _____
10 _____	50 _____	80 _____	95 _____
5 _____	40 _____	85 _____	30 _____
4 _____	60 _____	100 _____	34 _____
6 _____	65 _____	90 _____	23 _____

IV. Show on the number lines:

$4 + 2$

$4 - 2$

4×2

$4 \div 2$

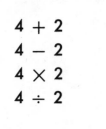

V. Add. Show the two-number combinations of 10.

1	3	3	6	4	4	1
2	4	8	2	2	2	6
4	0	0 ⟩10	5	2	4	1
4	6	2	0	5	2	2

2	3	2	7	6	3	7
7	6	8	3	4	1	1
3	1	0	2	1	5	1
1	2	3	1	1	4	3

5	2	4	3	2	3	5
1	8	4	3	0	4	4
1	1	4	3	6	2	3
6	1	0	3	1	2	1

VI. Add (carrying).

6	16	26	46	66	44	7
4	4	4	4	4	6	5

17	27	37	47	45	6	16
5	5	5	5	7	9	9

26	36	46	49	8	18	28
9	9	9	6	6	6	6

38	58	56	22	13	34	27
6	6	8	8	7	6	3

17	16	28	27	36	28	32
9	7	6	6	7	7	6

59	45	87	78	66	78	64
5	37	79	22	59	74	79

48	88	67	69	99	85	43
85	94	73	71	83	27	89

VII. Add (carrying).

48	65	5	16	89	77	3
9	21	14	90	50	24	90
90	9	28	3	26	19	8

87	69	4	9	4	58	49
79	20	78	88	65	84	2
5	37	87	64	52	1	66

75	56	39	3	57	67	57
3	2	99	88	9	4	94
66	89	4	49	20	87	20

68	95	75	97
20	30	2	3
53	47	68	68

VIII. Add (carrying).

$.89	$.33	$.75	$.88	$.69	$.79
.86	.58	.57	.57	.45	.37

$.52	$.93	$.56	$.73	$.34	$.46
.58	.37	.26	.19	.28	.29

$.29	$.48	$.07	$.89	$.17	$.20
.35	.37	.76	.08	.24	.07
				.35	.48

$.35	$.26	$.75	$.44	$.26	$.25
.26	.18	.18	.49	.39	.63
.29	.37	.10	.15	.15	.37

IX. Add.

456	106	247	529	857	378
219	484	328	426	135	418

237	755	465	267	438	274
447	219	328	619	157	519

505	677	259	173	117	171
476	316	721	95	28	87

392	142	138	481	911	183
16	78	229	142	358	275

X. Add.

$2.85	$6.67	$7.55	$4.59	$3.46
3.07	3.23	1.18	5.34	1.46

$3.25	$5.28	$7.59	$5.45	$4.75
1.35	1.68	1.29	2.39	4.18

$8.05	$2.39	$3.26	$2.57	$4.56
1.86	3.31	6.64	7.39	3.24

$5.00	$ .46	$ .85	$2.75	$ .75
3.00	.30	.75	.50	2.83

$ .84	$ .06	$ .95
.93	.08	1.10

$ .84	$2.75	$2.73	$4.60	$4.20
.55	.46	.65	2.07	3.60
.28	3.82	.43	4.80	4.80

$ .05	$3.00	$1.50	$5.00	$1.00
.04	2.00	.10	.05	1.75
.06	4.00	.01	.50	1.50

$ .57	$ .98
1.00	1.98
.10	2.98

XI. Subtract.

6	6	8	9	3	8	6
−3	−5	−4	−2	−1	−5	−2

4	7	5	9	5	10	9
−2	−1	−3	−7	−5	−1	−5

6	9	7	15	11	17	13
−1	−6	−2	−4	−6	−1	−6

19	17	12	15	18	19	21
−4	−9	−7	−8	−7	−6	−7

XII. Subtract (some borrowing).

$.65 − .40	$.95 − .75	$.60 − .50	$.34 − .25	$.56 − .38
$.65 − .35	$.98 − .45	$.97 − .85	$.98 − .32	$.75 − .17
$.49 − .19	$.58 − .06	$.95 − .29	$.34 − .27	$.87 − .29
$.46 − .37	$.45 − .29	$.38 − .19	$.10 − .09	$.21 − .18
$.24 − .17	$.37 − .15	$.49 − .16	$.65 − .18	$.27 − .19

XIII. Subtract (borrowing).

$ .60 − .36	$ .84 − .57	$ .45 − .28	$ .98 − .29	$3.85 −2.07	$6.62 −3.23
$7.55 − 1.18	$5.53 −4.34	75 −26	87 −39	93 −64	81 −28
54 −18	82 −48	73 −59	$ .91 − .86	$ .84 − .77	$ .76 −.69
$ .52 − .48	$ .43 − .37	$ .75 − .67	$ .63 − .58	$ .50 − .29	$5.17 −3.79

XIV. Subtract (borrowing twice).

$5.17	$6.28	$7.60	$6.41	$9.32	$8.53
− 3.79	− 2.69	− 1.78	− 3.66	− 6.87	− 4.74

$9.17	$8.24	685	438	823	976
− 4.98	− 6.37	−396	−249	−545	−589

712	361	734	452	641	540
−385	−187	−269	−266	−386	−285

XV. Subtract.

865	728	373	884	916	778
−570	−285	−129	−636	−124	−399

$6.00	$7.00	$9.00	400	800	500
− 3.46	− .58	− 4.35	−167	−271	−316

600	300	900	700	200	400
−428	−226	− 65	−539	− 87	− 24

XVI. Multiply.

4 × 5 =	5 × 8 =	2 × 3 =	2 × 4 =
4 × 3 =	3 × 6 =	5 × 8 =	5 × 3 =
5 × 6 =	8 × 3 =	3 × 4 =	2 × 8 =
2 × 6 =	3 × 5 =	5 × 5 =	5 × 7 =
3 × 7 =	2 × 6 =	5 × 9 =	4 × 5 =
2 × 4 =	2 × 3 =	5 × 2 =	5 × 1 =
3 × 3 =	2 × 7 =	3 × 6 =	3 × 4 =
3 × 5 =	3 × 3 =	4 × 2 =	5 × 7 =

$5 \times 7 =$ $3 \times 7 =$ $3 \times 1 =$ $2 \times 5 =$

$5 \times 2 =$ $5 \times 6 =$ $2 \times 7 =$ $2 \times 9 =$

$5 \times 9 =$ $5 \times 3 =$ $3 \times 2 =$ $8 \times 2 =$

$2 \times 3 =$ $3 \times 8 =$ $2 \times 9 =$ $5 \times 4 =$

$2 \times 2 =$ $2 \times 7 =$ $5 \times 5 =$ $2 \times 4 =$

XVII. Multiply (carrying).

22	12	25	$.15	52	59
2	9	8	4	5	5

12	$.25	22	12	51	$.52
8	7	3	7	4	4

22	15	22	$.55	25	12
5	3	4	8	6	6

15	$.52	22	15	52	$.55
2	3	6	7	2	7

55	12	15	$.22	21	51
6	5	9	7	4	7

52	25	15	15	52	$.42
6	9	9	7	8	5

$.12	$.25	$.21	$.12	$.52	$.15
3	8	7	4	8	7

XVIII. Divide.

2/4̄	2/6̄	2/8̄	2/1̄0̄	2/1̄2̄	2/1̄8̄

2/1̄6̄	2/1̄4̄	4/8̄	6/1̄2̄	7/1̄4̄	8/1̄6̄

3/6̄	2/4̄	1/2̄	5/1̄0̄

½ of 6 =　　　½ of 12 =　　　½ of 4 =　　　½ of 18 =

XIX. Divide (some have remainders).

3/6̄0̄	4/8̄0̄	5/1̄0̄0̄	2/1̄6̄8̄	5/2̄5̄0̄	4/1̄2̄8̄
3/6̄7̄	2/8̄5̄	5/1̄5̄6̄	2/4̄7̄	5/1̄0̄5̄	2/1̄0̄6̄
5/1̄5̄	2/6̄5̄	5/5̄6̄	6/1̄2̄	4/2̄0̄8̄	2/8̄4̄
5/2̄5̄8̄	2/1̄4̄3̄	2/1̄6̄2̄	2/1̄8̄8̄	5/3̄0̄9̄	2/2̄9̄
5/3̄5̄7̄	2/4̄6̄	5/4̄0̄5̄	5/4̄5̄6̄	2/1̄0̄6̄	2/8̄5̄
5/1̄0̄9̄	2/6̄4̄	5/5̄8̄	2/1̄2̄3̄	2/1̄4̄2̄	5/1̄5̄5̄
2/6̄2̄	5/2̄5̄5̄	2/1̄8̄5̄	5/1̄5̄7̄	3/6̄3̄3̄	5/3̄5̄6̄
2/2̄9̄	5/2̄0̄6̄	2/1̄4̄3̄	2/4̄9̄	5/3̄0̄9̄	2/1̄0̄6̄

XX. Watch the sign.

5	17	5	16	15	14
+8	−8	×3	−7	−6	−5

13	5	9	5	12	8
−7	×9	×5	×1	−4	×5

7	7	6	5	5	8
×5	+4	+4	×2	×8	+3

5	6	4	5	7	2
+7	×5	+9	×7	+7	×5

$20 \div 5 =$ $25 \div 5 =$ $30 \div 5 =$

$20 - 5 =$ $6 \times 5 =$ $20 + 5 =$

$2 \times 5 =$ $2 \times 6 =$ $10 \div 5 =$

$\frac{1}{5}$ of $5 =$ $40 \div 5 =$ $\frac{1}{2}$ of $10 =$

$5 \times 5 =$ $4 \times 5 =$ $8 \times 5 =$

$9 \times 5 =$ $5 + 3 =$ $9 + 6 =$

$\frac{1}{5}$ of $45 =$ $10 - 5 =$

XXI. Fill in the blanks.

1. 1 dollar = _____ quarters
2. 1 dime = _____ cents
3. 1 dollar = _____ dimes
4. 1 dollar = _____ nickels
5. 1 dollar = _____ cents
6. one year = _____ months
7. one pound = _____ ounces
8. one quart = _____ pints
9. one yard = _____ inches
10. one yard = _____ feet
11. one foot = _____ inches
12. one week = _____ days
13. one gallon = _____ quarts
14. 1 dozen = _____ things
15. ½ dozen = _____ things
16. ¼ dozen = _____ things
17. ½ pound = _____ ounces
18. 1 hour = _____ minutes
19. ½ year = _____ months
20. ½ dollar = _____ cents

XXII. Answer.

1. ½ of 12 = _____
2. ½ of 128 = _____
3. ½ of 16 = _____
4. ½ of 146 = _____
5. ½ of 80 = _____
6. ½ of 162 = _____
7. ½ of 106 = _____
8. ½ of 22 = _____
9. ½ of 168 = _____
10. ½ of 18 = _____
11. ⅓ of 99 = _____
12. ⅓ of 51 = _____
13. ⅓ of 45 = _____
14. ⅓ of 501 = _____
15. ⅓ of 150 = _____
16. ⅓ of 336 = _____
17. ⅓ of 21 = _____
18. ⅓ of 29 = _____
19. ⅕ of 75 = _____
20. ⅓ of 46 = _____
21. ⅕ of 25 = _____
22. ⅕ of 45 = _____
23. ⅕ of 29 = _____
24. ⅕ of 405 = _____
25. ⅕ of 400 = _____
26. ⅕ of 575 = _____
27. ⅕ of 255 = _____

XXIII. Thought problems.

1. Ann took 75¢ to the store. She bought a watermelon and had 12¢ left. The melon cost _____ .

2. Bob had a rope 34 inches long. He cut off a foot of the rope. He had _____ inches of rope left.

3. Tim has 48¢. Bob has a quarter. Tim has _____ ¢ more than Bob.

4. Tom paid 3¢ for a stamp, 1¢ for an envelope, and 5¢ for a pad of paper. Altogether he spent _____ ¢.

5. It takes Betty 10 minutes to go from her home to the library. If she starts at 5 minutes after 4, she will reach the library at _____ minutes after 4.

workbook answers   third grade

reading exercises

I.
2. chair
3. set
4. tied
5. flies
6. broke
7. eggs
8. stocking
9. tickets
10. pretend
11. woodshed
12. trembled
13. together
14. Whiskers
15. seasons

II.
1. jumped jumps jumping jumper
2. cried cries crying crier
3. farmed farms farming farmer
4. skated skates skating skater
5. finds finding finder
6. throws throwing thrower
7. liked likes liking
8. winds winding windy
9. emptied empties emptying emptiness
10. gives giving giver
11. watched watches watching watcher
12. ordered orders ordering orderer
13. played plays playing player
14. hurts hurting
15. carried carries carrying carrier
16. knitted knits knitting knitter
17. grinned grins grinning
18. spotted spots spotting spotter spotless
19. wiped wipes wiping wiper
20. snowed snows snowing
21. dried dries drying drier driest

III.
1. smile
2. whip
3. noise
4. sweet
5. trip
6. mad
7. gaze
8. candy
9. supply
10. loud
11. shade
12. swim
13. skate
14. boil
15. dish
16. calf
17. freeze
18. hammer
19. wife
20. try

IV.
2. make believe
3. shook
4. got away
5. someone with news
6. stupid
7. dried
8. broke quickly
9. knew about
10. sank to the bottom
11. boy
12. keep from harm
13. rush out to hurt
14. caught
15. small house
16. signs
17. bravery
18. throws about
19. not sunny
20. a small town
21. part of an arm
22. stop living
23. wander
24. hunt for
25. eats a big meal
26. a loud noise
27. be afraid
28. try to move without being seen
29. branch
30. get down on your knees
31. little bird
32. long stick
33. ask
34. fine
35. dark
36. allow to enter
37. line
38. trusting
39. crying
40. very enjoyable
41. unable to remember
42. kind
43. weak
44. foolish

192

V. A. 4, 5, 2, 7, 6, 3, 1
B. 3, 6, 5, 7, 1, 4, 2
C. 3, 5, 7, 1, 4, 6, 2

VI. (Mother, check with a dictionary if you are in doubt about some of the words your child has chosen that do not appear in these answers.)

1. queer   question   quiet
2. screen   scamp   scowl
3. snore   sneeze   snare
4. two   twenty   twice
5. blow   blue   blast
6. brown   breeze   brother
7. spill   spell   splash
8. sweater swell   swim
9. slip   sled   slow
10. smile   smell   smother
11. close   clash   clutch
12. straight stream   string

VII. Every child's dictionary will be different.

VIII. 1. Then she heard more splashing and a loud grunt.
2. Baby slid down from her seat.
3. Tracks was a puppy with black and white spots.
4. The weather is turning cold.
5. He led Tripper out of the barn.
6. The cow didn't give a drop of milk.
7. Jim likes to collect different kinds of stamps.
8. Spot wears a collar around his neck.

IX. 2. jam
3. fly
4. black
5. store
6. end
7. stone
8. board
9. crawl
10. dark
11. long
12. sick
13. eat
14. smile
15. tall
16. lost
17. sleep
18. arm
19. flat
20. sit
21. wash
22. hole
23. work
24. hour
25. number

X. 1. mud dauber
2. one
3. size of a small thimble
4. It eats the spiders in the cell.
5. It may take several weeks.

XI. 1. screen door
2. feed for his animals, chiefly corn
3. one stomach with four sections (sometimes it is said they have four stomachs.)
4. tadpole
5. It has a tail like a fish and no back legs.
6. none
7. needles
8. It eats harmful insects.
9. mole
10. web

XII. Cross out the sentences beginning:
1. Mr. Gray likes . . .
2. The floor was . . .
3. The lady wore . . .
4. She gave him an . . .
5. Mother lets me . . .

english exercises

I. Sentences 1, 3, 6, 7, 8, 10, 11, 13, 14, 15, 17, 19, and 20 use *are*.

Sentences 2, 4, 5, 9, 12, 16, 18, 21, 22, 23, and 24 use *is*.

II. Sentences 2, 3, 7, 8, 10, 12, 15, 16, 18a, 19, 20, 21, and 22 end with a period.

Sentences 1, 4, 5, 6, 9, 11, 13, 14, 17, 18b, 23, and 24 end with a question mark.

III.
1. My, Charles
2. My, Fidio
3. Last, Monday
4. We, New York, Saturday
5. Did, I
6. May, I, Edith
7. Susan's
8. Our, Tuesday
9. Father, I, Lake Como
10. Did, Mary
11. Gretchen, Peter
12. What, Miss Hall
13. Tommy's
14. David, Mrs. Lane
15. Did
16. Yes, Dr. Smith
17. It, Christmas
18. I, Thanksgiving
19. Our, Mittens
20. Our, Brookfield Zoo
21. I, American
22. The, Velva, North Dakota
23. They, Houston, Texas
24. Mimi, Michigan
25. Carl, Chicago

IV.
1. No, he isn't here.
2. I saw three puppies.
3. Six of us are ready to go.
4. These pictures are pretty.
5. Oh, yes, I have seen many bears.
6. Why have the children come here?
7. They boys have come with their sleds.
8. Jack and I will help you.
9. We were just leaving.
10. Have they gone home yet?

V.
1. men
2. feet
3. houses
4. dresses
5. books
6. friends
7. sticks
8. children
9. bells
10. farms
11. letters
12. coats
13. boxes
14. meetings
15. bananas
16. baseballs
17. ropes
18. names
19. holidays
20. teachers

VI.
1. tight
2. comb
3. wrong
4. sign
5. thumb
6. knee
7. listen
8. chalk
9. autumn
10. calf

VII.
1. a
2. e
3. i
4. e
5. o
6. a
7. o
8. e
9. a
10. i
11. a
12. a
13. i
14. o
15. o
16. e
17. i
18. a
19. u
20. e

VIII.
1. wouldn't
2. isn't
3. didn't
4. can't
5. don't
6. I'm
7. couldn't
8. won't
9. it's
10. aren't

IX.
1. hour
2. weak
3. airplane
4. calf
5. colt
6. quart
7. Tuesday
8. freeze
9. eleven
10. board

X.
1. You are a good cook.
2. My sister's name is Gretchen.
3. Cindy and Penny are at our house.
4. Their dog's name is Mr. Dickens.
5. They are the daughters of Mr. and Mrs. Hall.
6. They go to Lincoln School.
7. They live in Nyack, New York.
8. They were here yesterday, too.
9. Does Joe play on your team?
10. I have a puppy. (omit "got")
11. I bought a new pencil.
12. My teacher's name is Miss Crawford.

XI.
1. outside
played
baseball
summer
than
2. rainy
scrapbook
magazines
pictures
pictures

XII. My uncle is a shoemaker. On Saturdays he locks his store and goes fishing with us. He catches many big fish. He gives them to Aunt Mary to cook for us.

XIII. Martha came over to play. We made mud pies. We pretended they were cherry pies because it was Washington's birthday. We didn't really eat the pies.

XIV. Notice whether your child's story is written in complete sentences, with correct spelling and punctuation. Express an interest, so that he will be encouraged to write more.

XV. Check the placement of the address on the envelope.

arithmetic exercise answers

I. Fill blanks.
- a) 9, 18, 27
- b) 12, 24, 36
- c) 18, 36, 54
- d) 21, 42, 63
- e) 24, 48, 72
- f) 27, 54, 81

II. Write.

510	5,000
1,206	911
6,115	2,003
4,254	75
893	436

III. Roman numerals.

VIII
X
V
IV
VI

XV
L
XL
LX
LXV

LXX
LXXX
LXXXV
C
XC

CX
XCV
XXX
XXXIV
XXIII

IV. Number lines.

V. Add.

11	13	13	13	13	12	10
13	12	13	13	12	13	12
13	12	12	12	9	11	13

VI. Add (carrying).

10	20	30	50	70	50	12
22	32	42	52	52	15	25
35	45	55	55	14	24	34
44	64	64	30	20	40	30
26	23	34	33	43	35	38
64	82	166	100	125	152	143
133	182	140	140	182	112	132

VII. Add (carrying).

147	95	47	109	165	120	101
171	126	169	161	121	143	117
144	147	142	140	86	158	171
		141	172	145	168	

VIII. Add (carrying).

$1.75	$ .91	$1.32	$1.45	$1.14	$1.16
$1.10	$1.30	$ .82	$ .92	$ .62	$ .75
$ .64	$ .85	$ .83	$ .97	$ .76	$ .75
$ .90	$ .81	$1.03	$1.08	$ .80	$1.25

IX. Add.

675	590	575	955	992	796
684	974	793	886	595	793
981	993	980	268	145	258
408	220	367	623	1269	458

X. Add.

$5.92	$9.90	$8.73	$ 9.93	$ 4.92
$4.60	$6.96	$8.88	$ 7.84	$ 8.93
$9.91	$5.70	$9.90	$ 9.96	$ 7.80
$8.00	$ .76	$1.60	$ 3.25	$ 3.58
	$1.77	$ .14	$ 2.05	
$1.67	$7.03	$3.81	$11.47	$12.60
$ .15	$9.00	$1.61	$ 5.55	$ 4.25
	$1.67	$5.94		

XI. Subtract.

3	1	4	7	2	3	4
2	6	2	2	0	9	4
5	3	5	11	5	16	7
15	8	5	7	11	13	14

XII. Subtract (some borrowing).

$ .25	$ .20	$ .10	$ .09	$ .18
$ .30	$ .53	$ .12	$ .66	$ .58
$ .30	$ .52	$ .66	$ .07	$ .58
$ .09	$ .16	$ .19	$ .01	$ .03
$ .07	$ .22	$ .33	$ .47	$ .08

XIII. Subtract (borrowing).

$ .24	$ .27	$ .17	$ .69	$1.78	$3.39
$6.37	$1.19	49	48	29	53
36	34	14	$ .05	$ .07	$ .07
$ .04	$ .06	$ .08	$ .05	$ .21	$1.38

XIV. Subtract (borrowing twice).

$1.38	$3.59	$5.82	$2.75	$2.45	$3.79
$4.19	$1.87	289	189	278	387
327	174	465	186	255	255

XV. Subtract.

295	443	244	248	792	379
$2.54	$6.42	$4.65	233	529	184
172	74	835	161	113	376

XVI. Multiply.

20	40	6	8
12	18	40	15
30	24	12	16
12	15	25	35
21	12	45	20
8	6	10	5
9	14	18	12
15	9	8	35
35	21	3	10
10	30	14	18
45	15	6	16
6	24	18	20
4	14	25	8

XVII. Multiply (carrying).

44	108	200	$ .60	260	295
96	$1.75	66	84	204	$2.08
110	45	88	$4.40	150	72
30	$1.56	132	105	104	$3.85
330	60	135	$1.54	84	357
312	225	135	105	416	$2.10
$ .36	$2.00	$1.47	$ .48	$4.16	$1.05

XVIII. Divide.

2	3	4	5	6	9
8	7	2	2	2	2
	2	2	2	2	
3	6			2	9

XIX. Divide (some have remainders).

20	20	20	84	50	32
22R1	42R1	31R1	23R1	21	53
3	32R1	11R1	2	52	42
51R3	71R1	81	94	61R4	14R1
71R2	23	81	91R1	53	42R1
21R4	32	11R3	61R1	71	31
31	51	92R1	31R2	211	71R1
14R1	41R1	71R1	24R1	61R4	53

XX. Watch the sign.

13	9	15	9	9	9
6	45	45	5	8	40
35	11	10	10	40	11
12	30	13	35	14	10

4	5	6
15	30	25
10	12	2
1	8	5
25	20	40
45	8	15
	9	5

XXI. Fill in the blanks.

1. 4	11. 12
2. 10	12. 7
3. 10	13. 4
4. 20	14. 12
5. 100	15. 6
6. 12	16. 3
7. 16	17. 8
8. 2	18. 60
9. 36	19. 6
10. 3	20. 50

XXII. Answer.

1. 6	2. 64	3. 8
4. 73	5. 40	6. 81
7. 53	8. 11	9. 84
10. 9	11. 33	12. 17
13. 15	14. 167	15. 50
16. 112	17. 7	18. 9R2
19. 15	20. 15R1	21. 5
22. 9	23. 5R4	24. 81
25. 80	26. 115	27. 51

XXIII. Thought problems.

1. $.63 or 63¢
2. 22
3. $.23 or 23¢
4. $.09 or 9¢
5. 15

final tests   third grade

reading and english

(Give these as one test. Allow 5 points for each correct answer. Total 100%.)

Part I. Read this paragraph twice. Then cover it and answer the questions below it.

The clown stood on the table. His face was painted pink and blue. Large circles were painted around his eyes. The tip of his nose was red. He wore a very large green suit with a green ruffle around his neck. The big wooden buttons on his suit were shaped like balloons.

1. Whom is the paragraph about? _____
2. What color was his nose? _____
3. What was painted pink and blue? _____
4. What did he have around his neck? _____
5. Where was he standing? _____
6. What part of his suit looked like balloons? _____
7. What color was his suit? _____
8. What part of his suit was made of wood? _____
9. Where were large circles painted? _____
10. Is this paragraph a story? _____

Part II. On another piece of paper, copy the following paragraph, correcting all the mistakes you can find (there are 10 of them). Look for (1) misspelled words, (2) wrong punctuation or no punctuation where there should be some, (3) capital letters in the wrong places or forgotten, (4) unnecessary words, and (5) mistakes in grammar.

Little insecks that make there homes of paper are called paper wasps they make the paper from the soft wood that is on the outside of a old dead tree? They chew the wood and mix it with a glew from out their mouths. It becomes awful strong and Rain will not make it soft again.

arithmetic test

I. (2 points each)

1. There are _____ cents in $5.00.
2. There are _____ dimes in a dollar.
3. Two quarters, one dime, and twenty-three pennies are $ _____ .
4. There are _____ nickels in $1.50.
5. One-half dollar is _____ cents.

II. Write: (2 points each)

Five hundred fifteen _____

Five thousand fifteen _____

Three thousand one hundred _____

Seven hundred eighteen _____

Nine hundred sixty-four _____

III. Write the Roman numerals for: (2 points each)

5 _____

10 _____

50 _____

100 _____

46 _____

IV. Add: (5 points)

$6.28
5.46
.23
4.35

V. Multiply: (5 points)

313
×3

VI. Subtract: (5 points)

853
−428

VII. Subtract: (5 points)

$9.66
− 8.99

VIII. Divide: (5 points)

3/249

IX. Divide: (5 points)

3/241

X. (2 points each)

1. $\frac{1}{2}$ foot = _____ inches
2. 1 yard = _____ inches
3. $\frac{1}{2}$ yard = _____ inches
4. 2 feet = _____ inches
5. 2 yards = _____ feet

IX.
1. $\frac{1}{2}$ hour = _____ minutes
2. $\frac{1}{2}$ year = _____ months
3. $\frac{1}{2}$ pound = _____ ounces
4. $\frac{1}{2}$ dozen = _____ things
5. 1 gallon = _____ quarts

XI. Estimate the answers. Circle the one you think is almost right. (2 points each)

1. One sweater sells for $4.50 and another sweater sells for $3.98. How much more does the first one cost than the second one? ($.50, $1.00, $1.50)

2. John had 60 papers to sell. He has 32 left. How many papers has he sold already? (10, 20, 30)

3. There are 125 pupils in Jane's school. 27 are absent today. How many are present? (30, 50, 100)

4. Joe's mother had $9.00 in her purse. She bought $4.95 worth of groceries. How much money did she have left? ($1.50, $4.00, $5.00)

5. A radio on sale was marked $12.95. The regular price was $15.00. How much could you save at the sale? ($2.00, $2.50, $3.00)

XII. (2 points each)

1. Jane put three layers of caramels in a box. She put 24 caramels in each layer. She put _____ caramels in the box.

2. Sue and two friends have 39¢ to divide equally among them. Each will get _____ ¢.

3. Ben has 18 chairs to carry to the assembly hall. If he carries them two at a time, he will have to make _____ trips.

4. For 38¢ you can get _____ 5-cent pencils and have _____ ¢ left.

5. Tom's teacher told him to write the answers to 70 subtraction problems. There are 10 problems in each row. Tom has to do _____ rows.

final test answers   third grade

reading and english

Part I. 1. a clown
2. red
3. his face
4. a green ruffle
5. on a table

6. the buttons
7. green
8. the buttons
9. around his eyes
10. no

Part II.

Little insects that make their homes of paper are called paper wasps. They make the paper from the soft wood that is on the outside of an old dead tree. They chew the wood and mix it with a glue from ~~out~~ their mouths. It becomes very strong and rain will not make it soft again.

arithmetic test answers

I. 1. 500
2. 10
3. $.83
4. 30
5. 50

II. 515
5,015
3,100
718
964

III.   V
X
L
C
XLVI

IV. $16.32

V. 939

VI. 425

VII. $.67

VIII. 83

IX. 80R1

X. 1. 6
2. 36
3. 18
4. 24
5. 6

6. 30
7. 6
8. 8
9. 6
10. 4

XI. 1. $.50
2. 30
3. 100
4. $4.00
5. $2.00

XII. 1. 72
2. 13¢
3. 9
4. 7, 3¢
5. 7

contents | fourth grade

workbook _____ 228

final tests _____ 255

helping your child in fourth grade

YOUR CHILD is now about nine years old—too old to be considered a child, but not yet an adolescent. He wants very much to do things on his own, to plan and carry through projects challenging to him. You will both get along fine *if* you don't lecture him too often. Don't always tell him what to do. Show him sometimes by example. If your actions indicate that you realize he is growing up, he will respond in a way that will warm your heart. In spite of the fact that he is beginning to grow away from his family, this can be a good year for family life and for learning.

reading | fourth grade

BY THE TIME he has reached the fourth grade, your child has learned to recognize hundreds of words. Many of these he knows how to spell. He knows the sounds of letters and of combinations of letters. All the basic reading skills, as they are called, are pretty well learned by this time, so that now your child will concentrate even more than last year on reading to find out what happens.

reading to learn

In his classroom he has practice in picking out the central thought in what he reads. He is encouraged to "browse around" in his reading. He is introduced to verse and poetry, fiction, adventure, and science. Visits to the library make him aware of how important books can be in answering his questions. He learns to use a card catalog in the library, so that from now on he knows where to find books that

tell about his special interests. Is he interested in jet planes, puppet shows, baseball? If he can't find all the information he wants in his school library, encourage him to visit the public library near you. Go with him if he wants you to.

Books can answer questions for your child about his family, his friends, his neighbors, his country—the world. Encourage him to read books. He needs to know what fun he can get from literature and that there are books and stories on anything and everything that interests him.

Books can help him understand his own problems. Help him get in the habit of turning to books to learn the answers to a simple question such as, "How many wings does a honey bee have?" Later in life when his problems have become so much more complex, he'll have the answers to a lot of them at his fingertips. He will if you help him learn *now* to depend on books.

unwillingness to read

By the time your child has reached the fourth grade it is becoming clear whether or not he is a "natural" reader. If he doesn't like to read, if he doesn't like it at all, it may be for one of several reasons. Don't scold or blame him! Find out what the trouble is. It may be that because of the fast pace and the many new words he has had to learn, he has reached a point where he simply wants to stand still for a while. Or it may be that his eyes need correction.

Children vary a lot in reading readiness; maybe he just isn't ready to read as much as you would like him to. It may be several years yet before he reaches his highest interest level. If there seems to be any real trouble, try to locate it with the help of his teacher and the school physician.

In his school class there is enough re-teaching of the basic skills for his teacher to see clearly where your child needs extra practice. Find out from her where it is.

By the end of this fourth year your child should read easy material silently at the rate of about 155 words a minute, with good understanding of what he reads. You won't stand over him with a stop watch, of course, but since he does learn to read by *reading*, the more reading you can encourage him to do, the better reader he will become. But remember this above all else: *The book he reads must be one that interests him.* A book he reads unwillingly will not help him much—any more than it would you.

For exercises to help your child improve his reading ability, see the section at the end of this book.

books your fourth-grade child may enjoy

All About Dinosaurs—*Andrews, Roy Chapman*
Lonesome Boy—*Bontemps, Arna*
Squanot, Friend of the White Men
    Bulla, Clyde Robert
The Adventures of Pinocchio—*Collodi, C.*
Rockets into Space—*Crosby and Larrick*
The Birdman (Story of Leonardo da Vinci)
    Foster, Mitchell
My Father's Dragon—*Gannett, Ruth S.*
Sal Fisher, Brownie Scout—*Gardner, Lillian*
The Wind in the Willows—*Grahame, Kenneth*
Grimm's Fairy Tales—*Grimm, Jakob and Wilhelm*
Young Voyageur—*Gringhuis, Richard H.*
Uncle Remus: His Songs and His Sayings
    Harris, Joel Chandler
Betsy and the Circus—*Haywood, Carolyn*
Benjamin West and His Cat Grimalkin
    Henry, Marguerite
Billy's Clubhouse—*Holland, Marion*
Just So Stories—*Kipling, Rudyard*
Little Pear—*Lattimore, Eleanor*
Johnny Appleseed—*Lindsay, Vachel*
Homer Price—*McCloskey, Robert*

Tangle-Britches—*Peckham, Betty*
Pepper and Salt—*Pyle, Howard*
Florence Nightingale
Joan of Arc
    Richards, Laura E.
Bambi—*Salten, Felix*
Silver Mink—*Sanderson, Ivan T.*
Horton Hears a Who!
McElligott's Pool
Scrambled Eggs Super
    Dr. Seuss
Heidi—*Spyri, Johanna*
The Story of Daniel Boone—*Steel, William O.*
Cub Scout Mystery—*Sterling, Dorothy*
Mary Poppins—*Travers, Pamela*
Rebel Mail Runner—*Wellman, Manly W.*
The Story of Serapina—*White, Anne H.*
Little House in the Big Woods—*Wilder, Laura*
Frogs and Toads
Insects
Lightning and Thunder
Mice, Men and Elephants
    Zim, Herbert S.

writing | fourth grade

IN THE BUSY days of a fourth-grade class there is little time for special writing-practice periods. However, the teacher is constantly aware that your child still needs supervision over his writing and she helps him all she can. You can help too by keeping an eye on how he writes at home. Good writing habits are as easy to establish as bad ones, and will last as long.

By this time all school work is done in the writing style (cursive) where the letters are connected, except in those few schools where manuscript writing is continued through all grades. Your child probably uses the manuscript style of writing only in such things as poster and project work.

rules for good writing

Here is a check list of writing rules. Review them once in a while with your child.

> ▶ Sit in a comfortable position for writing. Hold the pencil easily; fingers should not be cramped.
> ▶ Make the letters correctly.
> ▶ Make all letters slant in the same direction.
> ▶ Make connecting strokes and ending strokes short.
> ▶ Leave the width of the letter o between words.
> ▶ Make loops correctly, so that there will be a "path of light" between the lines of writing.
> ▶ Make capital letters and tall letters twice the height of small letters.
> ▶ You should be able to see through each e.
> ▶ The letter *t* is not quite as tall as the letter *l*.
> ▶ The lines that connect the letters *b e* or *w e* do not come down to the line.
> ▶ Numbers are the same height as *t*.
> ▶ The downward stroke of *f* is straight.
> ▶ A period is *on* the line.
> ▶ Be sure to dot *i* above the *i*, and to cross the *t*.
> ▶ Point the small handwritten *s*.
> ▶ There is no loop in a small *d* or *p* or *t*.
> ▶ Do not use unnecessary beginning and ending strokes and flourishes.
> ▶ Rounded-letter forms are more easily read than angular ones. Watch your *m*'s and *n*'s.
> ▶ The o and *a* should always be closed.

ENGLISH

grammar

GRAMMAR is taught as a part of all the language arts. Your child cannot learn reading, spelling, or English without learning something about grammar at the same time. He understands that grammar is nothing more than a system of rules for speaking or writing. If he wants to write something to you, and wants to be sure you will understand it, he knows that he must learn the rules for such things as spelling, punctuation, capitalization, sentence and paragraph building, letter forms, and outlining.

the sentence

Your child may have difficulty grasping the difference between a group of related words and a complete thought. When is a group of words a sentence? He knows that a sentence has a capital letter at the beginning and a period at the end. However, a capital and a period at the beginning and ending of some words do not necessarily make a sentence. They do not necessarily make a complete thought.

Your fourth-grade child, then, has a great deal of practice work on the sentence. He has to *want* to recognize a sentence when he sees one. He has to *want* to make good sentences. He wants to when he realizes that with good sentences he can make his needs more clearly understood; that he can write better letters, tell better stories, make better reports, and even write a better diary.

punctuation rules a fourth-grader should know

Before the end of the year your child should know certain simple rules of punctuation without even stopping to think. Some of these he learned in the third grade. He uses one or more every time he writes or talks. So do you. So does everybody.

▶ End a question with a question mark.

▶ Begin every sentence with a capital letter.

▶ Use a capital letter to begin the name of a holiday; the names of the days of the week and the names of the months; a title before a name (Aunt May); the titles of books, names of countries, titles of records, names of schools, names of streets and roads; names of people; the titles *Mr., Miss, Mrs.* (Mr. and Mrs. are abbreviations and should end with periods); to begin the first word in the greeting and the first word in the closing of a letter; and always use a capital letter for *I.*

▶ Use a period after initials.

▶ Use a comma between the day and the year (Jan. 6, 1958). Use it also between the name of a city and a state (Bangor, Maine). Use it after the greeting in a friendly letter, and after the closing (Dear Jane,— Yours truly,).

▶ Use an exclamation mark after sentences that show surprise.

▶ Use quotation marks around the actual words that people speak.

▶ Separate a quotation from the rest of the sentence with a comma.

the correct use of words

Pick a word. Pick any word. There are correct ways to use it and many wrong ways. If your child learns to use his words in the right way, it will be easier for him to make himself understood all the rest of his life. If people understand him, he will probably get along with them better, be happier, and make a better living for his family. If you can help your child to understand this, you will be doing him a service for which he will grow up to thank you. If you can help him to understand even a glimmering of this, he may approach the business of learning to use the right word in the right place with some enthusiasm. It will be so much easier for him now and later if he does.

You might think up some horrible examples of bad speech to bring to his attention. He *probably* wouldn't say, "I ain't brang home no schoolbooks." He *might* think it was funny to hear so many mistakes in one sentence. But perhaps you can show him that it wouldn't be funny if he talked even a little like this later on when applying for a job. He wouldn't get the job!

Here are some of the good-use rules he will be taught in school during the year.

▶ *Have, has, had, is, are, was,* and *were* are helping words, and one of them should be used with such words as *seen, eaten, done, written, drawn, known, come.*

EXAMPLES:

She *has eaten* her dinner.

Have you *done* your homework?

My dog *has come* home.

▶ Do not use a helping word with words such as *saw, came, ate, did, wrote, drew, knew.*

EXAMPLES:

He *ate* his dinner.

You *did* a good job.

My dog *came* home.

▶ Say *brought,* not *brung.*

EXAMPLE:

Daddy *brought* home some ice cream.

▶ *Good* is used to describe something.

EXAMPLES:

It was a *good* story, Anne.

The apples were *good.*

▶ *Well* tells how some action is done.

EXAMPLES:

You told the story *well,* Anne.

Jane sings *well.*

Tom does not swim *well.*

▶ Do not use *got* when it isn't needed.

NOT GOOD:

We haven't *got* many books.

BETTER:

We haven't many books.

▶ Use *may* when you ask permission. Use *can* when you talk of what someone is able to do.

EXAMPLES:

May I help the committee?

You *can* print very well, Tom.

▶ *Is* and *isn't* are used in talking of one thing. *Are* and *aren't* are used in talking of more than one person or thing.

EXAMPLES:

Next week *is* Book Week.

Those stories *are* fairy tales.

▶ It is never right to use *ain't.*

▶ When it is right to use *I* alone, it is right to use it with another name. When it is right to use *me* alone, it is right to use it with another name. Remember always to name yourself last.

EXAMPLES:

I am on the squad.

Joe and *I* are on the squad.

Sister copies *me*.

Sister copies Sue and *me*.

▶ It is right to use *any* with a contraction that ends in *n't* (which means *not*).

YOU MAY SAY:

hasn't any   *haven't any*

wasn't any   *aren't any*

weren't any

▶ It is not right to say *hasn't no* or *isn't no*.

▶ It is right to use *was* and *wasn't* when you talk about one person or thing. Use *were* and *weren't* when you talk about more than one.

EXAMPLES:

The child *wasn't* careful.

The boys *weren't* at home.

▶ *Let* means allow.
Leave means go away.
Left means went away.
Do not use *leave* or *left* instead of *let*.

EXAMPLES:

WRONG:

Will you *leave* me help you?

RIGHT:

Will you *let* me help you?

WRONG:

Who *left* the kitten in?

RIGHT:

Who *let* the kitten in?

▶ Say *himself*, not *hisself*.
Say *themselves*, not *theirselves*.

▶ Do not use unnecessary words.

EXAMPLE:

WRONG:

John he came to my house.

RIGHT:

John came to my house.

▶ You *learn* what someone else *teaches* you.

EXAMPLES:

RIGHT:

My father will *teach* me how to swim.

RIGHT:

I can *learn* how to make fudge.

parts of speech

Because so much work is done with words in this grade, it is necessary to have names for different groups of words referred to. Therefore, your child, with little effort, learns to call the *name of something* a noun. He calls a word that *describes a noun* an adjective. He may even go so far as to call an *action word* a verb.

EXAMPLE:

noun   verb   adjective   noun

John came to my piano lesson with me.

your child learns to co-operate

As soon as he learns a new skill in school your child is eager to put it to use. Your fourth-grade child, for example, may participate with his classmates in writing and printing a class newspaper or magazine. He may contribute an original story or verse, an article on one of his school or home interests, a book review, etc. This kind of project develops initiative and originality. It is also an excellent way of impressing him with the need for co-operation in certain enterprises. He begins to see that *everyone* has a talent for *something,* and that everyone may have a part in the success of the whole.

pen pals

To put newly acquired knowledge to use at home, how about helping your child find a Pen Pal? This can be an exciting experience for him. But be sure he shows an interest in the idea before going ahead. It may be that he isn't ready yet. If not, just wait a year or two.

To get the name of a fourth-grader in another country with whom your child may correspond, contact friends, relatives, or your child's teacher. If this fails, then write to your State Department of Education. They will give you the names of other fourth-grade teachers who, in turn, will give you names of children in foreign lands. A place where you can write directly and get the name of a Pen Pal for a very small fee is The Students' Exchange, Waseca, Minnesota.

giving a puppet show

An excellent way to use language arts is by writing and giving a puppet show. This can be done by your child's class in school, or by a Brownie Scout or Cub Scout group, or by any group of children in your neighborhood. It is a wonderful group activity. If your child is shy, a production of this kind will help him overcome his shyness. It will be necessary for him to speak slowly and clearly. He will have a chance to use many kinds of creative expression.

There are many committees necessary for a school activity of this kind—one for handling tools, one for making and painting puppets, making the stage, sewing costumes, writing the script, etc. If you feel capable of helping in any of these areas, ask the teacher

if she can use an extra pair of hands. It may not be practical for you to meet in the classroom, but she would appreciate it if you could have your committee at your home after school for short work sessions.

ORAL ENGLISH

Because everyday living depends upon the ability to speak easily and well, your child has training in oral English. Training is based on real situations and includes:

▶ **greetings and good-bys;**
▶ **conversations;**
▶ **story telling;**
▶ **group discussions;**
▶ **dramatizations;**
▶ **formal reports;**
▶ **use of a telephone;**
▶ **introductions;**
▶ **club meetings;**
▶ **correction of common grammatical errors.**

In his speech training these things are stressed: voice quality, pronunciation, enunciation, correct usage, enrichment of vocabulary, and thought organization.

You can help the teacher and your child by continuing this training at home. If you find that your child is talking too loudly, don't scold—*you* relax and ask him to relax and to lower his voice. If he mispronounces a word, correct him respectfully, as one responsible person to another. If you can't understand him, ask him to slow down and start again. If he makes a mistake in grammar, correct him.

You will also notice that your child responds more quickly to a soft voice than to a harsh voice, which is sure to irritate him.

mistakes to avoid

Here are some common mistakes you can help your child avoid or overcome:

▶ **Wrong vowel pronunciations. The vowels are the five sounds in our alphabet that change:**

a, e, i, o, u.

kin	for	can
ketch	for	catch
extry	for	extra
uv	for	of
er	for	or

► Slighting final *d* or *t* in words like *slept, first, next, told, around.*

► Lazy speech in omitting some sounds entirely:

p'r'aps	for	perhaps
hist'ry	for	history
b'long	for	belong
fam'ly	for	family

speaking well

Your child needs to realize the importance of speaking well, and so his teacher creates situations where speaking is the tool he uses to get his ideas across to others. When he was younger, he did not have so many suggestions to make, but now that he is nine years old he has had enough experiences so that he has quite a few ideas to draw from. He sees that the better he makes his ideas understood, the better the response to them is.

All children acquire bad speech habits through what they hear. Therefore much oral work is done in the classroom to train the ear to hear the correct forms. Your child is likely to become confused, however, if too many right and wrong forms are taught at one time. If you are trying to correct bad speech habits at home, work on one at a time. When using the correct form becomes a well-established habit, then take up the next wrong usage.

story telling

Your child is a born story teller. He likes to spin yarns. These may be more or less factual accounts of what has happened to him or to others during the day, a retelling of a book story, or fanciful things created wholly out of his imagination. There are a few simple rules for effective story telling. Your child may appreciate being reminded of them.

► Keep the story short . . . tell the steps in the right order.
► There is usually *one* *important idea* in one story.
► Don't join sentences with *ands*.
► Use good descriptive words (adjectives).
► Have plenty of action.
► Show by your voice where each sentence ends.
► Say each word clearly.
► Look right at your audience.

letter writing

Your child learns the correct form and punctuation for writing a friendly letter. Study the example on the following page. A letter to a friend should be written as though he were talking to the friend. It should be interesting and entertaining. It should make the receiver glad to get it.

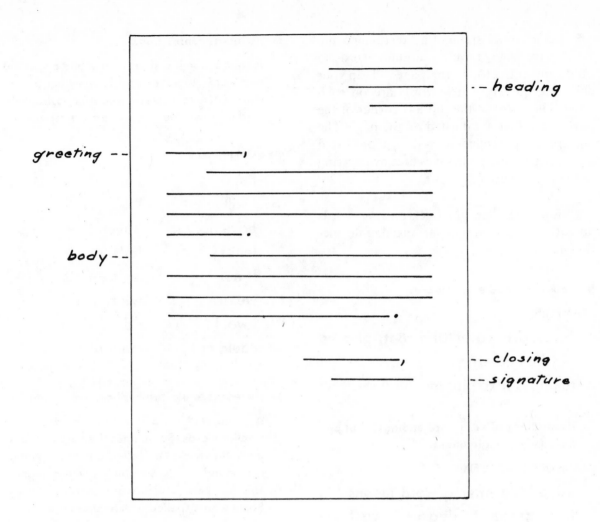

SPELLING

Your child will use a dictionary every day. He learns that it helps him to:

a. **spell words;**
b. **pronounce words;**
c. **divide words into parts called syllables (for example, *but-ter*);**
d. **know which syllable to accent, which one to say the hardest (for example, *eve'ning*);**
e. **know the meaning of words.**

Diacritical marks are the marks made over the vowels to show your child how to pronounce them. A straight line indicates a long sound (a sound like the name of the letter). A curved line indicates a short sound.

examples of diacritical marks

LONG		SHORT	
ā	make	ă	hat
ē	heat	ĕ	bed
ī	kite	ĭ	sit
ō	pole	ŏ	hot
ū	cute	ŭ	rub

Other diacritical marks are explained in the front of the dictionary.

Guide words are another dictionary aid. Dictionary pages have these guide words in bold type at the top of the page to help your child see quickly which words are on each page. The word at the top left corner of the page is the first word listed on the page. The one at the top right corner is the last one listed on the page. Your child saves time by referring to the guide words.

Sometimes he practices putting words into *abc* order, as they are arranged in the dictionary.

▶ **Your child studies *root words*.**

EXAMPLES:

> *covered* is *cover* (the root) plus *ed* (the ending);
>
> *taking* is *take* plus *ing*.

▶ **He studies *suffixes* (word endings) and *prefixes* (word beginnings).**

EXAMPLE OF A SUFFIX:

> *est* added after a word means "in the greatest degree"—fast*est*, high*est*, etc.
>
> Some other suffixes are *ing, ly, en*.

EXAMPLE OF A PREFIX:

> *bi* added before a word means "two." A *bi*cycle has two wheels. *Bi*annually means every two years.

▶ **He learns *abbreviations*.**

  a. The days of the week are abbreviated: Mon., Tue., Wed., Thurs., Fri., Sat., Sun.
  b. The months of the year are abbreviated: Jan., Feb., Mar., Apr., Aug., Sept., Oct., Nov., Dec. (The short names, May, June, and July, are not abbreviated.)
  c. Other common abbreviations are: Mr., Mrs., P.S., A.M., P.M.
  d. Each abbreviation must end with a period.

▶ **He learns *contractions*.**

A contraction is a short form made by putting two words together and leaving out one or more letters in their spelling. An apostrophe is used to show where the letters are left out.

EXAMPLES:

I am	I'm
I will	I'll
have not	haven't
let us	let's
is not	isn't
we are	we're
I would	I'd
could not	couldn't

▶ **He learns to use the *hyphen*.**

A compound word is a word made of two smaller words. Sometimes they are joined by a small straight line called a hyphen. Not all compound words are spelled with a hyphen. This is where a dictionary comes in handy. Some words spelled with hyphens are:

> *good-by, self-respect, half-hour* (but not *halfway*).

▶ **He learns what *homonyms* are.**

A *homonym* is a word which sounds like another word but is spelled differently.

EXAMPLES:

blue	blew	hole	whole
board	bored	I	eye
brake	break	meet	meat
cents	sense	new	knew
dear	deer	no	know
fourth	forth	one	won
grown	groan	our	hour

reel	real		stares	stairs
role	roll		sun	son
sail	sale		threw	through
sea	see		write	right
		to	two	too

▶ **He learns to make *plurals***—to take a word that means only one and make it mean more than one.

To make plurals we sometimes add only *s*.

EXAMPLES:

shoe	shoes
fist	fists

We add *es* to words which already end in *s* or *sh* or *ch*.

EXAMPLES:

dress	dresses
wish	wishes
witch	witches

Sometimes we change the spelling.

EXAMPLES:

man	men
wolf	wolves

A child's dictionary gives the plural spelling of a word if the plural form is irregular.

six steps to correct spelling

Here is a study plan your child can use for learning to spell new words. Ask him to:

▶ **Look at the word carefully.**

▶ **Pronounce the word correctly. If the word has more than one syllable, say each syllable clearly while looking at it.**

▶ **Look to see if the word is spelled the way you expect it to be spelled. Notice if it is different from what you expected.**

▶ **Write the word.**

▶ **See if you spelled it correctly. If you did, cover the word and write it three or four times.**

▶ **If you spelled it wrong, find out why you missed it. Then write it a few times correctly.**

Your child is taught about ten to fifteen new words a week. In order not to lose the meaning of a word, the teacher dictates it in a sentence, asking the class to write the complete sentence with proper punctuation and capitals.

A good dictionary for home use for children from nine to twelve years of age is *The American College Dictionary.*

spelling word list

Your child should be able to spell all the following words by the time he has finished the fourth grade. When you dictate them to him, do not give him more than 20 words at a time.

(Taken from the New York State Department of Education spelling list for the fourth grade.)

able	bottle	count	eye	hearing
above	bottom	couple	fair	heart
across	bought	course	family	hello
address	branch	crack	faster	history
afraid	brave	cream	feast	hoping
against	breakfast	creek	February	horn
ahead	bridge	cute	fence	hospital
all right	broom	dead	field	hour
alone	brush	decided	fifteen	hungry
among	building	die	fifty	hurry
animal	bunch	doctor	filled	ice cream
answer	butter	doesn't	finger	important
anyone	buying	dollar	finish	inch
anyway	canal	downstairs	firecracker	insects
anywhere	candle	dream	flies	instead
April	capital	dried	flour	interested
aren't	careful	drive	flower	iron
arrow	carried	dropped	flying	January
atom	carrots	drove	folks	July
August	cattle	duck	follow	June
avenue	cause	during	fool	kept
awful	center	ear	football	kitchen
awhile	central	east	fourth	kitten
balloon	chairs	easy	fox	knife
baseball	chalk	eaten	fresh	knock
basketball	chew	eighth	friendly	ladder
beach	chief	either	fruit	laid
beat	circus	electric	furniture	language
being	cities	elephant	gather	larger
believe	clear	eleven	geography	laugh
belong	climate	else	germs	learning
below	climb	engine	getting	least
berries	closer	English	gift	lessons
beside	clothing	enjoy	given	library
between	clown	evening	giving	lie
bicycle	coffee	everybody	goose	life
bigger	company	everyone	group	lion
biggest	cookies	examination	handle	listen
blew	corner	except	happen	living
board	cotton	excuse	health	load

lonesome	parents	ribbon	stopped	track
loose	pasture	rice	stores	trick
loud	peanuts	ruler	stories	trouble
lovely	pencil	running	storm	truck
lucky	penny	salt	stove	Tuesday
machine	person	scared	straight	turkey
match	picnic	schoolhouse	strange	twelve
meal	pigeons	seat	strong	twenty
means	playhouse	September	stuck	twice
middle	pleased	sewing	studies	unknown
minute	poem	shoe	such	upstairs
missed	popcorn	shoot	sudden	uses
month	porch	shot	sugar	valley
mountain	potato	silver	suit	wagon
moving	potatoes	sincerely	suppose	wait
muddy	president	size	surely	walked
music	prevent	skate	surprise	washing
myself	prize	sleigh	sweater	watching
nail	program	slide	swimming	wears
nearly	proud	soap	swing	Wednesday
neck	public	somebody	tables	west
needle	pudding	someone	taken	whole
noise	pupils	sooner	taking	whose
north	puppies	sore	talking	wild
nose	queen	south	taught	windows
November	quickly	speak	tea	without
number	quiet	spell	teaching	woke
ocean	quit	spent	team	wolf
October	rabbits	squirrel	tear	woman
office	rained	stain	telephone	women
often	raise	stairs	theater	won
oil	rather	stand	thick	wonderful
orange	reach	state	thirty	wool
others	reads	station	though	world
ought	really	stationery	thousand	wouldn't
ours	reason	stepped	threw	written
own	receive	sticks	Thursday	wrong
package	recess	stocking	tiger	young
pail	reindeer	stone	tired	yours
painted	report	stood	tooth	yourself

arithmetic | fourth grade

WORK IN arithmetic during the fourth grade continues to be practical and related to your child's everyday experiences. During the first two or three months he will review what he learned in the third grade. Your child is given many problems now because he is able to "think through." Arithmetic becomes even more challenging and exciting as the children find new paths to lead them to their discoveries of right answers.

numbers and numerals

He learns to read and write numerals to 1,000,000 (one million). He uses place-value boxes to show how the numerals are grouped by threes. When he writes large numerals, he separates the groups of threes by commas.

EXAMPLE

BILLIONS			MILLIONS			THOUSANDS			ONES		
Hundreds	Tens	Ones	Hundreds	Tens	Ones	Hundreds	Tens	Ones	Hundreds	Tens	Ones
			1	5	3	2	7	1	3	4	2

153,271,342

Read: one hundred fifty-three million, two hundred seventy-one thousand, three hundred forty-two.

He reads and writes the Roman numerals through 1,000. For an explanation of how Roman numerals are written, see the third-grade ARITHMETIC section.

1. I	11. XI	21. XXI	31. XXXI	50. L
2. II	12. XII	22. XXII	32. XXXII	60. LX
3. III	13. XIII	23. XXIII	33. XXXIII	70. LXX
4. IV	14. XIV	24. XXIV	34. XXXIV	80. LXXX
5. V	15. XV	25. XXV	35. XXXV	90. XC
6. VI	16. XVI	26. XXVI	36. XXXVI	100. C
7. VII	17. XVII	27. XXVII	37. XXXVII	500. D
8. VIII	18. XVIII	28. XXVIII	38. XXXVIII	1000. M
9. IX	19. XIX	29. XXIX	39. XXXIX	
10. X	20. XX	30. XXX	40. XL	

measures

In the area of measures your child:

▶ **Changes inches to feet and feet to inches.**

1 foot (1') = 12 inches (12")

(the mark " means inches, ' means feet.)

½ foot = 6 inches

1½ feet = 18 inches (12 + 6)

▶ **Perfects the telling of time.**

He learns that a quarter of one means 15 minutes before 1; that 12:15 means 15 minutes after 12.

▶ **Is introduced to the metric system.**

1 centimeter is a little less than one half an inch.

▶ **Learns the measures of length.**

12 inches = 1 foot

3 feet = 1 yard

5,280 feet = 1 mile

▶ **Learns liquid measures.**

2 cups = 1 pint

2 pints = 1 quart

4 quarts = 1 gallon

▶ **Learns dry measures.**

2 pints = 1 quart

8 quarts = 1 peck

4 pecks = 1 bushel

▶ **Learns weight measures.**

16 ounces = 1 pound

2,000 pounds = 1 ton

▶ **Learns the measures of time.**

60 seconds = 1 minute

60 minutes = 1 hour

24 hours = 1 day

7 days = 1 week

12 months = 1 year

365 days = 1 year

366 days = 1 leap year

▶ **Learns the abbreviation of:**

inch = in.	second = sec.
foot = ft.	minute = min.
mile = mi.	week = wk.
pint = pt.	hour = hr.
quart = qt.	month = mo.
peck = pk.	year = yr.
bushel = bu.	pound = lb.
ton = T.	ounce = oz.

geometry

In the modern method of learning mathematics, your child spends much time manipulating actual objects and it is necessary that he becomes familiar with their **properties**. Properties of figures are their characteristics, such as shape, dimensions (height, width, length), etc.

He learns to use many new terms in his work with figures:

▶ **Intersecting lines** are those that cross each other.

▶ **Parallel lines** never meet, no matter how far they are extended.

▶ A **parallelogram** is any four-sided figure whose opposite sides are parallel.

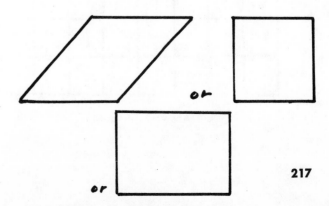

or

or

217

▶ The **perimeter** is the distance around an object.

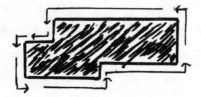  

EXAMPLE: Find the perimeter of the shaded area if each square measures 1 inch.

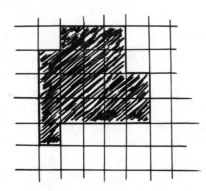

Answer: 20 inches

▶ A **right angle** is formed by one quarter of a complete rotation. When one line, AB, is **perpendicular** (vertical) and the other, BC, is **horizontal,** the angle formed (X) is a right angle.

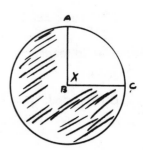

▶ **Area** is the measurement of flat surfaces. Example: Each square measures 1 inch on each side and is called a square inch. What is the area in square inches of these figures?

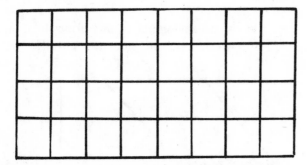 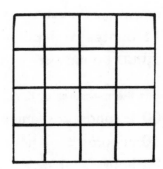

Answer: 32 sq. in.　　　　　Answer: 16 sq. in.

218

Your child will discover that the number of squares across the top times the number of squares on the side will tell him the number of square inches on the entire surface.

▶ The **radius** is the distance from the center of a circle to the edge, the line from B to C.

▶ The **diameter** of a circle is the distance from one edge through the center to the opposite edge, the line from A through B, to C.

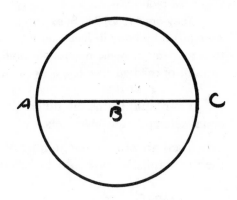

▶ A **cube** is a solid form that has 6 faces of equal size, and 12 edges of equal length, and 8 vertices.

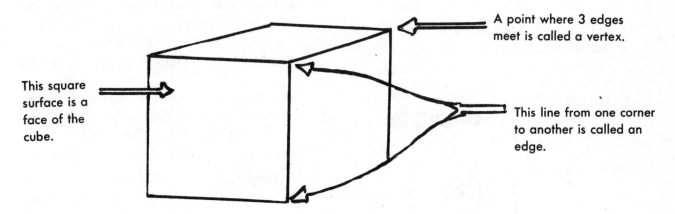

This square surface is a face of the cube.

A point where 3 edges meet is called a vertex.

This line from one corner to another is called an edge.

sets and subsets

The concept of sets unifies your child's world of mathematics. The term "set" and related terms should be used whenever possible.

The objects used to make up a set are called the elements of the set. A subset can be made up of many elements, or only one element, or none. A set with no elements is called an **empty set.** The symbol for an empty set is 0, the word name is zero.

EXAMPLE:

A set of 20 elements.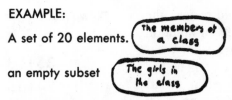

an empty subset

The subset is empty because these sets refer to classes in a boys' school.

Your child will continue to have practice in identifying sets. He will learn to write them with brackets, separating the elements with commas.

EXAMPLE: Name the set of children in the class who have birthdays in June.

They are {Mary, Jane, John, Kate}.

219

Your child will discover that different sets may have common elements.

EXAMPLE: Name the set of children in the class who take piano lessons.

They are {Jane, Bill, Sue, Judy}.

Jane has a birthday in June and takes piano lessons too, so her name appears in both sets. The two sets of children have one element in common.

Your child learns the difference between **equal sets** and **equivalent sets.**

When sets are alike in the number of elements they contain, they are said to be equivalent.

EXAMPLE:
Set A { △ △ }

Set B { ○ ○ }

Sets are said to be equal only if their elements are identical, not necessarily in the same order.

EXAMPLE:
Set A { ¢ ¢ ¢ ¢ ¢ }

Set B { 5¢ }

addition and subtraction

Your child reviews the basic facts of addition and subtraction. What a time saver if he has learned them well! Don't lose the flash cards you made when he was in the third grade. Review them with him once in a while.

Addition will be extended this year to the adding of six 5-place numbers.

EXAMPLE:

	35123
	24135
the addends	48146
	96351
	16101
	28191
the sum	248,047

Subtraction will be extended to include 4-place minuends and 4-place subtrahends.

EXAMPLE:

the minuend	4831
the subtrahend	2810
the difference	2021

Add the subtrahend and the difference. The answer will be the minuend if the problem has been worked correctly. This shows your child how addition and subtraction are related—that one is used to check the other.

The teacher will stress the property of:

▶ **Distributivity of numbers:** This may be called the "breaking apart" of numbers to make adding or subtracting easier and quicker to do.

EXAMPLE:

$$25 + 42 = n$$
$$\text{think } (20 + 5) + (40 + 2) = n$$
$$60 + 7 = 67$$

▶ **Commutativity:** The sums of two or more numbers is the same regardless of the order in which you add them.

EXAMPLE:

$$30 + 18 = 18 + 30$$

▶ **Associativity:** When adding more than two numbers, you can change the grouping and the sum is the same.

EXAMPLE:

$$2 + 1 + 9 + 3 = n$$
$$\text{regroup} \quad 2 + 10 + 3 = 15$$
$$\text{or} \quad 3 + 9 + 3 = 15$$
$$\text{or} \quad 10 + 5 = 15$$

The answer, no matter how you group the numbers, is 15.

Your child will discover that 10 is the key to easy arithmetic. He will try to regroup numbers to find the sums of ten first.

The teacher will not generally use these terms in class but you should be familiar with them and their meanings.

The following table can be used to add or subtract any combination through 18. Ask your child to make one to use for easy reference.

+/−	1	2	3	4	5	6	7	8	9
1	2	3	4	5	6	7	8	9	10
2	3	4	5	6	7	8	9	10	11
3	4	5	6	7	8	9	10	11	12
4	5	6	7	8	9	10	11	12	13
5	6	7	8	9	10	11	12	13	14
6	7	8	9	10	11	12	13	14	15
7	8	9	10	11	12	13	14	15	16
8	9	10	11	12	13	14	15	16	17
9	10	11	12	13	14	15	16	17	18

Using n to represent an unknown number, ask him to solve equations like the following by referring to his +/− table.

$$n + 8 = 14$$
$$n = 6$$

$$14 - n = 8$$
$$n = 6$$

Your child will subtract numbers where the numeral in the ones column of the subtrahend is larger than the numeral in the ones column of the minuend.

EXAMPLE: 32 is 3 tens and 2 ones
          − 7 7 ones cannot be
               subtracted from 2 ones

Borrow a ten from the 3, add it to the 2. This makes it large enough for 7 to be subtracted. The problem becomes:

```
  2 1
  3 2    (1st step: borrow)
  − 7
  25    (2nd step: 12 ones − 7 ones is 5 ones)
```
(3rd step: 2 tens − 0 tens is 2 tens)

Remember: 10 is the easy number to use in arithmetic. Use a multiple of 10 to solve equations like this:

$$75 - 19 = n$$

Think: "19 is almost 20. I'll subtract 20 from 75 first and then add 1 back to the answer."

$$75 - 20 = 55$$
$$55 + 1 = 56$$

Check the answer: $19 + 56 = 75$

multiplication

Your child reviews the basic multiplication facts he learned in the third grade. Did you make a set of flash cards for this kind of practice? They will be useful this year.

Ask him to explain to you what he is doing. He must understand what multiplication means before he can use it. His explanation will be something like this:

$$3 \times 5 = 15$$
(three 5s are 15)

11111   11111   11111
  5   5   5

The commutative property can be applied to multiplication:

$$5 \times 3 = 15$$
(five 3s are 15)

111   111   111   111   111
 3   3   3   3   3

He learns the multiplication tables of 4s, 6s, 7s, 8s, and 9s. Help him drill on these at home. If he knows them well, arithmetic will be easier for him the rest of his life.

Your child learns to multiply two-digit numbers, and uses the correct names for each part of the problem.

EXAMPLE:

the multiplicand	24 means 2 tens and 4 ones
the multiplier	× 3 means times 3 of each
the product	72 12 (3 × 4 ones)
	+60 (3 × 2 tens)
	72 (added together)

He will soon shorten his work by "carrying."

EXAMPLE: 24   1st step: (3 × 4 are 12, write
           × 3   the 2 and carry the 1)

            72

(2nd step: 2 × 3 = 6, plus the 1 = 7)

Your child also multiplies by a two-digit number. He multiplies by 10 simply by adding a zero to the right side of a number. If he writes 8 and places a zero at its right side, then he has 80. He has multiplied it by 10. He has made 8 ten times larger than it was.

He can multiply a number by 100 in the same way, by adding two zeros to the right side. To multiply by 1000, he adds three zeros to the right side.

Suppose he is multiplying by a number larger than 10.

EXAMPLE:

How many eggs are in 12 dozen?

Write:
```
      12
    × 12
      24  ( 2 dozen)
     120  (10 dozen)
     144
```

Think: 1 dozen is 12;

12 dozen are 2 dozen and 10 dozen;

2 dozen is 24;

10 dozen is 120 (add a zero to the right);

24 and 120 are 144 things in 12 dozen.

How much easier it is to multiply:
```
      12
    × 12
      24
      12
     144
```

The next step is to multiply by more tens and ones.

EXAMPLE: 36 × $.25

First think: 6 × $.25 = $1.50
Then think: 30 × $.25 =   7.50
Then add the two products $9.00

But write the numbers one under the other this way:
```
      $.25
    ×  36
      1.50   (6 × 25)
      7.50   (30 × 25)
      $9.00
```

222

This is the short way, by multiplying with carrying:
```
       3
      $.25
    ×  36
      150
       75
     $9.00
```

In some schools fourth-graders even multiply by three-place numbers.

EXAMPLE:
```
         324
      ×  523
         972
        6 48
      162 0
     169,452
```

This is really three problems in one:

(1)
```
      324
    ×   3
      972
```
(2)
```
      324
    ×  20
     6480
```
(3)
```
        324
    ×   500
     162000
```

The following table can be used to find products to 81 quickly.

X ÷	1	2	3	4	5	6	7	8	9
1	1	2	3	4	5	6	7	8	9
2	2	4	6	8	10	12	14	16	18
3	3	6	9	12	15	18	21	24	27
4	4	8	12	16	20	24	28	32	36
5	5	10	15	20	25	30	35	40	45
6	6	12	18	24	30	36	42	48	54
7	7	14	21	28	35	42	49	56	63
8	8	16	24	32	40	48	56	64	72
9	9	18	27	36	45	54	63	72	81

division

Division is a big subject in fourth-grade arithmetic. Your child learns even the long-division form. To help him understand it better, it is explained to him that division is a *short way of subtracting.*

EXAMPLE: Find out how many sandwiches we can make from 18 slices of bread.

Draw 18 slices of bread, a set of 18.

This is how we subtract 2 slices each time we make a sandwich. Each sandwich is a subset of 2.

18 slices of bread
— 2 slices for one sandwich

16 slices left
— 2 slices for the second sandwich

14 slices left
— 2 slices for the third sandwich

12 slices left
— 2 slices for the fourth sandwich

10 slices left
— 2 slices for the fifth sandwich

8 slices left
—2 slices for the sixth sandwich

6 slices left
—2 slices for the seventh sandwich

4 slices left
—2 slices for the eighth sandwich

2 slices left
—2 slices for the ninth sandwich

0 no slices left

We discover there are 9 twos in 18, 9 sandwiches from the 18 slices of bread. But we can find the answer quicker by dividing.

Write it this way: $2\overline{)18}^{\,9}$

Or this way: $18 \div 2 = 9$

Division is a way of changing a large group into smaller groups.

EXAMPLE:

Mother bought 27 pieces of candy because she wanted each child at the party to have 3 pieces. Can you tell how many children were at the party?

$$27 \div 3 = 9 \text{ or: } 3\overline{)27}^{\,9}$$

or: there are 9 groups of 3 in 27

```
0 0    0 0    0 0    0 0    0 0
 0      0      0      0      0
 1      2      3      4      5
    0 0    0 0    0 0    0 0
     0      0      0      0
     6      7      8      9
```

dividing short numbers

Your child learns the division facts of 4s, 6s, 7s, 8s, and 9s. He also repeats the division facts learned in the third grade. He uses the same table for quick division facts that he uses for multiplication facts, but reverses his thinking.

He sees that with small divisors the short form is easier; with divisors of 4, 6, 7, 8, and 9 the long form is easier. The use of the long form now acquaints him with this form for later use in the fifth grade, where he learns to divide by two-place numbers.

EXAMPLES:

Short form: $6 \div 2 = 3$

Long form:
$$2\overline{)6}^{\,3}$$
$$\underline{6}$$

(Write what 3 twos are. No remainder after subtracting 6 from 6.)

223

He continues practice with uneven division facts.

EXAMPLE: 11 ÷ 5 = 2, and 1 left over. This 1 is called a remainder.

Good practice can be had at home by finding how many nickels there are in any number of pennies.

EXAMPLE: How many nickels in fourteen pennies?

WORK:
$$5\overline{)14}$$
2 (this is the number of nickels there are)

$$\frac{10}{4}$$ (this is what 2 fives are)
(this is the remainder)

THINK: "Because there are 5 pennies in each nickel divide 14 by 5."

THE ANSWER IS: 2 nickels and 4 pennies remaining.

dividing large numbers

He should know the names of the parts of a division problem. The teacher uses them in her explanations.

EXAMPLE: divisor $\overline{)\text{dividend}}^{\text{quotient}}$

In dividing one number into a three-place number, your child takes the following steps:

HE WORKS: $7\overline{)252}$ HE THINKS:

A. Are there more than ten 7s in 252? Ten times 7 are only 70. So there must be more than ten 7s in 252.

B. Are there as many as 100 7s in 252? One hundred times 7 is 700. Oh no! Not that many.

C. Conclusion: If there are more than 10 and fewer than 100, then the answer will be a two-place number.

$7\overline{)252}$

D. The first digit in the quotient will be in the tens house and written over the tens house of the dividend.

$7\overline{)252}$ (3 above)

E. Now he thinks: 25 ÷ 7 = 3 (and some left over, but not as much as another seven). This tells him that the number in the tens place is 3.

$7\overline{)252}$ (3 above)
$$\frac{210}{42}$$

F. With the 3 in the tens place, the answer will be 30-something.

224

$$\begin{array}{r} 36 \\ 7\overline{)252} \\ \underline{210} \\ 42 \\ \underline{42} \\ 00 \end{array}$$

G. With the three in the tens place standing for 30, he then takes thirty 7s out of 252.

$$30 \times 7 = 210$$
$$252 - 210 = 42$$

H. Now there are 42 left over. How many 7s are there in 42? Recalling the multiplication facts, he finds that there are 6. The 6 is written in the one's place.

$$42 - 42 = 0$$

(So there are none left over.)

Now he has found that there are thirty-six 7s in 252. To prove the answer, he multiplies the answer by the divisor to find out how much thirty-six 7s are. If it is the same as the dividend, he has divided correctly.

EXAMPLE: $\begin{array}{r} 36 \\ \times\ 7 \\ \hline 252 \end{array}$ He is right!

Your child will go on dividing larger numbers that have remainders, and dividing money. Be sure he always checks his division by multiplying the quotient by the divisor. This shows that division is an inverse or opposite operation of multiplication.

fractions

The flannel board that you made for use in the kindergarten where your child was introduced to fractions can be used again for work in fractions. Circles and squares can be cut to show that there are 2 halves in a whole, 3 thirds in a whole, or 5 fifths or 8 eighths in a whole. Your child can easily see that the more parts into which a circle is divided, the smaller the parts are—that $\frac{1}{8}$ is smaller than $\frac{1}{2}$.

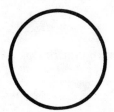 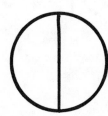  

Cut the circle into sections as indicated by the lines. Your child can put two of the eighths on one fourth and learn that $\frac{2}{8} = \frac{1}{4}$.

He can also see from the circles and sections of circles on the flannel board that $\frac{1}{2}$ is the same as $\frac{4}{8}$ and the same as $\frac{2}{4}$. Use three circles of the same size but of different colors to show this.

225

numerator and denominator

If he sets out to find $\frac{1}{5}$ of 15, this means he wants to know how many fives are in 15. The number under the line (called the denominator) tells him how many equal parts are in the whole. The number above the line (called the numerator) tells how many of these equal parts he will use. Therefore, to find $\frac{1}{5}$ of 15, he thinks:

$15 \div 5 = 3$. So $\frac{1}{5}$ of 15 is 3.

$\frac{15}{15}$ is all the pieces, or the whole circle, or 1.

$\frac{16}{15}$ is one circle and one extra piece, or it is 1 and $\frac{1}{15}$.

Your child can see that there are 3 parts in each fifth. How many parts are there in 2 fifths? How many parts in 3 fifths?

The circle with 15 even pieces will look like this.

facts about fractions

The following number bars will help your child to understand some fractional facts.

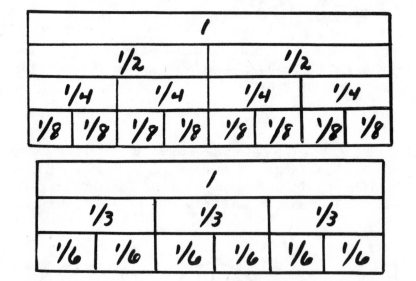

2/2 = 1 whole
4/4 = 1 whole
2/4 = 1/2
8/8 = 1 whole
4/8 = 1/2
2/8 = 1/4

3/3 = 1 whole
2/6 = 1/3
6/6 = 1 whole

Your fourth-grade child adds and subtracts fractions that have the same denominator:

1/6 + 1/6 = 2/6 or 1/3; 5/6 − 1/6 = 4/6 or 2/3

He adds and subtracts fractions that have unlike denominators. First the denominators must be changed so they are alike without changing the value of the fraction. The table above will help your child see quickly that $\frac{1}{2}$ and $\frac{2}{4}$ are the same.

EXAMPLE:

1/2 + 1/4 = n
(1/4 + 1/4) + 1/4 = n
2/4 + 1/4 = 3/4

226

Your child learns to call fractions in which the numerator is smaller than the denominator **proper fractions.** Example: $\frac{1}{4}$. Those fractions in which the numerator is larger than the denominator are called **improper fractions.** The value of a proper fraction is less than a whole. The value of an improper fraction is more than a whole.

EXAMPLE: 1/4 is only one of the 4/4 that makes a whole

5/4 is 4/4 and 1/4 more

Your child will have practice in changing improper fractions to mixed numbers.

He multiplies a whole number by a mixed number. (A mixed number is a whole number and a fraction.) Practical situations are used. It is easier for him to handle a problem of this kind as if it were two separate problems. First he multiplies by the whole number, and then by the fraction. Then he adds the two answers.

EXAMPLE: Cookies are $.40 a pound, I buy 1¼ pounds.

How much will I have to pay for them?

$.40	Cost per pound.
× 1¼	Number of pounds I bought.
.40	1 multiplied by 1.
.10	1 multiplied by ¼.
$.50	Cost of 1¼ pounds of cookies.

Your child learns that to cut a number in half means to divide it by 2, that to find $\frac{1}{3}$ of a number means to divide it by 3, that $\frac{1}{4}$ of a number is the number divided by 4.

EXAMPLES: $1/2$ of $4 = 4 \div 2 = 2$

$1/3$ of $6 = 6 \div 3 = 2$

$1/4$ of $8 = 8 \div 4 = 2$

A problem asking him to find $\frac{2}{3}$ of 6 has two steps to perform: First find $\frac{1}{3}$ of 6, then multiply that answer by 2. If $\frac{1}{3}$ of $6 = 2$ then $\frac{2}{3}$ is 2×2 or 4.

thought problems

Another strong feature of the fourth-grade arithmetic program is problem solving. A problem has to be thought through carefully before it can be solved. First, your child must know what facts are stated, and then understand what is asked in the problem.

Your child is constantly urged to practice estimating answers and do problems in his mind before working them out on paper. It is a practical tool for everyday living. It teaches your child to see what is a reasonable and what is a foolish answer in day-to-day living.

reading exercises

I. Choose the right word.

1. Mary fed the ___deer___ .   (deer, dime, date)

2. A winter day is _____ .   (frosty, balmy, billowy)

3. Janey found a _____ .   (tree, hair, seat)

4. Janice made a _____ .   (chair, chain, chill)

5. Alice feels _____ .   (tried, tired, true)

6. Put the water in the _____ .   (paste, pail, plate)

7. The cat caught a _____ .   (ride, rat, rate)

8. The cat is as _____ as coal.   (blue, blow, black)

9. Pat wants to read a _____ .   (bake, book, bike)

10. Daddy smokes a big _____ .   (pile, pipe, pole)

II. Write as many short words as you can find in the long words.

noon (no, on)	kitchen	brays	sister	lesson
grand	flour	roars	Sunday	package
mother	hour	crushed	turnip	kneel
grasshopper	howl	shrugged	goes	paper
snowflakes	crown	button	shatter	string
teapot	shower	donkey	worship	cereal
painful	ground	goldfish	world	bridge
horse	shout	store	cheat	crashed
shoelace	crowd	clown	clothes	important
unload	growl	glitter	train	vowel

III. In one sentence write the central thought of each of the following paragraphs.

A. Thelma liked to find out about things. On the way to school she saw some bushes. The leaves on the bushes had tiny spots on them. When she looked closer, she saw that the spots were really little bugs. She wondered if bugs have laws about going to school. But she knew she did not need any law to force her to go to school. She liked it. She could learn so many new things in school!

B. One day a friend brought a little canary to the queen. It was like no other canary. It had yellow designs on its wings. She had a gold cage built for it. The cage was beautiful.

IV. Follow these directions.

Put **1** beside the words below that make you think of sounds.
Put **2** beside the words below that name countries.
Put **3** beside the first name of a man or lady.
Put **4** beside the name of a place that is not a river or a nation.
Put **5** beside an act a person might have done.
Put **6** beside something an animal might have done.
Put **7** beside each one that tells when an event happened.
Put **8** beside the one that means you should listen.

1. ___1___ loud
2. _____ Lois
3. _____ hugged her doll
4. _____ one November day
5. _____ comforted the child
6. _____ whistling
7. _____ France
8. _____ Wilmington
9. _____ wagged its tail
10. _____ dishes breaking

11. _____ Alamo
12. _____ Hear ye! hear ye!
13. _____ when his age was fourteen
14. _____ during recess
15. _____ Bob
16. _____ Germany
17. _____ used its snout
18. _____ sewed
19. _____ shook a finger
20. _____ Sunday morning

V. Read the story, then answer the questions below.

A year is the time it takes the earth to go around the sun. It is the time from one birthday to another. Many things happen in a year—one Easter, one Thanksgiving, one Christmas, one spring, one summer, one autumn, one winter.

Spring is the morning of the year when everything wakes up. Leaves begin to grow, flower plants come out of the ground, and animals that have slept all winter wake up. Spring is the time for planting.

Summer is the daytime of the year. The sun is hot and bright, and all growing things stretch up to meet it. Plants cannot be strong and healthy without the sun. Flowers get bright, and fruits ripen, and birds sing.

Autumn is the evening of the year. Fruits and grains are harvested. Some animals grow thicker coats so they will be warm through the winter. Some animals store food so they will not be hungry when there is no food to find. Flower plants make their seeds. Leaves fall off the trees and become part of the soil.

Winter is the night of the year, the time for resting. In cold places, gardens and fields rest. Many animals rest in their homes and hardly do anything but breathe. This is the time of the year when the days are short and the nights are long.

A. Write what you have learned about

leaves

1. _____

2. _____

3. _____

flowers

4. _____

5. _____

6. _____

winter nights

7. _____

B. Choose the best title for this selection:

1. The Morning of the Year   2. The Four Seasons

3. A Time for Resting   4. The Evening of the Year

english exercises

1. She seen her cat run from the dog.
2. Two children was called upon to sing.
3. They is known by a different name.
4. The boys was last seen crossing the river.
5. Many watermelons was eaten at the picnic.
6. The letter was wrote on Friday.
7. She has did her work well.
8. The package come yesterday morning.
9. The picture were drawn with crayon.
10. Is these for you to carry?
11. Daddy brung home some friends.
12. You did the cooking very good.
13. Can I help the gardener?
14. Joe and me put up the tent.
15. The ice cream was saved for you and I.
16. The children wasn't careful enough.
17. Her and I wanted to feed the fish.
18. He didn't mean to cut hisself.
19. Ten gooses were in the farmyard.
20. Leave me be your helper.

II. There are three mistakes in each sentence. Can you find them?

1. the books jacket was torn?
2. she said, my name is Mary.
3. I and gretchen have a secret?
4. she gave it to Penny, cindy, and I.
5. the story was about two wolfs?
6. Aunt jane and aunt Mae are sisters?
7. They ain't painters but they is builders?
8. did you like dorothy's story.
9. lila is a girl from germany?
10. its not right to say ain't?
11. don't he know about our club.
12. miss lee talks to fast.
13. we go to the library on wednesday?
14. The fourth of july is in April.
15. a Stone went through the Window.
16. May we visit the lincoln park zoo?
17. the johnsons bought an new oven.
18. mrs. johnson baked a apple pie.
19. Gerry asked, did you make this pie
20. Miss nelsons friend john came too.

III. **Put each list of words in alphabetical order.**

A. grass
    tree
    report
    animal
    creature
    winter
    baby
    audience
    green
    dog

B. froze
    frost
    freeze
    frog
    friend
    frolic
    frown
    free
    fry
    funny

IV. **Use *ate* or *eaten* (*eaten* needs a helper—*have*, *has*, or *had*).**

1. Have you _____ your dessert?

2. Yes, I _____ it first.

3. We all have _____ well.

4. Has the bait been _____ by the fish?

5. We _____ the picnic lunch at home.

V. **Use *good* or *well* (*well* tells *how*).**

1. You did your job very _____ .

2. It was a _____ story.

3. Mother makes _____ porridge.

4. She paints _____ .

5. Don't you hear _____ ?

VI. **Use *is* or *are* (*is* is singular; *are* is plural, and is also used with *you*).**

1. There _____ more than ten here.

2. _____ you satisfied?

3. Two bears _____ talking to each other.

4. What book _____ you reading?

5. A book _____ a good friend.

VII. Use *come* or *came* (*came* is the past tense; *come* is the present tense, and is also the form used with a helper—*have, has, had, will, would,* or *should*).

1. We _____ too late to save them.

2. A gentleman _____ to the door.

3. We thought we would _____ earlier.

4. They _____ an hour ago.

5. We have never _____ late before.

VIII. Use *wrote* or *written* (*written* needs a helper—*have, has,* or *had*).

1. Aunt Mary has _____ to all of us.

2. We've _____ our invitations.

3. I think she _____ it herself.

4. Joseph has _____ a poem.

5. Everybody _____ a story.

IX. Use *can* or *may* (*can* means " is able to"; *may* means "do I have permission").

1. _____ we have a rest?

2. You _____ have a rest at any time.

3. _____ you climb a flagpole?

4. I don't think I _____ paint a house.

5. _____ I see your butterflies?

X. Use *I* or *me* (where it is correct to use *I* or *me* alone, it is correct to use them with other names).

1. Is this for you or _____ ?

2. Jerry and _____ are going swimming.

3. Susie and _____ both look like Mother.

4. Father went fishing with Joe and _____ .

5. Ray and _____ made a safety poster.

XI. Use *any* or *no* (use *any* with *haven't, isn't,* and other negative contractions).

1. The girls haven't _____ money left.

2. There are _____ more fish in the bowl.

3. Don't you obey _____ signs?

4. We don't need _____ more blankets.

5. Isn't the ice _____ thicker today?

XII. Use *knew* or *known* (*known* needs a helper—*have, has, had*).

1. I'd never have _____ it was true.

2. They _____ me with my mask on.

3. Have you _____ her very long?

4. Ruth _____ my secret.

5. The boys _____ the way to the cave.

XIII. Use *let* or *leave* (*let* means "allow").

1. _____ me help you carry the bags.

2. Please _____ me alone for a while.

3. _____ Mary tell her story first.

4. _____ John finish his work.

5. Anne _____ the dog come into the house.

XIV. Use *drew* or *drawn* (*drawn* needs a helper—*have, has, had, is, was,* or *will be*).

1. Mary has _____ a good poster.

2. The picture was _____ by Ray.

3. The children _____ pictures of a horse.

4. They all have _____ good pictures.

5. Have you _____ your slip out of the hat?

XV. Use *wasn't* or *weren't* (*weren't* is plural, and is used with *you*).

1. There _____ enough room for us.

2. There _____ enough seats on the bus.

3. We _____ invited to the party.

4. It _____ important anyway.

5. Mary and Charles _____ tall enough.

XVI. Circle the number before each group of words that makes a complete sentence.

1. A warm pleasant morning.
2. He found many acorns.
3. Where do you go swimming?
4. The large brick building.
5. Thank you for a lovely party.
6. I do not like angry words.
7. For a long walk through the woods.
8. Had stolen a piece of cheese.
9. The long, low, gray car.
10. She wrapped herself in fur.
11. We will help you carry the logs.
12. How to write a story.
13. The foolish, talkative crow.
14. At least eight years old.
15. Once upon a time.
16. I ride on the school bus.
17. She writes long sentences.
18. The boy who wore the green and white sweater.

XVII. These two paragraphs are poorly written. Rewrite them. Do everything necessary to make them easy to read and easy to understand.

A. The canary is a little bird and it has its name from some islands at the coast of africa where it has a native home and it is about 300 years before these birds began to be raise for cage birds.

B. Whales have no gills and they breathe air as you do but they are made so that they can remain under water for a much longer time than you can but if a whale is kept under water too long he drowns.

spelling exercises

I. **Make as many words as possible, using only the following combinations of vowels:** *oo oi oa ai ie ea ee ay.*

1. l —— ves
   (leaves, loaves)
2. tr —— s
3. p —— d
4. h ——
5. yesterd ——
6. r —— ch
7. thr ——
8. b —— t
9. t —— d
10. t —— ch

11. t ——
12. w ——
13. gr —— n
14. s —— nt
15. p —— nt
16. ch —— ce
17. dr —— d
18. —— sy
19. s —— t
20. sw —— t

21. tr —— t
22. t —— st
23. ch —— se
24. —— ch
25. r —— sin
26. p —— n
27. p ——
28. gr —— f
29. gr —— t
30. m —— n

31. pl —— se
32. tr —— l
33. st —— p
34. p —— k
35. st ——
36. b —— ch
37. p —— ch
38. s ——
39. r —— d
40. gr ——

II. **By changing the order of the letters you can make one or more new words from each word in this list. Try it.**

1. tea (eat, ate)
2. net
3. sag
4. who
5. nip
6. bat
7. loop
8. mane
9. vile
10. felt
11. peal
12. mate
13. deal
14. mace
15. least

16. miles
17. sale
18. risen
19. slump
20. step
21. verse
22. charm
23. strap
24. board
25. snail
26. quite
27. grown
28. shrub
29. file
30. palm

31. care
32. pans
33. tone
34. scat
35. pace
36. dray
37. silo
38. dear
39. sift
40. hops
41. rote
42. reap
43. tale
44. odor
45. now

46. ours
47. owe
48. snug
49. male
50. angel
51. there
52. sore
53. tapes
54. peels
55. rate
56. nest
57. inch
58. taps
59. pots
60. wings

III. Mark the vowels in these words either long (example: ā) or short (example: ă) or silent (example: a). Use your dictionary.

1. David	6. clean	11. running	16. engine
2. tub	7. unhappy	12. begin	17. excited
3. tube	8. cute	13. smokestack	18. behind
4. creature	9. slope	14. stagecoach	19. folding
5. snapping	10. speak	15. wheeling	20. spread

IV. Write the plural of each of the following words.

1. igloo _____	9. dress _____	17. iceberg _____
2. chalet _____	10. church _____	18. bottle _____
3. wigwam _____	11. woman _____	19. reward _____
4. potato _____	12. foot _____	20. puppy _____
5. beech _____	13. teacher _____	21. man _____
6. tooth _____	14. dime _____	22. goose _____
7. place _____	15. talk _____	23. Indian _____
8. box _____	16. speech _____	24. story _____

V. Some words look very much alike. In the sentences below, select the correct word from the group that is given and write it in the blank space.

1. Ten women hunted _____ the haystack for the needle.
   (though   thought   through)
2. Sam thought of a trick but he kept _____ .
   (quite   quit   quiet)
3. The storekeeper watched _____ the boy twirled his cap.
   (white   with   while)
4. The bandits _____ captured by the police.
   (where   were   when)
5. He was so excited that he _____ all over.
   (trembled   troubled)
6. John carried the box on his _____ .
   (shoulder   soldier)
7. On the farm we _____ sheep and cows.
   (was   saw)

arithmetic exercises

I. Read:

1,762	4,812	403	200,002	16,425
25,601	17,120	100,000	10,010	8,931

Write:
    Five thousand
    Sixteen thousand six hundred sixty-six
    Eight thousand twenty
    Three hundred ten
    Ninety thousand

II. Geometry. Fill the blanks.

1.   ◱   is called a _____.
       ◻   is called a _____.
       ▭   is called a _____.
       △   is called a _____.
       ○   is called a _____.

2. The perimeter of a square that measures 2 inches on each side is _____ inches.

3. There are _____ square inches on the surface of that square.

4. The perimeter of this triangle is _____ inches.

5. When the six faces of a block are the same size, it is called a _____.

6. Angle X is called a _____ angle.

7. Line AB is called the _____.

8. Line CB is called the _____.

9. Lines CB and DE are said to _____ at point A.

10. Lines FG and YZ are called _____ lines.

III. Sets and subsets.

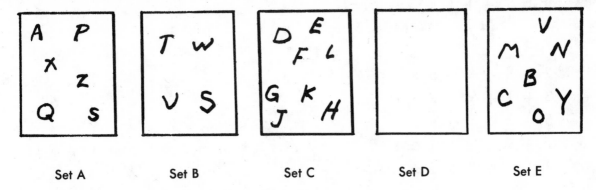

Set A	Set B	Set C	Set D	Set E

Write an addition equation to answer each of the following questions.

How many elements are in sets A and B?

How many elements are in sets C and D?

How many elements are in sets A and B and E?

2. Write a subtraction equation to answer each of the following questions.

How many more elements are there in set C than in set B?

What is the difference in the number of elements in sets E and B?

How many more elements does set B need to be as large as set A?

3. Set D is called an _____ set.

4. The common element in sets B and E is _____.

5. A subset in set E are the letters that come before F in the alphabet. They are _____.

6. Which pairs of sets are equal?

7. Which pairs are equivalent?

first pair $\{\triangle \triangle \triangle\}$ $\{\triangle \triangle \triangle\}$

second pair $\{ \text{①} \text{①} \text{①} \text{①} \text{①} \}$ $\{ \text{⑤¢} \}$

third pair $\{\triangle \square \bigcirc\}$ $\{\bigcirc \text{し} \triangledown\}$

fourth pair $\{\boxed{\$1.00}\}$ $\{\text{⑩⑩⑩⑩⑩}\ \text{⑩⑩⑩⑩⑩}\}$

fifth pair $\{6\ 1\ 2\ 5\ 0\}\{3\ 3\ 3\ 3\ 2\}$

IV. Add. Show your association of numbers with parentheses.

EXAMPLE:
$$4 + 1 + 3 + 5 = n$$
$$(4 + 1) + (3 + 5) = n$$
$$5 + 8 = 13$$

$2 + 8 + 4 + 6 = n$

$8 + 1 + 9 + 2 = n$

$5 + 3 + 5 + 9 = n$

$7 + 9 + 3 + 1 = n$

$2 + 4 + 7 + 5 = n$

$9 + 0 + 1 + 10 = n$

$3 + 4 + 5 + 6 = n$

$7 + 4 + 9 + 2 = n$

$5 + 5 + 1 + 6 = n$

$6 + 7 + 3 + 4 = n$

V. Add.

$2.45	$1.50	$6.21	$9.56	$2.28	$8.41
.27	.40	2.43	2.48	.79	.36
1.05	5.53	8.27	3.75	.64	.27

$2.45	463	475	$3.54	$9.67	346
.43	284	286	6.82	.28	287
5.00	29	347	4.73	.25	936
	408	903	8.55	2.76	423

567	$6.45	$2.80	284	$7.56	$ .78
208	.87	.57	365	2.84	4.65
435	4.00	4.39	283	3.05	.29
928	.95	.10	195	2.89	5.00

VI. Subtract.

400	600	140	130	170	190
− 189	− 590	− 50	− 70	− 82	− 84

180	160	246	465	530	287
− 93	− 57	− 83	− 92	− 64	− 56

387	460	563	234	$.89	$.37
− 29	− 87	− 98	− 72	− .75	− .28

$.46	$.57	$.98	$.86	$.65	$.79
− .39	− .48	− .79	− .47	− .58	− .33

VII. Give the change in the smallest number of coins or bills.

COINS RECEIVED IN CHANGE

	Amt. Spent	Amt. Given Clerk	Pennies	Nickels	Dimes	Quarters	Half Dollars	Dollar Bills	5-Dollar Bills
1.	2¢	10¢	3	1					
2.	4¢	10¢							
3.	21¢	25¢							
4.	17¢	25¢							
5.	8¢	25¢							
6.	42¢	50¢							
7.	36¢	50¢							
8.	20¢	50¢							
9.	13¢	50¢							
10.	52¢	60¢							
11.	58¢	75¢							
12.	66¢	75¢							
13.	91¢	$1.00							
14.	70¢	$1.00							
15.	28¢	$1.00							
16.	33¢	$1.00							
17.	$1.72	$2.00							
18.	$ .94	$2.00							
19.	$ .32	$2.00							
20.	$4.17	$5.00							
21.	$3.43	$5.00							
22.	$ .86	$5.00							
23.	$3.40	$10.00							

VIII. Multiply.

347 8	829 9	409 7	$7.15 9	$6.06 9	$2.59 5

$2.35 25	$2.93 25	$1.44 15	876 367	564 459	548 740

$3.18 176	$7.38 385	892 864	719 396	728 830	$6.54 951

$9.13 537	825 619	586 741	829 950	$3.75 381	$4.83 926

174 246	275 832	351 350	$4.85 104	$4.63 206	$1.32 106

475 209	162 405	247 608	234 304	$29.18 9

IX. Divide (do by long division method).

6/79   6/243   6/345   6/276   6/438   6/276

6/438   6/484   6/416   6/206   6/514   6/373

6/515   6/450   4/163   6/198   5/285   6/468

3/262   6/393   6/284   4/260   5/485   6/336

$5\overline{)298}$ $7\overline{)639}$ $7\overline{)595}$ $5\overline{)380}$ $8\overline{)584}$

$9\overline{)6786}$ $6\overline{)5070}$ $5\overline{)4763}$ $8\overline{)5896}$ $8\overline{)5649}$

$7\overline{)5089}$ $6\overline{)5608}$ $6\overline{)4816}$ $8\overline{)4575}$ $9\overline{)5879}$

$7\overline{)6531}$ $7\overline{)3220}$ $6\overline{)5640}$ $5\overline{)2680}$ $6\overline{)4578}$

$7\overline{)4935}$ $8\overline{)7259}$ $7\overline{)1792}$ $8\overline{)2474}$ $9\overline{)4052}$

$5\overline{)3765}$ $6\overline{)2873}$ $5\overline{)1795}$ $7\overline{)4959}$ $8\overline{)6408}$

X. Divide.

$6\overline{)3603}$ $7\overline{)3504}$ $9\overline{)5406}$ $8\overline{)7208}$ $6\overline{)\$24.06}$

$5\overline{)\$20.10}$ $8\overline{)809}$ $6\overline{)4205}$ $9\overline{)6300}$ $8\overline{)5656}$

$5\overline{)\$40.45}$ $7\overline{)\$21.03}$ $7\overline{)4205}$ $9\overline{)7281}$ $6\overline{)4800}$

$7\overline{)4949}$ $8\overline{)\$64.00}$ $9\overline{)\$18.27}$ $8\overline{)4802}$ $7\overline{)4903}$

$9\overline{)8102}$ $6\overline{)5401}$ $5\overline{)\$25.05}$ $6\overline{)\$18.24}$ $9\overline{)4536}$

XI. Fractions.

½ of 4 = _____   ⅓ of 6 = _____   ⅓ of 21 = _____

½ of 6 = _____   ½ of 12 = _____   ⅓ of 18 = _____

⅓ of 12 = _____   ⅓ of 15 = _____   ⅕ of 45 = _____

½ of 10 = _____   ⅕ of 30 = _____   ½ of 18 = _____

⅓ of 27 = _____   ⅕ of 25 = _____   ⅕ of 35 = _____

½ of 14 = _____   ¼ of 12 = _____   ½ of 40 = _____

⅕ of 40 = _____   ⅕ of 10 = _____   ½ of 60 = _____

½ of 8 = _____   ⅓ of 9 = _____   ½ of 80 = _____

XII. Fractions.

1/3 of 1500 = _____   1/8 of 32 = _____   1/2 of 400 = _____

1/5 of 255 = _____   1/6 of 12 = _____   1/8 of 408 = _____

1/9 of 72 = _____   1/4 of 28 = _____   1/9 of 81 = _____

1/4 of 36 = _____   2/7 of 21 = _____   1/6 of 360 = _____

1/6 of 54 = _____   2/5 of 35 = _____   1/8 of 360 = _____

1/5 of 360 = _____   3/7 of 49 = _____   1/5 of 25 = _____

1/7 of 56 = _____   2/3 of 30 = _____   1/6 of 36 = _____

1/8 of 40 = _____   4/5 of 25 = _____   1/9 of 54 = _____

XIII. Fractions.

5/6 of 36 = _____   3/10 of 80 = _____   4/5 of 35 = _____

7/9 of 54 = _____   4/7 of 21 = _____   4/7 of 49 = _____

4/5 of 40 = _____   5/8 of 72 = _____   3/3 of 30 = _____

2/3 of 12 = _____   3/8 of 64 = _____   5/8 of 40 = _____

3/8 of 40 = _____   4/5 of 20 = _____   5/8 of 64 = _____

3/5 of 45 = _____   5/6 of 48 = _____   5/9 of 45 = _____

5/6 of 36 = _____   2/7 of 63 = _____   5/9 of 63 = _____

5/7 of 28 = _____   1/4 of 36 = _____   2/5 of 40 = _____

XIV. Mixed numbers.

Find the cost of:

2½ yds. of ribbon at 20¢ a yd. _____

2¾ lbs. of lard at 32¢ a lb. _____

2⅔ yds. of lace at 30¢ a yd. _____

3⅝ yds. of rope at 16¢ a yd. _____

2⅝ lbs. of candy at 40¢ a lb. _____

6½ ft. wire at 10¢ a ft. _____

4½ yds. of ribbon at $1.00 a yd. _____

3⅜ lbs. of cheese at 80¢ a lb. _____

3¼ yds. of ribbon at 20¢ a yd. _____

2¾ lbs. of cookies at 48¢ a lb. _____

3½ yds. of canvas at $2.00 a yd. _____

2¼ oz. of seed at 40¢ an oz. _____

XV. Change these improper fractions to mixed numbers.

5/3 – _____   11/4 – _____   5/4 – _____

8/5 – _____   5/2 – _____   9/7 – _____

10/3 – _____   13/6 – _____   27/3 – _____

XVI. Using measures.

1 ft. = _____ in.   ⅝ yd. = _____ in.   1 lb. = _____ oz.

1 mi. = _____ ft.   ¾ mi. = _____ ft.   1 da. = _____ hr.

1 hr. = _____ min.   ½ T. = _____ lb.   1 yr. = _____ wk.

1 yr. = _____ mo.   ¼ hr. = _____ min.   1 pt. = _____ cups

1 leap yr. = __ da.   4 hr. = _____ min.   1 gal. = _____ qt.

1 qt. = _____ cups   ⅓ yr. = _____ mo.   ½ doz. = __ things

1 doz. = __ things   ⅙ ft. = _____ in.   ½ yd. = _____ in.

¼ yd. = _____ in.   1 yd. = _____ ft.   ½ mi. = _____ ft.

XVII. Thought problems.

1. Patsy bought a blouse for $1.69, a green corduroy skirt for $3.75, and a sweater for $3.19. In all Patsy's new clothes cost $_____ .

2. Fred wants to buy a handlebar basket for his bicycle. The basket costs $3.15. Fred has only $2.77. He needs _____ more.

3. Six boys in the Outdoor Club are sending away for wrist flashlights. The lights cost $.98 each. For the 6 lights they must send _____ .

4. Find the cost of ¼ pound of candy at 80¢ a pound. _____ .

5. If 6 children divide 144 cherries equally among them, each child will get _____ cherries.

6. How many 4-inch bookmarks can Ted cut from a strip of leather 48 inches long? _____ .

7. A salesgirl knew that there were 8⅔ yards of cloth on a bolt of material. She sold 2⅓ yards. How much material was left on the bolt?

8. The Scouts hiked 9⅛ miles one day, and 8⅝ miles the next day. How far did they hike on both days?

9. There are 4,375 books in the school library. Last year there were 2,126 books in the library. How many more books are in the library this year than last year?

10. Find the cost of the fence for a rectangular yard that measures 50 feet by 75 feet. The fence material costs $.50 a foot.

workbook answers   fourth grade

reading answers

I 1. deer   2. frosty   3. seat   4. chain   5. tired
6. pail   7. rat   8. black   9. book   10. pipe

II

no, on	kit, it, itch, hen	ray, rays	is	less, son, on
ran, an, and	our	oar, oars	sun, day	pack, age
other, he, her	our	crush, us, rush, shed	turn, urn, nip	knee, eel
grass, ass, shop, hop, per	how, owl	shrug, rug, rugged	go	ape, per
snow, now, flake, lake	crow, row, own	but, ton	hat, at	ring, in
tea, pot	show, how	on, key	or, ship, hip	real
pain, in	round	gold, old, fish, is	or	rid, ridge
or	out	tore, or, ore	heat, eat, at	rash, ash, shed
shoe, hoe, lace, ace	crow, row	low, own	clot, lot, cloth, the, clothe, he	imp, import, port, or an, ant
load	grow, row, owl	lit, litter, it	rain, in	vow, owe

III.   A. Thelma enjoyed going to school.
B. The queen had a beautiful gold cage built for an unusual canary she received from a friend.

IV. 1. _1_   6. _1_   11. _4_   16. _2_
2. _3_   7. _2_   12. _8_   17. _6_
3. _5_   8. _4_   13. _7_   18. _5_
4. _7_   9. _6_   14. _7_   19. _5_
5. _5_   10. _1_   15. _3_   20. _7_

V. A. 1. Leaves begin to grow in the spring.
2. Leaves fall off the trees in the autumn.
3. Leaves become part of the soil.
4. Flowers begin to grow in the spring.
5. Flowers cannot be strong and healthy without the sun.
6. Flowers get bright in the summer.
7. Winter nights are long.
B. The Four Seasons

english answers

I.

1. seen	saw	6. wrote	written	11. brung	brought	16. wasn't	weren't
2. was	were	7. did	done	12. good	well	17. Her	She
3. is	are	8. come	came	13. Can	May	18. hisself	himself
4. was	were	9. were	was	14. me	I	19. gooses	geese
5. was	were	10. Is	Are	15. I	me	20. Leave	Let

II.
1. The book's jacket was torn.
2. She said, "My name is Mary."
3. Gretchen and I have a secret.
4. She gave it to Penny, Cindy, and me.
5. The story was about two wolves.
6. Aunt Jane and Aunt Mae are sisters.
7. They aren't painters but they are builders.
8. Did you like Dorothy's story?
9. Lila is a girl from Germany.
10. It's not right to say ain't.
11. Doesn't he know about our club?
12. Miss Lee talks too fast.
13. We go to the library on Wednesday.
14. The Fourth of July is in July.
15. A stone went through the window.
16. May we visit the Lincoln Park Zoo?
17. The Johnsons bought a new oven.
18. Mrs. Johnson baked an apple pie.
19. Gerry asked, "Did you make this pie?"
20. Miss Nelson's friend John came too.

III.

A.	B.
animal	free
audience	freeze
baby	friend
creature	frog
dog	frolic
grass	frost
green	frown
report	froze
tree	fry
winter	funny

IV.
1. eaten
2. ate
3. eaten
4. eaten
5. ate

V.	**VI.**	**VII.**	**VIII.**
1. well	1. are	1. came	1. written
2. good	2. Are	2. came	2. written
3. good	3. are	3. come	3. wrote
4. well	4. are	4. came	4. written
5. well	5. is	5. come	5. wrote

IX.	**X.**	**XI.**	**XII.**
1. May	1. me	1. any	1. known
2. may	2. I	2. no	2. knew
3. Can	3. I	3. any	3. known
4. can	4. me	4. any	4. knew
5. May	5. I	5. any	5. knew

XIII.	**XIV.**	**XV.**
1. Let	1. drawn	1. wasn't
2. leave	2. drawn	2. weren't
3. Let	3. drew	3. weren't
4. Let	4. drawn	4. wasn't
5. let	5. drawn	5. weren't

XVI. Numbers 2, 3, 5, 6, 10, 11, 16, and 17 are complete sentences.

XVII.

A.   The canary is a little bird. It got its name from some islands off the coast of Africa, from which it originates. It is about three hundred years since these birds began to be raised for cage birds.

B.   Whales have no gills. They breathe air as you do, but they are made so that they can remain under water for a much longer time than you can. However, if a whale is kept under water too long, he drowns.

spelling answers

I.

1. leaves, loaves	21. trait, treat
2. trees, trays, tries	22. toast
3. paid	23. choose, chaise, cheese
4. hay	24. each
5. yesterday	25. raisin
6. reach, roach	26. pain
7. three	27. pie, pea, pay, poi
8. beat, beet, boat	28. grief
9. toad, tied	29. great, greet, groat
10. teach	30. mean, main, moan, moon, mien
11. too, tea	31. please
12. way, woo, wee	32. trail
13. green, groin, grain	33. stoop, steep
14. saint	34. peak, peek
15. paint, point	35. stay
16. choice	36. beach, beech
17. dried, dread	37. poach, peach, pooch
18. easy	38. sea, see, say
19. soot, seat	39. read, road, raid, reed
20. sweet, sweat	40. gray

II.

1. eat, ate
2. ten
3. gas
4. how
5. pin
6. tab
7. pool, polo
8. name, mean
9. live, evil
10. left
11. leap, pale
12. tame, team, meat
13. lead
14. came
15. steal, stale, tales, slate
16. smile, slime, limes
17. ales, seal
18. siren, reins
19. lumps, plums
20. pest, pets
21. serve, sever
22. march
23. traps
24. broad
25. nails, slain
26. quiet
27. wrong
28. brush
29. life
30. lamp
31. race
32. naps, snap, span
33. note
34. cats
35. cape
36. yard
37. soil, oils
38. read, dare
39. fist, fits
40. shop
41. tore
42. pear, pare
43. late
44. door
45. won, own
46. sour
47. woe
48. sung, guns
49. lame, meal
50. angle, glean
51. three
52. rose
53. paste
54. sleep
55. tear
56. sent, nets, tens
57. chin
58. pats, spat
59. tops, spot
60. swing

III.

1. Dāvĭd
2. tŭb
3. tūbe̸
4. crēa̸tūre̸
5. snăppĭng
6. clēa̸n
7. ŭnhăppy
8. cūte̸
9. slōpe̸
10. spēa̸k
11. rŭnnĭng
12. bēgĭn
13. smōke̸stăck
14. stāge̸cōa̸ch
15. whēe̸lĭng
16. ĕngĭne̸
17. ĕxcītĕd
18. bēhīnd
19. fōldĭng
20. sprĕa̸d

IV.

1. igloos
2. chalets
3. wigwams
4. potatoes
5. beeches
6. teeth
7. places
8. boxes
9. dresses
10. churches
11. women
12. feet
13. teachers
14. dimes
15. talks
16. speeches
17. icebergs
18. bottles
19. rewards
20. puppies
21. men
22. geese
23. Indians
24. stories

V.

1. through
2. quiet
3. while
4. were
5. trembled
6. shoulder
7. saw

arithmetic answers

I. Write:
5,000
16,666
8,020
310
90,000

II. Geometry. Fill the blanks.

1. parallelogram
   square
   rectangle
   triangle
   circle
2. 8
3. 4
4. 25
5. cube
6. right
7. radius
8. diameter
9. intersect
10. parallel

III. Sets and subsets.

1. $6 + 4 = 10$
   $8 + 0 = 8$
   $6 + 4 + 7 = 17$
2. $8 - 4 = 4$
   $7 - 4 = 3$
   $6 - 4 = 2$
3. empty
4. V
5. {C, B}
6. First.
7. First, third, and fifth.

IV. Add.

20	20
20	18
22	22
20	17
18	20

V. Add.

$3.77	$7.43	$16.91	$15.79	$3.71	$9.04
$7.88	1184	2011	$23.64	$12.96	1992
2138	$12.27	$7.86	1127	$16.34	$10.72

VI. Subtract.

211	10	90	60	88	106
87	103	163	373	466	231
358	373	465	162	$.14	$.09
$.07	$.09	$.19	$.39	$.07	$.46

VII. Change.

1. 3 pennies, 1 nickel
2. 1 penny, 1 nickel
3. 4 pennies
4. 3 pennies, 1 nickel
5. 2 pennies, 1 nickel, 1 dime
6. 3 pennies, 1 nickel

7. 4 pennies, —— , 1 dime
8. —— , 1 nickel, —— , 1 quarter
9. 2 pennies, —— , 1 dime, 1 quarter
10. 3 pennies, 1 nickel
11. 2 pennies, 1 nickel, 1 dime
12. 4 pennies, 1 nickel
13. 4 pennies, 1 nickel
14. —— , 1 nickel, —— , 1 quarter
15. 2 pennies, —— , 2 dimes, —— , 1 half dollar
16. 2 pennies, 1 nickel, 1 dime, —— , 1 half dollar
17. 3 pennies, —— , —— , 1 quarter
18. 1 penny, 1 nickel, —— , —— , —— , 1 dollar
19. 3 pennies, 1 nickel, 1 dime, —— , 1 half dollar, 1 dollar
20. 3 pennies, 1 nickel, —— , 1 quarter, 1 half dollar
21. 2 pennies, 1 nickel, —— , —— , 1 half dollar, 1 dollar
22. 4 pennies, —— , 1 dime, —— , —— , 4 dollars
23. —— , —— , 1 dime, —— , 1 half dollar, 1 dollar, 1 five-dollar bill

VIII. Multiply.

2776	7461	2863	$64.35	$54.54	$12.95
$58.75	$73.25	$21.60	321,492	258,876	405,520
$559.68	$2,841.30	770,688	284,724	604,240	$6,219.54
$4,902.81	510,675	434,226	787,550	$1,428.75	$4,472.58
42,804	228,800	122,850	$504.40	$953.78	$139.92
99,275	65,610	150,176	71,136	$262.62	

IX. Divide (long division).

13R1	40R3	57R3	46	73	46
73	80R4	69R2	34R2	85R4	62R1
85R5	75	40R3	33	57	78
87R1	65R3	47R2	65	97	56
59R3	91R2	85		76	73

754	845	952R3	737	706R1
727	934R4	802R4	571R7	653R2
933	460	940	536	763
705	907R3	256	309R2	450R2
753	478R5	359	708R3	801

X. Divide.

600R3	500R4	600R6	901	$4.01
$4.02.	101R1	700R5	700	707
$8.09	$3.00R3	600R5	809	800
707	$8.00	$2.03	600R2	700R3
900R2	900R1	$5.01	$3.04	504

XI. Divide.

2	2	7
3	6	6
4	5	9
5	6	9
9	5	7
7	3	20
8	2	30
4	3	40

XII. Fractions.

500	4	200
51	2	51
8	7	9
9	6	60
9	14	45
72	21	5
8	20	6
5	20	6

XIII. Fractions.

30	24	28
42	12	28
32	45	30
8	24	25
15	16	40
27	40	25
30	18	35
20	9	16

XIV. Fractions.

50¢
88¢
80¢
58¢
$1.05
65¢
$4.50
$2.70
65¢
$1.32
$7.00
90¢

XV. Mixed numbers.

$1\tfrac{2}{3}$	$1\tfrac{1}{4}$
$1\tfrac{3}{5}$	$1\tfrac{2}{7}$
$3\tfrac{1}{3}$	9
$2\tfrac{3}{4}$	
$2\tfrac{1}{2}$	
$2\tfrac{1}{6}$	

XVI. Change these improper fractions.

12 in.	30 in.	16 oz.
5280 ft.	3960 ft.	24 hr.
60 min.	1000 lb.	52 wk.
12 mo.	15 min.	2 cups
366 da.	240 min.	4 qt.
4 cups	4 mo.	6 things
12 things	2 in.	18 in.
9 in.	3 ft.	2640 ft.

XVII. Using measures.

1. $8.63
2. $.38
3. $5.88
4. 20¢
5. 24
6. 12
7. $6\tfrac{1}{3}$ yards
8. $17\tfrac{3}{4}$ miles
9. 2,249
10. $125.00

final tests   fourth grade

reading

Read the selection and answer the questions that follow it. (100 points)

Would you like to learn how to recognize some of our common birds? This article will help you.

The meadow lark has a yellow breast with a large, black V on it. There are patches of white on either side of its tail. It has a warbling, whistling song.

The yellow warbler looks like a butterfly as it flits about. It has a very slender beak. It looks yellow when it flies; however its back is darker than the rest of its body.

The goldfinch is smaller than a sparrow but it has the same short, thick beak and short body. You can tell it by its black wing tips and the black cap over its eyes.

The bluejay has a bright blue back. It is larger than a robin and much larger than a bluebird. Its lower side is almost white. It has a black band across its throat and on its head is a crest. A crest is a bunch of feathers which stand up above the rest.

The cardinal is smaller than a robin. Its beak is like a sparrow's beak. It is red all over except for a large spot of black on its throat. It, too, has a crest. It is the only red bird that has a crest.

The flicker is larger than a robin. It is brown with some bright marks. On each side of its beak is a streak of black. It has a red mark on the back of its head and a black mark under its throat. The upper part of its body, just in front of its tail, is white.

Write your answers in complete sentences.

1. Which word in the story means *identify*?
2. Which word means *most usual* or *familiar*?
3. What is the main idea of this selection?
4. How does a goldfinch compare in size with a sparrow?
5. Name two birds mentioned in the selection that have crests.
6. What is the difference between a cardinal and any other red bird?
7. Which bird looks like a butterfly when it flits about?
8. Which bird has a yellow breast marked with a black V?
9. Compare the size of a bluejay with a bluebird.
10. Write a good title for this selection.

english

I. Rewrite the following selection. Correct the mistakes in grammar, punctuation, and capitalization. Take out the unnecessary words and sentences. There are 20 mistakes. (20 points)

Johnny he made a feeding station for the bird's this Winter. The first day of spring is in March. He though it was lots of fun to watch the birds eat. Most of the birds they realy seemed hungery.

John he made the feeding station from a old lamy chimey he used too of his mothers pie plates for the floor and the roof he hanged it on the branch of a tree.

John plans to use the feeding station agin next Winter.

II. Select more interesting words in place of those that are underlined. You will find suggestions below the paragraph. (10 points)

My friend is reading a <u>nice</u> book. It is about a little <u>wooden doll</u> named Pinocchio. He was often very <u>bad</u>. Once when <u>he didn't feel well</u>, he wouldn't take his medicine. The fairy <u>bawled him out</u>. Then he said he would <u>be good</u>. This is only one of the <u>happenings</u> in the book that <u>you can get at the</u> <u>library</u>. The <u>writer</u> of the book is Collodi.

events	naughty	author	puppet	find
promised	behave	was ill	scolded him	an interesting

III. Mark the long and short vowels. Cross out the silent vowels. (10 points)

1. plum   3. white   5. grape   7. fort   9. little
2. late   4. apple   6. bandit   8. blade   10. quiet

IV. Write the plural of each word. (20 points)

1. puppy _____   6. bridge _____   11. roast _____   16. speech _____
2. monkey _____   7. dress _____   12. suit _____   17. foot _____
3. baby _____   8. box _____   13. chair _____   18. coach _____
4. inch _____   9. church _____   14. bottle _____   19. tube _____
5. bird _____   10. yolk _____   15. potato _____   20. woman _____

V. Choose the correct word for each sentence. (20 points)

(though, thought)   1. We came because we _____ we could help you.

(let, leave)   2. Please _____ me alone.

(teach, learn)   3. My friend says he will _____ me to swim.

(left, let)   4. Who _____ the dog in?

(may, can)   5. Did your mother say you _____ come along?

(done, did)   6. He has _____ many interesting tricks.

(was, were)   7. I didn't know that you _____ entering the contest.

(came, come)   8. The bus has _____ earlier than usual this week.

(good, well)   9. She does very _____ in her art class.

(brought, brung)   10. Nobody _____ hot dogs for the picnic.

(ain't, aren't)   11. There _____ enough sandwiches to go around.

(eaten, ate)   12. Those girls have already _____ lunch.

(is, are)   13. Where _____ the baseball team?

(wrote, written)   14. We have _____ our compositions.

(I, me)   15. Mother made a cake for him and _____ .

(any, no)   16. She didn't have _____ sugar left for the icing.

(knew, new)   17. The class _____ it was my birthday.

(wasn't, weren't)   18. Our teacher said that we _____ going on a trip this year.

(saw, seen)   19. I haven't ever _____ the Statue of Liberty.

(scent, sent, cent)   20. Grandmother _____ me on an errand.

VI. Before each word in the left-hand column, write the *letter* preceding the word in the right-hand column that has almost the same meaning. (20 points)

EXAMPLE: __*g*__ 1. love   g. adore

A.				B.			
	_____	1. pause	a. keep		_____	1. tell	a. desire
	_____	2. slap	b. close		_____	2. trade	b. dim
	_____	3. save	c. strike		_____	3. part	c. exchange
	_____	4. seat	d. carriage		_____	4. want	d. begin
	_____	5. near	e. glisten		_____	5. start	e. relate
	_____	6. hates	f. close		_____	6. faint	f. darn
	_____	7. coach	g. tutor		_____	7. roam	g. mold
	_____	8. sparkle	h. wait		_____	8. mend	h. copy
	_____	9. shut	i. dislikes		_____	9. shape	i. wander
	_____	10. coach	j. chair		_____	10. trace	j. separate

arithmetic

I. Copy and add. (10 points)
1. $2.53 + $.87 + $.69 + $7.54 + $9.83
2. $7.84 + $6.75 + $9.87 + $3.46 + $.95
3. $2.78 + $4.65 + $9.56 + $1.25 + $.50
4. $4.78 + $9.34 + $3.51 + $1.25 + $.50
5. $5.68 + $7.73 + $2.80 + $1.25 + $.50

II. Copy and subtract. (10 points)
1. $6.75 − $1.87
2. $5.74 − $1.90
3. 803 − 252
4. 2786 − 1978
5. $2.01 − $.90

III. Copy and multiply. (10 points)
1. $1.13 × 9
2. $6.46 × 7
3. $2.35 × 25
4. $6.54 × 951
5. 234 × 304

IV. Copy and divide. (10 points)
1. 686 ÷ 7
2. $67.41 ÷ 7
3. $35.50 ÷ 5
4. $73.98 ÷ 9
5. 6372 ÷ 9

V. How much change will you get from $5.00 if you spend: (10 points)
1. $.10 _____
2. $3.15 _____
3. $.35 _____
4. $1.75 _____
5. $3.40 _____
6. $1.00 _____
7. $4.99 _____
8. $1.50 _____
9. $2.50 _____
10. $2.99 _____

VI. Fractions. (10 points)
1. $\frac{1}{2}$ of 50 = _____
2. $\frac{1}{3}$ of 30 = _____
3. $\frac{1}{5}$ of 45 = _____
4. $\frac{1}{6}$ of 12 = _____
5. $\frac{2}{5}$ of 50 = _____
6. $\frac{4}{6}$ of 36 = _____
7. $\frac{3}{8}$ of 40 = _____
8. $\frac{1}{9}$ of 54 = _____
9. $\frac{3}{7}$ of 49 = _____
10. $\frac{3}{4}$ of 48 = _____

VII. Find the cost of: (10 points)
1. $2\frac{1}{2}$ yards of ribbon at 16¢ a yard. _____
2. $3\frac{3}{8}$ pounds of cheese at 96¢ a pound. _____
3. 12 boxes of cookies at 40¢ a box. _____
4. $7\frac{1}{2}$ feet of wire at 10¢ a foot. _____
5. 4 yards of gingham at 89¢ a yard. _____
6. $3\frac{1}{3}$ yards of lace at $1.29 a yard. _____
7. 9 chairs at $13.00 each. _____
8. $\frac{1}{2}$ dozen cookies at 50¢ a dozen. _____
9. $\frac{3}{4}$ pound of butter at $1.00 a pound. _____
10. 2 dozen pencils at 5¢ per pencil. _____

VIII. All kinds of measures. (10 points)
1. $\frac{1}{3}$ yd. = _____ ft.
2. $\frac{3}{4}$ T. = _____ lb.
3. $\frac{1}{2}$ hr. = _____ min.
4. 2 yr. = _____ mo.
5. $\frac{2}{3}$ yr. = _____ mo.
6. 3 wk. = _____ da.
7. $\frac{1}{4}$ doz. = _____ things
8. 4 hr. = _____ min.
9. 90 min. = _____ hr.
10. 1 qt. = _____ cups

IX. Write only the answer on the blank line. Do your work on scratch paper. (10 points)

1. Mary bought 6 postcards for 25¢. She sold them for 5¢ each. She made a profit of _____ ¢.
2. Jane has a quarter and 7 pennies. She can buy ——— 8¢ tickets.
3. Tom had 6 white rabbits and 8 brown rabbits. He gave 9 rabbits away. He had _____ rabbits left.
4. Gretchen had 17¢. She lost 9¢. Then she earned a nickel. Then she had _____ ¢.
5. Jane bought 3 yards of red material, 3 yards of white material, and 3 yards of blue material for Fourth of July decorations. At 19¢ a yard the material cost _____ .
6. A jeep traveling at 28 miles an hour can go _____ miles in 4 hours.
7. Peter's father has 8 gallons of maple syrup. If he sells it at $.75 a quart, he will get _____ for it.
8. The total cost of $\frac{1}{2}$ yard of cloth at 68¢ a yard and a 15¢ card of buttons is _____ .
9. If Allen buys 2 pairs of socks at 39¢ a pair, he will get _____ change from $1.00.
10. James paid $1.00 for a box of 24 greeting cards. He sold the cards at 5¢ each. He made _____ .

X. Sets and subsets. (10 points)

1. Using brackets.
   Separate this list of words into sets of
   A. The number words.
   B. The words used in measuring length or distance.
   C. The words used in measuring weight.

two	mile	pound
inch	centimeter	four
eight	one	ounce
nine	yard	sixteen
ton	twelve	foot

2. Show in brackets a subset of
   Set A, giving the names of numbers under ten.
   Set B, giving the measures of lengths over 12 inches.
   Set C, giving the measure(s) of weight used in buying coal.

3. Write as an equation in fractions:

4. True or False—All objects in a set must be alike.
5. True or False—1, 2, 3, 4, 5 is a set of cardinal numbers.
6. True or False—Grouping sets of numbers when adding is called the associative principle of numbers.

final test answers   fourth grade

reading

1. *Recognize* is the word that means *identify*.
2. *Common* is the word that means *most usual* or *familiar*.
3. The main idea of this selection is that birds can be recognized by such things as size, color, and markings.
4. A goldfinch is smaller than a sparrow.
5. Cardinals and bluejays have crests.
6. The cardinal is the only red bird that has a crest.
7. The yellow warbler looks like a butterfly as it flits about.
8. The meadow lark has a yellow breast with a black **V** on it.
9. A bluejay is much larger than a bluebird.
10. A good title for this selection is How to Identify Birds.

(Mother, the answers need not be expressed in exactly this way. Be sure the sentences are complete, with proper punctuation, spelling, capitalization, and grammar, as well as correct in their information.)

english

I.   Johnny ~~he~~ made a feeding station for the bird's this <u>winter</u>. ~~The first day of spring is in March~~. He <u>thought</u> it was lots of fun to watch the birds eat. Most of the birds ~~they~~ really seemed <u>hungry</u>.

John ~~he~~ made the feeding station from <u>an</u> old lamp <u>chimney</u>. <u>He</u> used <u>two</u> of his mother's pie plates for the floor and the roof. <u>He</u> <u>hung</u> it on the branch of a tree.

John plans to use the feeding station <u>again</u> next <u>winter</u>.

II.   My friend is reading <u>an interesting</u> book. It is about a little <u>puppet</u> named Pinocchio. He was often very <u>naughty</u>. Once when he <u>was</u> <u>ill</u>, he wouldn't take his medicine. The fairy <u>scolded</u> <u>him</u>. Then he <u>promised</u> he would <u>behave</u>. This is only one of the <u>events</u> in the book that you can find at the library. The <u>author</u> of the book is Collodi.

III.

1. plŭm	3. whīte̸	5. grāpe̸	7. fŏrt	9. lĭttle̸
2. lāte̸	4. ăpple̸	6. băndīt	8. blāde̸	10. quĭĕt

IV.

1. puppies	6. bridges	11. roasts	16. speeches
2. monkeys	7. dresses	12. suits	17. feet
3. babies	8. boxes	13. chairs	18. coaches
4. inches	9. churches	14. bottles	19. tubes
5. birds	10. yolks	15. potatoes	20. women

V.
1. thought
2. leave
3. teach
4. let
5. may
6. done
7. were
8. come
9. well
10. brought
11. aren't
12. eaten
13. is
14. written
15. me
16. any
17. knew
18. weren't
19. seen
20. sent

VI. A.
	h	1.	i	6.
	c	2.	d or g	7.
	a	3.	e	8.
	j	4.	b or f	9.
	b or f	5.	d or g	10.

B.
	e	1.	b	6.
	c	2.	i	7.
	j	3.	f	8.
	a	4.	g	9.
	d	5.	h	10.

arithmetic

I. Add.
1. $21.46
2. $28.87
3. $18.74
4. $19.38
5. $17.96

II. Subtract.
1. $4.88
2. $3.84
3. 551
4. 808
5. $1.11

III. Multiply.
1. $10.17
2. $45.22
3. $58.75
4. $6,219.54
5. 71,136

IV. Divide.
1. 98
2. $9.63
3. $7.10
4. $8.22
5. 708

V. Change.
1. $4.90
2. $1.85
3. $4.65
4. $3.25
5. $1.60
6. $4.00
7. $.01
8. $3.50
9. $2.50
10. $2.01

VI. Fractions.
1. 25
2. 10
3. 9
4. 2
5. 20
6. 24
7. 15
8. 6
9. 21
10. 36

VII. Find cost.
1. 40¢
2. $3.24
3. $4.80
4. 75¢
5. $3.56
6. $4.30
7. $117.00
8. 25¢
9. 75¢
10. $1.20

VIII. Measures.
1. 1
2. 1500
3. 30
4. 24
5. 8
6. 21
7. 3
8. 240
9. $1\frac{1}{2}$
10. 4

IX. Thought problems.
1. 5¢
2. 4
3. 5
4. 13¢
5. $1.71
6. 112
7. $24.00
8. 49¢
9. 22¢
10. 20¢

X. Sets and subsets.
1. Set A = {two, eight, nine, one, twelve, sixteen, four}
   Set B = {mile, inch, centimeter, foot, yard}
   Set C = {ton, pound, ounce}
2. Subset of A = {two, eight, nine, one, four}
   Subset of B = {mile, yard}
   Subset of C = {ton}
3. $\frac{4}{4} - \frac{3}{4} = \frac{1}{4}$
4. False
5. True
6. True

contents | fifth grade

helping your child in fifth grade

YOUR CHILD is about ten years old, between childhood and adolescence. Those of us who remember that period in our lives will recall that it is a more trying time than may appear on the surface. If you remember this and work as closely with him as before it should prove a rewarding experience. After all, at this particular stage of your child's growth he is generally relaxed and easygoing and he is eager to learn all kinds of things. However, he is not as independent as he would like you to believe. It is still a confusing world, and his understanding is pretty superficial. He needs you to help him develop his ideas and deepen his understanding.

reading | fifth grade

YOUR CHILD'S reading skill is increasing rapidly now. He is using more and more difficult materials, and is applying his knowledge more widely. His reading is helping him "grow up."

His range of reading interests is widening. He enjoys reading magazines, bulletins, newspapers, and books. His vocabulary is growing because of this increased reading, and he should be able to read aloud with expression.

You can help him develop a taste for good literature by helping him in his selection of books. (See the book list at the end of this READING section.) Have good literature available at home, and see that your child gets the public-library habit.

A fifth-grade schoolroom should have a well-stocked library because there is such a wide range of interests among the children—also a wide range of reading ability. If your school library is not all you would like it to be, perhaps you can do something about adding books to it through your parent-teacher group.

when your child can read, but doesn't know what he is reading

Sometimes your child still has difficulty reading. If he has difficulty interpreting what he reads, he can benefit from practice in listening. If you are a good reader yourself, then read aloud fifth-grade-level material to him. Let him tell you about what he hears; let him tell it in his own words to find out how much he understands. After several lessons like this, let him again try to interpret what he reads to himself.

Often the trouble is that he is a slow, and not very good, silent reader. This makes interpretation of what he reads almost impossible to him. Maybe he reads without expression, reading only words, not thoughts.

Ask him to read aloud for you. Check him on the above points.

If your child asks you to help every time he stumbles over a word and you tell him the word, you are making him dependent on you; he will not be able to read very much without your help. By this time he knows how to use a dictionary. In many cases he should also be able to figure out a word and its meaning from the way it is used in the story. Encourage him to do things for himself rather than ask you.

what your child learns from reading this year

Reading at fifth-grade level gives your child practice in:

▶ **Reading to find the main idea of an article.**
▶ **Reading to get all the details on a certain topic.**
▶ **Reading to draw a conclusion.**
▶ **Reading to find and remember events in sequence.**

With the above in mind, ask your child to read a story from one of his own magazines. When he has finished, ask him questions about it. You will be able to see how much he really gets from his reading. By doing this at different times during the year you can keep track of the progress he is making.

Speaking, writing, reading, and listening—the language arts—are closely related to each other. When your child reads an interesting story, it will help him to construct a good story for himself. When he struggles through a poorly organized paragraph, he is learning some things he must not do. If he can form a picture in his mind of the things he reads about, he is learning to make vivid descriptions of his own when he speaks and writes to others.

reading problems

Special remedial help in reading may still be necessary for some children. If you think your child would benefit from it, see his teacher about it. She will show you how you can help in working with your child on a remedial program.

books your fifth-grade child may enjoy

The Pony Express—*Adams, Samuel Hopkins*
Little Women—*Alcott, Louisa M.*
Andersen's Fairy Tales—*Andersen, Hans C.*
Pecos Bill—*Bowman, James C.*
Alice's Adventures in Wonderland
Through the Looking Glass
　　Carroll, Lewis
Five Boys in a Cave—*Church, Richard*
Great Caesar's Ghost—*Coles, Manning*
Robinson Crusoe—*Defoe, Daniel*
The Personal History of David Copperfield
　　Dickens, Charles
Hans Brinker—*Dodge, Mary Mapes*
Cruise of the Jeannette—*Ellsberg, Edward*
The Black Stallion—*Farley, Walter*
Fun with Science—*Freeman, Mae and Ira*
Tomás and the Red Headed Angel
　　Garthwaite, Marion
Lady and the Tramp—*Greene, Ward*
A Wonder Book and Tanglewood Tales
　　Hawthorne, Nathaniel
The Jungle Book—*Kipling, Rudyard*
Big Red—*Kjelgaard, Jim*
Lassie Come-home—*Knight, Eric M.*

Tales from Shakespeare
　　Lamb, Charles and Mary
Judy's Journey
Prairie School
　　Lenski, Lois
The Story of Dr. Dolittle—*Lofting, Hugh*
At the Back of the North Wind
　　MacDonald, George
King Arthur and His Knights of the Round Table
　　Malory, Sir Thomas
Abe Lincoln: Log Cabin to White House
　　North, Sterling
My Friend Flicka—*O'Hara, Mary*
The Merry Adventures of Robin Hood
Otto of the Silver Hand
　　Pyle, Howard
Roller Skates—*Sawyer, Ruth*
Mojave Joe—*Scott, D. C.*
Black Beauty—*Sewell, Anna*
Paul Bunyan—*Shephard, Esther*
Ballet Shoes—*Streatfeild, Noel*
Highpockets—*Tunis, John R.*
Lions on the Hunt—*Waldeck, Theodore J.*
All About the Stars—*White, Anne Terry*

WRITING is not included as a subject in the curriculum in most fifth, sixth, seventh and eighth grades. It is a well-established tool to be used in connection with other work, though when time permits, writing practice periods are set aside. However, if your child is careless about his writing and you have difficulty reading it, help him practice at home.

To write well, he must be relaxed. His posture must be good—he must be sitting straight, with his feet on the floor and both arms to the elbows on the table. He should hold the pencil loosely and easily—the lines will flow more smoothly and evenly.

In good writing all the small letters are the same height, and the letters are slanted the same way throughout. Have you ever noticed what happens when some letters slant back, some stand straight, and some lean forward?

This is hard to read.

In the fifth grade your child will begin to use pen and ink for some of his work. A good fountain or ball point pen would be a thoughtful Christmas gift.

ENGLISH

capital letters and punctuation

Your child reviews the uses of capital letters and punctuation rules, and also learns to:

▶ Begin each new line of poetry with a capital letter.

▶ Begin each main topic and each subtopic in an outline with a capital letter.

▶ Put a period after each Roman numeral and capital letter which is used to indicate parts of an outline.

EXAMPLE:
I.
A.

▶ Use commas to separate the single words or groups of words in a series.

EXAMPLE:

My pencils are red, blue, green, and yellow.

▶ Use a comma to separate the name of the person who is addressed from the rest of the sentence.

EXAMPLE:

Mary, can you come to my house?

▶ Use a comma after the words *No* or *Yes* when either is the first word in a statement.

EXAMPLE:

Yes, I would like to come.

▶ Use an apostrophe to show where one or more letters are left out.

EXAMPLE:

No, I can't come.

▶ Show possession by adding an apostrophe and s to the name of a person or an animal, even if the singular form ends in s.

EXAMPLES:

I think it is Fido's collar.

This is Lois's book.

267

► Show possession by adding an apostrophe and *s* to the name of a group of persons that does not end in *s*.

EXAMPLE:

Those are the children's boots.

► Show possession by adding only an apostrophe to the plural form that ends in *s*.

EXAMPLE:

The boys' lockers were installed.

► Put the words of a direct quotation in quotation marks.

EXAMPLE:

He exclaimed loudly, "Hurrah!"

paragraphing

Your child has work on paragraphing. Good paragraphs make good stories. Here are some rules for making good paragraphs:

► Make every sentence in a paragraph tell about one and only one topic: the topic of the paragraph.
► Put all the sentences that tell about one particular topic into one paragraph.
► Begin a new paragraph for each change of speaker when writing exact quotations.
► When writing a paragraph, arrange the sentences so that they tell things in the order they did, or should, develop.

outlines

Your child learns to make outlines according to certain rules.

► Number each main topic with a Roman numeral followed by a period. Arrange the numerals in a column so that the periods form a straight line.
► Indent each subtopic under its main topic. Put a capital letter followed by a period before each subtopic. Arrange the letters in a column so that the periods form a straight line.
► Begin each main topic and each subtopic with a capital letter.
► If there are subtopics under subtopics, use arabic numerals followed by a period.

EXAMPLE:

  I.
    A.
      1.
    B.
      1.
      2.

stories and reports

Your child learns to make reports, tell stories, and give book reviews. This is one of the reasons why he makes outlines and practices paragraphing. When your child is allowed to choose his own subject, help him select one that he will find interesting and that will interest the rest of the class, something about which he can get information, and something not too big for him to handle (such as atomic power).

descriptions

Your child also learns to make descriptions. He learns to point out the features of an object that make it different from other things that might be mistaken for it.

EXAMPLE:

Which description would help you find a lost sweater?

1. "It is brown. It has pockets. There is a row of buttons down the front."

2. "Nearly all the sweater is tan. The strip of cloth that goes around the neck and down the front on each side is blue. There are six dark blue buttons down the front. The first button is broken. Each pocket has a strip of blue ribbon across the top."

directions

Your child learns to give directions clearly. Has your child ever failed when you asked him to get something for you that you had carefully put away, or been unable to make something according to your directions? Did it occur to you that perhaps your directions were at fault? You can teach yourself to give directions clearly, and you can help your child do a good job. Be sure that he tells *all* the important things that need to be done. He must not leave out important steps. He must tell things in the order in which they must be done. He must say exactly what he means.

EXAMPLE:

Bad directions.

To go from our school to the post office, walk up the street about four blocks. Then turn left about two blocks and you'll see the big red-and-white building that is the post office.

Good directions.

Walk north from our school building exactly four and one-half blocks. Turn west on Lawrence Street. Walk exactly two blocks. The post office is the big red brick building with white pillars on the northwest corner of Lawrence and Madison streets.

letter writing

Your child has practice in writing business letters. The form of a business letter is important. It must clearly give all necessary information. Study the diagram.

The *heading* is the writer's address—his house number and street on the first line, the city and state on the second—and the date on which the letter is being written on the third.

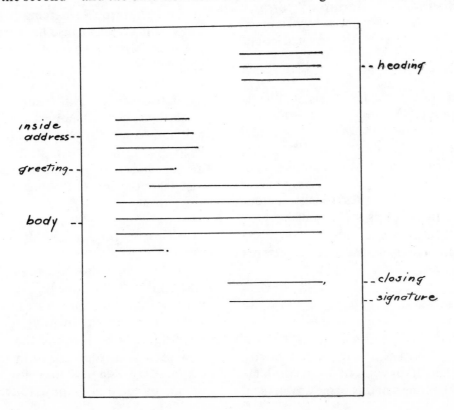

The *inside address* is the name and address of the firm or person being written to. It should be as complete as it is on the envelope. This is necessary in case the envelope later becomes lost or separated from the letter.

The *salutation* (greeting) should be courteous but short, such as *Gentlemen:* or *Dear Sir:*.

The *body* should tell (1) the purpose of the letter; (2) everything the other person will need to know in order to do what is wanted of him; (3) nothing unnecessary and nothing that has been said before.

The most acceptable *complimentary close* is *Yours truly,*.

The name of the writer should be *signed* in full.

A business letter should not be cluttered with unnecessary punctuation. Study the diagram as a correct example.

Two forms of letter writing are correct. Your child's school may suggest that one form is acceptable over the other form in certain areas of the country.

EXAMPLES:

block form	indented form
(generally accepted for business letters)	(generally accepted for personal letters)

If the block form (lines begin directly under one another) is used in the heading, it should be used also in the inside address and the closing, as well as on the envelope. If the indented form is used it should be used throughout.

Your child also writes friendly letters. The form is the same as for the business letter, without the inside address. The greeting and complimentary close are somewhat warmer in tone.

parts of speech

Your child has been gradually taught parts of speech, so by this time he can pick out nouns, adjectives, and verbs without formal drill. He knows that common nouns name any person,

place, or thing; proper nouns name special persons, places, or things. He knows that adjectives describe nouns and that verbs are words that express an action, an occurrence, or a state-of-being.

EXAMPLES:

The big *dog* barked at me. (noun)

The *big* dog barked at me. (adjective)

The big dog *barked* at me. (verb-action)

The big dog *seemed* angry. (verb-seems to be)

SPELLING

By the end of this grade your child will have about 2,000 well-selected basic words in his writing vocabulary; they will be useful to him throughout his life. New words are continually added. Your child uses the dictionary regularly.

If he has trouble learning new words each week, it may be because he is trying to learn them as separate words. If he is given a chance to *use* the new words, he will come to know them. Give him writing chores at home. Let him write his own thank-you notes and invitations. If he has an exciting story to tell, ask him to write it out as a story for you to keep. Ask to see the compositions and letters he does in school, so that they don't become just school exercises to him, to be left in his schoolroom and forgotten.

spelling is important, but . . .

When a composition is assigned an English class, it is with the hope that the children will express their thoughts in fresh and effective ways. Teachers frequently do not correct spelling mistakes, feeling that the children may become discouraged in their attempts at original expression if they are burdened by details of spelling, handwriting, etc. This is right, but at home you can make a list of those misspelled words and use them in your games and practice periods with your child.

spelling games

To help him drill on the new spelling words, continue to use the games you used in previous grades. For example:

▶ **Scramble the letters and let him unscramble them.**

utboa (about)
denhlicr (children)

▶ **Write words, leaving out some of the troublesome letters, and let him complete the words.**

rec —— ve (receive)
sho —— d (should)

▶ **Give your child the meaning and let him select from a list the words that fit.**

a) ten cents (dime)
b) in any place (anywhere)
c) most of the time (usually)

▶ **Write sentences or a story, leaving blank spaces that are to be filled in with the week's spelling words.**

WORDS
invention invented faster

STORY
The printing press was _____ about five hundred years ago. Today there would be no books or newspapers without this _____ . Of course, things can be printed much _____ nowadays than they could then.

▶ **Have fun finding antonyms (words that mean the opposite of other words, *i.e.*, lose —find, well—ill).**

FIND ANTONYMS FOR:
front easy
behind war
for cold
win run

spelling word list

Before your child moves on to the sixth grade he should be able to use and spell the following words. Do not study more than 25 of them at one time. (From the list prepared by the New York State Education Department.)

absent	angry	attic	battle
account	ankle	auditorium	beauty
ache	answering	aunt	beginning
acres	appreciate	author	bench
adventure	apron	automobile	blackboard
afterward	army	average	blanket
airplane	arrived	barrel	boards
alive	artist	basement	borrow
although	ashamed	baskets	bother
amount	attend	bathing	bowl

bucket	dangerous	figure	knives
buried	daughter	flight	laughing
button	deal	float	lawn
calves	death	followed	lazy
camera	decide	foreign	leather
canary	dentist	forgotten	length
candles	department	forty	lettuce
canoe	depot	fourteen	level
captain	desert	fruits	limb
captured	destroy	fuel	listen
catalogue	difference	furnace	marble
celebrate	dining	garage	march
cellar	disease	giant	married
cement	distance	glasses	master
certain	ditch	gloves	matter
chain	dozen	golf	measles
change	driver	grain	measure
check	drug	grammar	medicine
cheese	earn	groceries	mistake
cherry	earth	habit	motor
chest	edge	handkerchiefs	movies
chimney	education	headache	museum
chocolate	eighteen	healthy	nature
choose	empty	heavy	neat
chose	enter	herd	neighbor
circle	envelope	holiday	nephew
classmate	especially	honey	newspaper
closet	etc.	honor	nickel
coast	examination	hunter	niece
collar	excellent	idea	notice
correct	exciting	imagine	nurse
costume	exercise	Indians	oatmeal
cough	exhibit	interest	obey
court	expect	invite	offer
crazy	extra	island	operetta
cries	factory	jail	orchestra
crowd	fail	journey	order
curly	fasten	juice	oven
daily	favorite	junior	owner
damage	fever	keen	paid

palace	ranch	shut	tank
parade	regards	sidewalk	tennis
patch	regular	sign	term
penmanship	remain	sixth	terrible
perhaps	remembered	ski	themselves
persons	reports	skis	thread
phone	respect	slaves	throat
pieces	return	slept	tied
pillow	rifle	slipper	tight
pitcher	rivers	smell	tiny
plain	rooster	smile	toe
pleasant	roots	smooth	tomatoes
pleasure	rough	soldiers	tools
plenty	rubber	socks	touch
pocketbook	rule	soup	traffic
police	safety	spare	trail
policeman	sail	speed	travel
polite	salmon	split	treasure
pool	scare	spoil	treat
post office	scarf	spoke	tribe
pour	scout	sport	true
powder	screen	spot	truth
practice	season	spread	umbrella
prepare	sentence	square	useful
press	separate	stable	vegetables
price	serve	stamp	violin
probably	settle	steal	weigh
property	seventh	steel	welcome
protect	several	stiff	wheat
pumpkin	sharp	stream	wheel
purple	sheet	stuff	whether
purse	shining	subject	whistle
quarter	shirt	sweep	wrist
question	shoulder	swell	writes
railroad	shovel	tablet	zero

EVERY CHILD has trouble with some part of arithmetic. Perhaps it's fractions, long division, decimals. . . . Find the areas in which your child needs help. By using the drills at the end of the fourth-grade book, you can help your child to a better start in the fifth grade. Help him approach his new work with confidence by making sure of each step as he comes to it.

In modern mathematics emphasis is put upon estimating answers before the actual work of solving the problems is begun. The aim of today's system is to develop *logical reasoning* in young people and to give them the *opportunity to think*.

numbers and numerals

This year your child will develop the ability to read and write numbers up to 1,000,000,000. Review place-value of digits with him. He uses letters to name the houses in which he places the digits to determine their value. Such a table is called a **place-value grid.**

EXAMPLE:

B	HM	TM	M	Hth	Tth	th	H	T	O
1	0	0	0	0	0	0	0	0	0

The number in the grid is one billion. When there are no elements in a set, such as the tens set in the grid above (wherever a zero appears), the set is said to be empty.

We have only ten **basic symbols** in our number system: 0, 1, 2, 3, 4, 5, 6, 7, 8, 9. When we name numbers through 9, a single symbol is sufficient. When we name numbers greater than 9, we use the same set of basic symbols over and over again. To read the numerals for large numbers easily, we group them in sets of 3 digits.

EXAMPLE: 561, 021

A **digit** is a numeral within a numeral. It gets its value from its position in the numeral. Example: In the numeral above, 2 is in the tens place and therefore has the value of 2 tens.

Numbers can have direction. A **negative whole number** is one whose value is less than zero. It must be preceded by a negative sign.

EXAMPLE:

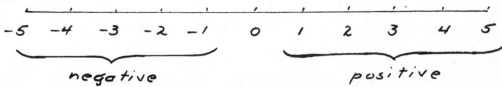

A number without a sign (+ or −) preceding it, is read as a positive number. Zero marks the starting point. All the positive numbers and the negative numbers and the zero are called integers. For every positive number there is a matching negative number. Just as there is no end to positive numbers, so there is no end to negative numbers. They go on forever. Think of the largest number you can. You can always add 1 to it.

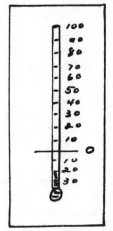

A practical use for negative numbers is on a thermometer. Those numbers above the zero are positive, those below are negative. If the temperature goes below zero we can see if it is −2° or −10°, etc.

Your child is introduced to **exponents,** which are another way of naming large numbers. Three tens (10 × 10 × 10) are 1000, or we say 10 to the third power. We write 10³. The little 3 is called the exponent and is a short way of telling how many times the factor 10 (called the base) is used (10 × 10 × 10).

Your child learns that **prime numbers** are those whole numbers greater than one (the positive integers) which can be divided only by one and by themselves with no remainder. Prime numbers can have only two factors.

EXAMPLE: 11 is a prime number. It can be divided by 1 (11 ÷ 1 = 11) and by itself (11 ÷ 11 = 1). It cannot be evenly divided by any other number.

EXAMPLE: 4 is NOT a prime number because it can be also divided by 2: 4 ÷ 1 = 4, 4 ÷ 4 = 1, 4 ÷ 2 = 2.

The numbers other than 1 and the prime numbers are called **composite numbers** and have more than two factors.

EXAMPLES:

6 is a composite number and has 4 factors.
6 ÷ 1 = 6,   6 ÷ 6 = 1,   6 ÷ 3 = 2,   6 ÷ 2 = 3
(Your child learned that the two numbers in a multiplication problem are called factors.
6 × 1 = 6,   1 × 6 = 6,   2 × 3 = 6,   3 × 2 = 6. Can you see how multiplication and division are related?)
21 is a composite number: 21 ÷ 7 = 3, 21 ÷ 3 = 7.
3 and 7 are both prime numbers as well as factors of 21. Therefore 3 and 7 are called prime factors of 21.
24 is a composite number and has 8 factors: Count them. They are underlined.

1 × 24 = 24	24 × 1 = 24
2 × 12 = 24	12 × 2 = 24
3 × 8 = 24	8 × 3 = 24
4 × 6 = 24	6 × 4 = 24

The study of Roman numerals is continued this year. Using the rules for writing Roman numerals, compare the system the Romans used to our own number system based on 10.

Your child writes the Roman numerals to 2000 (MM) or more if he wishes. He learns to use a bar over his Roman numerals to denote thousands.

EXAMPLE: XXV is 25, but X̄X̄V̄ is 25,000.

Review with him the rules for writing Roman numerals (grade three).

Notice and remember:

▶ **Repetition may occur no more than 3 times.**
I written three times is III, or 3.
X written twice is XX, or 20.

▶ **Subtraction may occur only once.**
I left of V means 1 from 5, or 4 (IV)
I left of X means 1 from 10, or 9 (IX)
X left of L means 10 from 50, or 40 (XL)
C left of M means 100 from 1000, or 900 (CM)

sets and subsets

Your child continues to review the idea of equal and equivalent sets.

EXAMPLES:

{8, 3}, {3, 8}   {1, 3, 5, 8}, {9, 6, 5, 4}
equal   equivalent

He learns the operations of **union** and **intersection** of sets, using capital letters as the names of his sets.

The union of two sets contains all the members of both sets. The symbol used to show union is ∪.

EXAMPLE:
Set A = {apple, pear, grape}
Set B = {banana, orange}
A ∪ B = {apple, pear, grape, banana, orange}

The intersection of two sets contains only the element or elements common to both sets. The symbol to show intersection is ∩.

EXAMPLE:
Set X = {apple, pear, grape}
Set Y = {banana, orange, apple}
X ∩ Y = {apple}

Practice problems:

1. Set A = all the boys in the class who have red hair
Set B = all the girls in the class who have red hair
A = {John, Tom}
B = {Grace, Susan, June}
A ∪ B =

Ans. A ∪ B = {John, Tom, Grace, Susan, June}

2. Set X boys in the class who have red hair
Set Y = boys in the first row who have red hair
X = {John, Tom}
Y = {Tom}
X ∩ Y =

Ans. X ∪ Y = {Tom}

3. Set A = {4, 5, 6, 7, 8}
Set B = {1, 2, 3, 4}
A ∪ B =

Ans. A ∪ B = {1, 2, 3, 4, 5, 6, 7, 8} (4 is mentioned once as a member of the union. It is not necessary to repeat it.)

4. Set X = {1, 2, 3, 4, 5}
Set Y = {3, 4, 5, 6, 7}
X ∩ Y =

Ans. X ∪ Y = {3, 4, 5}

Intersection can be shown by diagrams.

EXAMPLE:

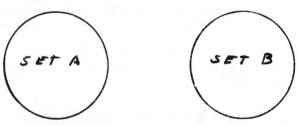

A and B are separate sets. If they have no elements in common, they are called **disjoint** sets. If they do have some elements in common, it is shown like this:

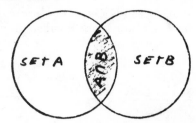

The shaded area indicates the elements they have in common.

276

addition, subtraction, multiplication, division

Your child does much of his work in arithmetic sentences. He must remember that work written in parentheses must be done first. When only multiplication and division are called for, work from left to right.

EXAMPLE:
$$8 \div 2 \times 4 = \square$$
$$4 \times 4 = 16$$

When only addition and subtraction are called for, work from left to right.

EXAMPLE:
$$4 - 2 + 6 = \square$$
$$2 + 6 = 8$$

When three or four processes are called for, multiply and/or divide first, working from left to right. Then add and subtract, also working from left to right.

EXAMPLE:
$$3 + 2 \times 5 \div 2 - 4 = \square$$

Multiply first	(2×5):	$3 + 10 \div 2 - 4 = \square$
Divide next	$(10 \div 2)$:	$3 + 5 \quad - 4 = \square$
Add next	$(3 + 5)$:	$- 8 \quad - 4 = \square$
Finally, subtract		4

Your child continues to maintain his skills in addition, subtraction, multiplication, and division of whole numbers. He solves problems with larger numbers than he has used before. (See the workbook section for practice problems.)

fractions

Your child has practice in writing sets of equivalent and equal fractions. Use number bars (grade 4) and diagrams.

EXAMPLE:

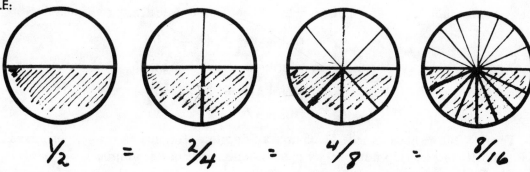

$$\tfrac{1}{2} = \tfrac{2}{4} = \tfrac{4}{8} = \tfrac{8}{16}$$

He learns that a fraction means the numerator (number above the line) divided by the denominator (number below the line). That is, in $\frac{1}{4}$ it means $1 \div 4$. If one apple is to be divided by four boys, each boy will get $\frac{1}{4}$. If three apples are to be divided by four boys, each one will get $\frac{3}{4}$ of an apple.

Your fifth-grade child should have visual help and actual handling of objects to understand this kind of division.

adding and subtracting fractions

Your child adds and subtracts fractions that are alike. First he will have to understand that the denominator (number below the line) is only the *name* of the pieces he is working with. These pieces have to be alike before he can add or subtract them. He adds halves to halves, thirds to thirds, fourths to fourths, etc.

EXAMPLES:

$$\tfrac{1}{3} + \tfrac{2}{3} = \tfrac{3}{3} \text{ (or 1)} \qquad \tfrac{2}{3} - \tfrac{1}{3} = \tfrac{1}{3} \qquad \tfrac{1}{4} + \tfrac{2}{4} = \tfrac{3}{4}$$

improper fractions

Your child learns to change *improper* (top-heavy) fractions to whole and mixed numbers. A mixed number is a whole number and a fraction, such as $1\frac{1}{2}$. If you still have the flannel board you made for your child in kindergarten, get it out.

EXAMPLE:

Change the improper fraction $\frac{9}{4}$ to a mixed number.

First lay out the 9 fourths.

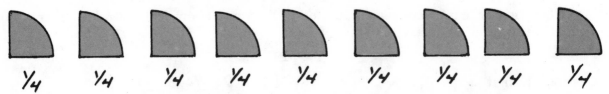

Then assemble them into circles.

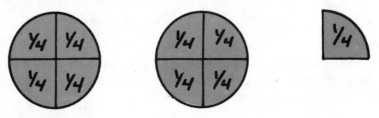

There are 2 wholes and one quarter.

It is written: $\frac{9}{4} = 2\frac{1}{4}$.

After several examples, your child sees that division is the fastest way to do the work.

$$\frac{9}{4} = (\text{think: } 9 \div 4) = 2\frac{1}{4}$$
$$\frac{6}{3} = (\text{think: } 6 \div 3) = 2$$
$$\frac{8}{5} = (\text{think: } 8 \div 5) = 1\frac{3}{5}$$
$$\frac{7}{2} = (\text{think: } 7 \div 2) = 3\frac{1}{2}$$

This is what he has learned: To change an improper fraction to a whole or mixed number, divide the numerator (top number) by the denominator (bottom number).

mixed numbers

Your child adds and subtracts mixed numbers. Use actual objects or the flannel board to help him understand the problems.

EXAMPLE:

Add $1\frac{1}{2}$ and $1\frac{1}{2}$. $1\frac{1}{2} + 1\frac{1}{2} = 2\frac{2}{2}$ or 3

adding and subtracting fractions with different denominators

He adds and subtracts fractions that have different denominators (numbers under the line). Then it is necessary to find a *common* denominator first. One cannot add bananas and basketballs—what would one label the result?

EXAMPLE:

> If Susie needs ½ yard of cloth for a doll's dress, and ¼ yard for the jacket, she must think: How much is ¼ and ½? According to the diagram, ½ is the same as ²⁄₄; ²⁄₄ and ¼ are ¾. She learns that she needs ¾ of a yard of material.

The following diagram will help your child find equal fractions:

1							
½				½			
¼		¼		¼		¼	
⅛	⅛	⅛	⅛	⅛	⅛	⅛	⅛
1/16 1/16	1/16 1/16	1/16 1/16	1/16 1/16	1/16 1/16	1/16 1/16	1/16 1/16	1/16 1/16

Remember, fractions cannot be added unless the denominators are alike. In adding $\frac{3}{4}$ and $\frac{3}{8}$, we will try to change them both to eighths. Always try first to use the largest of the given denominators. If not, try 2 times that denominator, or 3 times, etc.

In this problem, $\frac{3}{4}$ plus $\frac{3}{8}$, we can change both fractions to eighths: $\frac{3}{8}$ will remain $\frac{3}{8}$, but $\frac{3}{4}$ will become $\frac{6}{8}$ (*see* the diagram above). We can add $\frac{3}{8}$ and $\frac{6}{8}$. The answer is $\frac{9}{8}$ or $1\frac{1}{8}$. If the answer is an improper (top-heavy) fraction, change it to a whole or mixed number.

To understand "like" fractions, use the diagram again. But your child must not lean on a diagram always. To change $\frac{3}{4}$ to ?/8, think: 4 into 8 is 2, 2 × 3 are 6; $\frac{3}{4} = \frac{6}{8}$.

To change $\frac{1}{6}$ to $\frac{?}{12}$, think: 6 into 12 is 2, 2 × 1 are 2; then $\frac{1}{6} = \frac{2}{12}$.

Change these to like fractions before adding:

1. $\frac{1}{3}$
   $\frac{1}{6}$

2. $\frac{2}{5}$
   $\frac{1}{10}$

3. $\frac{1}{6}$
   $\frac{1}{3}$
   $\frac{1}{3}$

Answers: 1. $\frac{2}{6}$ 2. $\frac{4}{10}$ 3. $\frac{1}{6}$
$\frac{1}{6}$ $\frac{1}{10}$ $\frac{2}{6}$
$\frac{3}{6}$ or $\frac{1}{2}$ $\frac{5}{10}$ or $\frac{1}{2}$ $\frac{2}{6}$
$\frac{5}{6}$

Be sure your child can visualize what he is doing. Use charts and objects. For example, in changing $\frac{1}{4}$ to twelfths (a fraction with a *higher* term), he must first know that there are $\frac{12}{12}$ in a whole. $\frac{1}{4}$ of 12 is 4 into 12 or 3. Then $\frac{1}{4}$ of $\frac{12}{12}$ is $\frac{3}{12}$.

1											
$\frac{1}{12}$	$\frac{1}{12}$	$\frac{1}{12}$	$\frac{1}{12}$	$\frac{1}{12}$	$\frac{1}{12}$	$\frac{1}{12}$	$\frac{1}{12}$	$\frac{1}{12}$	$\frac{1}{12}$	$\frac{1}{12}$	$\frac{1}{12}$
$\frac{1}{2}$						$\frac{1}{2}$					
$\frac{1}{4}$			$\frac{1}{4}$			$\frac{1}{4}$			$\frac{1}{4}$		
$\frac{1}{3}$				$\frac{1}{3}$				$\frac{1}{3}$			

In changing to *lower* terms (or to fractions with the smallest denominator possible), it can readily be seen by making a chart that $\frac{6}{12}$ is equal to $\frac{1}{2}$. It is always advisable to reduce fractions to lowest terms. In this case, how much easier it is to work with $\frac{1}{2}$ than with $\frac{6}{12}$!

subtracting fractions from whole numbers

EXAMPLE:

How much of 2 cakes is left after ¾ of one cake is eaten?

First draw the two cakes. We are working with fourths, so divide them into fourths.

shaded fourths have been eaten

1 cake   1 cake

The problem is $2 - \frac{3}{4}$. It is necessary to think of the 2 cakes as $1\frac{4}{4}$ cakes. Then the problem becomes

$$\begin{array}{r} 1\frac{4}{4} \\ -\ \frac{3}{4} \\ \hline 1\frac{1}{4} \end{array}$$

This way we have a fraction from which to subtract the $\frac{3}{4}$. Think: $\frac{4}{4} - \frac{3}{4}$ is $\frac{1}{4}$; 1 minus nothing is still 1. The answer is $1\frac{1}{4}$ cakes left.

EXAMPLE:

How much is left of 3 pies if ⅖ of one pie is eaten?

First draw the pies and divide them into fifths.

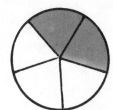

1 pie   1 pie   1 pie ($\frac{5}{5}$ pie)

The problem is   3

$$-\ \frac{2}{5}$$

We have no fraction from which to subtract the $\frac{2}{5}$, so we think of the pies as being $2\frac{5}{5}$ pies.

The problem then is $2\frac{5}{5}$

$$-\ \frac{2}{5}$$

$2\frac{3}{5}$ pies are left.

subtracting fractions from mixed numbers

Subtracting fractions from mixed numbers is very like subtracting fractions from whole numbers. Again, to help your child, use real objects—circles of paper, pictures of apples, etc.

EXAMPLE:

There were 2¼ pies in the pantry cut into fourths. Joe took a piece, Sally took one, and Tom took one. How many pies were left?

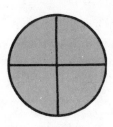

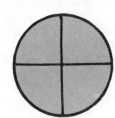

1 pie   1 pie $\frac{1}{4}$ pie

The problem is $2\frac{1}{4}$

$$-\ \frac{3}{4}$$

You cannot subtract $\frac{3}{4}$ from $\frac{1}{4}$, so you must borrow a whole one from the 2 (a whole is $\frac{4}{4}$) and add it to the fraction beside the 2. This reduces the 2 to 1 and increases the $\frac{1}{4}$ to $\frac{5}{4}$.

Write it this way: $2\frac{1}{4} = 1\frac{5}{4}$
$$-\frac{3}{4} = \quad\frac{3}{4}$$
$$\overline{\qquad 1\frac{2}{4} \text{ or } 1\frac{1}{2}}$$

EXAMPLES:

1. $2\frac{1}{6} = 1\frac{7}{6}$
$$-\frac{5}{6} = \quad\frac{5}{6}$$
$$\overline{\qquad 1\frac{2}{6} \text{ or } 1\frac{1}{3}}$$

2. $\quad 4 = 3\frac{9}{9}$
$$-1\frac{5}{9} = 1\frac{5}{9}$$
$$\overline{\qquad 2\frac{4}{9}}$$

multiplying fractions, whole numbers, and mixed numbers

In multiplying a fraction times a whole number, try to solve the problem by illustrating it with a real situation. Your child will understand his work in fractions if he can see for himself why he should learn it.

EXAMPLE:

Five girls need headbands, each ¾ yards long. How much material do they need to buy?

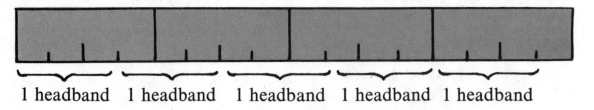

1 headband   1 headband   1 headband   1 headband   1 headband

By reading on the measure, it can be seen that $3\frac{3}{4}$ yards of ribbon are needed, or that $5 \times \frac{3}{4}$ are $\frac{15}{4}$ or $3\frac{3}{4}$.

The next example is a problem in multiplying a mixed number by a whole number. This becomes a practical problem when your child buys $1\frac{1}{2}$ pounds of candy. Let's say the price of candy is 70 cents per pound. He wants to know how much it will cost him. The problem is $1\frac{1}{2} \times \$.70$.

This is worked as though it were *two* problems.

$$\begin{array}{r} \$ \ .70 \\ \times \ \ 1\frac{1}{2} \\ \hline .35 \\ .70 \\ \hline \$1.05 \end{array}$$

$.35$ $(\frac{1}{2} \times .70)$
$.70$ $(1 \times .70)$
$\$1.05$ the cost of $1\frac{1}{2}$ pounds of candy.

First multiply the fraction by 70¢; then the whole number by 70¢. Add the two answers together.

The work of multiplying fractions by fractions is developed further in the sixth grade.

measurements

The tables of measurements of length, liquid, weight, and time and money are reviewed (*see* the ARITHMETIC section for the fourth grade) and are applied to problems. Review them with your child. Show him how often you use this information during your daily tasks.

EXAMPLES:

▶ **How much will 27 inches of material cost at 40¢ a yard.**

THINK: There are 36 inches in a yard; 27 inches is $\frac{27}{36}$ of a yard. Both 27 and 36 can be divided by 9 to reduce the fraction, so $\frac{27}{36}$ is $\frac{3}{4}$ of a yard; $\frac{3}{4}$ of 40¢ is 30¢ ($\frac{1}{4}$ of 40¢ is 10¢; $\frac{3}{4}$ of 40¢ is 3 times 10¢ or 30¢).

▶ **10 minutes is what part of an hour?**

There are 60 minutes in one hour; 10 minutes are $\frac{10}{60}$ or $\frac{1}{6}$ of an hour.

▶ **4 ounces is what part of a pound?**

There are 16 ounces in a pound; 4 ounces is $\frac{4}{16}$ of a pound, $\frac{4}{16}$ is $\frac{1}{4}$, 4 ounces is $\frac{1}{4}$ of a pound.

area and perimeter

Your child learns to find area in square inches, square feet, and square yards. *Area* is the measurement of a surface. A *square foot* is a square that measures one foot long and one foot wide: one foot times one foot is one *square* foot.

To find the area of a rectangle, multiply the length times the width.

To find the area of a rectangle 10 feet long and 9 feet wide, think: 9 feet × 10 feet = 90 square feet.

In area measurements your child learns that:

9 square feet = 1 square yard

144 square inches = 1 square foot

160 square rods = 1 acre

640 acres = 1 square mile

Your child also has problems in finding perimeters of rectangles. *Perimeter* means "the distance around." Given a rectangle 6 feet long and 2 feet wide, the perimeter can be found in any of three ways:

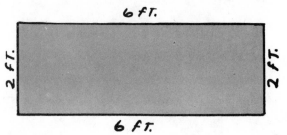

THINK:

A. 6 feet plus 2 feet are 8 feet, the distance around two sides; 2 × 8 feet are 16 feet, the perimeter or distance around all four sides.

B. 6 feet and 6 feet are 12 feet, the length of opposite sides; 2 feet and 2 feet are 4 feet; 12 feet plus 4 feet are 16 feet, the perimeter of the rectangle.

C. 6 feet plus 2 feet are 8 feet; 8 feet plus 8 feet are 16 feet, the perimeter.

Additional length measures are learned.

16½ feet = 1 rod

5½ yards = 1 rod

320 rods = 1 mile

There is a complete table of measurements at the end of the book.

decimals

Decimal fractions are another way of writing common fractions. Decimal fractions are written with a decimal point, or dot. $\frac{7}{10}$ and .7 are both read the same way; $1\frac{4}{10}$ and 1.4 are read the same way.

Your child learns that the decimal system, like our whole number system, is based on tens. It is a fraction when there are fewer than ten tenths. But ten tenths ($\frac{10}{10}$) is one, and is the beginning of whole numbers. Whole numbers are written on the left side of the decimal point. Parts of whole numbers are written on the right side of the decimal point.

The name of the first place to the right of the decimal point is tenths place; the second place is hundredths place; the third place is thousandths place.

EXAMPLES:

.1 is $\frac{1}{10}$ of a whole

.2 is $\frac{2}{10}$ of a whole

.3 is $\frac{3}{10}$ of a whole

.4 is $\frac{4}{10}$ of a whole

.5 is $\frac{5}{10}$ of a whole

.6 is $\frac{6}{10}$ of a whole

.7 is $\frac{7}{10}$ of a whole

.8 is $\frac{8}{10}$ of a whole

.9 is $\frac{9}{10}$ of a whole

1.0 ($\frac{10}{10}$ becomes a whole number)

Your child has learned two ways of writing tenths. There are also two ways of writing hundredths. There are *two* places after the decimal point in hundredths.

COMMON FRACTION:

$\frac{12}{100}$ $\frac{85}{100}$ $4\frac{10}{100}$ $\frac{1}{100}$

DECIMAL FRACTION:

.12   .85   4.10   .01

Your child makes practical use of decimals.

EXAMPLE:

100 gallons of oil were put into the oil tank. Then when it was measured, the measuring stick showed it was .5 full. How much oil would the tank hold if it were filled?

THINK: .5 is $\frac{5}{10}$ or $\frac{1}{2}$. If $\frac{1}{2}$ is 100 gallons, the full tank will hold 200 gallons, because there are 2 halves in a whole and 2×100 is 200.

Your child practices writing equivalent common and decimal fractions.

EXAMPLES:

$\frac{1}{2} = .5$ or .50

$\frac{3}{4} = .75$

money is written in decimals

Money is written in decimal fractions: $\frac{1}{10}$ of a dollar is 10 cents. There are 100 cents in the whole dollar; 10 cents is $\frac{10}{100}$ of the whole dollar; $\frac{10}{100}$ is written .10.

$\frac{1}{100}$ of a dollar is written .01 or 1 cent.

$1.57 can be read "one dollar and fifty-seven cents" or "one and fifty-seven one hundredths dollars."

The cents point and the decimal point are the same thing.

How would you write 6 and 3 tenths dollars? It is $6.3. However, cents is always written with *two* places, so it is $6.30— .3 or $\frac{3}{10}$, and .30 or $\frac{30}{100}$, are the same.

The use and placement of decimal points are very important. Can you see what difference the placement of the decimal point makes in these sentences?

1. Boots cost $475. a pair.
2. Boots cost $4.75 a pair.
3. Boots cost $47.5 a pair.

adding and subtracting decimals

In adding and subtracting decimals your child must be careful to place the decimal points directly under each other. This automatically puts the tenths in one column, the hundredths in another column, etc. The whole numbers fall naturally into place, too; the tens are in one column, hundreds together, etc.

EXAMPLES:

Add: $5.61   Subtract: 28.6
      .27   16.4
     3.03   12.2
    $8.91

How would you write this subtraction problem?

Forty-five and 7 tenths minus twenty-three.

45.7
−23

284

thought problems

Your child will have trouble with word problems unless he has mastered all the basic facts of addition, subtraction, multiplication, and division. He continues to search for patterns and relationships to help him remember those basic facts.

Many of his word problems require him to read charts and maps, line and bar graphs, tables, and simple scale drawings. Give your child opportunities to use his ability by asking him to chart his weekly spelling grades, to draw a scale map of the route to Uncle John's house, etc.

▶ **a line graph**

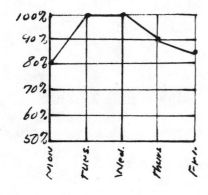

Spelling grades for one week.

▶ **a scale drawing**

My room.   Scale: ¼" = 2'

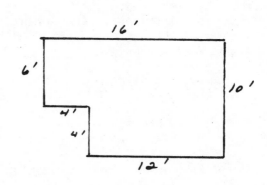

▶ **a bar graph**

Newspapers sold in one month.

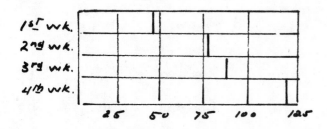

english exercises

I. Use "sit," "sat," or "set."

1. She can _____ still for almost a half hour.   2. They all _____ quietly at the theater.   3. _____ the can of oil on the paper.   4. She always _____ a beautiful table.   5. It's no joke to _____ on a tack.

II. Use "don't" or "doesn't."

1. We _____ believe we will go on the trip.   2. She _____ care for cherry pie.   3. Hundreds of people _____ want this serv-ice.   4. He says he _____ want to buy it.   5. It _____ always act so sleepy.

III. Use "rang" or "rung."

1. Have you _____ the dinner bell yet?   2. She _____ the school bell too early.   3. She said she had already _____ it.   4. Has he _____ the tardy bell?   5. The telephone _____ at six o'clock.

IV. Use "sang" or "sung."

1. The choir _____ a beautiful hymn.   2. Have you ever _____ with a choir?   3. The children _____ Christmas carols.   4. She _____ with the group last year.   5. We have all _____ nursery rhymes.

V. Use "a" or "an."

1. This is _____ good example.   2. It took her _____ hour to read the story.   3. She is _____ happy baby.   4. That rug is _____ family heirloom.   5. _____ heirloom must be handled carefully.

VI. Use "well" or "good."

1. That is a _____ use of the word.   2. Our team made a _____ record.   3. They played _____ in every game.   4. They planned the party _____ .   5. She is an expert at _____ planning.

VII. Use "any" or "no."

1. We haven't _____ time left to do it.   2. There isn't _____ more apple pie.   3. Haven't you _____ time to make a picture?   4. We mustn't waste _____ time.   5. There is _____ reason for being careless.

VIII. Use "was" or "were."

1. There _____ only one apple left.   2. There _____ many in the box.   3. We _____ not supposed to be late.   4. They _____ very good swimmers.   5. She _____ not feeling well yesterday.

IX. Put capital letters where they belong.

1. jane came home from camp addison boyce on tuesday.

2. i gave the book named sandy to my friend paula.

3. dr. smith is a good friend of mine.

4. yesterday we celebrated independence day.

5. independence day is on july fourth.

6. the zoo in bronx park is very very big.

7. aunt mae baked it and bob ate it.

8. the lazy daisy club meets on friday afternoon.

9. mexico was explored by spaniards.

10. the mississippi river is called the father of waters.

11. the amazon river flows through brazil to the atlantic ocean.

12. the pacific ocean is connected with the atlantic ocean by the panama canal.

X. Punctuate these sentences.

1. Dont stop now   2. Dr J C Wilkes lives in Boston Mass   3. Do you really think it will rain   4. What an important decision to make   5. Anns books were ruined by the rain   6. Mary is visiting her Aunt Mae in Chicago Illinois   7. The party will be on October 3 1959   8. Yes we will all be in costume   9. Tell us Jane what your costume will be   10. Our teacher always says Good morning children   11. This looks like Marks cap Jane said   12. Her poster is painted orange green gray and black

XI. Find the mistakes—they may be in punctuation, grammar, or in use of word forms.

1. As they set there and listened the train left.   2. An huge eagle landed on the top of the mountain?   3. It must have been the doorbell that rung.   4. Everyone say it is a good book.   5. I worked for a hour, a whole hour!   6. This is a ugly but a useful gadget.   7. This problem is a easy one.   8. The jet plane flowed across the country.   9. Everyone, came Jane, just everyone!   10. The world book company prints beautiful books.   11. Leave me see the puppy Joe.   12. I and Maggie have coats alike.

XII. Name the parts of this business letter. Then punctuate the letter and put the capital letters where they belong.

clinton school

avon texas

november 10 1957

mr fred m smith

chief of the fire department

avon texas

dear mr smith

    our class would like to learn more about fire prevention and about what we can do if fires break out can you or one of your men come to our school and tell us about it our teacher will call you for your answer

yours very truly

miss owens class

XIII. Why isn't this a good invitation?

Dear Mary,

    You are invited to come to my party. Wear blue jeans. We are going to cook our supper outside. I hope you can come.

Your friend,

Marty

XIV. Address an envelope to

Miss Patsy Leinhart

57 Yarmon Avenue

Velva, North Dakota

Put your return address on it.

XV. Pick out all the nouns, common and proper, singular and plural.

1. Two airplanes crashed in the sky.   2. Mt. Ash is covered with pine trees.   3. Both chairs needed new seats.   4. Our shells are on the table.   5. The house is on the shore.   6. Jane and Ellen made a birdhouse.   7. Joey

plays football well.   8. Friday is wash day at our house.   9. The Grand Canyon is a breath-taking sight.   10. Mount Vernon is the name of a city. 11. The boys went fishing in Lake Como.   12. The seeds were scattered over the yard.

XVI. Write the plural forms of these nouns. (Use a dictionary if necessary.)

1. calf   _____
2. engineer _____
3. man   _____
4. company   _____
5. child   _____
6. half   _____

7. boy   _____
8. country   _____
9. dress   _____
10. auctioneer _____
11. box   _____
12. dish   _____

XVII. Underline the verbs.

1. The children <u>helped</u> each other.   2. News spreads quickly.   3. Many people are listening to the news reports.   4. She plays the piano very well.   5. They came immediately.   6. The children had eaten earlier. 7. There are many books on the shelf.   8. They have sung all the songs. 9. Four children knew the right answer.   10. Stems of trees give us wood for fuel.

XVIII. Underline the adjectives.

1. <u>Many</u> children sang <u>interesting folk</u> songs.   2. Four boys sang a cowboy ballad.   3. One girl played a piano selection.   4. The youngest boy gave a short report on the whole program.   5. Eskimos wear soft animal skins. 6. The clown has bright red hair.   7. Cotton dresses are cool.   8. Soft, fine, wool fibers make wonderful warm sweaters.   9. Healthy children are happy children.   10. The little country school was heated by an iron coal stove.

arithmetic exercises

I. Write the numerals for:

1. One million, five hundred ten. _____

2. Four hundred seventy-five thousand, four hundred four. _____

3. Thirty-seven million, one hundred eleven. _____

4. Eight hundred nine million, four hundred thirteen thousand, two hundred twelve. _____

5. One billion, one hundred million, one hundred thousand, one hundred.

   _____

6. Four hundred thirty-five thousand. _____

7. Two thousand ten. _____

8. Seventy-four thousand, one hundred forty-seven. _____

   _____

9. One billion, one million, one thousand, one. _____

10. Two million, two hundred twenty-two thousand, two hundred twenty-two.

    _____

II. Write the exponent form for:

1. $10 \times 10 \times 10 =$
2. $4 \times 4 =$
3. $5 \times 5 \times 5 =$
4. $2 \times 2 \times 2 \times 2 =$
5. $8 \times 8 =$
6. $10 \times 10 \times 10 \times 10 \times 10 =$
7. $3 \times 3 \times 3 \times 3 =$
8. $6 \times 6 =$
9. $7 \times 7 \times 7 \times 7 =$
10. $9 \times 9 \times 9 =$

III. Circle the prime numbers.

1	11	21	31
2	12	22	32
3	13	23	33
4	14	24	34
5	15	25	35
6	16	26	36
7	17	27	37
8	18	28	38
9	19	29	39
10	20	30	40

IV. Write the Roman numerals for:

1. 63,000
2. 2,000
3. 2,431
4. 756
5. 1,000

6. 380
7. 201
8. 1,492
9. 1,776
10. 98

V. Show the union of sets.

1. Set A = {Harry, Dale, Bob, Pete}
   Set B = {Charles, Mike, Bob, Pete}
   A ∪ B =

2. Set A = {1, 2, 3}
   Set B = {3, 4, 5}
   A ∪ B =

3. Set A = {1, 2, 3}
   Set B = {4, 5, 6}
   A ∪ B =

4. Set A = {1, 2, 3, 4}
   Set B = {1, 2}
   A ∪ B =

5. Set A = {a, b, c, d}
   Set B = {b, d, f, h}
   A ∪ B =

VI. Show the intersection of sets.

1. Set A = {Harry, Dale, Bob, Pete}
   Set B = {Charles, Mike, Bob, Pete}
   A ∩ B =

2. Set A = {1, 2, 3}
   Set B = {3, 4, 5}
   A ∩ B =

3. Set A = {1, 2, 3}
   Set B = {4, 5, 6}
   A ∩ B =

4. Set A = {Fords, Plymouths, Dodges}
   Set B = {Plymouths, Dodges, Chevrolets, Chryslers}
   A ∩ B =

5. Set A = {a, e, i, o, u}
   Set B = {a, b, c, d, e}
   A ∩ B =

VII. Watch the symbol.

1. Set A = {x, y, z}
   Set B = {v, w, x}
   A ∪ B =

2. Set A = {x, y, z}
   Set B = {v, w, x}
   A ∩ B =

3. Set A = {Judy, Carol, Ann}
   Set B = {Sue, Ruth, Carol}
   Set C = {Jane, Mary, Carol}
   A ∩ B ∩ C =

4. Set A = {dog, cat, cow}
   Set B = {horse, mule}
   A ∪ B =

5. Set A = {5, 6, 7}
   Set B = {1, 2, 3}
   Set C = {4, 8}
   A ∪ B ∪ C =

VIII. Add.

1. $1.68	2. $4.38	3. $ 4.63	4. $ 2.76
7.05	6.28	25.87	.32
9.42	7.29	9.74	12.67
3.01	8.35	.23	3.03

5. $27.39	6. $24.98	7. $46.32	8. 2381
86.23	86.94	87.31	246
40.79	3.08	46.75	50
			1245

9. $6.24	10. $3.56	11. 256	12. 364
3.39	2.87	386	285
.47	.97	95	297
.98	.65	672	672
2.63	2.53	70	836
.48	.49	380	207

13. $4.53	14. $4.57	15. $6.73	16. $2.56
2.78	9.25	8.25	4.82
.94	6.38	9.39	7.95
8.24	.45	.87	.87
.67	2.38	5.00	.93
2.56	.46	.10	.50

17. 287	18. 374	19. 186	20. 384
849	863	349	875
932	95	873	291
45	847	58	400
87	68	64	675
608	270	95	283

21. $4.95	22. $4.56	23. 653	24. 278
6.87	2.89	485	96
.45	9.74	962	854
.83	.86	784	37
.97	.03	96	92
5.64	5.00	43	407

IX. Subtract.

1. $14.58	2. $23.67	3. $32.76	4. $69.00	5. 600
6.59	14.30	23.21	47.74	469

6. 800	7. 900	8. 546	9. 4689	10. $25.00
259	557	298	1736	17.49

11. $47.08	12. $80.00	13. $7.09	14. $8.00	15. $7.00
3.94	2.75	2.87	2.54	1.84

16. $5.30	17. $25.00	18. $13.00	19. $13.84	20. $15.68
2.56	17.65	9.54	9.58	2.80

21. $12.00	22. $25.00	23. $30.00	24. $74.60	25. 5009
9.32	18.49	13.75	28.75	2873

26. 2546	27. 1567	28. 2146
1883	935	1306

X. Multiply.

1. $9.27	2. $8.18	3. $7.29	4. $6.30	5. $4.52
42	53	64	75	97

6. 741
   33

7. 392
   56

8. 526
   91

9. 174
   64

10. 238
    55

11. 903
    46

12. 401
    73

13. 372
    60

14. 591
    83

15. 221
    47

16. 306
    51

17. 463
    284

18. 165
    601

19. 274
    739

20. 383
    848

21. 501
    167

22. 682
    531

23. $7.63
    24

24. $2.75
    83

25. $6.08
    64

26. 346
    608

27. 800
    19

28. 509
    59

29. 570
    38

30. 139
    200

31. 724
    50

32. 246
    35

33. 506
    95

34. 283
    46

35. $5.78
    40

36. $3.89
    56

37. 583
    94

38. 607
    85

39. 439
    46

40. 584
    903

XI. Divide.

1. $7\overline{)\$58.38}$

2. $5\overline{)\$3.75}$

3. $6\overline{)\$28.98}$

4. $5\overline{)\$12.95}$

5. $6\overline{)\$5.76}$

6. $7\overline{)\$66.92}$

7. $32\overline{)480}$

8. $21\overline{)677}$

9. $32\overline{)992}$

10. $32\overline{)162}$

11. $30\overline{)692}$ 12. $13\overline{)299}$ 13. $11\overline{)495}$ 14. $42\overline{)465}$ 15. $14\overline{)350}$

16. $52\overline{)629}$ 17. $21\overline{)969}$ 18. $41\overline{)533}$ 19. $40\overline{)974}$ 20. $23\overline{)489}$

21. $42\overline{)882}$ 22. $62\overline{)695}$ 23. $23\overline{)496}$ 24. $32\overline{)736}$ 25. $31\overline{)664}$

26. $21\overline{)682}$ 27. $22\overline{)902}$ 28. $44\overline{)3564}$ 29. $63\overline{)5193}$ 30. $80\overline{)6400}$

XII. Fractions.

Change to whole or mixed numbers.

1. $\dfrac{7}{4} =$ 2. $\dfrac{13}{4} =$ 3. $\dfrac{16}{5} =$

4. $\dfrac{12}{4} =$ 5. $\dfrac{11}{3} =$ 6. $\dfrac{23}{6} =$

7. $\dfrac{8}{4} =$ 8. $\dfrac{3}{3} =$ 9. $\dfrac{33}{4} =$

10. $\dfrac{18}{6} =$ 11. $\dfrac{25}{4} =$ 12. $\dfrac{9}{5} =$

13. $\dfrac{7}{3} =$ 14. $1\dfrac{3}{3} =$ 15. $\dfrac{27}{5} =$

16. $\dfrac{25}{8} =$ 17. $\dfrac{6}{6} =$ 18. $\dfrac{8}{6} =$

19. $\dfrac{11}{3} =$ 20. $\dfrac{25}{8} =$ 21. $\dfrac{8}{8} =$

22. $\dfrac{16}{5} =$ 23. $\dfrac{40}{10} =$ 24. $\dfrac{60}{10} =$

XIII. Fractions.

Change:

1. $\dfrac{1}{2} = \dfrac{}{12}$ 2. $\dfrac{1}{2} = \dfrac{}{6}$ 3. $\dfrac{6}{8} = \dfrac{}{16}$

4. $\dfrac{1}{3} = \dfrac{}{12}$ 5. $\dfrac{1}{3} = \dfrac{}{6}$ 6. $\dfrac{3}{4} = \dfrac{}{12}$

7. $\dfrac{2}{3} = \dfrac{}{12}$ 8. $\dfrac{2}{4} = \dfrac{}{12}$ 9. $\dfrac{1}{4} = \dfrac{}{20}$

10. $\dfrac{1}{6} = \dfrac{}{12}$ 11. $\dfrac{2}{6} = \dfrac{}{12}$ 12. $\dfrac{3}{5} = \dfrac{}{10}$

13. $\dfrac{5}{6} = \dfrac{}{12}$ 14. $\dfrac{3}{4} = \dfrac{}{12}$ 15. $\dfrac{4}{5} = \dfrac{}{20}$

16. $\dfrac{3}{4} = \dfrac{}{12}$ 17. $\dfrac{1}{4} = \dfrac{}{8}$ 18. $\dfrac{3}{4} = \dfrac{}{20}$

19. $\dfrac{1}{2} = \dfrac{}{4}$ 20. $\dfrac{3}{4} = \dfrac{}{8}$ 21. $\dfrac{3}{8} = \dfrac{}{16}$

22. $\dfrac{3}{4} = \dfrac{}{8}$ 23. $\dfrac{3}{8} = \dfrac{}{16}$ 24. $\dfrac{2}{6} = \dfrac{}{12}$

XIV. Fractions.

Reduce to lowest terms.

1. $\dfrac{2}{4} =$ 2. $\dfrac{10}{16} =$ 3. $\dfrac{6}{12} =$

4. $\dfrac{2}{16} =$ 5. $\dfrac{8}{12} =$ 6. $\dfrac{5}{10} =$

7. $\dfrac{3}{6} =$ 8. $\dfrac{4}{20} =$ 9. $\dfrac{7}{14} =$

10. $\dfrac{3}{12} =$ 11. $\dfrac{8}{16} =$ 12. $\dfrac{8}{24} =$

13. $\dfrac{4}{8} =$　　　14. $\dfrac{14}{16} =$　　　15. $\dfrac{9}{36} =$

16. $\dfrac{6}{16} =$　　　17. $\dfrac{9}{12} =$　　　18. $\dfrac{10}{20} =$

19. $\dfrac{2}{6} =$　　　20. $\dfrac{15}{20} =$　　　21. $\dfrac{15}{30} =$

22. $\dfrac{10}{12} =$　　　23. $\dfrac{4}{16} =$　　　24. $\dfrac{5}{15} =$

XV. Fractions. Add:

(If improper fractions result, change to mixed numbers.)

1. $\dfrac{4}{8}$ $\dfrac{3}{8}$　　2. $\dfrac{7}{8}$ $\dfrac{2}{8}$　　3. $\dfrac{2}{4}$ $\dfrac{1}{4}$　　4. $\dfrac{7}{10}$ $\dfrac{4}{10}$　　5. $\dfrac{3}{6}$ $\dfrac{2}{6}$

6. $\dfrac{1}{4}$ $\dfrac{3}{4}$　　7. $\dfrac{4}{8}$ $\dfrac{7}{8}$　　8. $\dfrac{4}{5}$ $\dfrac{3}{5}$　　9. $\dfrac{1}{2}$ $\dfrac{1}{2}$　　10. $\dfrac{7}{8}$ $\dfrac{6}{8}$

11. $4\frac{2}{3}$ 3　　12. $6\frac{5}{6}$ 4　　13. $9\frac{3}{4}$ 6　　14. $7\frac{3}{8}$ 2　　15. 4 $2\frac{1}{2}$

16. 6 $3\frac{5}{6}$　　17. 4 $3\frac{2}{3}$　　18. 5 $2\frac{3}{7}$　　19. 9 $4\frac{5}{8}$　　20. $6\frac{1}{2}$ $2\frac{1}{2}$

21. $3\frac{2}{3}$ $5\frac{1}{3}$　　22. $8\frac{1}{4}$ $9\frac{3}{4}$　　23. $5\frac{3}{4}$ $6\frac{2}{4}$　　24. $7\frac{4}{6}$ $8\frac{3}{6}$　　25. $4\frac{7}{10}$ $\frac{4}{10}$

XVI. Fractions. Add:

(Change any improper fractions to mixed numbers.)

1. $\frac{1}{2}$ $\frac{5}{8}$ $\frac{3}{4}$	2. $\frac{1}{4}$ $\frac{3}{8}$ $\frac{5}{8}$	3. $\frac{1}{2}$ $\frac{2}{3}$ $\frac{5}{6}$	4. $\frac{5}{8}$ $\frac{3}{16}$ $\frac{3}{4}$	5. $\frac{2}{3}$ $\frac{5}{6}$ $\frac{7}{12}$
6. $\frac{5}{16}$ $\frac{3}{4}$ $\frac{5}{8}$	7. $\frac{7}{8}$ $\frac{3}{4}$ $\frac{1}{2}$	8. $\frac{2}{3}$ $\frac{1}{6}$ $\frac{1}{12}$	9. $\frac{3}{8}$ $\frac{1}{2}$ $\frac{3}{4}$	10. $\frac{1}{2}$ $\frac{2}{3}$ $\frac{1}{3}$
11. $\frac{5}{8}$ $\frac{5}{16}$ $\frac{1}{4}$	12. $\frac{5}{12}$ $\frac{1}{6}$ $\frac{1}{2}$	13. $\frac{3}{4}$ $\frac{1}{6}$ $\frac{1}{2}$	14. $\frac{3}{8}$ $\frac{4}{8}$ $\frac{1}{2}$	15. $\frac{1}{6}$ $\frac{2}{3}$ $\frac{2}{6}$
16. $\frac{3}{5}$ $\frac{8}{10}$ $\frac{1}{2}$	17. $\frac{1}{2}$ $\frac{1}{3}$ $\frac{1}{6}$	18. $\frac{5}{8}$ $\frac{1}{2}$ $\frac{1}{4}$	19. $\frac{7}{16}$ $\frac{2}{16}$ $\frac{1}{8}$	20. $\frac{1}{3}$ $\frac{5}{6}$ $\frac{1}{2}$

XVII. Fractions. Add:

(Reduce answers to lowest terms.)

1. $7\frac{1}{3}$ $3\frac{5}{6}$	2. $3\frac{5}{8}$ $\frac{1}{2}$	3. $5\frac{7}{10}$ $2\frac{3}{5}$	4. $6\frac{7}{8}$ $5\frac{1}{4}$	5. $\frac{7}{8}$ $5\frac{1}{4}$
6. $7\frac{3}{10}$ $4\frac{4}{5}$	7. $5\frac{3}{4}$ $\frac{5}{8}$	8. $4\frac{5}{6}$ $3\frac{2}{3}$	9. $4\frac{3}{4}$ $2\frac{1}{2}$	10. $7\frac{5}{8}$ $4\frac{1}{2}$

11. $3\frac{2}{3}$
$5\frac{7}{12}$

12. $8\frac{7}{10}$
$2\frac{4}{5}$

13. $4\frac{1}{4}$
$7\frac{1}{2}$

14. $3\frac{1}{4}$
$\frac{1}{2}$

15. $8\frac{1}{2}$
$5\frac{1}{4}$

16. $5\frac{1}{2}$
$3\frac{1}{6}$

17. $4\frac{3}{5}$
$\frac{1}{10}$

18. $3\frac{2}{3}$
$\frac{1}{6}$

19. $7\frac{1}{6}$
$4\frac{1}{3}$

20. $3\frac{1}{2}$
$4\frac{1}{6}$

21. $7\frac{1}{8}$
$4\frac{5}{8}$

22. $6\frac{5}{12}$
$9\frac{1}{2}$

23. $3\frac{5}{8}$
$4\frac{1}{2}$

24. $3\frac{1}{2}$
$2\frac{3}{4}$

25. $7\frac{1}{6}$
$8\frac{1}{12}$

XVIII. Fractions. Add:

(Reduce answers to lowest terms.)

1. $3\frac{1}{2}$
$2\frac{2}{3}$
$5\frac{3}{4}$

2. 7
$2\frac{7}{12}$
$5\frac{3}{4}$

3. $8\frac{2}{3}$
$5\frac{5}{6}$
$3\frac{1}{2}$

4. $4\frac{2}{3}$
$5\frac{1}{4}$
$\frac{5}{6}$

5. $3\frac{1}{2}$
$9\frac{3}{4}$
$7\frac{1}{8}$

6. $7\frac{9}{10}$
$4\frac{3}{5}$
$8\frac{1}{2}$

7. $4\frac{1}{2}$
$\frac{1}{3}$
$9\frac{5}{6}$

8. $2\frac{1}{2}$
$\frac{1}{6}$
$6\frac{1}{12}$

9. $\frac{2}{3}$
$4\frac{1}{2}$
$\frac{5}{12}$

10. $\frac{1}{2}$
$\frac{1}{4}$
$2\frac{1}{3}$

11. $\frac{1}{2}$
$\frac{2}{6}$
$7\frac{2}{3}$

12. $5\frac{1}{2}$
$4\frac{1}{5}$
$2\frac{1}{10}$

13. $3\frac{1}{2}$
$4\frac{1}{8}$
$3\frac{3}{4}$

14. $5\frac{1}{3}$
$4\frac{1}{6}$
$2\frac{1}{4}$

15. $6\frac{1}{2}$
$\frac{2}{3}$
$4\frac{5}{6}$

XIX. Fractions. Subtract:

(Reduce answers to lowest terms.)

1. $\frac{5}{6}$
$\frac{4}{6}$

2. $\frac{7}{8}$
$\frac{2}{8}$

3. $\frac{3}{4}$
$\frac{2}{4}$

4. $\frac{4}{5}$
$\frac{1}{5}$

5. $\frac{6}{7}$
$\frac{1}{7}$

6. $\dfrac{3}{8}$ $\dfrac{1}{4}$

7. $\dfrac{7}{8}$ $\dfrac{3}{4}$

8. $\dfrac{5}{6}$ $\dfrac{1}{3}$

9. $\dfrac{1}{2}$ $\dfrac{1}{6}$

10. $\dfrac{7}{8}$ $\dfrac{1}{2}$

11. $\dfrac{3}{4}$ $\dfrac{5}{8}$

12. $\dfrac{5}{8}$ $\dfrac{1}{2}$

13. $\dfrac{5}{6}$ $\dfrac{1}{2}$

14. $\dfrac{1}{3}$ $\dfrac{1}{6}$

15. $\dfrac{1}{2}$ $\dfrac{1}{4}$

16. $\dfrac{5}{8}$ $\dfrac{1}{4}$

17. $\dfrac{1}{2}$ $\dfrac{1}{8}$

18. $\dfrac{2}{3}$ $\dfrac{1}{6}$

19. $\dfrac{7}{12}$ $\dfrac{1}{6}$

20. $\dfrac{9}{16}$ $\dfrac{1}{2}$

21. $\dfrac{11}{12}$ $\dfrac{3}{4}$

22. $\dfrac{7}{16}$ $\dfrac{1}{4}$

23. $\dfrac{7}{12}$ $\dfrac{1}{4}$

24. $\dfrac{5}{12}$ $\dfrac{1}{6}$

25. $\dfrac{3}{5}$ $\dfrac{1}{10}$

XX. Fractions. Subtract:

(Reduce answers to lowest terms.)

1. $2\frac{3}{4}$ $\frac{1}{2}$

2. $6\frac{1}{2}$ $2\frac{1}{4}$

3. $7\frac{5}{6}$ $2\frac{1}{3}$

4. $4\frac{5}{6}$ $\frac{2}{3}$

5. $4\frac{5}{6}$ $2\frac{1}{3}$

6. $7\frac{3}{5}$ $2\frac{1}{10}$

7. $4\frac{5}{6}$ $\frac{1}{6}$

8. $7\frac{2}{3}$ $5\frac{2}{3}$

9. $5\frac{3}{4}$ $2\frac{1}{2}$

10. $7\frac{2}{3}$ $2\frac{1}{3}$

11. $6\frac{3}{10}$ $2\frac{1}{5}$

12. $4\frac{5}{6}$ $2\frac{1}{2}$

13. $7\frac{5}{8}$ $3\frac{1}{8}$

14. $3\frac{5}{16}$ $\frac{1}{4}$

15. $8\frac{11}{12}$ $2\frac{1}{3}$

16. $7\frac{3}{4}$ $\frac{3}{8}$

17. $8\frac{7}{8}$ $3\frac{1}{4}$

18. $8\frac{1}{2}$ $3\frac{3}{8}$

19. $4\frac{5}{6}$ $2\frac{1}{3}$

20. $9\frac{3}{16}$ $2\frac{1}{8}$

21. $\frac{2}{3}$ 22. $5\frac{1}{4}$ 23. $\frac{5}{8}$ 24. $\frac{3}{4}$ 25. $7\frac{2}{3}$

    $\frac{1}{6}$ $3\frac{1}{12}$ $\frac{3}{8}$ $\frac{1}{4}$ $5\frac{1}{3}$

XXI. Fractions. Subtract:

(Reduce answers to lowest terms.)

1. 4 2. $7\frac{2}{3}$ 3. $3\frac{1}{4}$ 4. 7 5. 6

   $\frac{3}{8}$ $3\frac{3}{4}$ $1\frac{5}{8}$ $\frac{3}{4}$ $\frac{3}{8}$

6. 7 7. 2 8. 1 9. 5 10. 9

   $\frac{7}{10}$ $\frac{5}{6}$ $\frac{2}{5}$ $\frac{5}{8}$ $\frac{3}{10}$

11. 10 12. 5 13. 5 14. $7\frac{5}{8}$ 15. $8\frac{3}{4}$

    $\frac{2}{3}$ $\frac{1}{3}$ $2\frac{1}{6}$ $3\frac{7}{8}$ $7\frac{2}{3}$

16. $4\frac{1}{4}$ 17. 14 18. $4\frac{1}{4}$ 19. $16\frac{7}{10}$ 20. $15\frac{1}{2}$

   $2\frac{3}{8}$ $8\frac{1}{4}$ $1\frac{3}{4}$ $4\frac{2}{5}$ $2\frac{7}{8}$

21. $6\frac{1}{5}$ 22. $5\frac{1}{6}$ 23. $7\frac{11}{16}$ 24. $8\frac{1}{4}$ 25. 8

   $3\frac{4}{5}$ $2\frac{5}{6}$ $4\frac{3}{16}$ $2\frac{1}{3}$ $\frac{3}{4}$

XXII. Fractions. Multiply:

1. $\frac{1}{3}$ of 9 $=$ 2. $\frac{2}{3}$ of 9 $=$ 3. $\frac{1}{8}$ of $80 =$

4. $\frac{1}{8}$ of $32 =$ 5. $\frac{5}{8}$ of $32 =$ 6. $\frac{1}{9}$ of $81 =$

7. $\frac{1}{4}$ of $24 =$ 8. $\frac{3}{4}$ of $24 =$ 9. $\frac{3}{8}$ of $32 =$

10. $\frac{1}{5}$ of $25 =$ 11. $\frac{2}{5}$ of $25 =$ 12. $\frac{1}{4}$ of $60 =$

13. $\frac{1}{6}$ of $30 =$ 14. $\frac{5}{6}$ of $30 =$ 15. $\frac{3}{4}$ of $36 =$

16. $\frac{1}{8}$ of $24 =$ 17. $\frac{5}{8}$ of $24 =$ 18. $\frac{5}{9}$ of $45 =$

19. $\frac{1}{5}$ of $35 =$ 20. $\frac{2}{5}$ of $35 =$ 21. $\frac{7}{8}$ of $72 =$

22. $\frac{1}{8}$ of $32 =$ 23. $\frac{7}{8}$ of $32 =$ 24. $\frac{5}{8}$ of $32 =$

25. $\frac{1}{6}$ of $42 =$ 26. $\frac{5}{6}$ of $42 =$ 27. $\frac{1}{7}$ of $63 =$

28. $\frac{3}{4}$ of $36 =$ 29. $\frac{3}{8}$ of $32 =$ 30. $\frac{1}{5}$ of $45 =$

31. $\frac{7}{8}$ of $24 =$ 32. $\frac{2}{3}$ of $27 =$ 33. $\frac{5}{6}$ of $12 =$

34. $\frac{5}{6}$ of $48 =$ 35. $\frac{3}{5}$ of $45 =$ 36. $\frac{3}{4}$ of $100 =$

37. $\frac{1}{8}$ of $24 =$ 38. $\frac{3}{8}$ of $24 =$ 39. $\frac{2}{3}$ of $90 =$

40. $\frac{1}{4}$ of $12 =$ 41. $\frac{5}{6}$ of $12 =$ 42. $\frac{5}{8}$ of $56 =$

XXIII. Fractions. Multiply:

(Change improper fractions to mixed numbers.)

1. $7 \times \frac{2}{3} =$ 2. $7 \times \frac{2}{5} =$ 3. $7 \times \frac{3}{4} =$

4. $9 \times \frac{1}{4} =$ 5. $8 \times \frac{1}{2} =$ 6. $5 \times \frac{2}{3} =$

7. $8 \times \frac{1}{5} =$ 8. $7 \times \frac{2}{3} =$ 9. $24 \times \frac{7}{8} =$

10. $8 \times \frac{7}{12} =$ 11. $10 \times \frac{3}{4} =$ 12. $20 \times \frac{3}{5} =$

13. $7 \times \frac{3}{5} =$ 14. $6 \times \frac{3}{4} =$ 15. $18 \times \frac{2}{3} =$

16. $9 \times \frac{2}{3} =$ 17. $\frac{2}{5} \times 8 =$ 18. $16 \times \frac{3}{4} =$

19. $6 \times \frac{5}{12} =$ 20. $\frac{2}{5} \times 10 =$ 21. $10 \times \frac{1}{5} =$

22. $8 \times \frac{5}{6} =$ 23. $\frac{5}{8} \times 16 =$ 24. $\frac{2}{3} \times 27 =$

25. $5 \times \frac{4}{7} =$ 26. $\frac{2}{5} \times 24 =$ 27. $\frac{3}{5} \times 40 =$

28. $7 \times \frac{1}{3} =$ 29. $\frac{2}{3} \times 10 =$ 30. $\frac{5}{8} \times 40 =$

31. $8 \times \frac{3}{4} =$ 32. $\frac{2}{3} \times 15 =$ 33. $\frac{2}{3} \times 60 =$

34. $7 \times \frac{2}{3} =$ 35. $9 \times \frac{2}{5} =$ 36. $\frac{3}{4} \times 100 =$

37. $9 \times \frac{3}{5} =$ 38. $3 \times \frac{7}{8} =$ 39. $\frac{1}{4} \times 100 =$

XXIV. Fractions. Multiply:

1. $2\frac{3}{4}$ $\underline{3}$ 2. $2\frac{1}{3}$ $\underline{7}$ 3. $5\frac{1}{2}$ $\underline{8}$ 4. $5\frac{2}{3}$ $\underline{9}$ 5. $9\frac{5}{6}$ $\underline{6}$

6. $1\frac{3}{8}$ $\underline{7}$ 7. $8\frac{1}{2}$ $\underline{5}$ 8. $3\frac{3}{4}$ $\underline{5}$ 9. $5\frac{3}{5}$ $\underline{4}$ 10. $7\frac{3}{4}$ $\underline{8}$

11. $5\frac{3}{4}$ $\underline{8}$ 12. $4\frac{1}{2}$ $\underline{6}$ 13. $7\frac{2}{3}$ $\underline{8}$ 14. $9\frac{1}{4}$ $\underline{6}$ 15. $5\frac{5}{8}$ $\underline{5}$

16. $5\frac{7}{8}$ $\underline{4}$ 17. $7\frac{5}{6}$ $\underline{8}$ 18. $8\frac{1}{3}$ $\underline{3}$ 19. $6\frac{2}{3}$ $\underline{9}$ 20. $8\frac{1}{4}$ $\underline{8}$

21. $9\frac{1}{6}$ $\underline{8}$ 22. $8\frac{2}{5}$ $\underline{4}$ 23. $3\frac{11}{16}$ $\underline{2}$ 24. $6\frac{5}{12}$ $\underline{4}$ 25. $8\frac{3}{5}$ $\underline{5}$

XXV. Fractions. Multiply:

1. $24\frac{1}{4}$ $\underline{8}$ 2. $32\frac{1}{8}$ $\underline{8}$ 3. $12\frac{2}{3}$ $\underline{5}$ 4. $42\frac{7}{8}$ $\underline{7}$ 5. $17\frac{1}{6}$ $\underline{3}$

6. $17\frac{1}{2}$ $\underline{9}$ 7. $16\frac{2}{3}$ $\underline{4}$ 8. $15\frac{2}{3}$ $\underline{9}$ 9. $29\frac{5}{6}$ $\underline{6}$ 10. $12\frac{3}{4}$ $\underline{3}$

XXVI. Multiply. (Mixed problems.)

1. $7 \times \frac{2}{3} =$ 2. $9\frac{3}{4} \times 5 =$ 3. $18 \times \frac{5}{6} =$

4. $6 \times \frac{4}{7} =$ 5. $8\frac{5}{12} \times 3 =$ 6. $25 \times \frac{4}{5} =$

7. $5 \times \frac{2}{5} =$ 8. $5\frac{4}{5} \times 9 =$ 9. $64 \times \frac{5}{8} =$

10. $8 \times \frac{5}{12} =$ 11. $\frac{3}{4} \times 8 =$ 12. $\frac{3}{7} \times 8 =$

13. $9 \times \frac{3}{4} =$ 14. $\frac{2}{3} \times 7 =$ 15. $\frac{3}{4} \times 24 =$

16. $9 \times \frac{2}{3} =$ 17. $\frac{5}{6} \times 12 =$ 18. $\frac{3}{5} \times 15 =$

19. $7 \times \frac{2}{5} =$ 20. $\frac{3}{4} \times 9 =$ 21. $\frac{2}{3} \times 36 =$

22. $12 \times \frac{5}{6} =$ 23. $\frac{4}{7} \times 28 =$ 24. $9 \times \frac{4}{5} =$

XXVII. Decimals. (Change to decimals.)

1. $\frac{5}{10} =$ 2. $\frac{6}{10} =$ 3. $\frac{9}{10} =$ 4. $\frac{1}{10} =$

5. $\frac{7}{10} =$ 6. $\frac{8}{10} =$ 7. $\frac{3}{10} =$ 8. $\frac{2}{10} =$

9. $\frac{4}{10} =$ 10. $2\frac{3}{10} =$ 11. $4\frac{5}{10} =$ 12. $3\frac{1}{10} =$

XXVIII. Decimals.

Change to common fractions or mixed numbers (do not reduce the answers).

1. $.8 =$ 2. $.6 =$ 3. $.9 =$ 4. $.5 =$

5. $.3 =$ 6. $.2 =$ 7. $1.7 =$ 8. $2.3 =$

9. $3.6 =$ 10. $4.8 =$ 11. $5.6 =$ 12. $2.1 =$

13. $3.06 =$ 14. $7.87 =$ 15. $8.9 =$ 16. $3.24 =$

17. 1.02 =   18. .05 =   19. .08 =   20. .01 =

21. 4.02 =   22. .73 =   23. 5.16 =   24. .97 =

25. .11 =   26. 2.05 =   27. .28 =   28. .13 =

29. .06 =   30. 4.04 =

XXIX. Decimals. Add:

1. 3.2	2. 5.4	3. 7.9	4. 6.3
4.5	3.3	4.2	2.6

5. 9.4	6. 5.8	7. 6.2	8. 11.5
6.3	3.5	4.5	7.2

9. 24.6	10. 92.7	11. 84.8	12. 5.1
95.3	35.6	98.5	.9

XXX. Decimals. Subtract:

1. 92.2	2. 87.6	3. 9.7	4. 7.3
14.7	42.3	4.2	2.8

5. 8.7	6. 7.2	7. 4.00	8. .76
4.5	5.1	.05	.07

9. 11.00	10. 9.4	11. 7.2	12. 50.00
7.32	3.7	2.0	27.98

XXXI. Common Measures.

1. 5 feet = _____ inches
2. 24 inches = _____ feet
3. $\frac{1}{2}$ hour = _____ minutes
4. 5 minutes = _____ seconds
5. 6 bushels = _____ pecks
6. $\frac{1}{2}$ bushel = _____ pecks
7. 6 quarts = _____ pints
8. $\frac{1}{2}$ gallon = _____ quarts
9. 28 pecks = _____ bushels
10. 4 bushels = _____ pecks
11. 4 pecks = _____ quarts
12. $2\frac{1}{2}$ feet = _____ inches
13. 36 months = _____ years
14. $\frac{3}{4}$ pound = _____ ounces
15. 15 feet = _____ yards
16. 21 days = _____ weeks
17. 120 seconds = _____ minutes
18. 20 pecks = _____ bushels
19. $5\frac{1}{2}$ bushels = _____ pecks
20. 24 pints = _____ quarts
21. 12 pints = _____ gallons
22. $7\frac{1}{2}$ quarts = _____ pints
23. 48 ounces = _____ pounds
24. $\frac{3}{4}$ year = _____ months
25. 6 days = _____ hours
26. $\frac{1}{2}$ mile = _____ feet

27. $\frac{1}{4}$ mile = _____ feet
28. $\frac{3}{8}$ pound = _____ ounces
29. $1\frac{1}{2}$ yards = _____ inches
30. $1\frac{1}{2}$ pounds = _____ ounces
31. 7 yards = _____ inches
32. 2 pounds = _____ ounces
33. 5 weeks = _____ days
34. 5 days = _____ hours
35. $\frac{1}{2}$ peck = _____ quarts
36. 24 quarts = _____ gallons
37. 12 quarts = _____ pints
38. 4000 pounds = _____ tons
39. 96 hours = _____ days
40. $\frac{3}{8}$ peck = _____ quarts
41. $\frac{5}{6}$ foot = _____ inches
42. $\frac{5}{8}$ pound = _____ ounces
43. $\frac{3}{4}$ yard = _____ inches
44. $\frac{3}{4}$ hour = _____ minutes
45. $\frac{5}{6}$ hour = _____ minutes
46. 8 yards = _____ feet
47. 72 inches = _____ yards
48. 3 years = _____ months
49. 16 quarts = _____ pecks
50. 3 pecks = _____ quarts
51. 64 quarts = _____ pecks
52. $5\frac{1}{2}$ gallons = _____ quarts

53. 4 gallons = _____ pints

54. 3 pounds = _____ ounces

55. $2\frac{1}{2}$ hours = _____ minutes

56. $\frac{7}{8}$ pound = _____ ounces

57. 5 gallons, 3 quarts = _____ quarts

58. 6 feet, 2 inches = _____ inches

59. 5 pounds, 5 ounces = _____ ounces

60. 7 bushels, 3 pecks = _____ pecks

61. 3 hours, 15 minutes = _____ minutes

62. 12 feet, 3 inches = _____ inches

63. 1 quart = _____ cups

64. 1 bushel = _____ pints

65. 60 days = _____ months

66. 17 inches = _____ feet _____ inches

67. 19 ounces = _____ pounds _____ ounces

68. 370 days = _____ years _____ days

69. 75 minutes = _____ hours _____ minutes

70. 27 months = _____ years _____ months

71. 15 pecks = _____ bushels _____ pecks

72. 10 feet = _____ yards _____ feet

73. 38 inches = _____ feet _____ inches

74. 32 feet = _____ yards _____ feet

75. 32 days = _____ weeks _____ days

76. 33 ounces = _____ pounds _____ ounces

77. 38 pecks = _____ bushels _____ pecks

78. 20 ounces = _____ pounds _____ ounces

79. 17 feet = _____ yards _____ feet

80. 65 inches = _____ feet _____ inches

XXXII. Thought Problems.

1. For a Scout Rally 225 paper napkins are needed. The napkins come 75 to the package. How many packages of napkins shall the scouts buy?

_____

WORK SPACE

2. Miss Turner has 12 dozen pencils for her class this year. If she divides the pencils equally among her 36 pupils how many pencils will each pupil get during the year? _____

3. Alice needs $\frac{1}{2}$ cup of corn syrup for ice cream and $\frac{3}{8}$ cup for cookies. To make both, she needs _____ cups of syrup.

4. Peter started to ride his bike from Ashton to Conover, a distance of $8\frac{3}{4}$ miles. When he had gone $6\frac{1}{2}$ miles, a tire went flat. He had to walk _____ miles to Conover to get a patch for the tire.

5. Jane is making a costume. She measured and finds she needs 216 inches of material. She needs _____ yards of material.

6. Mrs. Brown had $\frac{1}{2}$ pound of beans. She told Mary to take half of them for a bean bag. Mary may take _____ of a pound of beans.

7. A navy plane flew these distances on four different days: 225 miles, 324 miles, 903 miles, 756 miles. The average distance flown per day was _____ miles.

8. A plane flew 1000 miles in 5 hours, or an average rate of _____ miles per hour.

9. If oranges are selling at 3 pounds for 35¢, 9 pounds will cost _____ .

10. Farmer Jones has some animals. $\frac{1}{4}$ were horses. $\frac{1}{2}$ were cows. The rest were pigs. He had 8 pigs. How many horses and how many cows did he have?

11. Suppose you put 2¢ in a bank on February 1, 4¢ on February 2, 8¢ on February 3, and so on, doubling the amount each day. After you made your last deposit on February 14th, would you have enough money to buy a $5.00 box of candy? How much would you have?

12. Draw a figure like the one shown. Cut it out. Cut along the dotted lines. Now fit the four pieces together to make a square.

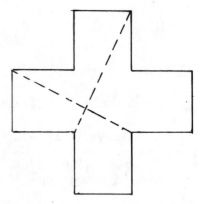

13. What is the size of this plot of land if the scale to which it is drawn is $\frac{1}{2}'' = 10$ feet.

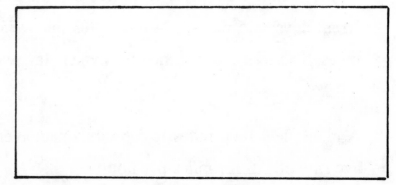

14. Using the table of facts, make a bar graph show-
    ing the increase in your school enrollment in the
    last 10 years.

In-	Your school had
1956	350 pupils
1957	375 "
1958	450 "
1959	490 "
1960	525 "
1961	550 "
1962	600 "
1963	700 "
1964	750 "
1965	800 "
1966	850 "

I.
1. sit
2. sat
3. set
4. sets
5. sit

1. don't
2. doesn't
3. don't
4. doesn't
5. doesn't

III.
1. rung
2. rang
3. rung
4. rung
5. rang

1. sang
2. sung
3. sang
4. sang
5. sung

V.
1. a
2. an
3. a
4. a
5. An

1. good
2. good
3. well
4. well
5. good

VII.
1. any
2. any
3. any
4. any
5. no

1. was
2. were
3. were
4. were
5. was

IX.
1. Jane–Camp Addison Boyce–Tuesday.
2. I–Sandy–Paula.
3. Dr. Smith.
4. Yesterday–Independence Day.
5. Independence Day–July.
6. The–Bronx Park.
7. Aunt Mae–Bob.
8. The–Lazy Daisy Club–Friday.
9. Mexico–Spaniards.
10. The–Mississippi River–Father–Waters.
11. The–Amazon River–Brazil–Atlantic Ocean.
12. The–Pacific Ocean–Atlantic Ocean–Panama Canal.

X.
1. Don't stop now!
2. Dr. J. C. Wilkes lives in Boston, Mass.
3. Do you really think it will rain?
4. What an important decision to make!
5. Ann's books were ruined by the rain.
6. Mary is visiting her Aunt Mae in Chicago, Illinois.
7. The party will be on October 3, 1959.
8. Yes, we will all be in costume.
9. Tell us, Jane, what your costume will be.
10. Our teacher always says, "Good morning, children."
11. "This looks like Mark's cap," Jane said.
12. Her poster is painted orange, green, gray, and black.

XI.
1. As they sat there and listened, the train left.
2. A huge eagle landed on the top of the mountain.
3. It must have been the doorbell that rang.
4. Everyone says it is a good book.
5. I worked for an hour, a whole hour!

6. This is an ugly but a useful gadget.
7. This problem is an easy one.
8. The jet plane flew across the country.
9. Everyone came, Jane, just everyone!
10. The World Book Company prints beautiful books.
11. Let me see the puppy, Joe.
12. Maggie and I have coats alike.

A.   Heading
Inside address
Salutation or greeting
         Body

                 Closing
                 Signature
B.

            Clinton School
            Avon, Texas
            November 10, 1957
Mr. Fred M. Smith
Chief of the Fire Department
Avon, Texas

Dear Mr. Smith:
     Our class would like to learn more about fire prevention and about what we can do if fires break out. Can you or one of your men come to our school and tell us about it? Our teacher will call you for your answer.

            Yours very truly,
            Miss Owen's Class

XIII. The date of the party was omitted.

XIV.

Mary Van Atta
Skyview Acres
Pomona, New York

Miss Patsy Leinhart
57 Yarmon Avenue
Velva
North Dakota

XV.
1. airplanes	—	common, plural
sky	—	common, singular
2. Mt. Ash	—	proper, singular
trees	—	common, plural
3. chairs	—	common, plural
seats	—	common, plural
4. shells	—	common, plural
table	—	common, singular
5. house	—	common, singular
shore	—	common, singular
6. Jane	—	proper, singular
Ellen	—	proper, singular
birdhouse	—	common, singular
7. Joey	—	proper, singular
football	—	common, singular

8. Friday   —proper, singular
    day   —common, singular
    house   —common, singular
9. Grand Canyon—proper, singular
    sight   —common, singular
10. Mount Vernon—proper, singular
    name   —common, singular
    city   —common, singular
11. boys   —common, plural
    Lake Como   —proper, singular
12. seeds   —common, plural
    yard   —common, singular

XVI.
1. calves
2. engineers
3. men
4. companies
5. children
6. halves
7. boys
8. countries
9. dresses
10. auctioneers
11. boxes
12. dishes

XVII.
1. helped
2. spreads
3. are listening
4. plays
5. came
6. had eaten
7. are
8. have sung
9. knew
10. give

XVIII.
1. Many, interesting, folk
2. Four, a, cowboy
3. One, a, piano
4. The, youngest, a, short, the, whole
5. soft, animal
6. The, bright, red
7. Cotton
8. Soft, fine, wool, wonderful, warm
9. Healthy, happy
10. The, little, country, an, iron, coal

I. Write numerals:
1. 1,000,510
2. 475,404
3. 37,000,111
4. 809,413,212
5. 1,100,100,100
6. 435,000
7. 2,010
8. 74,147
9. 1,001,001,001
10. 2,222,222

II. Exponent form:
1. 10^3
2. 4^2
3. 5^3
4. 2^4
5. 8^2
6. 10^5
7. 3^3
8. 6^2
9. 7^4
10. 9^3

III. Prime numbers:
2, 3, 5, 7, 11, 13, 17, 19, 23, 29, 31, 37

IV. Roman numerals:
1. $\overline{\text{LXIII}}$
2. MM or $\overline{\text{M}}$
3. MMCDXXXI
4. DCCLVI
5. M
6. CCCLXXX
7. CCI
8. MCDXCII
9. MDCCLXXVI
10. XCVIII

V. Union of sets:
1. A ∪ B = {Harry, Dale, Bob, Pete, Charles, Mike}
2. A ∪ B = {1, 2, 3, 4, 5}
3. A ∪ B = {1, 2, 3, 4, 5, 6}
4. A ∪ B = {1, 2, 3, 4}
5. A ∪ B = {a, b, c, d, f, h}

VI. Intersection of sets:
1. A ∩ B = {Bob, Pete}
2. A ∩ B = {3}
3. A ∩ B = φ
4. A ∩ B = {Plymouths, Dodges}
5. A ∩ B = {a, e}

VII. Watch the symbol:
1. A ∪ B = {x, y, z, v, w}
2. A ∩ B = {x}
3. A ∩ B ∩ C = {Carol}
4. A ∪ B = {dog, cat, cow, horse, mule}
5. A ∪ B ∪ C = {1, 2, 3, 4, 5, 6, 7, 8}

VIII. Add.
1. $21.16
2. $26.30
3. $40.47
4. $18.78
5. $154.41
6. $115.00
7. $180.38
8. 3922
9. $14.19
10. $11.07
11. 1859
12. 2661
13. $19.72
14. $23.49
15. $30.34
16. $17.63
17. 2808
18. 2517
19. 1625
20. 2908
21. $19.71
22. $23.08
23. 3023
24. 1764

IX. Subtract.
1. $7.99
2. $9.37
3. $9.55
4. $21.26
5. 131
6. 541
7. 343
8. 248
9. 2953
10. $7.51
11. $43.14
12. $77.25
13. $4.22
14. $5.46
15. $5.16
16. $2.74
17. $7.35
18. $3.46
19. $4.26
20. $12.88
21. $2.68
22. $6.51
23. $16.25
24. $45.85
25. 2136
26. 663
27. 632
28. 840

X. Multiply.
1. $389.34
2. $433.54
3. $466.56
4. $472.50
5. $438.44
6. 24,453
7. 21,952
8. 47,866
9. 11,136
10. 13,090
11. 41,538
12. 29,273
13. 22,320
14. 49,053
15. 10,387
16. 15,606
17. 131,492
18. 99,165
19. 202,486
20. 324,784
21. 83,667
22. 362,142
23. $183.12
24. $228.25
25. $389.12
26. 210,368
27. 15,200
28. 30,031
29. 21,660
30. 27,800
31. 36,200
32. 8,610
33. 48,070
34. 13,018
35. $231.20
36. $217.84
37. 54,802
38. 51,595
39. 20,194
40. 527,352

XI. Divide.
1. $8.34
2. $.75
3. $4.83
4. $2.59
5. $.96
6. $9.56
7. 15
8. 32 R5
9. 31
10. 5 R2
11. 23 R2
12. 23
13. 45
14. 11 R3
15. 25
16. 12 R5
17. 46 R3
18. 13
19. 24 R14
20. 21 R6
21. 21
22. 11 R13
23. 21 R13
24. 23
25. 21 R13
26. 32 R10
27. 41
28. 81
29. 82 R27
30. 80
31. 81 R10
32. 12
33. 93 R18
34. 21 R3
35. 82 R34

XII. Fractions.
1. $1\frac{3}{4}$
2. $3\frac{1}{4}$
3. $3\frac{1}{5}$
4. 3
5. $3\frac{2}{3}$
6. $3\frac{3}{6}$
7. 2
8. 1
9. $8\frac{1}{4}$
10. 3
11. $6\frac{1}{4}$
12. $1\frac{4}{5}$
13. $2\frac{1}{3}$
14. 2
15. $5\frac{4}{5}$
16. $3\frac{1}{8}$
17. 1
18. $1\frac{1}{4}$
19. $3\frac{4}{5}$
20. $3\frac{1}{8}$
21. 1
22. $3\frac{1}{5}$
23. 4
24. 6

XIII. Fractions.
1. $\frac{6}{12}$
2. $\frac{6}{12}$
3. $\frac{12}{16}$
4. $\frac{4}{12}$
5. $\frac{6}{9}$
6. $\frac{9}{12}$
7. $\frac{8}{12}$
8. $\frac{6}{12}$
9. $\frac{5}{20}$
10. $\frac{2}{12}$
11. $\frac{4}{12}$
12. $\frac{6}{10}$
13. $\frac{12}{12}$
14. $\frac{2}{12}$
15. $\frac{16}{12}$
16. $\frac{9}{12}$
17. $\frac{2}{8}$
18. $\frac{15}{20}$
19. $\frac{2}{4}$
20. $\frac{8}{6}$
21. $\frac{2}{16}$
22. $\frac{8}{6}$
23. $\frac{4}{16}$
24. $\frac{4}{12}$

XIV. Fractions.

1. $\frac{1}{2}$
2. $\frac{5}{8}$
3. $\frac{1}{2}$
4. $\frac{1}{8}$
5. $\frac{2}{3}$
6. $\frac{1}{2}$
7. $\frac{1}{4}$
8. $\frac{1}{5}$
9. $\frac{1}{2}$
10. $\frac{1}{4}$
11. $\frac{1}{4}$
12. $\frac{1}{4}$
13. $\frac{1}{2}$
14. $\frac{7}{8}$
15. $\frac{1}{4}$
16. $\frac{3}{8}$
17. $\frac{3}{4}$
18. $\frac{1}{4}$
19. $\frac{1}{4}$
20. $\frac{3}{8}$
21. $\frac{1}{4}$
22. $\frac{2}{5}$
23. $\frac{2}{4}$
24. $\frac{1}{3}$

XV. Fractions. Add:

1. $\frac{7}{8}$
2. $1\frac{1}{8}$
3. $\frac{3}{4}$
4. $1\frac{1}{10}$
5. $\frac{5}{6}$
6. 1
7. $1\frac{3}{8}$
8. $1\frac{4}{5}$
9. 1
10. $1\frac{5}{8}$
11. $7\frac{2}{3}$
12. $10\frac{5}{6}$
13. $15\frac{3}{4}$
14. $9\frac{3}{8}$
15. $6\frac{1}{4}$
16. $9\frac{5}{6}$
17. $7\frac{2}{3}$
18. $7\frac{3}{7}$
19. $13\frac{5}{8}$
20. 9
21. 9
22. 18
23. $12\frac{1}{2}$
24. $16\frac{1}{4}$
25. $5\frac{1}{10}$

XVI. Fractions. Add:

1. $1\frac{7}{8}$
2. $1\frac{1}{4}$
3. 2
4. $1\frac{9}{16}$
5. $2\frac{1}{2}$
6. $1\frac{11}{16}$
7. $2\frac{1}{8}$
8. $\frac{11}{12}$
9. $1\frac{3}{8}$
10. $1\frac{1}{2}$
11. $1\frac{3}{16}$
12. $1\frac{1}{12}$
13. $1\frac{5}{12}$
14. $1\frac{3}{8}$
15. $1\frac{1}{6}$
16. $1\frac{9}{10}$
17. 1
18. $1\frac{3}{8}$
19. $1\frac{1}{16}$
20. $1\frac{2}{3}$

XVII. Fractions. Add:

1. $11\frac{1}{6}$
2. $4\frac{1}{8}$
3. $8\frac{3}{10}$
4. $12\frac{1}{8}$
5. $6\frac{1}{8}$
6. $12\frac{1}{10}$
7. $6\frac{3}{8}$
8. $8\frac{1}{2}$
9. $7\frac{1}{4}$
10. $12\frac{1}{8}$
11. $9\frac{1}{4}$
12. $11\frac{1}{2}$
13. $11\frac{3}{4}$
14. $3\frac{3}{4}$
15. $13\frac{3}{4}$
16. $8\frac{2}{3}$
17. $4\frac{7}{10}$
18. $3\frac{5}{6}$
19. $11\frac{1}{2}$
20. $7\frac{2}{3}$
21. $11\frac{3}{4}$
22. $15\frac{11}{12}$
23. $8\frac{1}{4}$
24. $6\frac{1}{4}$
25. $15\frac{1}{4}$

XVIII. Fractions. Add:

1. $11\frac{11}{12}$
2. $15\frac{1}{3}$
3. 18
4. $10\frac{3}{4}$
5. $20\frac{3}{8}$
6. 21
7. $14\frac{2}{3}$
8. $8\frac{3}{4}$
9. $5\frac{7}{12}$
10. $3\frac{1}{12}$
11. $8\frac{1}{2}$
12. $11\frac{4}{5}$
13. $11\frac{3}{8}$
14. $11\frac{3}{4}$
15. 12

XIX. Fractions. Subtract:

1. $\frac{1}{6}$
2. $\frac{5}{8}$
3. $\frac{1}{4}$
4. $\frac{3}{5}$
5. $\frac{5}{7}$
6. $\frac{1}{8}$
7. $\frac{1}{8}$
8. $\frac{1}{2}$
9. $\frac{1}{3}$
10. $\frac{3}{8}$
11. $\frac{1}{8}$
12. $\frac{1}{8}$
13. $\frac{1}{3}$
14. $\frac{1}{6}$
15. $\frac{1}{4}$
16. $\frac{3}{8}$
17. $\frac{3}{8}$
18. $\frac{1}{2}$
19. $\frac{5}{12}$
20. $\frac{1}{16}$
21. $\frac{1}{6}$
22. $\frac{3}{16}$
23. $\frac{1}{3}$
24. $\frac{1}{4}$
25. $\frac{1}{2}$

XX. Fractions. Subtract:

1. $2\frac{1}{4}$
2. $4\frac{1}{4}$
3. $5\frac{1}{2}$
4. $4\frac{1}{6}$
5. $2\frac{1}{2}$
6. $5\frac{1}{2}$
7. $4\frac{2}{3}$
8. 2
9. $3\frac{1}{4}$
10. $5\frac{1}{3}$
11. $4\frac{1}{10}$
12. $2\frac{1}{3}$
13. $4\frac{1}{2}$
14. $3\frac{1}{16}$
15. $6\frac{7}{12}$
16. $7\frac{3}{8}$
17. $5\frac{5}{8}$
18. $5\frac{1}{8}$
19. $2\frac{1}{2}$
20. $7\frac{1}{16}$
21. $\frac{1}{2}$
22. $2\frac{1}{6}$
23. $\frac{1}{4}$
24. $\frac{1}{2}$
25. $2\frac{1}{3}$

XXI. Fractions. Subtract:

1. $3\frac{5}{8}$
2. $3\frac{11}{12}$
3. $1\frac{5}{8}$
4. $6\frac{1}{4}$
5. $5\frac{5}{8}$
6. $6\frac{3}{10}$
7. $1\frac{1}{6}$
8. $\frac{3}{5}$
9. $4\frac{3}{8}$
10. $8\frac{7}{10}$
11. $9\frac{1}{3}$
12. $4\frac{2}{3}$
13. $2\frac{5}{6}$
14. $3\frac{3}{4}$
15. $1\frac{1}{12}$
16. $1\frac{7}{8}$
17. $5\frac{3}{4}$
18. $2\frac{1}{2}$
19. $12\frac{3}{10}$
20. $12\frac{5}{8}$
21. $2\frac{2}{5}$
22. $2\frac{1}{3}$
23. $3\frac{1}{2}$
24. $5\frac{11}{12}$
25. $7\frac{1}{4}$

XXII. Fractions. Multiply:

1. 3
2. 6
3. 10
4. 4
5. 20
6. 9
7. 6
8. 18
9. 12
10. 5
11. 10
12. 15
13. 5
14. 25
15. 27
16. 3
17. 15
18. 25
19. 7
20. 14
21. 63
22. 4
23. 28
24. 20
25. 7
26. 35
27. 9
28. 27
29. 12
30. 9
31. 21
32. 18
33. 10
34. 40
35. 27
36. 75
37. 3
38. 9
39. 60
40. 3
41. 10
42. 35

XXIII. Fractions. Multiply:

1. $4\frac{2}{3}$
2. $2\frac{4}{5}$
3. $5\frac{1}{4}$
4. $2\frac{1}{4}$
5. 4
6. $3\frac{1}{4}$
7. $1\frac{3}{5}$
8. $4\frac{2}{3}$
9. 21
10. $4\frac{2}{3}$
11. $7\frac{1}{2}$
12. 12
13. $4\frac{1}{5}$
14. $4\frac{1}{2}$
15. 12
16. 6
17. $3\frac{1}{4}$
18. 12
19. $2\frac{1}{2}$
20. 4
21. 2
22. $6\frac{2}{3}$
23. 10
24. 18
25. $2\frac{6}{7}$
26. $9\frac{3}{5}$
27. 24
28. $2\frac{1}{4}$
29. $6\frac{2}{3}$
30. 25
31. 6
32. 10
33. 40
34. $4\frac{2}{3}$
35. $3\frac{3}{4}$
36. 75
37. $5\frac{2}{3}$
38. $2\frac{5}{8}$
39. 25

XXIV. Fractions. Multiply:

1. $8\frac{1}{4}$
2. $16\frac{1}{3}$
3. 44
4. 51
5. 59
6. $9\frac{5}{8}$
7. $42\frac{1}{2}$
8. $18\frac{3}{4}$
9. $22\frac{2}{5}$
10. 62
11. 46
12. 27
13. $61\frac{1}{3}$
14. $55\frac{1}{2}$
15. $28\frac{1}{8}$
16. $23\frac{1}{2}$
17. $62\frac{2}{3}$
18. 25
19. 60
20. 66
21. $73\frac{1}{3}$
22. $33\frac{3}{5}$
23. $7\frac{3}{8}$
24. $25\frac{2}{3}$
25. 43

XXV. Fractions. Multiply:

1. 194
2. 257
3. $63\frac{1}{3}$
4. $300\frac{1}{8}$
5. $51\frac{1}{2}$
6. $157\frac{1}{2}$
7. $66\frac{2}{3}$
8. 141
9. 179
10. $38\frac{1}{4}$

XXVI. Multiply. (Mixed problems.)

1. $4\frac{2}{3}$
2. $48\frac{3}{4}$
3. 15
4. $3\frac{3}{7}$
5. $25\frac{1}{4}$
6. 20
7. 2
8. $52\frac{1}{5}$
9. 40
10. $3\frac{1}{3}$
11. 6
12. $3\frac{3}{7}$
13. $6\frac{3}{4}$
14. $4\frac{2}{3}$
15. 18
16. 6
17. 10
18. 9
19. $2\frac{4}{5}$
20. $6\frac{3}{4}$
21. 24
22. 10
23. 16
24. $7\frac{1}{5}$

XXVII. Decimals.
Change to decimals:

1. .5
2. .6
3. .9
4. .1
5. .7
6. .8
7. .3
8. .2
9. .4
10. 2.3
11. 4.5
12. 3.1

XXVIII. Decimals.
Change to common fractions or mixed numbers:

1. $\frac{8}{10}$
2. $\frac{6}{10}$
3. $\frac{9}{10}$
4. $\frac{5}{10}$
5. $\frac{3}{10}$
6. $\frac{2}{10}$
7. $1\frac{7}{10}$
8. $2\frac{3}{10}$
9. $3\frac{6}{10}$
10. $4\frac{8}{10}$
11. $5\frac{6}{10}$
12. $2\frac{1}{10}$
13. $3\frac{6}{100}$
14. $7\frac{87}{100}$
15. $8\frac{9}{10}$
16. $3\frac{24}{100}$
17. $1\frac{2}{100}$
18. $\frac{5}{100}$
19. $\frac{9}{100}$
20. $\frac{1}{100}$
21. $4\frac{2}{100}$
22. $\frac{73}{100}$
23. $5\frac{16}{100}$
24. $\frac{97}{100}$
25. $\frac{11}{100}$
26. $2\frac{5}{100}$
27. $\frac{28}{100}$
28. $\frac{13}{100}$
29. $\frac{6}{100}$
30. $4\frac{4}{100}$

XXIX. Decimals. Add:

1. 7.7
2. 8.7
3. 12.1
4. 8.9
5. 15.7
6. 9.3
7. 10.7
8. 18.7
9. 119.9
10. 128.3
11. 183.3
12. 6.0

XXX. Decimals. Subtract:

1. 77.5
2. 45.3
3. 5.5
4. 4.5
5. 4.2
6. 2.1
7. 3.95
8. .69
9. 3.68
10. 5.7
11. 5.2
12. 22.02

XXXI. Common Measures.

1. 60 inches   2. 2 feet   3. 30 minutes   4. 300 seconds   5. 24 pecks   6. 2 pecks   7. 12 pints   8. 2 quarts   9. 7 bushels   10. 16 pecks   11. 32 quarts   12. 30 inches   13. 3 years   14. 12 ounces   15. 5 yards   16. 3 weeks   17. 2 minutes   18. 5 bushels   19. 22 pecks   20. 12 quarts   21. $1\frac{1}{2}$ gallons   22. 15 pints   23. 3 pounds   24. 9 months   25. 144 hours   26. 2640 feet   27. 1320 feet   28. 6 ounces   29. 54 inches   30. 24 ounces   31. 252 inches   32. 32 ounces   33. 35 days   34. 120 hours   35. 4 quarts   36. 6 gallons   37. 24 pints   38. 2 tons   39. 4 days   40. 3 quarts   41. 10 inches   42. 10 ounces   43. 27 inches   44. 45 minutes   45. 50 minutes   46. 24 feet   47. 2 yards   48. 36 months   49. 2 pecks   50. 24 quarts   51. 8 pecks   52. 22 quarts   53. 32 pints   54. 48 ounces   55. 150 minutes   56. 14 ounces   57. 23 quarts   58. 74 inches   59. 85 ounces   60. 31 pecks   61. 195 minutes   62. 147 inches   63. 4 cups   64. 64 pints   65. 2 months   66. 1 foot 5 inches   67. 1 pound 3 ounces   68. 1 year 5 days   69. 1 hour 15 minutes   70. 2 years 3 months   71. 3 bushels 3 pecks   72. 3 yards 1 foot   73. 3 feet 2 inches   74. 10 yards 2 feet   75. 4 weeks 4 days   76. 2 pounds 1 ounce   77. 9 bushels 2 pecks   78. 1 pound 4 ounces   79. 5 yards 2 feet   80. 5 feet 5 inches

XXXII. Thought Problems.

1. 3 packages   2. 4 pencils   3. $\frac{7}{8}$ cup   4. $2\frac{1}{4}$ miles   5. 6 yards   6. $\frac{1}{4}$ pound   7. 552 miles   8. 200 mi. per hr.   9. $1.05   10. 8 horses, 16 cows   11. Yes. $327.66
12.

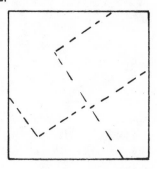

13. 80 feet   35 feet
14.

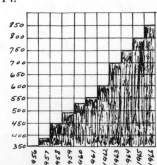

reading

Read the story below and answer the questions that follow it.

A GERM FIGHTER

Dr. Alexander Fleming of London, England, was a special kind of gardener. He raised germs in his gardens. Each garden was no larger than an ordinary flat dish.

One day he noticed something strange about one of his gardens. In the center was a spot of green mold. He looked closely at it. It looked like the mold you sometimes see on bread. Dr. Fleming noticed that around the mold there were no germs at all, but that some distance away from it they continued to grow thickly. This made him think. He had discovered something new. It is something used today, about thirty years later, to fight against the growth of germs. It is called penicillin.

Mold is a simple kind of plant. There are many kinds of molds. All mold seeds are so small that you cannot see them without a microscope. They float in the air. They grow only if they land someplace where they can grow, as on bread or cheese.

Dr. Fleming's mold began to grow in just that way. A mold seed had fallen into his germ garden. Because no germs grew around the mold, he concluded that it was the mold that prevented the germs from growing.

Other scientists began to study that kind of mold and kept on studying it for years. Little by little they found out many things. They learned that penicillin does not kill germs. Instead it checks the growth and increase of germs. It is the white corpuscles in your blood that kill the germs that are present.

Other germ fighters have been developed since Dr. Fleming's discovery, but penicillin is still one of our most useful medicines.

I. Write the answers in complete sentences. (40 points)

1. Who discovered penicillin?
2. Where did he live?
3. How does a germ garden compare to a vegetable garden?
4. About how long ago was penicillin discovered?
5. What was different about one of the germ gardens that led to the discovery of penicillin?
6. How does penicillin act to make you well?
7. What does the word *checks* mean as it is used in this story?
8. What is the main idea of this story?

II. Write *true* or *false* after each statement. (50 points)

1. Penicillin was developed in six months. _____
2. There are other medicines that fight germs. _____
3. Mold will grow on bread. _____

4. Mold is an animal. _____

5. Penicillin is no longer used as a medicine. _____

6. A microscope is necessary to study molds. _____

7. Mold seeds float in the air. _____

8. Penicillin is a good germ killer. _____

9. Penicillin is a new drug. _____

10. All mold is harmful. _____

III. Arrange these sentences in the proper order. (10 points)

1. Dr. Fleming raised germ gardens.
2. Penicillin is still used to check disease germs.
3. Dr. Fleming noticed a mold growing in one of his gardens.
4. Eventually the drug penicillin was developed from this kind of mold.
5. Other scientists studied the same kind of mold.
6. Dr. Fleming noticed that germs would not grow near the mold.

english

I. Make an outline for the following article. (10 points)

A TERRARIUM

You can make a terrarium from a fish bowl. Begin by sinking a little pan of water into some soil in the bottom of the bowl. Set the plants into the soil so that the roots are covered. Arrange them so the tall plants do not hide or crowd the small ones.

There are certain things to remember in selecting the plants for the terrarium. Do not choose plants that grow very fast. Do not choose plants that grow very tall. Select the kinds of plants that like warm, damp air.

Only a little care is needed for the plants. Put a cover on the bowl to keep the moisture in the air and soil. You seldom need to add more water, but you must take the cover off once a day to let the plants have fresh air.

II. Divide this selection into paragraphs. Tell what fact about the shrew is discussed in each paragraph. (20 points)

THE SHREW

A shrew is a tiny animal. It is about as heavy as a teaspoonful of water. It has a long, pointed snout, beady little eyes, and short, rounded ears. It is covered with soft brown or gray fur. The shrew is a hungry animal. It hunts for food all the time, day and night. It likes to eat crickets, grasshoppers, and earthworms. Because it eats so many of the harmful insects, it is one of the farmer's best friends. Shrews are fierce little animals. They even kill each other.

III. Draw two envelopes. Address them properly. (10 points)

    A. Address the first one to your friend Mary Smith, 24 Linden Avenue, New City 17, New York. Don't forget the return address.

    B. Address the second one to The J. M. Crane Company, 534 Oak Street, Davenport 15, Iowa. Don't forget the return address.

IV. Write the possessive forms of these words. (10 points)

    1. boy   2. boys   3. children   4. Lois   5. class   6. fox
    7. mouse   8. country   9. child   10. deer

V. Write the plural forms of these words. (10 points)

    1. child   2. country   3. man   4. wife   5. mouse   6. deer
    7. answer   8. party   9. class   10. ox

VI. Tell whether each underlined word is a proper noun (p.n.), common noun (c.n.), adjective (adj.), verb of being (v.b.), or verb of action (v.a.). Use the abbreviations. (20 points)

    1. The new girl in the class made a beautiful blue dress for herself.
    2. The answer to this subtraction problem seems unreasonable.
    3. A huge black bird flew over the high stone wall.
    4. Grandma Moses is old.

VII. Rewrite these sentences. Correct the mistakes you find in punctuation, grammar, word usage, capitalization, and spelling. (20 points)

    1. He says he don't want to buy the knew bycicle horn untill Wedensday.
    2. She ain't having the party on may 3 because that day it ain't her birthday.
    3. The whistel seemed to say who-who-who-who.
    4. Never again the Teacher exclaimed.
    5. Does alaska have a star in are Flag.

arithmetic test

I. Mixed numbers. Change each answer to its simplest form. (10 points)

1. $7\frac{1}{8} + 4\frac{3}{8}$ 6. $4\frac{6}{7} - 1\frac{3}{7}$
2. $5\frac{2}{7} + 3\frac{3}{7}$ 7. $14\frac{3}{10} - 7\frac{1}{10}$
3. $4\frac{1}{12} + 6\frac{11}{12}$ 8. $6\frac{1}{2} - 4$
4. $10\frac{3}{16} + 6\frac{15}{16}$ 9. $9 - 7\frac{2}{7}$
5. $1\frac{3}{7} + 2\frac{4}{7}$ 10. $12 - 6\frac{5}{10}$

II. Fractions. Change to whole or mixed numbers. (10 points)

1. $\frac{9}{4}$ 6. $\frac{19}{4}$
2. $\frac{16}{5}$ 7. $\frac{21}{7}$
3. $\frac{10}{2}$ 8. $\frac{60}{10}$
4. $\frac{40}{5}$ 9. $\frac{23}{4}$
5. $\frac{33}{4}$ 10. $\frac{25}{8}$

III. Fractions with different denominators. (10 points)

1. $\frac{1}{2} + \frac{2}{12}$ 6. $2\frac{3}{4} - \frac{1}{2}$

2. $3\frac{1}{4} + \frac{1}{2}$ 7. $4\frac{5}{6} - 2\frac{1}{3}$

3. $\frac{3}{8} + \frac{4}{8} + \frac{1}{2}$ 8. $\frac{9}{16} - \frac{1}{2}$

4. $\frac{7}{8} + 5\frac{1}{4}$ 9. $8\frac{1}{2} - 3\frac{3}{8}$

5. $\frac{1}{3} + \frac{5}{6} + \frac{1}{2}$ 10. $7\frac{2}{3} - 2\frac{1}{4}$

IV. Fractions. Multiply. (10 points)

1. $\frac{3}{4} \times 8$ 6. $19 \times 6\frac{3}{4}$

2. $\frac{2}{3} \times 9$ 7. $18 \times 6\frac{1}{2}$

3. $\frac{2}{3} \times 36$ 8. $25 \times \frac{3}{25}$

4. $64 \times \frac{5}{8}$ 9. $15 \times 3\frac{2}{3}$

5. $10 \times \frac{4}{5}$ 10. $21 \times 2\frac{3}{7}$

V. Decimals. Change to common fractions or mixed numbers. (10 points)

1. .5   3. 2.3   5. .8   7. .1   9. 6.7

2. .7   4. 1.5   6. .9   8. .2   10. 23.4

VI. A. What is the area of a rectangle that measures 4 feet in length and 5 feet in width? (5 points)
B. What is the perimeter of the same rectangle? (5 points)

VII. Divide and check. (10 points)

1. $2994 \div 32$ 4. $3888 \div 72$

2. $2870 \div 35$ 5. $4180 \div 54$

3. $3276 \div 63$

VIII. Measures. (10 points)

1. $\frac{1}{2}$ bu. = _____ pk.   6. $\frac{1}{3}$ min. = _____ sec.

2. $\frac{1}{8}$ lb. = _____ oz.   7. $\frac{1}{2}$ T. = _____ lb.

3. 16 pt. = _____ qt.   8. 36 = _____ doz.

4. 1000 lb. = _____ T.   9. $\frac{1}{2}$ da. = _____ hr.

5. 3 mo. = _____ yr.   10. 12 ft. = _____ in.

IX. Show the union or intersection of sets.

1. Set A = {Joe, Bill, Tom}
   Set B = {Harry, Dick, Tom}
   A ∩ B =

3. Set A = {2, 4, 6, 8}
   Set B = {1, 3, 5, 7}
   A ∪ B =

2. Set A = {Mary, Kate}
   Set B = {Lil, Nancy}
   A ∪ B =

4. Set A = {2, 4, 6, 8}
   Set B = {4, 8, 12}
   A ∩ B =

5. Set A = {red, green, blue}
   Set B = {blue, red}
   A ∪ B =

X. Problem. (10 points)

1. Ted is putting up 4 shelves for his mother. Each shelf is $16\frac{1}{2}$ inches long. Ted has a board 60 inches long. Can he make the four shelves out of that?

final test answers   fifth grade

reading

I.
1. Dr. Alexander Fleming discovered penicillin.
2. He lived in London, England.
3. A germ garden is very much smaller than a vegetable garden. It is the size of a flat dish.
4. Penicillin was discovered about thirty years ago.
5. A mold grew in one of the germ gardens.
6. Penicillin prevents germs from increasing, giving the white corpuscles in your blood a chance to kill the germs already present.
7. Check, as used in this story, means prevent.
8. The main idea of the story is to tell about the discovery and development of a useful drug.

II. 1. F, 2. T, 3. T, 4. F, 5. F, 6. T, 7. T, 8. F, 9. F, 10. F

III. 1, 3, 6, 5, 4, 2.

english

I.   A Terrarium
   I. Make the terrarium
      A. Use a fish bowl
      B. Sink pan of water in soil
      C. Arrange tall and short plants
   II. Select proper plants
      A. Not fast-growing
      B. Not tall
      C. Suited to warm, damp air
   III. Little care needed
      A. Cover bowl
      B. Provide fresh air daily

II.   The Shrew
   A shrew is a tiny animal. It is about as heavy as a teaspoon-ful of water. — size

   It has a long, pointed snout, beady little eyes, and short, rounded ears. It is covered with soft brown or gray fur. — appearance

   The shrew is a hungry animal. It hunts for food all the time, day and night. It likes to eat crickets, grasshoppers, and earth-worms. Because it eats so many of the harmful insects, it is one of the farmer's best friends. — eating habits

   Shrews are fierce little animals. They even kill each other. — temperament

III.
A.
Your name
   Your street
      Your town, state

       Miss Mary Smith
       24 Linden Avenue
       New City 17
       New York

B.
Your name
Your street
Your town, state

The J. M. Crane Company
534 Oak Street
Davenport 15
Iowa

IV.
1. boy's
2. boys'
3. children's
4. Lois's
5. class's
6. fox's
7. mouse's
8. country's
9. child's
10. deer's

V.
1. children
2. countries
3. men
4. wives
5. mice
6. deer
7. answers
8. parties
9. classes
10. oxen

VI.

new	adj.	seems	v.b.
girl	c.n.	huge	adj.
class	c.n.	black	adj.
made	v.a.	bird	c.n.
beautiful	adj.	flew	v.a.
blue	adj.	high	adj.
dress	c.n.	stone	adj.
answer	c.n.	wall	c.n.
subtraction	adj.	Grandma Moses	p.n.
problem	c.n.	is	v.b.

VII.
1. He says he doesn't want to buy the new bicycle horn until Wednesday.
2. She isn't having the party on May 3 because that day ∧ isn't her birthday.
3. The whistle seemed to say, "Who-who-who-who."
4. "Never again!" the teacher exclaimed.
5. Does Alaska have a star in our flag?

arithmetic test answers

I. Mixed numbers.
1. $11\frac{1}{2}$ 6. $3\frac{3}{7}$
2. $8\frac{5}{7}$ 7. $7\frac{1}{3}$
3. 11 8. $2\frac{1}{2}$
4. $17\frac{1}{8}$ 9. $1\frac{5}{7}$
5. 4 10. $5\frac{1}{2}$

II. Fractions.
1. $2\frac{1}{4}$ 6. $4\frac{3}{4}$
2. $3\frac{1}{5}$ 7. 3
3. 5 8. 6
4. 8 9. $5\frac{3}{4}$
5. $8\frac{1}{4}$ 10. $3\frac{1}{8}$

III. Fractions.
1. $\frac{2}{3}$ 6. $2\frac{1}{4}$
2. $3\frac{3}{4}$ 7. $2\frac{1}{2}$
3. $1\frac{3}{8}$ 8. $\frac{1}{16}$
4. $6\frac{1}{8}$ 9. $5\frac{1}{8}$
5. $1\frac{2}{3}$ 10. $5\frac{5}{12}$

IV. Fractions.
1. 6 6. $128\frac{1}{4}$
2. 6 7. 117
3. 24 8. 3
4. 40 9. 55
5. 8 10. 51

V. Decimals.
1. $\frac{1}{2}$ 6. $\frac{9}{10}$
2. $\frac{7}{10}$ 7. $\frac{1}{10}$
3. $2\frac{3}{10}$ 8. $\frac{1}{5}$
4. $1\frac{1}{2}$ 9. $6\frac{7}{10}$
5. $\frac{4}{5}$ 10. $23\frac{2}{5}$

VI.
A. 20 sq. ft.
B. 18 ft.

VII. Divide and check.
1. 93 R18
2. 82
3. 52
4. 54
5. 77 R22

VIII. Measures.
1. 2 pk. 6. 20 sec.
2. 2 oz. 7. 1000 lb.
3. 8 qt. 8. 3 doz.
4. $\frac{1}{2}$ T. 9. 12 hr.
5. $\frac{1}{4}$ yr. 10. 144 in.

IX. Sets.
1. $A \cap B$ = {Tom}
2. $A \cup B$ = {Mary, Kate, Lil, Nancy}
3. $A \cup B$ = {1, 2, 3, 4, 5, 6, 7, 8}
4. $A \cap B$ = {4, 8}
5. $A \cup B$ = {red, green, blue}

X. Problem.
1. No

contents | sixth grade

helping your child in sixth grade

YOUR CHILD is about eleven years old and starting adolescence. In school he is highly competitive and curious about everything. He may need your help in various subjects, but he is unlikely to accept it if he feels he is being "bossed" too much.

The following sections tell what your child will be learning in the sixth grade, and will aid you in giving him the help he may need.

reading | sixth grade

BY THIS TIME your child can recognize, understand, and use many words. He does a great deal of reference reading, comparing books by different authors to get contrasting views. He is making longer and better book reports—indicating that he is thinking more deeply.

Remedial reading is still given in school. If you feel your child could benefit by it, don't neglect it any longer. Talk it over with his teacher. She can help—and she can show you how you can help too.

Your child uses his reading ability for different purposes. He learns to skim materials for main ideas, to read materials to give summaries, to follow directions for hobbies and activities. He reads for fun, for adventure, to acquire knowledge. Reading brings him beauty and emotional experience. It helps him develop his own set of ideals.

help your child find good books

You can help your child by surrounding him at home with good reading matter, and this need not be limited to the textbook kind used in school. The reading you help him select should not only be interesting and popular, but have lasting qualities as well. His choice will be stories with plot, suspense, movement, and humor, and preferably written from a child's point of view. Stories of lasting value for your child will have morals. These morals need not be too pointed; they can simply be stories in which virtues such as honesty, loyalty, sincerity, courage, and faith are shown to be important.

Your sixth-grade child is a pretty good judge of character and actions. He is apt to develop a hero worship for adults about whom he reads. Books that have great appeal at this age are the stories of famous Americans like Thomas Edison or Benjamin Franklin, and stories of famous incidents in history such as the story of the pony express. Your child is beginning to wonder what it will be like to be grown up. He will identify himself in some way with many of the characters about whom he reads. He will appreciate the things they have done, and will set a few goals for himself.

unwillingness to read

You can't, of course, *force* your child to read. You can tell him how much fun he can get out of reading or how much he will learn—but even that may not impress him. He has to *want* to find these things out for himself; he has to experience the thrill of discovery.

One thing you can do is to give him as many first-hand experiences as possible—field trips, displays, projects, interviews. Indirect experiences are good too—some radio and TV programs, recordings, charts, models, etc. Once his curiosity is aroused, your child will want to know more and more—and will then be ready to try finding the answers in books. When he reaches the point of getting real enjoyment and profit from his reading, you will feel rewarded for any effort you have made to bring this about.

reading out loud

In this grade your child sometimes reads aloud. This is helpful to him because it is a check on comprehension, accuracy, and interpretation. He may read something to the rest of his class that he wants to share with them. This means he has to understand what he is reading, and speak pleasantly and clearly. It helps him to moderate his own voice and to read expressively in order to bring out the meaning for the rest of the class. Exercises like this also help him build up his speaking vocabulary. You can help him by encouraging him to read sometimes at home —and listening to him when he does.

His reading program at school includes practical, informal discussions. These are important; they give him a feeling of being an active part of a group and teach him how to contribute his share. They help him to sort out significant and important points from a welter of words, and in general give him confidence in himself as a member of society.

what your child learns from reading

By the end of the sixth year in school, with your help at home, your child will be able to:

▶ Show skill in using a table of contents.
▶ Use an encyclopedia.
▶ Extract important and unimportant information.
▶ Sift out fact from opinion.
▶ Use several sources of information to solve a problem.
▶ Take ideas gained in reading and use them in new situations.
▶ Follow directions.
▶ Take notes.
▶ Classify, outline, and summarize.

All the language arts are interrelated. If your child speaks well, he tends to become a good reader. A good reader usually acquires a large vocabulary which enables him to write well. But remember: don't compare your child with your neighbor's child; don't feel badly if he doesn't seem to show the same interest in reading. Let him develop at his own pace. Children vary greatly as to achievement, growth, interest, and needs, and as they get older this variation increases. *Your* aim is to help *your* child. You can have fun doing it; you can learn together.

reading aids

There are ways of helping your sixth-grade child improve his reading through playing games. You can buy board games and card games, but games you make yourself can be just as attractive and just as helpful. Part of the learning process is in the making of the game. Let your child help you. Here are some suggestions.

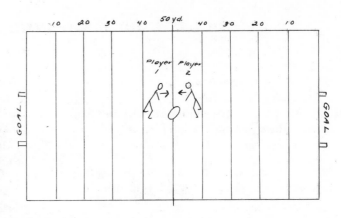

▶ Wordball (for two players)

On a large piece of paper draw a football field with sections to represent ten yards each. The game begins at the fifty-yard line, where a cardboard ball is placed. A set of cards with a word on each card is used. Make the cards from cardboard. Select words your child has stumbled over. Include some new words that you find in his library book.

The first player, chosen by tossing a coin, reads the word on the first card. If he reads the word correctly, he moves the ball ten yards toward the goal ahead of him. If he reads it incorrectly, it is considered a fumble and the ball goes ten yards back toward his own goal. Players take turns, drawing only one card at a time.

When a player crosses the opposite goal line, he gets a score of 6. If he reads the next word correctly, he adds one point to his score. Whenever a score is made, both players start again at the fifty-yard line.

There is no limit to the number of cards you may use. Before you begin, however, you should decide on a time limit and whether you want to play off a tie score, should there be one.

▶ Letter toss (for one or more players)

Prepare 59 pieces of cardboard, each about one inch square. On one side of each card print a letter of the alphabet. Because they appear in our language in different frequencies, print *e* on four of the pieces; print three squares each of *a, b, d, i, l, m, n, o, r, s,* and *t;* print two each of *c, f, g, h, p, u, w,* and *y;* make only one each of *j, k, q, v, x,* and *z.* You also need a covered container just large enough to hold the 59 squares loosely.

Put all the squares into the container. To determine who will be the first player, everyone draws a letter. Players take turns as their letters occur in the alphabet—*a* will be first, *b* next, etc. In case of a draw, both players draw again.

The first player returns all of the letters to the container and shakes them up well. Then he tosses them out on a table. Those that land with the letter side up are his to use to make words of four or more letters each. He is not allowed to use abbreviations or proper names. He may not use a word in more than one form (Ex. *sing, singing*). His score is determined by counting 1 point for each letter used in a completed and correctly spelled word. For words with 8 or more letters he gets an extra point. When he has made as many words as he can, all the letters are returned to the container and passed to the next player. A point limit should be agreed upon as a goal toward which to work; 100 is suggested. A time limit for each player should also be set at the start of the game.

word list

Use an inexpensive notebook in which your child can keep a list of new words and their definitions. They may be words learned in school, heard in conversations, heard on radio or television. Be sure your child becomes familiar with every word before it is added to the list. You will be surprised and pleased to see and hear the growth in your child's vocabulary, and in yours, too.

books your sixth-grade child may enjoy

Jo's Boys
Little Men
     Alcott, Louisa May
Peter Pan—*Barrie, James*
Stories of the Gods and Heroes—*Benson, Sally*
Summerfield Farm—*Black, Mary M.*
The Iliad of Homer—*Church, Alfred*
Boomer—*Clark, Denis*
Amigo, Circus Horse—*Cooper, Page*
All About Satellites and Space Ships
     Dietz, David
Mascots—*Downey, Fairfax D.*
The Three Musketeers—*Dumas, Alexandre*
Horses, Horses, Horses—*Fenner, Phyllis R.*
Tuffy—*Franklin, George C.*
Justin Morgan Had a Horse—*Henry, Marguerite*
Kon-Tiki—*Heyerdahl, Thor*
Outlaw Red—*Kjelgaard, Jim*
The Wonderful Adventures of Nils
     Lagerlöf, Selma

Arabian Nights—*Lang, Andrew*
Burma Boy—*Lindquist, Willis*
Blue Palomino—*Meigs, Elizabeth B.*
Amahl and the Night Visitors
     Menotti, Gian-Carlo
Amikuk—*Montgomery, Rutherford G.*
Little Lame Prince—*Mulock, D. M.*
Old Bones, the Wonder Horse—*Pace, Mildred M.*
The King of the Golden River—*Ruskin, John*
Abe Lincoln Grows Up—*Sandburg, Carl*
Call It Courage—*Sperry, Armstrong*
Kidnapped
Treasure Island
     Stevenson, Robert Louis
Gulliver's Travels—*Swift, Jonathan*
Adventures of Tom Sawyer—*Twain, Mark*
Remember the Alamo—*Warren, Robert Penn*
Prehistoric America—*White, Anne Terry*
Charlotte's Web—*White, E. B.*
The Swiss Family Robinson—*Wyss, Johann D.*

AT THIS AGE writing is a tool your child uses almost every day. Don't let him neglect it or get careless. Praise him when he writes clearly and neatly. He will be able to pick out his own badly formed letters.

It is possible that he needs to practice *d* and *cl*, also *h* and *k*, then *m*, *n*, *i*, *u*, and *v* in a group so they can easily be read. The next group he should practice is *i*, *j*, *t*, *e*, *l*. Small *o* is apt to be carelessly made. The final stroke on *o* does *not* come down to the line, and he shouldn't forget to close the *a* and *g* and *o*.

If necessary, refer back to the samples in the third-grade book.

ENGLISH

Let's start out with *you* in this section. Your child learns by imitation, so why not check your own speech habits once in a while? Are you a good conversationalist? Do you speak at the same time someone else is speaking? Are you a good listener? Is your voice pleasant to listen to? Can you tell a story well?

In telling a story your child learns to state the situation first—the who, when, and where of his story. Then he tells the part that creates suspense. Then he ends it with the solution, or climax. He tries to make his points interesting, tell them in their proper order, make himself heard without shouting, and avoid the *and-uh* habit.

While you are helping your child, you will be improving your own conversation and storytelling techniques. Do you speak clearly? Your child can check you on that. Maybe you are not aware that you sometimes mumble words or drop letters from words, or that you pronounce some words incorrectly.

say:	not:
which	wich
slept	slep
just	jist
catch	ketch
figure	figger
take them	takem
want to	wanta

punctuation

Rules for quotation marks, as well as uses of capital letters and punctuation marks, are reviewed this year. Remember, quotation marks are used to set off from the rest of the sentence the actual words spoken.

EXAMPLE:

Aunt Mary said, "I'll come tomorrow."

sentence structure

So that he can make himself understood more easily, your child learns how a sentence is constructed.

He has already learned that a sentence is a group of words that gives a complete thought. It says something one can understand. Now he learns that every sentence must have a subject and predicate. The *complete subject* tells about what or whom the sentence is written. The *complete predicate* tells something about the subject.

EXAMPLES:

_____ subject; _____ predicate

1. Henry's father told a funny story.

2. The fish couldn't see the orange tie.

The most important word in the complete subject is called the *simple subject*. The most important word in the predicate is the *verb* or *verb phrase,* which is the word (or words) that shows action or state of being.

EXAMPLES:

_____simple subject;

_____predicate (verb)

1. My father gave my sister a puppy.

2. The puppy was named Sparky.

When there is more than one simple subject in a sentence, we call it a *compound* subject.

EXAMPLE:

Dogs and cats do not talk.

When there is more than one verb it is called a *compound* predicate.

EXAMPLES:

Sparky talked and whistled.
The dog and bird both add and subtract.

the four kinds of sentences

▶ A *declarative* sentence makes a statement. It is followed by a period.

EXAMPLE:

Poochie is a dog.

▶ An *interrogative* sentence asks something. It is a question. It is followed by a question mark.

EXAMPLE:

Do you have a dog?

To find the subject of an interrogative sentence, simply turn it into a declarative sentence.

EXAMPLE:

You do have a dog.

▶ An *exclamatory* sentence shows surprise or excitement. It is followed by an exclamation point.

EXAMPLE:

What a wonderful idea!

Sometimes an exclamatory sentence has to be changed to a simple declarative form before it is clear what the subject and predicate are.

EXAMPLE:

A. Exclamatory:

How Winky and Blinky hate each other!

B. Declarative form of the same sentence:

Winky and Blinky hate each other, how.

▶ An *imperative* sentence gives a command. It is followed by either a period or an exclamation point.

EXAMPLE:

Tell me what happened!

In an imperative sentence the word *you* is always understood to be the subject.

EXAMPLE:

(You) tell me what happened!

synonyms, antonyms, and homonyms

These names aren't as difficult as they sound. Your child has known the meaning, if not the formal words, since the earlier grades.

Synonyms are words that mean almost the same thing.

EXAMPLES:

The synonym for cry is scream, for woman is lady, for gift is present.

Read the following two paragraphs. In the first one the dull, overworked words are underlined. In the second paragraph more interesting synonyms have been substituted. Which paragraph do you like better?

1. All at once there was a loud cry in the attic. We knew that my little brother and his buddies were hunting for things up there. We ran upstairs in a hurry and found that one of the kids had gotten inside a trunk. The top had come down, and there he was inside. Father pulled him out, and he was okay but scared. That was the last of hunting for things in our attic.

2. Suddenly there was a shrill scream in the attic. We knew that my little brother and his friends were searching for treasure up there. We dashed wildly upstairs and discovered that one of the boys had crawled inside a trunk. The lid had banged shut, and there he was inside. Father dragged him out, and he was all right but frightened. That was the end of searching for treasure in our attic.

Antonyms are word opposites.

EXAMPLES:

The antonym for dull is bright, for cheap is expensive, for black is white.

Homonyms are words that sound alike but have different meanings and are usually spelled in different ways.

EXAMPLES:

The homonym for eye is I, for knight is night, for one is won.

building vocabulary

Although the proper use of words is stressed in all grades, you will be surprised at how many words your child will add to his vocabulary this year. You might find it helpful at this time to refer back to the rules your child learned in the fourth and fifth grades.

Keep a dictionary always handy. You can take advantage of dull moments by playing word games. Open the dictionary at random and choose any word. Encourage your child to read it, study it, use it, learn how to spell it, see what part of speech it is, pronounce it correctly, and remember it.

Your child improves his art of communication this year by continuing to write personal and business letters in the correct form. He is encouraged to use his new words in the letters and stories and reports he writes through the year.

There is no more important use of word-of-mouth communication than in conducting a meeting. Your child's class will probably organize a classroom club, establish a purpose, elect officers, and hold regular meetings. The real aim will be, of course, to teach rules of parliamentary procedure, to make and keep reports (secretary, treasurer, and committee heads), and to share in discussions and decisions.

parts of speech

Some schools offer a great deal of work this year on parts of speech: verbs, nouns, pronouns, adjectives, adverbs, prepositions, conjunctions, interjections. The more he understands about words, the jobs they do, and meanings, the more easily he will use words and remember them. Other schools only mention parts of speech in this grade and work thoroughly on them in the seventh grade.

verbs

Your child has learned that verbs are words that show action or state-of-being.

Verbs of action transfer the action to an object. They are called *transitive* verbs.

EXAMPLE:

I ate an apple.

State-of-being verbs are: am, is, are, was, were, shall be, could be, has been, had been. They are called *intransitive* verbs. They do not take an object. Instead they refer the words that follow back to the subject.

EXAMPLE:

The apple was sour.

All verbs have one form when they show present time, another form when they show the simple past time, a third form when they show past time but are used with a *helper*. Helpers are: was, were, have, has, had.

EXAMPLES:

present

give	write	eat	see
go	come	run	do
break	speak	am	

simple past

gave	wrote	ate	saw
went	came	ran	did
broke	spoke	was	

past with a helper (have)

given	written	eaten	seen
gone	come	run	done
broken	spoken	been	

Verbs have different forms according to whether they are singular or plural.

EXAMPLES:

1. Alice writes well.   (singular)
2. Those girls write well.   (plural)

A dictionary gives all forms of verbs.

nouns

Your child studies the noun, a word that names a person, place or thing.

334

EXAMPLE:

The nouns in the following paragraph are underlined.

Last <u>Tuesday</u> this <u>school</u> had a fine <u>assembly</u> <u>program</u>. <u>Dr. T. W. Andrew</u> talked about his <u>trip</u> through the <u>Black Hills</u>. He showed us <u>pictures</u> of the <u>faces</u> of the <u>men</u> which <u>Borglum</u>, the <u>sculptor</u>, has blasted out of the <u>mountain</u>.

The name of a *particular* person, place, or thing is called a *proper noun*. It begins with a capital letter.

EXAMPLES:

Tuesday, Dr. T. W. Andrew, Black Hills and *Borglum* in the above paragraph.

The name of *any* person, place, or thing is called a *common noun*.

EXAMPLES:

mountain, men

A noun in the predicate that refers to the same person or thing as the subject is called a predicate noun. It is linked with the subject by a verb-of-being such as: am, is, are, was, were, shall be, will be, has been, have been, had been, could be.

EXAMPLES:

1. The <u>show</u> was a double <u>feature</u>.
2. The <u>movie</u> is a <u>comedy</u>.
3. <u>Charlie</u> will be a <u>hero</u>.

The noun that names the receiver of the action of the verb is an object noun or *direct object*.

EXAMPLES:

1. David carried the <u>ball</u>.
2. Arthur kicked the <u>pigskin</u>.
3. The boys chose a <u>captain</u>.

Important rules to remember in making plural nouns:

▶ **Most nouns are made plural by adding s.**

EXAMPLE:

boy	boys

▶ **Nouns ending in *sh, ch, s,* or *x* are made plural by adding *es*.**

EXAMPLES:

bush	bushes
church	churches
dress	dresses
box	boxes

▶ **With nouns ending in a *y* that has a consonant just before it, change the *y* to *i* and add *es*.**

EXAMPLES:

city	cities
lady	ladies

▶ **When a vowel comes before the final *y*, the plural is made by just adding *s*.**

EXAMPLE:

monkey	monkeys

▶ **Some nouns ending in *f* or *fe* are made plural by changing the *f* or *fe* to *ves*. Here are thirteen common ones:**

loaf	loaves
life	lives
thief	thieves
shelf	shelves
half	halves
wolf	wolves
sheaf	sheaves
wife	wives
leaf	leaves
elf	elves
calf	calves
self	selves
knife	knives

► Other nouns ending in *f* are made plural in the regular way—by adding *s*.

EXAMPLE:

roof   roofs

► A few nouns follow no rule in forming the plural.

EXAMPLES:

man	men
child	children
goose	geese
tooth	teeth
mouse	mice

► A few nouns are the same in both singular and plural.

EXAMPLES:

deer,   sheep,   trout

Rules to remember regarding nouns when they show ownership:

► Singular nouns show possession by adding an apostrophe (') and *s*.

EXAMPLES:

James's   girl's   boy's

► Plural nouns that end in *s* show possession by adding just the apostrophe.

EXAMPLES:

pupils'   girls'   boys'

► Plural nouns that do not end in *s* are made to show possession by adding an apostrophe and *s*.

EXAMPLES:

women's   children's

pronouns

A word that takes the place of a noun is called a pronoun. The pronouns we use most often are:

I, me, my, mine

you, your, yours

he, him, his

she, her, hers

it, its

we, us, our, ours

they, them, their, theirs

Because pronouns can take the place of nouns, they can be used as subjects, or predicate pronouns, or objects, just as nouns are. They can also show singular or plural or possession, as nouns do. They do this by changing their forms.

EXAMPLES:

	singular	plural
subject	he	they
predicate pronoun	he	they
object	him	them
possessive	his	their, theirs

adjectives and adverbs

A word that modifies or describes a noun or pronoun is an adjective.

EXAMPLES:

1. There on his rug lay a <u>tiny</u> <u>black</u> and <u>white</u> kitten.
2. Do you like <u>that</u> book?
3. <u>The</u> cat had <u>five</u> kittens.

Some adjectives *describe*, others tell *how many*, some *point out*, and some are articles like *a, an, the*. They are all called adjectives.

Sometimes the adjective is in the predicate, but modifies the noun or pronoun in the subject. Then it is called a predicate adjective.

EXAMPLE:

The story is exciting.

When an adjective comes from a proper noun, it is called a *proper adjective* and it starts with a capital letter.

EXAMPLE:

I read about Dutch boys and girls as well as about Chinese children.

Adverbs modify verbs, adjectives, and other adverbs. They answer the questions How? When? Where? and How much?

EXAMPLES:

1. **The girl behaved badly. (how)**
2. **She ran home immediately. (when)**
3. **She put the book there. (where)**
4. **She was too young to know. (how much)**

Adjectives and adverbs have three degrees of *comparison*. The simplest form is the *positive* degree. When two persons or things are *compared*, we use the *comparative* degree. When *more* than two persons or things are compared, the *superlative* degree is used.

EXAMPLE using the adjective lonely:

POSITIVE FORM: **The boy was lonely.**

COMPARATIVE DEGREE: **He was lonelier than Mary.**

SUPERLATIVE DEGREE: **He was the loneliest child in school.**

EXAMPLE using the adverb fast:

POSITIVE FORM: **Mary ran fast.**

COMPARATIVE DEGREE: **Steve ran faster than Mary.**

SUPERLATIVE DEGREE: **Dick could run fastest of all.**

Your child can think of other examples—and there are more included in the ENGLISH EXERCISES in the workbook section.

Most adjectives and adverbs of one syllable and some of two syllables are compared by adding *er* or *est* to the positive degree. Some adjectives and adverbs of two syllables and all adjectives and adverbs of three or more syllables are compared by adding either *more* or *less* to make the comparative degree, and either *most* or *least* to make the superlative degree.

EXAMPLES of the comparison of adjectives:

POSITIVE	COMPARATIVE	SUPERLATIVE
old	older	oldest
happy	happier	happiest
pleasant	more pleasant	most pleasant
difficult	less difficult	least difficult
good	better	best
bad	worse	worst
many	more	most
little	less	least

EXAMPLES of the comparison of adverbs:

POSITIVE	COMPARATIVE	SUPERLATIVE
early	earlier	earliest
cheerfully	more cheerfully	most cheerfully
carefully	less carefully	least carefully
well	better	best
much	more	most
little	less	least

tricky adjectives and adverbs

Some adverbs and adjectives are tricky. Be careful to use these correctly.

Sure is an adjective when it modifies a noun or pronoun. *Surely* is always an adverb.

EXAMPLES:

A <u>sure</u> sign of spring is the robin. (adjective)

A dime is <u>surely</u> not too much to pay. (adverb)

Good is an adjective used to describe a person, place, or thing. *Well* is an adverb when it tells how something is done.

EXAMPLES:

Mary gets <u>good</u> marks in school. (adjective)

She reads very <u>well</u>. (adverb)

prepositions

A *preposition* is a word that shows the relation between a noun or pronoun and some other word in the sentence. The word preposition is made of two parts: *pre,* meaning "before," and *position,* meaning "place." It is a linking word. It helps to tie the parts of a sentence together.

Some of the words most often used as prepositions are:

about	behind	from	through
above	beside	in	to
across	between	into	toward
against	by	of	under
among	except	on	upon
at	for	over	with

EXAMPLES of prepositions in sentences:

1. The children looked <u>to</u> her <u>for</u> help.
2. He walked <u>into</u> the store <u>on</u> Adam Street.

The noun or pronoun that comes after the preposition is called the *object of the preposition*. The preposition plus the noun or pronoun following it are called the *prepositional phrase*. Prepositional phrases are used as either adjectives or adverbs.

EXAMPLES:

1. This is a land <u>of winter sunshine</u>. (adjective)
2. Visitors walk <u>in the park</u>. (adverb)

Help your child use prepositions correctly:

▶ *Into* shows motion from the outside to the inside.

▶ *In* shows that something is already inside.

EXAMPLES:

We climbed <u>into</u> the bus.

The driver was already <u>in</u> his seat.

▶ *To* usually shows motion toward a person, place, or thing.

▶ *At* usually shows that something is already in place.

▶ *Between* is used in speaking of two persons, places, or things.

▶ *Among* is used in speaking of more than two.

EXAMPLES:

Washington was a great favorite <u>among</u> his men.

Once he came <u>between</u> two soldiers who were fighting.

Let your child read the following sentences to try to discover some mistakes. The corrected sentences are given just below.

1. We stopped by the museum for a while.
2. We bought a ticket off the man.
3. These weapons are different than those.
4. Please don't pick anything off of the table.
5. Where is Washington's coach at?

Corrected sentences:

1. We stopped at the museum for a while.
2. We bought a ticket from the man.
3. These weapons are different from those.
4. Please don't pick anything off the table.
5. Where is Washington's coach?

conjunctions

A word that is used to link words, phrases, or sentences is called a conjunction.

Some of the common ones are: and, but, or. They link parts of equal value such as two nouns, two verbs, two adjectives, two adverbs, two phrases, or two sentences, and so are called *co-ordinate conjunctions*.

EXAMPLES:

> We must choose the good things,
> <u>or</u> we may fail at everything.
> Men <u>and</u> women belong to the club.

Other conjunctions often used are: when, where, while, although, because, until, after, for, as, if, unless. They are used in linking short, choppy sentences.

interjections

An exclamatory word that is thrown into a sentence, but is not really a part of it, is called an interjection. It usually shows a strong feeling and is followed by an exclamation point. If it shows mild feeling, it is followed by a comma.

EXAMPLES:

> <u>Goodness</u>, I'm glad to see you.
> <u>Ouch!</u> Stop that.

Some common interjections are:

oh	alas	well
O	hush	there
goodness	ouch	indeed
hurrah	pooh	look

review of abbreviations

Your child continues his study of abbreviations. He will review those he already knows and add new ones. He should know the following:

Dr.	Doctor
Ave.	Avenue
Capt.	Captain
Supt.	Superintendent
Mrs.	Mistress
Gen.	General
Mr.	Mister
Maj.	Major
B.C.	Before Christ

A.D.	Anno Domini
P.S.	postscript
C.O.D.	cash on delivery
P.M.	post meridian, after noon
A.M.	ante meridian, before noon
R.F.D.	rural free delivery

punctuation review

Your child reviews punctuation rules and continues their study.

A *period* is used:
► At the end of a declarative sentence.
► After an initial.
► After an abbreviation.
► In outlining after the Roman numerals and capital letters used as subheads.

A *question mark* is used at the end of a question.

An *exclamation point* is used:
► After an interjection that shows strong feeling.
► After an exclamatory sentence.

Quotation marks are used:
► Around the exact words of a speaker.
► Around the titles of short stories, booklets, poems, and songs.

A *comma* is used:
► After a mild interjection.
► After a person's last name when it is written before his first name.
► After the closing of a letter.
► After the greeting of a friendly letter.
► Between the name of a town or city and the name of the state.
► Between the day of the month and the year.
► In linking two sentences with a conjunction.
► In a series.
► To separate a direct quotation from the rest of the sentence.
► To set off the name of the person addressed.

▶ To set off words like *too*, *however*, *more-over*.

▶ To set off words like *yes* and *no* when they come at the beginning of a sentence.

An *apostrophe* is used:
▶ In a contraction.
▶ To show possession.

A *colon* is used:
▶ After the greeting of a business letter.
▶ In writing time, to separate hours from minutes.
▶ To introduce a list.

A *hyphen* is used to separate words used in combination, such as *forget-me-not*.

Your child adds many words to his writing vocabulary this year, as well as to his reading and speaking vocabularies. Every week he will surprise you with new words casually used.

He continues to have at least twenty new words a week. He learns to spell them in much the same manner he learned in the lower grades. He must know the meaning of a word and be able to use it before he can be expected to remember it and spell it.

studying words

Your child has words with more than one meaning, and uses his dictionary to clear up his questions.

EXAMPLES:

CURRENT
1. flow of electricity
   or
2. belonging to the present time

BOIL
1. to be excited with anger
   or

2. to make very hot

He learns that the accent mark over a syllable of a word in the dictionary shows which syllable is pronounced with the most force. It is an important part of the pronunciation of the word.

EXAMPLE:

re cord′ (verb) to set down in writing or some permanent form; to record some fact.

rec′ ord (noun) an account in writing or some permanent form—phonograph record.

rec′ ord (adjective) notable in degree of accomplishment —a record year for sales.

Your child studies root words and other words made from those root words. He reviews those he has learned before.

EXAMPLE:

Light is a root word. Other words made from it are: lights, lighting, lighted, lighter.

A compound word is a word made of two smaller words.

EXAMPLES:

whatever, cupboard, sidewalk, pocketbook, policeman.

Sometimes a compound word is written as two words: post office.

spelling rules

The sound of <u>ee</u> can be spelled several ways, but the two that cause confusion are <u>ie</u> and <u>ei</u>. The more general spelling is <u>ie</u> (p<u>ie</u>ce, hyg<u>ie</u>ne, n<u>ie</u>ce, ch<u>ie</u>f, bel<u>ie</u>ve). The <u>ei</u> spelling occurs (1) after a <u>c</u> (c<u>ei</u>ling, rec<u>ei</u>ve, conc<u>ei</u>t), (2) when sounded like <u>a</u> (n<u>ei</u>ghbor, sl<u>ei</u>gh), and (3) in a few special cases (either, neither, foreign, leisure). There is an old jingle that holds good to a certain extent—but only to a certain extent:

> I before e,
> Except after c,
> Or when sounded like a
> As in neighbor or weigh.

Your child learns how to add suffixes to base words. Most common suffixes are ed, s, es, ing, ly, ion, er, ment, and y. They can be added to many words without changing the base.

EXAMPLES:

add	added
car	cars

When one adds a suffix beginning with a vowel to a word that ends in a single consonant preceded by a single vowel, one doubles the final consonant before adding the suffix.

EXAMPLES:

set	setting
big	bigger
forgot	forgotten
rob	robbed

When a root word ends in a consonant and y, the y has to be changed to i before adding the suffix.

EXAMPLES:

lady	ladies
fry	fried
carry	carries
dairy	dairies

If the word ends in a vowel and y, then just add the suffix.

EXAMPLES:

boy	boys
play	playing

Your child discovers that in a word like *carry,* the y must be changed to i before adding es. However, when the suffix begins with i, like ing, it can just be added without making changes.

EXAMPLES:

carry	carrying
fry	frying
marry	marrying
fly	flying
copy	copying
empty	emptying

A root word is also changed when the final e is *dropped* before adding a suffix that begins with a vowel. The final e is *kept* before adding a suffix that begins with a consonant.

EXAMPLES:

amuse	amusement
arrange	arranged
bathe	bathing
prepare	preparing
file	filing
use	using
	useful
shine	shined

There are always exceptions. For example, the root word in *peaceable* and *changeable* is not changed because the final e affects the pronunciation of the word. Use a dictionary when in doubt about the spelling of a word.

Your child practices writing contractions, using an apostrophe to show where a letter or letters are omitted.

EXAMPLES:

I am	I'm
have not	haven't
is not	isn't
will not	won't

Continued work with antonyms, homonyms, and synonyms makes him familiar with many new words. (*See* the sixth grade ENGLISH section.) The language arts are so closely related that when topics such as synonyms are taught in English, they are carried over at the same time into reading and spelling.

arithmetic | sixth grade

YOUR CHILD learns many new arithmetic concepts this year and continues to add new words to his arithmetic vocabulary. Be sure he has a sound knowledge of the concepts he has learned in earlier grades so that he will have the confidence he needs to tackle the more difficult problems ahead of him.

He gets a taste of business arithmetic this year: per cents, banking, accounts, bill forms, receipts, etc. Children of this age are ready and eager to learn these things, although of course such information needs to be closely tied to their own experiences and level of understanding.

numbers and numerals

Your child is encouraged to do as much of his work mentally as possible. It is helpful when he estimates answers to be able to "round-out" numbers.

EXAMPLES:

a)   41 is thought of as 40 (rounded to the nearest ten)

53 is thought of as 50 (rounded to the nearest ten)

740 is thought of as 700 (rounded to the nearest hundred)

Rules: When the digit in ones place is 1, 2, 3, or 4 show it as 0.
When the digit in tens place is 1, 2, 3, or 4 show it as 0.

b)   86 is thought of as 90 (rounded to nearest ten)

98 is thought of as 100 (rounded to nearest ten)

170 is thought of as 200 (rounded to nearest hundred)

Rules: When the digit in ones place is 1, 6, 7, 8, or 9, show it as 0 and increase the digit in tens place by 1. When the digit in tens place is 5, 6, 7, 8, or 9, show it as 0 and increase the digit in hundreds place by 1.

Our common number system is based on 10 because man first began counting on his 10 fingers. There are 10 digits in the base ten system: 0, 1, 2, 3, 4, 5, 6, 7, 8, 9. Any other number can also be used as a base for a number system. Computers use a system based on 2— a "yes–no" system. There are also systems based on 12, since there are 12 in a dozen and 12 inches in a foot. Knowledge of other systems helps your child to understand better the structure of the common base ten system.

To count in systems with bases other than 10, use the same method as used in the base ten system.

When the number 5 is used as the base, it is called the base five system. It has 5 symbols: 0, 1, 2, 3, 4. Any number written in the base five system must have a small "five" placed on the lower right side of the numeral.

EXAMPLE: 31_{five}. A number written without a small word number to the right is considered to be a base ten numeral. Numbers written in base systems other than the base ten system are read by digits. The number in this example is read "three, one, base five."

In the base ten system we keep track of how many sets of one, how many sets of 10, how many sets of 100, etc. In base five we state how many sets of one, how many sets of 5, how many sets of 25, etc. because each place has a value 5 times as great as the place to the right of it.

Place-value grid for base five:

125	25	5	1
5^3	5^2	5^1	1

Examples of base five numbers:

41_{five} means 4 fives + 1 one

324_{five} means 3 twenty-fives + 2 fives + 4 ones

Your child can keep base five place value straight by thinking of the ones place as pennies, the 5s place as nickels (worth 5 pennies), the 25s place as quarters (worth 5 nickels).

Use the place value grid above to count in the base five system: Remember, you have only five digits to use.

0_{five}

1_{five}

2_{five}

3_{five}

4_{five}

10_{five} (1 in the 5s place and no ones)

11_{five} (1 in the 5s place and 1 one)

12_{five} (1 in the 5s place and 2 ones)

13_{five} (1 in the 5s place and 3 ones)

14_{five} (1 in the 5s place and 4 ones)

20_{five} (2 in the 5s place and no ones)

30_{five} (3 in the 5s place and no ones)

100_{five} (1 in the 25s place and no 5s and no ones)

It is easy to change base five numbers to base ten numbers.

EXAMPLES:

23_{five} is $(2 \times 5) + 3$, or $10 + 3$, or 13 in base ten.

312_{five} is $(3 \times 25) + (1 \times 5) + 2$, or $75 + 5 + 2$, or 82 in base ten

Make place-value grids for other number base systems.

EXAMPLES:

1. Base three system has 3 digits: 0, 1, 2. Place value grid for base three:

27	9	3	1
3^3	3^2	3^1	1

Each place in the base three system has the value 3 times as great as the place to the right of it.

34_{three} means 3 three and 4 ones

343_{three} means 3 nines and 4 threes and 3 ones

1251_{three} means 1 twenty-seven, 2 nines, 5 threes, and 1 one

Counting in base three: 0_{three}, 1_{three}, 2_{three}, 10_{three}, 11_{three}, 12_{three}, 20_{three}, etc.

2. Base seven system has 7 digits: 0, 1, 2, 3, 4, 5, 6. Place value grid for base seven:

343	49	7	1
7^3	7^2	7^1	1

Each place in the base seven system has the value 7 times as great as the place to the right of it. (Do you see where 343 came from? (Answer: 7×49.)

34_{seven} means 3 sevens and 4 ones

643_{seven} means 6 forty-nines, 4 sevens, 3 ones

1251_{seven} means 1 three hundred forty-three, 2 forty-nines, 5 sevens, 1 one

Counting in base seven: 0_{seven}, 1_{seven}, 2_{seven}, 3_{seven}, 4_{seven}, 5_{seven}, 6_{seven}, 10_{seven}, 11_{seven}, 12_{seven}, 13_{seven}, 14_{seven}, 15_{seven}, 16_{seven}, 20_{seven}, etc.

3. Base two system has 2 digits: 0, 1. Place-value grid for base two:

8	4	2	1
2^3	2^2	2^1	1

Each place in the base two system has the value 2 times as great as the place to the right of it.

11_{two} means 1 two and 1 one

101_{two} means 1 four and 0 twos and 1 one

1111_{two} means 1 eight, 1 four, 1 two and 1 one

Counting in base two: 0_{two}, 1_{two}, 10_{two}, 11_{two}, 100_{two}, 101_{two}, 110_{two}, 111_{two}, etc.

sets and subsets

Your child continues to work with the concepts of union and intersection of sets. He uses a symbol, $\emptyset$, to signify an empty set, or he may use brackets enclosing nothing, { }.

Set A = the set of elephants on the moon = $\emptyset$ or { }.

He uses a symbol, $\subset$, to designate "subset of."

EXAMPLE:

Set A = all the children in the class
Set B = all the boys in the class
Set B is a subset of A: B $\subset$ A

EXAMPLES:

▶ Union:
1) Set A = {1, 2, 3}
   Set B = {3, 4, 5}
   A $\cup$ B = {1, 2, 3, 4, 5}

2) Set C = {1, 2, 3}
   Set D = {4, 5, 6}
   C $\cup$ D = {1, 2, 3, 4, 5, 6}

3) Set E = {1, 2, 3, 4}
   Set F = {1, 2}
   E $\cup$ F = {1, 2, 3, 4}

▶ Intersection:
Set A = boys in the sixth grade.
Set B = boys in the school chorus.
A $\cap$ B = sixth-grade boys in the school chorus.

▶ Subset:
Set A = all sixth-grade boys.
Set B = sixth-grade boys in the school chorus.
B $\subset$ A = sixth-grade boys in the school chorus.

Your child uses diagrams, called Venn diagrams after an English mathematician, to show the relationship between sets.

(They intersect, but the shading shows union)

(They are disjoint, but the shading shows union)

(F $\subset$ E but the shading shows union)

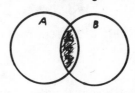

345

► **Equal Sets:** sets whose elements are identical, regardless of their order. Equal sets are also equivalent but the reverse is not true.

Set F = {a, f, h}
Set G = {h, f, a}
Set F = Set G

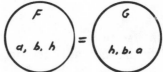

► **Equivalent sets:** sets which have the same number of elements, but whose members are not necessarily identical. Such sets are not equal. The sign for not equal is ≠. The sign for equivalent is ~

Set H = 2, 3, 4
Set J = 7, 8, 9
  H ≠ J
  H ~ J

addition, subtraction, multiplication, division

Your child continues to improve his ability in the four basic operations of arithmetic.

Whenever it is possible, he is encouraged to use number sentences. It is a visual way of expressing his thoughts in logical order. Remind him that work in parentheses must be done first. When three or four operations are called for, do the multiplication first, then the division, then the addition, and finally the subtraction. There are times when it is correct to work from left to right (see Grade 5).

Devise a scheme to help your child remember the correct order of these operations. For example: Use the first letter of each word: P (parentheses), M (multiplication), D (division), A (addition), S (subtraction). Put them together and they spell PMDAS. It is a ridiculous combination but not hard to remember. The trick of association with something familiar can be used. Maybe your child has classmates who are named Patsy, Mary, Dora, Annie, and Susie.

Not following the proper order of operations can lead to trouble.

EXAMPLE:

$$3 + 8 \times 2 - 9 \div 3 = n$$

Ignore the rule of order of operations and work from left to right.

Step one: $(3 + 8) \times 2 - 9 \div 3 = n$
Step two: $(11 \times 2) - 9 \div 3 = n$
Step three: $(22 - 9) \div 3 = n$
Step four: $(13 \div 3) = n$

$4\frac{1}{3} = n$ This is the wrong answer.

Now follow the correct order of operations. PMDAS

Step one: $3 + (8 \times 2) - 9 \div 3 = n$
Step two: $3 + 16 - (9 \div 3) = n$
Step three: $(3 + 16) - 3 = n$
Step four: $(19 - 3) = n$

$16 = n$ This is the correct answer.

SIXTH GRADE

fractions

Your child shows both common and decimal fractions on number lines. This helps him to compare one kind of fraction to the other.

EXAMPLES:

1. Common fractions
   Decimal fractions

2. Common fractions
   Decimal fractions

3. Common fractions
   Decimal fractions

Your child uses common fractions to express ratios. A **ratio** is a relation between two numbers. If in the group of 7 children there are 2 girls and 3 boys, the ratio of girls to boys is 2 to 5 and expressed as $\frac{2}{5}$.

EXAMPLES:

The baseball team won 8 games out of 12 games played. They won $\frac{8}{12}$ of their games. The fraction should be expressed in as small terms as possible. Because both the numerator 8 and the denominator 12 can be divided by the same number (4), it can be expressed as $\frac{2}{3}$ $\frac{8 \div 4 = 2}{12 \div 4 = 3}$.

The same team lost 4 games. The ratio of games won (8) to games lost (4) is $\frac{8}{4}$ or 2 (see Improper Fractions in Grade 5).

Your child continues his work in multiplying common fractions. It is often simpler to express whole or mixed numbers as improper fractions before multiplying.

EXAMPLES:

a) $2\frac{1}{2} \times 3\frac{2}{3} = \frac{5}{2} \times \frac{11}{3} = \frac{55}{6} = 9\frac{1}{6}$

b) $\frac{4}{5} \times 20 =$

$\frac{4}{5} \times \frac{20}{1} = \frac{80}{5} = 16$

Up to now your child has been multiplying the numerators and then multiplying the denominators, with the result that his answers are fractional numbers with large numerators and denominators which have to be reduced.

EXAMPLE: $\frac{3}{5} \times \frac{5}{7} = \frac{15}{35}$ or $\frac{3}{7}$

It is possible to reduce the fractions that are used as factors *before* multiplying by applying the commutative property of multiplication to the factors in either the numerator or the denominator (see Grade 4).

347

EXAMPLES:

a) $$\frac{3}{5} \times \frac{5}{7} = n$$ (Let n stand for the answer we are seeking to find)

Step one: $$\frac{3 \times 5}{5 \times 7} = n$$ (Show as one fraction)

Step two: $$\frac{3 \times 5}{7 \times 5} = n$$ (Commute the factors in the denominator)

Step three: $$\frac{3}{7} = n$$ (Since $\frac{5}{5} = 1$ and does not change values in multiplication, it can be eliminated)

b) $$\frac{13}{51} \times \frac{17}{13} = n$$ (The problem is to find n)

Step one: $$\frac{13 \times 17}{51 \times 13} = n$$ (Show as one fraction)

Step two: $$\frac{13 \times 17}{13 \times 51} = n$$ (Commute the factors in the denominator)

Step three: $$\frac{17}{51} = n$$ (Eliminate $\frac{13}{13}$ because it equals 1)

Step four: $$\frac{1}{3} = n$$ (Reduce answer to lowest terms)

Your child learns to divide by common fractions this year. The procedure for dividing fractions is the same as for dividing whole numbers, providing the denominators are alike.

EXAMPLES:

a) Problem: $$\frac{15}{16} \div \frac{3}{16} = n$$

Step one: $$\frac{15 \div 3}{16 \div 16} = n$$ (Make one fraction)

Step two: $$\frac{5}{1} = n$$

Step three: $$5 = n$$ (Dividing by 1 leaves the number unchanged)

b) Problem: $$1\frac{2}{3} \div \frac{2}{3} = n$$

Step one: $$\frac{5}{3} \div \frac{2}{3} = n$$ (Change the mixed number to an improper fraction. There are $\frac{3}{3}$ in 1. Therefore $1\frac{2}{3}$ is the same as $\frac{3}{3} + \frac{2}{3}$ or $\frac{5}{3}$)

Step two: $$\frac{5 \div 2}{3 \div 3} = n$$ (Make one fraction)

Step three: $$\frac{2\frac{1}{2}}{1} = n$$

Step four: $$2\frac{1}{2} = n$$

Dividing fractions with unlike denominators is done by first finding a denominator common to both fractions (see Grade 5). Proceed as with fractions with like denominators. A number line can be used to find the lowest common denominator.

EXAMPLE: To find the lowest common denominator for $\frac{1}{2}$ and $\frac{1}{3}$ and $\frac{1}{4}$, count by twos, threes, and fours, until they all meet for the first time. They meet at 12.

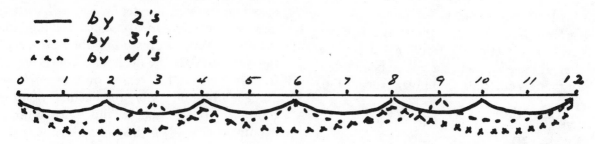

An easy way to divide fractions is to remember that the division process is the opposite of the multiplication process. Therefore, dividing by a fraction is the same as multiplying by its reciprocal. The **reciprocal** of a fraction is that number that produces 1 when it is multiplied by the original fraction. Since $\frac{2}{3} \times \frac{3}{2} = \frac{6}{6}$ or 1, $\frac{3}{2}$ is the reciprocal of $\frac{2}{3}$, and for the same reason $\frac{2}{3}$ is the reciprocal of $\frac{3}{2}$.

To divide one fraction by another, use the reciprocal of the divisor and multiply. Before the days of "New Math" we simply said "invert the divisor and multiply," but we didn't know why.

EXAMPLE:

a) $\frac{2}{3} \div \frac{2}{3} = n$ (The fraction to the right of the $\div$ sign is the divisor.)

$\frac{2}{3} \times \frac{3}{2} = n$ (The reciprocal of $\frac{2}{3}$ is $\frac{3}{2}$).

$\dfrac{2 \times 3}{2 \times 3} = n$ (Proceed as in multiplication. Use the commutative property of multiplication to shorten your work).

$1 \times 1 = n$ ($\frac{2}{2}$ are 1; $\frac{3}{3}$ are 1).
$1 = n$

b) $\frac{2}{3} \div \frac{1}{2} = n$
$\frac{2}{3} \times \frac{2}{1} = n$ (To commute the numerators or denominators
$\dfrac{2 \times 2}{3 \times 1} = n$ would not help in this problem)

$\frac{4}{3} = n$
$1\frac{1}{3} = n$

expressing money as fractions

Certain commonly used amounts of money are equal to easy fractional parts.

Let your child use these fractional parts. It will help him to work problems and costs in his head more quickly.

Here is a table that shows the number of cents in the common fractional parts of a dollar. It is a great help for you to be familiar with these. Your child should learn them too.

$$\$\tfrac{1}{10} = 10¢ \qquad \$\tfrac{3}{8} = 37\tfrac{1}{2}¢$$

$$\$\tfrac{3}{10} = 30¢ \qquad \$\tfrac{5}{8} = 62\tfrac{1}{2}¢$$

$$\$\tfrac{5}{10} = 50¢ \qquad \$\tfrac{7}{8} = 87\tfrac{1}{2}¢$$

$$\$\tfrac{7}{10} = 70¢ \qquad \$\tfrac{1}{4} = 25¢$$

$$\$\tfrac{9}{10} = 90¢ \qquad \$\tfrac{3}{4} = 75¢$$

$$\$\tfrac{1}{5} = 20¢ \qquad \$\tfrac{1}{6} = 16\tfrac{2}{3}¢$$

$$\$\tfrac{2}{5} = 40¢ \qquad \$\tfrac{5}{6} = 83\tfrac{1}{3}¢$$

$$\$\tfrac{3}{5} = 60¢ \qquad \$\tfrac{1}{3} = 33\tfrac{1}{3}¢$$

$$\$\tfrac{4}{5} = 80¢ \qquad \$\tfrac{2}{3} = 66\tfrac{2}{3}¢$$

$$\$\tfrac{1}{8} = 12\tfrac{1}{2}¢ \qquad \$\tfrac{1}{2} = 50¢$$

EXAMPLE:

Finding the cost of 16 balls of twine that cost $.37½ apiece means multiplying 16 × .37½ unless your child knows that .37½ is ⅜ of a dollar. Then he can simply multiply 16 × ⅜. Let's do it both ways and see if it comes out the same.

A.
$$\frac{\cancel{16}^{\,2}}{1} \times \frac{3}{\cancel{8}_{\,1}} = \$6.00$$

B.
$$\begin{array}{r} \$.37½ \\ \underline{16} \\ 8 \\ 222 \\ \underline{37} \\ \$6.00 \end{array}$$

Have your child do the problems in the workbook in his head, using the short method.

decimal fractions

Your child sees clearly that .7 and $\tfrac{7}{10}$ are two different ways of writing *seven tenths*. In a common fraction the denominator is written and can be seen. In a decimal fraction the denominator is expressed by the position of the number after the decimal point. Decimal fractions can be expressed only in terms of 10. The first place after the decimal point is tenths (.7 is $\tfrac{7}{10}$); the second place is hundredths (.07 is $\tfrac{7}{100}$); the third place is thousandths (.007 is $\tfrac{7}{1000}$), etc.

It is in science and business that decimal fractions are used more than common fractions.

The meaning of decimals can be explained with money: .1 or $\tfrac{1}{10}$ of a dollar is a dime or 10 cents or $.10.

There are 100 pennies in a dollar: $\tfrac{1}{100}$ of that dollar is one cent; $\tfrac{1}{100}$ is written .01; one cent is written $.01.

adding and subtracting decimals

Adding and subtracting decimals is a continuation of adding and subtracting money. In checking your child's work, be sure first that he has placed his numbers in straight columns, decimal point under decimal point, tenths under tenths, hundredths under hundredths, etc. The whole numbers, too, must be placed in straight columns, the tens under tens, hundreds under hundreds, etc.

EXAMPLE:

Add: $1.00, $3.45, $.50, $10.25

$$\begin{array}{r} \$1.00 \\ 3.45 \\ .50 \\ \underline{10.25} \\ \$15.20 \end{array}$$

changing decimals to common fractions

Your child learns to change decimal fractions to common fractions and vice versa.

EXAMPLE:

1.5 is read as $1\frac{5}{10}$. $\frac{5}{10}$ reduced to lowest terms is $\frac{1}{2}$. The point is read as *and*. 1.5 is read as one and five tenths or one and a half.

There are times when one form is simpler and quicker to use than the other. Would you ask for one and five tenths pounds of butter or $1\frac{1}{2}$ pounds? Would you pay one and five tenths dollars for something? You would, but you read it as one dollar and a half. You write it as $1.50.

Some decimal fractions changed to common fractions in lowest terms are:

$$.50 = \tfrac{50}{100} \text{ or } \tfrac{1}{2}$$
$$.1 = \tfrac{1}{10}$$
$$.20 = \tfrac{20}{100} \text{ or } \tfrac{1}{5}$$
$$2.8 = 2\tfrac{8}{10} \text{ or } 2\tfrac{4}{5}$$
$$.05 = \tfrac{5}{100} \text{ or } \tfrac{1}{20}$$
$$.75 = \tfrac{75}{100} \text{ or } \tfrac{3}{4}$$

changing common fractions to decimals

The line between the numerator and denominator means "divided by." To prove that $\frac{1}{4}$ = .25, actually divide 1 by 4.

To make the work possible, add a decimal point and zeros after the one. Add two zeros, which means your answer will be in hundredths. We use decimals in relation to dollars and cents most of the time and cents has two places. In changing per cent to decimals, we show two places because *per cent* means "hundredths." If it is obvious that more zeros are needed to make the division come out even, add them. You are not changing the value of the number.

EXAMPLE:

$$\begin{array}{r} .25 \\ 4\overline{)1.00} \\ \underline{8} \\ 20 \\ \underline{20} \end{array}$$

Always reduce common fractions first so the numbers will be smaller and easier to handle. To do this, divide the numerator and denominator by a number which will go into both of them evenly; the value of the fraction will not be changed.

EXAMPLE:

Change $\frac{15}{20}$ to a decimal.

$$\tfrac{15}{20} = \tfrac{3}{4}$$

First, reduce $\frac{15}{20}$ by dividing both 15 and 20 by 5. It will become $\frac{3}{4}$. Then, divide 3 by 4.

$$\begin{array}{r} .75 \\ 4\overline{)3.00} \\ \underline{2\,8} \\ 20 \\ \underline{20} \end{array}$$

Some common fractions changed to decimal fractions:

$$\tfrac{32}{100} = .32 \qquad 3\tfrac{4}{100} = 3.04$$
$$\tfrac{1}{10} = .1 \qquad 4\tfrac{1}{2} = 4.5$$
$$\tfrac{3}{100} = .03 \qquad \tfrac{1}{4} = .25$$

multiplying decimals

Your child has already learned to multiply money by whole numbers. Now he learns to multiply decimals. The rule he remembers in multiplying decimals is: Multiply decimals as if they were whole numbers. Then place the decimal point so there are as many decimal places in the product as there are in the multiplicand and multiplier together.

EXAMPLE:

$$\begin{array}{r} 4.03 \text{ multiplicand} \\ \times 2.4 \text{ multiplier} \\ \hline 16\,12 \\ 80\,6 \\ \hline 9.672 \text{ product} \end{array}$$

There are two decimal places (figures to the right of the decimal point) in the multiplicand, one in the multiplier. A total of three places must be pointed off in the product. Begin at the right and count three figures to the left and place the decimal point.

Sometimes it is necessary to add zeros in the product (answer) in front of the numbers to get the correct number of decimal places to point off.

EXAMPLES:

A.
$$\begin{array}{r} .012 \\ \times\ .06 \\ \hline .00072 \end{array}$$
multiplicand
multiplier
product

B.
$$\begin{array}{r} .001 \\ \times\ 9 \\ \hline .009 \end{array}$$
multiplicand
multiplier
product

Here is a helpful short cut: To multiply a decimal by 10, simply move the decimal point in the multiplicand one place to the right.

EXAMPLE:
$$\begin{array}{r} 6.375 \\ \times\ \ \ 10 \\ \hline 63.750 \end{array}$$ or think 63.75

To multiply a decimal by 100, move the decimal point in the multiplicand two places to the right.

EXAMPLE:
$$\begin{array}{r} 6.375 \\ \times\ \ \ 100 \\ \hline 637.500 \end{array}$$ or think 637.5

dividing decimals

In dividing decimals the important thing your child learns is the correct placement of the decimal point in the quotient (answer). Where would you place the decimal point in these quotients to make the answer sensible?

EXAMPLE:

$$\begin{array}{r} 3.2 \\ 3\overline{)9.6} \end{array}$$

THINK: How many 3s in 9? There are three 3s in 9. Then there would be three and a fraction 3s in 9 and a fraction. So the decimal point is placed after the 3. The answer is 3.2.

In dividing *a decimal by a whole number,* place the decimal point in the quotient right above the point in the dividend (number inside the box).

EXAMPLE:

$$\begin{array}{r} 1.25 \\ 7\overline{)8.75} \end{array}$$

Here is the rule for dividing by a decimal: Make the divisor a whole number by moving the decimal point to the right end of the number being used as the divisor. Then move the decimal point in the dividend as many places to the right as you moved the point in the divisor. Add zeros if necessary. Put a decimal point for the quotient above the new decimal point in the dividend. Divide as you do with whole numbers.

What you are actually doing is multiplying both the divisor and the dividend by the same number. This does not change the ratio of the numbers. The number of places in the divisor determines the numbers to multiply by. If the divisor is tenths, it is necessary to multiply by 10 to change it to a whole number. If the divisor is hundredths, it is necessary to multiply by 100 to change it to a whole number. The dividend must be multiplied by the *same number that was used to multiply the divisor.*

EXAMPLES:
a) *Problem*

$$.4\overline{).48}$$

Get Ready
The divisor is 4 tenths
so multiply by 10.
$$.4\ \times 10 = 4$$
$$.48 \times 10 = 4.8$$

Divide

$$\begin{array}{r} 1.2 \\ 4\overline{)4.8} \end{array}$$

b)

$$.25\overline{)1.50}$$

The divisor is 25 hundredths so multiply by 100.

$$\begin{array}{r} 6 \\ 25\overline{)150} \end{array}$$

$.25 \times 100 = 25$
$1.50 \times 100 = 150$

c)

$$.5\overline{).395}$$

The divisor is 5 tenths so multiply by 10.

$.5 \times 10 = 5$
$.395 \times 10 = 3.95$

$$\begin{array}{r} .79 \\ 5\overline{)3.95} \end{array}$$

per cent

Your child learns that *per cent* means "so many out of a hundred." A whole is 100 hundredths or 100 per cent. The meaning can be developed with a diagram divided into 100 squares.

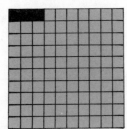

Three of the small squares are shaded. Three out of a hundred are shaded; $\frac{3}{100}$ or .03 or 3% are shaded.

If fifty out of a hundred were shaded, it would be $\frac{50}{100}$ or .50 or 50%; twenty out of a hundred are $\frac{20}{100}$ or .20 or 20%; six out of a hundred are $\frac{6}{100}$ or .06 or 6%.

Per cent of means "hundredths times." To find the per cent of a number, *change the per cent to a decimal and multiply.*

EXAMPLE:

Find 45% of 900

$$\begin{array}{r} 900 \\ \times\ .45 \\ \hline 4500 \\ 3600 \\ \hline 405.00 \end{array}$$

(45% is $\frac{45}{100}$ or .45)

EXAMPLE:

In Jim's Scout Troop, 75% of the 20 boys went to camp. How many went to camp?

$$\begin{array}{r} 20 \\ \times\ .75 \\ \hline 100 \\ 140 \\ \hline 15.00 \end{array}$$

(75% is $\frac{75}{100}$ or .75)
15 boys went to camp.

Remember that 75% or $\frac{75}{100}$ is also $\frac{3}{4}$. With some numbers it will be quicker and easier to switch to the common fraction form. In the problem just explained I could have thought:

$$\frac{3}{\cancel{4}} \times \frac{\cancel{20}^{5}}{1} = 15$$

Be sure that your child is familiar with the most commonly used decimals and the common fraction forms they equal, pages 25–6.

See the workbook section for some practical problems in per cent.

A more intensive study of percentages is made in the seventh grade.

geometry and measurement

Your child learns what a rod is in length. Let him measure off a rod along your driveway to help him get a clearer idea.

16½ feet = 1 rod (rd.)

5½ yards = 1 rod

320 rods = 1 mile

Farmland is measured in rods.

area

Your child learns to find area in square rods, acres, and square miles.

160 square rods = 1 acre

640 acres = 1 square mile

1 square mile is called a section.

The area of a rectangle equals the number of units in the width times the number of units in the length. Both the length and width must be in the *same unit of measure.*

EXAMPLE:

Instead of thinking, "6 inches by 2 feet," think, "½ foot by 2 feet." The answer will be in square feet. Or think, "6 inches by 24 inches." The answer will be in square inches. These units can be inches or feet or miles or yards, but the answer is always in *square units.*

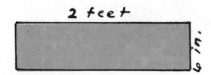

The acre is a unit of measure used in measuring land. An acre covers an area of 43,560 square feet. It does not need to be a square; it can also be a rectangle.

Your child learns to change measures of area from one unit to another. This is best understood by diagrams.

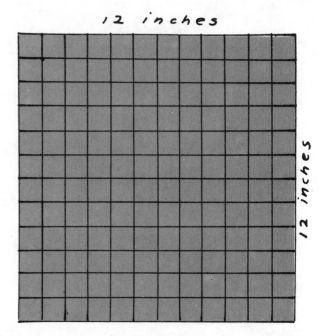

Draw a square, 1 foot on each side. Draw lines to divide it into square inches (12 inches = 1 foot). Now your drawing shows that there is 1 square foot and that *there are 144 square inches in 1 square foot.*

To change square inches to square feet, divide by 144. Divide 144 by 144 and it changes right back to 1 square foot.

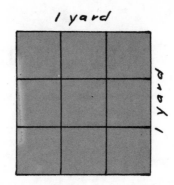

Draw a square yard. Divide it into square feet.
(3 feet = 1 yard)

The drawing shows that there are 9 square feet in 1 square yard. To change square feet to square yards, *divide* by 9. To change square yards to square feet, *multiply* by 9.

In a square that measures 2 yards or 6 feet on each side, we know that there are 4 square yards (2 yards $\times$ 2 yards = 4 square yards). The rule is that to change the 4 square yards to square feet, one must multiply by 9. Then there must be 36 square feet in 4 square yards (4 $\times$ 9 = 36). Count them.

Now let us change the 36 square feet to square yards. The rule is that to do this one must divide the number of square feet by 9. There must be 4 square yards in this surface (36 $\div$ 9 = 4). Count them to see if this is correct.

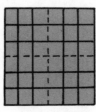

Do not confuse perimeter (distance around the outside) with area (surface in square units).

volume

Measurement of volume is also studied in the sixth grade. To find the volume of a box-shaped object, your child multiplies its length by its width by its height. The measurement units used must be the same on all three edges—they must be either inches, feet, or yards. The answer is in *cubic units.*

EXAMPLE:

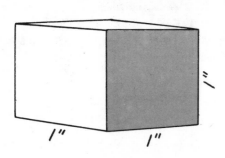

A CUBIC INCH

A cubic inch is a unit of measure 1 inch long, 1 inch wide, and 1 inch deep.

A CUBIC FOOT

A cubic foot is a unit of measure 1 foot long, 1 foot wide, and 1 foot high. A cubic foot is also 1728 cubic inches. Each foot has 12 inches, $12 \times 12 \times 12 = 1728$ cubic inches.

A CUBIC YARD

A cubic yard is a unit of measure 1 yard long, 1 yard wide and 1 yard high. Each yard has three feet, so a cubic yard is $3 \times 3 \times 3$, or 27 cubic feet. It can be written 3^3 and read "three cubed."

Your child adds more geometric terms to his arithmetic vocabulary.

▶ A **point** is an exact location. It does not have length, width, or thickness. It can be represented by making a dot.

▶ A **line** is a set of points. It has only one dimension—length.

▶ A **line segment** is a part of a line that lies between any two points on a line.

▶ A **ray** is a part of a line that has a fixed point at one end but goes on indefinitely at the other end.

▶ The **vertex** is the fixed point from which the ray starts.

▶ An **angle** is the figure formed by 2 rays having a common vertex. The symbol for the word angle is $\angle$.

Angles are named by letters with the vertex letter in the middle. Illustration is ABC.

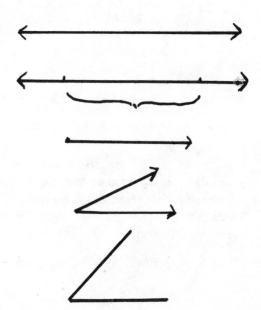

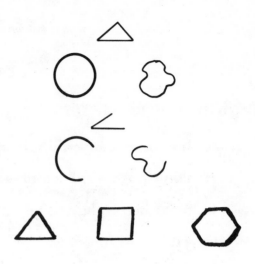

▶ A **closed figure** is made by a line that continues until it returns to its starting point. The line separates the area *inside* (I) from the area *outside* (B).

▶ An **open figure** is made by a line whose ends do not meet.

A **polygon** is any closed plane geometric shape with many sides ("Poly" is the Greek prefix meaning *many,* as different from the Greek prefix "mono" meaning *one*.)

thought problems

Your child becomes acquainted with problems in business arithmetic this year. He is asked to keep a personal account of his earnings and expenditures, real and imaginary. You can do something about making this experience real and meaningful to him.

If it is possible, let him open a savings account at the bank. Let him keep a personal budget. He will need help sticking to it, but in that way he will learn the usefulness of a budget. He will enjoy doing his own bookkeeping.

He learns the meanings of some new words: savings account, interest, deposit, deposit slip, passbook.

He continues to use and graph scale drawings to solve problems. He learns to organize numerical data.

workbook | sixth grade

english exercises

I. Put one line under the complete subject and two lines under the complete predicate.

1. <u>Healthy cows</u> <u><u>must have green grass</u></u>. 2. The boy who was digging looked at the stones on his shovel. 3. Your house is made of stone. 4. The dishes in your house are made of clay. 5. All your furniture is made of wood. 6. You would soon starve without food. 7. Can you catch fish without a hook? 8. Only living things can grow. 9. Plants are among the largest and smallest things in the world. 10. Very large trees are found in California. 11. In New Jersey I once saw a large hollow tree. 12. A piece of moss is a flowerless plant.

II. Put one line under the simple subject (or subjects) and two lines under the verb or simple predicate.

1. The <u>plants</u> with flowers <u><u>are</u></u> the most perfect plants. 2. A perfect plant has six parts. 3. A root is a plant's anchor. 4. Roots differ much in shape. 5. When I was a child I picked dandelions. 6. Plant stems are useful to men. 7. The part of the plant which you like best is the flower. 8. Soak the beans in water. 9. In a day or two you may dig up one plant. 10. Your climbing bean plant needs a stick to climb on. 11. All spring and summer your bean plant will grow. 12. Here, folded up in these hard dry beans, lie the bean vines of next year.

III. What kind of a sentence is each of the following—declarative, interrogative, exclamatory, or imperative?

1. I have traveled through five states. 2. Where did you live before you came here? 3. Please come to a meeting at my house tonight. 4. How you have changed! 5. Boys, line up; girls, remain seated. 6. What a large class we

have! 7. Did you ever see the tendrils on a morning glory? 8. Look at the strawberry beds. 9. Look at that huge melon! 10. There are more climbing plants in hot lands than in cool lands. 11. How many books did you read last month? 12. Berries of the mistletoe are white.

IV. Put the exact words of the person in quotation marks; add capitals if necessary.

1. Look at that queer old man with the long white beard, exclaimed the boy.

2. Teacher said, cut six pieces of wood exactly the same size.

3. A locust, the boy answered, is a cousin to a grasshopper.

4. The locust is a greedy animal, the boy read on.

5. Mrs. Cricket does not sing, our teacher told us. It is Mr. Cricket that makes all the noise.

6. Crickets are thirsty creatures. They drink water, milk, tea, soup, beer, or vinegar, Miss Mills read.

7. Father added, Crickets like vegetables.

8. Mother added, They'll eat anything they find.

9. They ate a woolen blanket at my house, Mrs. Jones said.

10. Crickets can fly but they would rather hop, Mr. Jones told us.

V. Write a synonym for each of these words.

1. ask _____   11. gay _____
2. pretty _____   12. material _____
3. brave _____   13. house _____
4. load _____   14. road _____
5. mob _____   15. empty _____
6. notorious _____   16. little _____
7. dirt _____   17. big _____
8. district _____   18. good _____
9. area _____   19. work _____
10. flowers _____   20. chose _____

VI. Choose an antonym for each word.

1. ancient _____
2. native _____
3. pretty _____
4. wholesale _____
5. victory _____
6. interior _____
7. enemy _____
8. easy _____
9. employee _____
10. feast _____

11. old _____
12. minority _____
13. wealthy _____
14. rare _____
15. often _____
16. fast _____
17. cold _____
18. priceless _____
19. busy _____
20. funny _____

VII. Choose a homonym for each word.

1. their _____
2. bear _____
3. by _____
4. sun _____
5. shown _____
6. great _____
7. hole _____
8. seen _____
9. here _____
10. stair _____

11. pause _____
12. plain _____
13. might _____
14. board _____
15. pray _____
16. medal _____
17. air _____
18. hour _____
19. ring _____
20. tale _____

VIII. Pick out the subject, predicate (or verb) and object in these sentences. (Not every sentence will have an object.)

1. Crickets will drink any liquid left in their way.
2. The field cricket runs into his hole.
3. He eats leaves and grass.

4. Little French children fish for crickets.

5. Finally the Scout leader found us.

6. Little crickets have no wings.

7. In Spain the people keep crickets in little cages to sing for them.

8. You may find a cricket in the woods.

9. Mrs. Cricket makes her nest soft and smooth.

10. After the eggs are laid, what do you think Mrs. Cricket does?

11. She sits and listens for the enemy.

12. She fights bravely.

13. Here was a little, live, pale green creature.

14. The hillside was covered with wild carrots.

15. I put all these things on a piece of white paper.

16. The butterfly wears an elegant, soft, velvet coat of fine hairs.

17. The butterfly builds no house.

18. The gentleman saw some orange and black butterflies.

19. A newborn peacock has no feathers.

20. You have told me many things.

IX. **Now go back and pick out the nouns.**

X. **Pick out the pronouns.**

XI. **Pick out the adjectives.**

XII. **Pick out the adverbs.**

XIII. **List the conjunctions used.**

XIV. **List the prepositions used.**

XV. **Write the abbreviations for:**

1. afternoon _____

2. before noon _____

3. postscript _____

4. rural free delivery _____

5. Mister _____

6. Mistress _____

7. Doctor _____

8. Avenue _____

9. Captain _____

10. Major _____

Punctuate the following sentences.

1. What story can a birds beak tell   2. Mary asked are you boys brothers
3. Dr J V Smith lives in Avon Oregon   4. Dont ever forget it again   5.
We all sang The Cradle Song   6. Yes we studied the butterfly last year
7. George Michael and John tied for third place   8. Byron said This
doesnt make sense   9. He ran the race in one hour 36 minutes   10.
Hurrah The parade is coming

XVII. **Punctuate and capitalize this friendly letter.**

velva north dakota
january 6 1958

dear aunt mary

the book you sent me for christmas was wonderful i have
read it already and now i am letting gretchen read it i have
always liked stories written by albert payson terhune

we are all well we missed having you with us for christmas this year but know you must have enjoyed being in florida
thank you again

lots of love
Mary Lynne

arithmetic exercises

I. **Round out these numbers to the nearest tens or nearest hundreds.**

46 ____	87 ____	42 ____	796 ____
35 ____	63 ____	118 ____	421 ____
101 ____	28 ____	767 ____	857 ____
967 ____	33 ____	890 ____	628 ____
430 ____	91 ____	534 ____	127 ____

II. **Exponents. Write the value.**

8^2 ____	10^5 ____	2^4 ____	3^4 ____
4^2 ____	2^{10} ____	3^2 ____	4^3 ____
3^3 ____	6^3 ____	9^2 ____	5^5 ____
5^3 ____	5^2 ____	7^3 ____	6^2 ____
4^4 ____	8^3 ____	2^5 ____	7^2 ____

III. What is the place-value of the 3 in each of these numerals?

1. 413
2. .3
3. 30
4. 300
5. 1.03

6. 103_{five}
7. 130_{five}
8. 300_{five}
9. 435_{five}
10. 39_{five}

11. 37_{four}
12. 300_{four}
13. 13_{four}
14. $1,731_{four}$
15. $8,319_{four}$

IV. Sets. Watch the symbol and complete the equation.

1. Set A = {1, 4, 6}
   Set B = {2, 4, 6}
   A $\cup$ B =

2. Set A = {a, b, g}
   Set B = {x, y, z}
   A $\cup$ B =

3. Set A = {A, H, Y}
   Set B = {B, Y, C}
   A $\cup$ B =

4. Set A = {4, 6, 8}
   Set B = {2, 3, 5}
   A $\cap$ B =

5. Set A = {a, c, f}
   Set B = {b, c, f}
   A $\cap$ B =

6. Set A = {D, B, O}
   Set B = {C, B, A}
   A $\cap$ B =

V. Sets. Show the relationships of sets. Use the symbols $\subset$, $=$, $\neq$, or $\sim$.

(Example: Set A = {4, 2, 1}. Set B = {1, 6, 2}. A $\neq$ B, and A $\sim$ B.)

1. Set A = {1, 2, 3}
   Set B = {1, 2, 3}
   ——— , ———

2. Set A = {1, 3, 2}
   Set B = {6}
   ———

3. Set A = {4, 5, 1}
   Set B = {1, 2, 3}
   ——— , ———

4. Set A = {a, b, c, d, e}
   Set B = {e, b, d, c, a}
   ——— , ———

5. Set A = {10^2}
   Set B = {100}
   ——— , ———

6. Set A = {5}
   Set B = {3, 5, 1}
   ——— , ———

VI. Problems with more than one operation. Find n.

1. $4 \times (7 + 2) - 3 = n$
2. $24 \div 3 \times 4 + 1 = n$
3. $5 \times (8 - 2) + 9 - 4 = n$
4. $14 - 7 + 16 \div 2 \times 4 = n$
5. $36 \div 9 \times 2 = n$

6. $5 \times 3 + (3 \times 5) \div 15 = n$
7. $3 \times 27 \div 9 - 2 = n$
8. $25 \times 4 \div 2 + 50 - 5 = n$
9. $42 - (27 \div 3) + 6 = n$
10. $13 + 120 - 14 \div 7 = n$

VII. Fractions. Add:

1. $\dfrac{1}{4}$
   $\dfrac{3}{8}$
   $\dfrac{1}{2}$

2. $\dfrac{1}{3}$
   $\dfrac{5}{6}$
   $\dfrac{1}{2}$

3. $\dfrac{5}{8}$
   $\dfrac{3}{4}$
   $\dfrac{1}{6}$

4. $\dfrac{1}{6}$
   $\dfrac{1}{2}$
   $\dfrac{2}{3}$

5. $\dfrac{3}{10}$
   $\dfrac{2}{5}$
   $\dfrac{1}{2}$

6. $\dfrac{3}{8}$
   $\dfrac{3}{4}$
   $\dfrac{1}{2}$

7. $\dfrac{2}{3}$
   $\dfrac{5}{12}$
   $\dfrac{1}{2}$

8. $\dfrac{7}{15}$
   $\dfrac{4}{5}$
   $\dfrac{1}{3}$

9. $\dfrac{4}{5}$
   $\dfrac{1}{2}$
   $\dfrac{7}{10}$

10. $\dfrac{3}{5}$
    $\dfrac{9}{10}$
    $\dfrac{1}{2}$

11. $\dfrac{5}{6}$
    $\dfrac{1}{3}$
    $\dfrac{3}{4}$

12. $\dfrac{4}{9}$
    $\dfrac{1}{3}$
    $\dfrac{2}{6}$

VIII. Fractions. Add:

1. $3\frac{1}{2}$
   $4\frac{1}{4}$
   $5\frac{1}{8}$

2. $6\frac{2}{3}$
   $7\frac{1}{2}$
   $8\frac{1}{6}$

3. $9\frac{9}{10}$
   $3\frac{3}{5}$
   $2\frac{1}{4}$

4. $1\frac{5}{6}$
   $6\frac{7}{12}$
   $5\frac{3}{4}$

5. $7\frac{1}{15}$
   $3\frac{2}{3}$
   $7\frac{4}{5}$

6. $1\frac{1}{3}$
   $3\frac{1}{4}$
   $2\frac{1}{2}$

7. $4\frac{2}{3}$
   $2\frac{1}{2}$
   $2\frac{5}{6}$

8. $5\frac{1}{2}$
   $3\frac{2}{5}$
   $4\frac{3}{10}$

9. $8\frac{1}{5}$
   $6\frac{3}{10}$
   $5\frac{1}{4}$

10. $2\frac{1}{3}$
    $6\frac{3}{4}$
    $4\frac{1}{6}$

11. $4\frac{2}{3}$
    $3\frac{3}{4}$
    $5\frac{1}{6}$

12. $3\frac{1}{2}$
    $4\frac{1}{3}$
    $2\frac{3}{4}$

IX. Fractions. Add:

1. $2\frac{5}{8}$
   $4\frac{7}{8}$
   $6\frac{1}{8}$
   $8\frac{5}{8}$

2. $2\frac{1}{3}$
   $9\frac{3}{8}$
   $8\frac{5}{6}$
   $6\frac{5}{12}$

3. $1\frac{1}{6}$
   $2\frac{3}{5}$
   $1\frac{2}{3}$
   $8\frac{1}{2}$

4. $8\frac{2}{3}$
   $5\frac{1}{6}$
   $8\frac{5}{12}$
   $2\frac{1}{2}$

5. $6\frac{3}{4}$
   $9\frac{1}{4}$
   $1\frac{3}{4}$
   $3\frac{3}{4}$

6. $6\frac{7}{16}$
   $6\frac{5}{8}$
   $3\frac{3}{4}$
   $7\frac{1}{2}$

7. $1\frac{1}{2}$
   $3\frac{3}{5}$
   $2\frac{7}{10}$
   $4\frac{1}{5}$

8. $2\frac{1}{5}$
   $6\frac{1}{2}$
   $8\frac{3}{4}$
   $4\frac{3}{10}$

9. $5\frac{1}{2}$
   $4\frac{1}{4}$
   $9\frac{2}{3}$
   $7\frac{5}{8}$

10. $9\frac{1}{2}$
    $8\frac{1}{6}$
    $7\frac{3}{8}$
    $5\frac{3}{4}$

11. $4\frac{1}{6}$
    $3\frac{3}{4}$
    $2\frac{1}{12}$
    $4\frac{2}{3}$

12. $5\frac{7}{8}$
    $2\frac{1}{16}$
    $5\frac{1}{2}$
    $3\frac{1}{4}$

X. Fractions. Subtract:

1. $6\frac{2}{3}$
   $4\frac{1}{3}$

2. $7\frac{5}{8}$
   $2\frac{1}{8}$

3. $8\frac{5}{6}$
   7

4. $2\frac{11}{12}$
   $1\frac{5}{12}$

5. $8\frac{5}{8}$
   $3\frac{1}{2}$

6. $12\frac{5}{6}$
   $4\frac{1}{2}$

7. $3\frac{3}{8}$
   $\frac{1}{4}$

8. $6\frac{1}{2}$
   $2\frac{1}{6}$

9. $10\frac{5}{6}$
   $5\frac{1}{3}$

10. $5\frac{7}{8}$
    $1\frac{3}{4}$

11. $7\frac{7}{12}$
    $5\frac{1}{3}$

12. $9\frac{3}{4}$
    $4\frac{5}{8}$

XI. Fractions. Subtract:

1. 26
   $13\frac{2}{5}$

2. 17
   $9\frac{1}{10}$

3. 3
   $1\frac{2}{3}$

4. 5
   $1\frac{1}{10}$

5. 3
   $1\frac{2}{3}$

6. 4
   $1\frac{3}{4}$

7. 5
   $2\frac{4}{7}$

8. 6
   $3\frac{3}{5}$

9. 5
   $3\frac{3}{8}$

10. 8
    $4\frac{2}{9}$

11. 18
    $13\frac{7}{8}$

12. 8
    $5\frac{3}{10}$

XII. Fractions. Subtract:

1. $3\frac{1}{8}$
   $1\frac{1}{2}$

2. $4\frac{1}{6}$
   $1\frac{1}{3}$

3. $6\frac{3}{8}$
   $2\frac{1}{2}$

4. $8\frac{2}{3}$
   $4\frac{5}{6}$

5. $9\frac{1}{10}$
   $3\frac{1}{5}$

6. $12\frac{1}{2}$
   $6\frac{5}{6}$

7. $9\frac{1}{5}$
   $3\frac{7}{10}$

8. $12\frac{1}{6}$
   $4\frac{1}{2}$

9. $14\frac{5}{8}$
   $11\frac{3}{4}$

10. $10\frac{1}{4}$
    $9\frac{7}{8}$

11. $18\frac{1}{12}$
    $13\frac{3}{4}$

12. $12\frac{4}{9}$
    $9\frac{8}{9}$

XIII. Fractions. Subtract:

1. $4\frac{3}{5}$
   $2\frac{1}{4}$

2. $7\frac{2}{5}$
   $4\frac{1}{7}$

3. $5\frac{5}{8}$
   $2\frac{1}{6}$

4. $2\frac{2}{3}$
   $1\frac{1}{8}$

5. $8\frac{7}{8}$
   $2\frac{2}{3}$

6. $10\frac{3}{4}$
   $6\frac{2}{5}$

7. $3\frac{1}{2}$
   $1\frac{2}{3}$

8. $6\frac{2}{5}$
   $4\frac{3}{4}$

9. $7\frac{2}{3}$
   $6\frac{1}{5}$

10. $9\frac{1}{8}$
    $3\frac{1}{3}$

11. $7\frac{3}{7}$
    $4\frac{2}{5}$

12. $8\frac{4}{9}$
    $6\frac{1}{2}$

13. $8\frac{5}{6}$
    $2\frac{3}{4}$

14. $3\frac{3}{10}$
    $1\frac{2}{3}$

15. $9\frac{5}{8}$
    $4\frac{4}{5}$

16. $12\frac{1}{2}$
    $2\frac{3}{7}$

XIV. Fractions. Multiply:

1. $6 \times \frac{1}{3} =$
2. $10 \times \frac{5}{6} =$
3. $6 \times \frac{2}{7} =$
4. $14 \times \frac{4}{7} =$
5. $16 \times \frac{3}{8} =$
6. $12 \times \frac{2}{9} =$
7. $6 \times \frac{7}{12} =$
8. $20 \times \frac{1}{10} =$

9. $9 \times \frac{5}{16} =$
10. $4 \times \frac{2}{5} =$
11. $5 \times \frac{5}{8} =$
12. $8 \times \frac{3}{4} =$
13. $13 \times \frac{1}{7} =$
14. $\frac{2}{3}$ of $6 =$
15. $\frac{1}{4}$ of $8 =$
16. $\frac{3}{4}$ of $10 =$

17. $\frac{4}{5}$ of $20 =$
18. $\frac{6}{7}$ of $9 =$
19. $\frac{4}{7}$ of $28 =$
20. $\frac{2}{9}$ of $36 =$
21. $\frac{1}{10}$ of $16 =$
22. $\frac{5}{8} \times 4 =$
23. $\frac{5}{7} \times 20 =$
24. $\frac{3}{8} \times 64 =$

XV. Fractions. Multiply:

1. $\frac{1}{3} \times \frac{3}{4} =$
2. $\frac{3}{5} \times \frac{5}{6} =$
3. $\frac{5}{8} \times \frac{1}{2} =$
4. $\frac{4}{5} \times \frac{2}{5} =$
5. $\frac{5}{8} \times \frac{3}{10} =$
6. $\frac{3}{4} \times \frac{1}{6} =$

7. $\frac{7}{8} \times \frac{3}{4} =$
8. $\frac{2}{3} \times \frac{4}{5} =$
9. $\frac{1}{2} \times \frac{2}{3} =$
10. $\frac{3}{4} \times \frac{1}{3} =$
11. $\frac{2}{5} \times \frac{5}{8} =$
12. $\frac{3}{4} \times \frac{2}{9} =$

13. $\frac{2}{3} \times \frac{3}{4} =$
14. $\frac{1}{8} \times \frac{2}{3} =$
15. $\frac{5}{6} \times \frac{3}{8} =$
16. $\frac{7}{8} \times \frac{2}{3} =$
17. $\frac{4}{5} \times \frac{7}{8} =$
18. $\frac{1}{16} \times \frac{9}{10} =$

XVI. Fractions. Multiply:

1. $6 \times 8\frac{3}{4} =$
2. $7 \times 4\frac{5}{6} =$
3. $3\frac{1}{2} \times 7 =$
4. $5\frac{5}{8} \times 8 =$
5. $10 \times 3\frac{2}{3} =$
6. $9 \times 7\frac{2}{5} =$

7. $14 \times 3\frac{1}{8} =$
8. $4\frac{2}{3} \times 9 =$
9. $2\frac{2}{7} \times 6 =$
10. $9\frac{1}{6} \times 9 =$
11. $8 \times 7\frac{3}{8} =$
12. $16 \times 5\frac{5}{9} =$

13. $7\frac{3}{4} \times 5 =$
14. $8\frac{1}{4} \times 7 =$
15. $12 \times 5\frac{5}{7} =$
16. $6 \times 2\frac{1}{3} =$
17. $8 \times 3\frac{3}{4} =$
18. $7 \times 4\frac{1}{2} =$

XVII. Fractions. Multiply:

1. $14\frac{1}{2}$
   4

2. $9\frac{2}{3}$
   7

3. $12\frac{5}{8}$
   8

4. $7\frac{5}{6}$
   5

5. $16\frac{4}{5}$
   10

6. $15\frac{3}{4}$
   3

7. 10
   $6\frac{2}{5}$

8. $11\frac{1}{2}$
   2

9. 9
   $6\frac{5}{9}$

10. $5\frac{3}{10}$
    5

11. 8
    $7\frac{5}{6}$

12. $7\frac{1}{3}$
    6

13. 12
    $7\frac{3}{4}$

14. 9
    $5\frac{2}{3}$

15. 18
    $6\frac{1}{6}$

16. $48\frac{1}{6}$
    12

17. 36
    $4\frac{3}{7}$

18. 25
    $2\frac{4}{5}$

XVIII. Fractions. Multiply:

1. $\frac{2}{3} \times 4\frac{1}{2} =$

2. $8\frac{1}{3} \times \frac{2}{5} =$

3. $9\frac{3}{8} \times \frac{3}{4} =$

4. $\frac{4}{5} \times 7\frac{3}{8} =$

5. $\frac{1}{2} \times 3\frac{1}{3} =$

6. $3\frac{1}{2} \times \frac{4}{5} =$

7. $7\frac{4}{9} \times \frac{5}{6} =$

8. $\frac{7}{10} \times 6\frac{3}{5} =$

9. $\frac{4}{5} \times 6\frac{1}{4} =$

10. $4\frac{3}{4} \times \frac{5}{8} =$

11. $12\frac{1}{6} \times \frac{7}{8} =$

12. $\frac{3}{4} \times 5\frac{2}{3} =$

13. $1\frac{1}{3} \times 2\frac{1}{2} =$

14. $7\frac{5}{6} \times 3\frac{2}{3} =$

15. $8\frac{2}{3} \times 3\frac{7}{8} =$

16. $1\frac{5}{12} \times 3\frac{4}{5} =$

17. $6\frac{2}{3} \times 4\frac{1}{4} =$

18. $3\frac{1}{8} \times 4\frac{3}{7} =$

XIX. Fractions. Multiply:

1. 16
   $1\frac{2}{3}$

2. 10
   $4\frac{1}{3}$

3. 18
   $2\frac{5}{6}$

4. 40
   $2\frac{3}{4}$

5. 12
   $5\frac{4}{5}$

6. 19
   $4\frac{1}{2}$

7. 16
   $2\frac{3}{8}$

8. 56
   $3\frac{3}{8}$

9. 12
   $4\frac{1}{5}$

10. 17
    $1\frac{3}{5}$

11. 15
    $5\frac{4}{5}$

12. 42
    $3\frac{5}{6}$

13. 10
    $5\frac{1}{3}$

14. 16
    $4\frac{3}{5}$

15. 14
    $9\frac{1}{2}$

16. 32
    $12\frac{3}{4}$

XX. Fractions. Divide:

1. $2 \div \frac{1}{4} =$

2. $6 \div \frac{1}{8} =$

8. $10 \div \frac{3}{4} =$

9. $4 \div \frac{1}{3} =$

15. $15 \div \frac{3}{4} =$

16. $5 \div \frac{1}{5} =$

22. $4 \div \frac{1}{10} =$

23. $12 \div \frac{3}{4} =$

3. $6 \div \frac{1}{4} =$ 10. $2 \div \frac{1}{9} =$ 17. $7 \div \frac{1}{7} =$ 24. $3 \div \frac{3}{5} =$

4. $4 \div \frac{2}{3} =$ 11. $3 \div \frac{7}{8} =$ 18. $3 \div \frac{1}{5} =$ 25. $7 \div \frac{2}{3} =$

5. $8 \div \frac{4}{5} =$ 12. $12 \div \frac{2}{3} =$ 19. $16 \div \frac{4}{5} =$ 26. $10 \div \frac{1}{2} =$

6. $6 \div \frac{3}{8} =$ 13. $8 \div \frac{5}{9} =$ 20. $8 \div \frac{1}{3} =$ 27. $17 \div \frac{1}{2} =$

7. $5 \div \frac{5}{8} =$ 14. $6 \div \frac{2}{5} =$ 21. $3 \div \frac{5}{6} =$

XXI. Fractions. Divide:

1. $5\frac{1}{4} \div 1\frac{3}{4} =$ 8. $3\frac{3}{5} \div 2\frac{1}{4} =$ 15. $9\frac{1}{3} \div 2\frac{1}{3} =$

2. $2\frac{4}{5} \div 1\frac{1}{2} =$ 9. $5\frac{5}{6} \div 16\frac{1}{2} =$ 16. $2\frac{1}{2} \div 3\frac{1}{5} =$

3. $3\frac{3}{5} \div 1\frac{4}{5} =$ 10. $6\frac{2}{3} \div 2\frac{2}{3} =$ 17. $5\frac{1}{3} \div 2\frac{3}{4} =$

4. $6\frac{1}{8} \div 3\frac{3}{4} =$ 11. $3\frac{1}{2} \div 8\frac{1}{6} =$ 18. $3\frac{1}{8} \div 1\frac{1}{4} =$

5. $2\frac{5}{8} \div 1\frac{3}{4} =$ 12. $9\frac{1}{6} \div 2\frac{3}{4} =$ 19. $3\frac{3}{5} \div 2\frac{1}{10} =$

6. $6\frac{1}{6} \div 2\frac{1}{5} =$ 13. $6\frac{2}{3} \div 3\frac{1}{3} =$ 20. $3\frac{1}{3} \div 6\frac{2}{3} =$

7. $9\frac{7}{8} \div 2\frac{3}{4} =$ 14. $8\frac{1}{4} \div 1\frac{3}{8} =$ 21. $6\frac{2}{5} \div 1\frac{3}{5} =$

XXII. Decimals. Copy in columns and add:

1. 3.75, 1.5, .875   6. 2.75, 2.375, 4.25   11. 1.375, 4.875, 9.25

2. 1.5, 5.833, 4.25   7. 2.625, 9.5, .75   12. 4.75, 4.125, 9.333

3. 1.333, 4.25, 9.667   8. 9.75, 8.875, 2.5   13. 25.5, 16.4, .2, 83.11

4. 1.25, 4.167, 5.75   9. 1.667, 4.5, 8.875   14. 1.62, 35.5, 9.45, .84

5. 4.875, 9.5, 8.333   10. 9.625, 8.25, 4.333   15. .225, 9.62, 36.8, 398.

XXIII. Decimals. Subtract:

1. 3.875 − .27   6. .806 − .242   11. 2.8 − 1.9

2. 2.52 − .19   7. 3. − .76   12. .72 − .40

3. 2.46 − 1.5   8. 34.501 − 8.998   13. 2.785 − .916

4. 1.632 − .461   9. 1.0 − .4   14. 8.625 − 1.25

5. .500 − .255   10. .943 − .176   15. 4.875 − 2.5

XXIV. Decimals. Multiply:

1. 12.5	2. .85	3. 36.4	4. 17.3	5. 65.4	6. 2.38
.05	2.3	.36	5.8	7.5	6.4

7. 4.29	8. 28.2	9. 6.25	10. 2.437	11. 5.33	12. 4.67
8.7	5.6	5.3	1.62	2.14	.09

13. .532	14. .0697	15. 15.7
.75	4.7	.06

XXV. Decimals. Multiply:

1. 5.76	2. .004	3. .009	4. .215	5. 5.76	6. .246
.18	.06	.07	.02	.12	.58

7. 25.9	8. .127	9. 5.78	10. .051	11. .201	12. .376
.26	1.7	9.2	6.2	7.8	5.6

13. .489	14. 8.406	15. .1934
7.3	.23	.16

XXVI. Decimals. Divide:

1. $3\overline{)\,.9}$ 2. $4\overline{)\,2.4}$ 3. $6\overline{)\,8.4}$ 4. $2\overline{)\,22.8}$ 5. $4\overline{)\,.16}$ 6. $8\overline{)\,.64}$

7. $5\overline{)\,4.55}$ 8. $7\overline{)\,22.61}$ 9. $4\overline{)\,.016}$ 10. $5\overline{)\,.200}$ 11. $8\overline{)\,.648}$ 12. $9\overline{)\,4.482}$

13. $3\overline{)\,9.006}$ 14. $6\overline{)\,8.454}$ 15. $16\overline{)\,20.928}$ 16. $34\overline{)\,72.080}$ 17. $12\overline{)\,220.8}$ 18. $5\overline{)\,282.70}$

XXVII. Decimals. Divide to nearest hundredth:

1. $8\overline{)2}$ 2. $5\overline{)3}$ 3. $28\overline{)14}$ 4. $21\overline{)14}$ 5. $65\overline{)48}$ 6. $72\overline{)60}$

7. $48\overline{)12}$ 8. $96\overline{)64}$ 9. $15\overline{)12}$ 10. $16\overline{)6}$ 11. $12\overline{)8}$ 12. $55\overline{)32}$

13. $12\overline{)9}$ 14. $84\overline{)28}$ 15. $39\overline{)16}$

XXVIII. Decimals. Divide to nearest hundredth:

1. $5\overline{)2.625}$ 2. $2\overline{)17.6}$ 3. $4\overline{)9.36}$ 4. $3\overline{)7.245}$ 5. $4\overline{)5.73}$

6. $7\overline{)2.56}$ 7. $8\overline{).985}$ 8. $5\overline{)1.823}$ 9. $9\overline{)5.35}$ 10. $6\overline{)8.3}$

11. $6\overline{)25.62}$ 12. $9\overline{)2.807}$ 13. $7\overline{).304}$ 14. $8\overline{)79.6}$ 15. $5\overline{)12.7}$

XXIX. Decimals. Divide to nearest thousandth:

1. $62\overline{)607.6}$ 2. $7.3\overline{).7008}$ 3. $.026\overline{)153.27}$ 4. $32.6\overline{).46455}$ 5. $2.84\overline{)37,630}$

6. $11.3\overline{)1.0283}$ 7. $65.3\overline{)4.8322}$ 8. $4.89\overline{)1124.7}$ 9. $12.5\overline{)1.1421}$ 10. $4.9\overline{)90.29}$

11. $.64\overline{)56.52}$ 12. $1.9\overline{)170.1}$ 13. $.28\overline{)198.8}$ 14. $.85\overline{)705.5}$ 15. $.64\overline{)460.8}$

XXX. Change to decimals:

1. $\frac{1}{10} = 10\overline{)1.0}^{.1}$

2. $\frac{1}{2} =$

3. $\frac{1}{4} =$

4. $\frac{2}{5} =$

5. $\frac{3}{4} =$

6. $\frac{3}{12} =$

7. $\frac{9}{5} =$

8. $\frac{1}{16} =$

9. $\frac{13}{20} =$

10. $\frac{24}{25} =$

11. $\frac{5}{16} =$

12. $\frac{13}{16} =$

13. $\frac{19}{50} =$

14. $\frac{11}{16} =$

15. $\frac{9}{25} =$

16. $\frac{11}{20} =$

17. $\frac{7}{16} =$

18. $\frac{1}{7} =$

XXXI. Measures:

A. Find the area of a rectangle:

1. 9 feet by 25 feet = _____ square feet

2. 12 feet by 9 yards = _____ square feet

3. 24 feet by 14 yards = _____ square yards

4. 16 feet by 21 yards = _____ square feet

5. 18 inches by 3 feet = _____ square feet

6. 3 feet by 9 feet = _____ square inches

7. 8 yards by 6 yards = _____ square yards

8. 48 rods × 66 rods = _____ square rods

9. $5\frac{1}{2}$ feet × 72 feet = _____ square feet

10. 40 rods × 40 rods = _____ acres

    (160 square rods = 1 acre)

11. 60 rods × 50 rods = _____ acres

12. 97 rods × 62 rods = _____ acres

13. 126 rods × 64 rods = _____ acres

14. 240 rods × 137 rods = _____ acres

15. 200 feet × 200 feet = _____ square feet

B. Find the *perimeter* of a rectangle:

1. 300 feet × 15 feet

2. 45 yards × 72 yards

3. 16 inches × 2 feet

4. 12 feet × 10 feet

5. $\frac{1}{2}$ foot × 9 inches

6. 6 inches × 8 inches

7. 4 feet × 1 yard

8. 4 yards × 1 foot

9. 25 feet × 15 feet

10. $25\frac{1}{2}$ feet × $10\frac{1}{2}$ feet

C. Find the volume of a cube:

1. 4 feet $\times$ 3 feet $\times$ 2 feet = _____ cubic feet

2. 6 feet $\times$ 7 feet $\times$ 5 feet = _____ cubic feet

3. 80 feet $\times$ 45 feet $\times$ 5 feet = _____ cubic feet

4. 8 yards $\times$ 6 yards $\times$ 3 yards = _____ cubic yards

5. 14 inches $\times$ 11 inches $\times$ 9 inches = _____ cubic inches or _____ gallons (1 gallon = 231 cubic inches)

6. 5 inches $\times$ 5 inches $\times$ $9\frac{1}{4}$ inches = _____ cubic inches

7. 5 feet $\times$ 4 feet $\times$ 3 feet = _____ cubic feet or _____ bushels (1 cubic foot = $\frac{8}{10}$ bushel)

8. 4 feet, 10 inches $\times$ 3 feet $\times$ 2 feet, 9 inches = _____ cubic feet

9. 150 feet $\times$ 500 feet $\times$ 6 feet = _____ cubic feet

10. 25 yards $\times$ 18 feet $\times$ 13 inches = _____ cubic inches or _____ cubic feet or _____ cubic yards

D. Equivalents:

1. $\frac{1}{2}$ pound = _____ ounces

2. 2 pecks = _____ bushels

3. 6 square yards = _____ square feet

4. $2\frac{1}{4}$ pounds = _____ ounces

5. 36 feet = _____ yard

6. 16 pints = _____ quarts

7. 1 gallon = _____ cups

8. 11 yards = _____ rods

9. 42 inches = _____ feet

10. 3 feet, 9 inches = _____ feet

11. 3 feet, 9 inches = _____ inches

12. 5 feet, 4 inches = _____ inches

13. 3 hours, 20 minutes = _____ minutes

14. 2 yards, 2 feet = _____ inches

15. 3 pounds, 12 ounces = _____ pounds

16. 16 feet, 6 inches = _____ yards

17. 7 gallons, 2 quarts = _____ quarts

18. 25 pecks = _____ bushels

19. 5 weeks, 3 days = _____ days

20. 6 quarts, 1 pint = _____ pints

21. 14 minutes, 10 seconds = _____ seconds

22. 125 minutes = _____ hours

23. 38 items = _____ dozen

24. 15 quarts = _____ gallons

25. 80 minutes = _____ hours

26. 21 inches = _____ feet

SIXTH GRADE

XXXII. Thought problems:

1. What is the number if .75 of it is 96? _____   WORK SPACE

2. What is the ratio of 18 to 27? _____

3. Sue has read 210 pages in her book. She has read $\frac{3}{4}$ of the book. How many pages are in the book? _____

4. A kitchen is 21 ft. long, and 18 ft. wide. How much will it cost to cover the floor with linoleum at $1.25 per square yard? _____

5. The Johnson family drove home from their vacation, a distance of 235 miles, in 7 hours. How many miles did they drive each hour on the average? _____

6. Bob bought 5 books at 25¢ each and 1 book for 75¢. How much did he pay for the 6 books? _____

7. Before Christmas ice skates sold at $2.50 a pair at the sports shop. In February these same skates were sold at 40% off. How much did the skates sell for in February? _____

8. Dick caught 3 fish. The fish weighed $1\frac{1}{8}$, $2\frac{1}{2}$, and $1\frac{1}{4}$ pounds. How many pounds did they weigh together? _____

9. Bill had 4 pounds of candy. He put $\frac{1}{3}$ pound in each bag. How many bags of candy did he have? _____

10. How many lengths $\frac{1}{16}$ of an inch long can be found in $\frac{2}{3}$ of a foot? _____

373

11. Jane bought 8 cans of dog food. Her dog eats $1\frac{1}{3}$ cans of food each day. How many days will the 8 cans last?

_____

12. Of the 96 plants in Tom's garden, 72 were tomato plants. What part of the plants were tomato plants?

_____

13. The combined thickness of 5 pieces of steel was 2.625 in. What was the average thickness of each piece?

_____

14. Mr. Lee is making a garage. He wants to put a concrete floor in it 24 ft. long and 15 ft. wide. How much will it cost to lay this floor at $3 a square yard?

_____

15. Find the total cost if your school buys:

40 maps for $13.65	$_____
1 desk @ $65.50	_____
3 tables @ $24.75 each	_____
1 chair @ $16.85	_____
18 chairs @ $5.30 each	_____
2 bookcases @ $37.20 each	_____
Total	$_____

16. Find the total cost of the following articles:

6 globes @ $10.45 each	$_____
8 cases of maps for $23.60	_____
12 outline maps for $6.80	_____
6 tables @ $24.75 each	_____
60 chairs @ $5.30 each	_____
5 bookcases @ $37.20 each	_____
1 office desk @ $75.00	_____
Total	$_____

ANSWERS

sixth grade english exercises

I. 1. Healthy cows must have green grass. 2. The boy who was digging looked at the stones on his shovel. 3. Your house is made of stone. 4. The dishes in your house are made of clay. 5. All your furniture is made of wood. 6. You would soon starve without food. 7. Can you catch fish without a hook? 8. Only living things can grow. 9. Plants are among the largest and smallest things in the world. 10. Very large trees are found in California. 11. In New Jersey I once saw a large hollow tree. 12. A piece of moss is a flowerless plant.

II.
1. plants—are
2. plant—has
3. root—is
4. Roots—differ
5. I—picked
6. stems—are
7. part—is
8. (You)—soak
9. You—may dig
10. plant—needs
11. plant—will grow
12. vines—lie

III.
1. dec.
2. int.
3. imp.
4. exc.
5. imp.
6. exc.
7. int.
8. imp.
9. exc.
10. dec.
11. int.
12. dec.

IV. 1. "Look at that queer old man with the long white beard," exclaimed the boy.
2. Teacher said, "Cut six pieces of wood exactly the same size."
3. "A locust," the boy answered, "is a cousin to a grasshopper."
4. "The locust is a greedy animal," the boy read on.
5. "Mrs. Cricket does not sing," our teacher told us. "It is Mr. Cricket that makes all the noise."
6. "Crickets are thirsty creatures. They drink water, milk, tea, soup, beer or vinegar," Miss Mills read.
7. Father added, "Crickets like vegetables."
8. Mother added, "They'll eat anything they find."
9. "They ate a woolen blanket at my house," Mrs. Jones said.
10. "Crickets can fly but they would rather hop," Mr. Jones told us.

V.
1. inquire
2. attractive
3. courageous
4. burden
5. crowd
6. famous
7. filth
8. area
9. district
10. blossoms
11. bright
12. cloth
13. abode
14. highway
15. vacant
16. small
17. large
18. excellent
19. toil
20. selected

VI.
1. modern
2. foreign
3. ugly
4. retail
5. defeat
6. exterior
7. friend
8. difficult
9. employer
10. famine
11. new
12. majority
13. poor
14. plentiful
15. rarely
16. slow
17. hot
18. worthless
19. idle
20. sad

VII.
1. there
2. bare
3. buy
4. son
5. shone
6. grate
7. whole
8. scene
9. hear
10. stare
11. paws
12. plane
13. mite
14. bored
15. prey
16. meddle
17. heir
18. our
19. wring
20. tail

VIII.
1. Crickets—will drink—liquid
2. cricket—runs
3. He—eats—leaves—grass
4. children—fish
5. leader—found—us
6. crickets—have—wings
7. people—keep—crickets
8. You—may find—cricket
9. Mrs. Cricket—makes—nest
10. You—do think—what
11. she—sits—listens
12. she—fights
13. creature—was
14. hillside—was covered
15. I—put—things
16. butterfly—wears—coat
17. butterfly—builds—house
18. gentleman—saw—butterflies
19. peacock—has—feathers
20. You—have told—things

IX.
1. crickets—liquid—way
2. cricket—hole
3. leaves—grass
4. children—crickets
5. leader
6. crickets—wings
7. Spain—people—crickets—cages
8. cricket—woods
9. Mrs. Cricket—nest
10. eggs—Mrs. Cricket
11. enemy
12. —
13. creature
14. hillside—carrots
15. things—piece—paper
16. butterfly—coat—hairs
17. butterfly—house
18. gentleman—butterflies
19. peacock—feathers
20. things

X.
1. their
2. his
3. He
4. —
5. us
6. —
7. them
8. You
9. her
10. you
11. She
12. She
13. —
14. —
15. I
16. —
17. —
18. —
19. —
20. You, me

XI.
1. any
2. The, field
3. —
4. Little, French
5. the, Scout
6. Little, no
7. the, little
8. a, the
9. soft, smooth
10. the
11. the
12. —
13. a, little, live, green
14. the, wild
15. all, these, a, white
16. The, an, elegant, soft, velvet, fine
17. The, no
18. The, some, orange, black
19. A, newborn, no
20. many

XII. 5. Finally   12. bravely   13. Here, pale

XIII. 3. and 9. and 10. After 11. and 18. and

XIV.
1. in
2. into
4. for
7. In, in, to, for
8. in
11. for
14. with
15. on, of
16. of

XV.
1. P.M.
2. A.M.
3. P.S.
4. R.F.D.
5. Mr.
6. Mrs.
7. Dr.
8. Ave.
9. Capt.
10. Maj.

XVI.
1. What story can a bird's beak tell?
2. Mary asked, "Are you boys brothers?"
3. Dr. J. V. Smith lives in Avon, Oregon.
4. Don't ever forget it again!
5. We all sang *The Cradle Song*. (Some schools underline titles, some use quotation marks.)
6. Yes, we studied the butterfly last year.
7. George, Michael, and John tied for third place.
8. Byron said, "This doesn't make sense."
9. He ran the race in one hour, 36 minutes.
10. Hurrah! The parade is coming!

XVII.

Velva, North Dakota
January 6, 1959

Dear Aunt Mary,

The book you sent me for Christmas was wonderful! I have read it already and now I am letting Gretchen read it. I have always liked stories written by Albert Payson Terhune.

We are all well. We missed having you with us for Christmas this year, but know you must have enjoyed being in Florida.

Thank you again.

Lots of love,
Mary Lynne

ANSWERS sixth grade arithmetic exercises

I. Round out numbers.

50	90	40	800
40	60	100	400
100	30	800	900
1000	30	900	600
400	90	500	100

II. Exponents.

64	100,000	16	81
16	1,024	9	64
27	108	81	3,125
125	25	147	36
256	512	32	49

III. Place-value.

1. one
2. tenth
3. ten
4. hundred
5. hundredth
6. one
7. five
8. twenty-five
9. five
10. five
11. four
12. sixteen
13. one
14. four
15. sixteen

IV. Sets.

1. $A \cup B = \{1,2,4,6\}$
2. $A \cup B = \{a,b,g,x,y,z\}$
3. $A \cup B = \{A,B,C,H,Y\}$
4. $A \cap B = \phi$
5. $A \cap B = \{c,f\}$
6. $A \cap B = \{B\}$

V. Sets.

1. $A = B, A \sim B$
2. $A = B$
3. $A \neq B, A \sim B$
4. $A = B, A \sim B$
5. $A = B, A \sim B$
6. $A \subset B, A \neq B$

VI. Multiple operations.

1. 33
2. 3
3. 35
4. 5
5. 2
6. 2
7. 7
8. 95
9. 39
10. 131

VII. Fractions. Add:

1. $1\frac{1}{8}$ 2. $1\frac{2}{3}$ 3. $1\frac{13}{24}$ 4. $1\frac{1}{3}$
5. $1\frac{1}{5}$ 6. $1\frac{5}{8}$ 7. $1\frac{7}{12}$ 8. $1\frac{3}{5}$
9. 2 10. 2 11. $1\frac{11}{12}$ 12. $1\frac{1}{9}$

VIII. Fractions. Add:

1. $12\frac{7}{8}$ 2. $22\frac{1}{3}$ 3. $15\frac{3}{4}$ 4. $14\frac{1}{6}$
5. $18\frac{8}{15}$ 6. $7\frac{1}{12}$ 7. 10 8. $13\frac{1}{5}$
9. $19\frac{3}{4}$ 10. $13\frac{1}{4}$ 11. $13\frac{7}{12}$ 12. $10\frac{7}{12}$

IX. Fractions. Add:

1. $22\frac{1}{4}$ 2. $26\frac{23}{24}$ 3. $13\frac{14}{15}$ 4. $24\frac{3}{4}$
5. $21\frac{1}{2}$ 6. $24\frac{5}{16}$ 7. 12 8. $21\frac{3}{4}$
9. $27\frac{1}{24}$ 10. $30\frac{19}{24}$ 11. $14\frac{2}{3}$ 12. $16\frac{11}{16}$

X. Fractions. Subtract:

1. $2\frac{1}{3}$ 2. $5\frac{1}{2}$ 3. $1\frac{5}{6}$ 4. $1\frac{1}{2}$
5. $5\frac{1}{8}$ 6. $8\frac{1}{3}$ 7. $3\frac{1}{8}$ 8. $4\frac{1}{3}$
9. $5\frac{1}{2}$ 10. $4\frac{1}{8}$ 11. $2\frac{1}{4}$ 12. $5\frac{1}{8}$

XI. Fractions. Subtract:

1. $12\frac{3}{5}$ 2. $7\frac{9}{10}$ 3. $1\frac{1}{3}$ 4. $3\frac{9}{10}$
5. $1\frac{1}{3}$ 6. $2\frac{1}{4}$ 7. $2\frac{3}{7}$ 8. $2\frac{2}{5}$
9. $1\frac{5}{8}$ 10. $3\frac{7}{9}$ 11. $4\frac{1}{8}$ 12. $2\frac{7}{10}$

XII. Fractions. Subtract:

1. $1\frac{5}{8}$ 2. $2\frac{5}{6}$ 3. $3\frac{7}{8}$ 4. $3\frac{5}{6}$
5. $5\frac{9}{10}$ 6. $5\frac{2}{3}$ 7. $5\frac{1}{2}$ 8. $7\frac{2}{3}$
9. $2\frac{7}{8}$ 10. $\frac{3}{8}$ 11. $4\frac{1}{3}$ 12. $2\frac{5}{9}$

XIII. Fractions. Subtract:

1. $2\frac{7}{20}$ 2. $3\frac{9}{35}$ 3. $3\frac{11}{24}$ 4. $1\frac{13}{24}$
5. $6\frac{5}{24}$ 6. $4\frac{7}{20}$ 7. $1\frac{5}{6}$ 8. $1\frac{13}{20}$
9. $1\frac{7}{15}$ 10. $5\frac{19}{24}$ 11. $3\frac{1}{35}$ 12. $1\frac{17}{18}$
13. $6\frac{1}{12}$ 14. $1\frac{19}{30}$ 15. $4\frac{33}{40}$ 16. $10\frac{1}{14}$

XIV. Fractions. Multiply:

1. 2   9. $2\frac{13}{16}$ 17. 16
2. $8\frac{1}{3}$ 10. $1\frac{3}{5}$ 18. $7\frac{5}{7}$
3. $1\frac{5}{7}$ 11. $3\frac{1}{8}$ 19. 16
4. 8   12. 6   20. 8
5. 6   13. $1\frac{6}{7}$ 21. $1\frac{3}{5}$
6. $2\frac{2}{3}$ 14. 4   22. $2\frac{1}{2}$
7. $3\frac{1}{2}$ 15. 2   23. $14\frac{2}{7}$
8. 2   16. $7\frac{1}{2}$ 24. 24

XV. Fractions. Multiply:

1. $\frac{1}{4}$ 7. $\frac{21}{32}$ 13. $\frac{1}{2}$
2. $\frac{1}{2}$ 8. $\frac{8}{15}$ 14. $\frac{1}{12}$
3. $\frac{5}{16}$ 9. $\frac{1}{3}$ 15. $\frac{5}{16}$
4. $\frac{8}{25}$ 10. $\frac{1}{4}$ 16. $\frac{7}{12}$
5. $\frac{3}{16}$ 11. $\frac{1}{4}$ 17. $\frac{7}{10}$
6. $\frac{1}{8}$ 12. $\frac{1}{6}$ 18. $\frac{9}{160}$

XVI. Fractions. Multiply:

1. $52\frac{1}{2}$ 7. $43\frac{3}{4}$ 13. $38\frac{3}{7}$
2. $33\frac{5}{6}$ 8. 42   14. $57\frac{3}{4}$
3. $24\frac{1}{2}$ 9. $13\frac{5}{7}$ 15. $68\frac{4}{7}$
4. 45   10. $82\frac{1}{2}$ 16. 14
5. $36\frac{2}{3}$ 11. 59   17. 30
6. $66\frac{3}{5}$ 12. $88\frac{8}{9}$ 18. $31\frac{1}{2}$

XVII. Fractions. Multiply:

1. 58   7. 64   13. 93
2. $67\frac{2}{3}$ 8. 23   14. 51
3. 101   9. 59   15. 111
4. $39\frac{1}{6}$ 10. $26\frac{1}{2}$ 16. 578
5. 168   11. $62\frac{2}{3}$ 17. $159\frac{3}{7}$
6. $47\frac{1}{4}$ 12. 44   18. 70

XVIII. Fractions. Multiply:

1. 3   7. $6\frac{11}{54}$ 13. $3\frac{1}{3}$
2. $3\frac{1}{3}$ 8. $4\frac{31}{50}$ 14. $28\frac{13}{18}$
3. $7\frac{1}{32}$ 9. 5   15. $33\frac{7}{12}$
4. $5\frac{9}{10}$ 10. $2\frac{31}{32}$ 16. $5\frac{23}{60}$
5. $1\frac{2}{3}$ 11. $10\frac{31}{48}$ 17. $28\frac{1}{3}$
6. $2\frac{4}{5}$ 12. $4\frac{1}{4}$ 18. $13\frac{47}{56}$

XIX. Fractions. Multiply:

1. $26\frac{2}{3}$ 2. $43\frac{1}{3}$ 3. 51   4. 110
5. $69\frac{3}{5}$ 6. $85\frac{1}{2}$ 7. 38   8. 189
9. $50\frac{2}{3}$ 10. $27\frac{1}{3}$ 11. 87   12. 161
13. $53\frac{1}{3}$ 14. $73\frac{3}{5}$ 15. 133   16. 408

XX. Fractions. Divide:

1. 8   10. 18   19. 20
2. 48   11. $3\frac{3}{7}$ 20. 24
3. 24   12. 18   21. $3\frac{3}{5}$
4. 6   13. $14\frac{2}{5}$ 22. 40
5. 10   14. 15   23. 16
6. 16   15. 20   24. 5
7. 8   16. 25   25. $10\frac{1}{2}$
8. $13\frac{1}{3}$ 17. 49   26. 20
9. 12   18. 15   27. 34

XXI. Fractions. Divide:

1. 3   8. $1\frac{3}{5}$ 15. 4
2. $1\frac{13}{15}$ 9. $\frac{35}{99}$ 16. $\frac{25}{32}$
3. 2   10. $2\frac{1}{2}$ 17. $1\frac{31}{33}$
4. $1\frac{19}{30}$ 11. $\frac{3}{7}$ 18. $2\frac{1}{2}$
5. $1\frac{1}{2}$ 12. $3\frac{1}{3}$ 19. $1\frac{5}{7}$
6. $2\frac{53}{66}$ 13. 2   20. $\frac{1}{2}$
7. $3\frac{13}{22}$ 14. 6   21. 4

XXII. Decimals. Add:

1. 6.125   6. 9.375   11. 15.5
2. 11.583   7. 12.875   12. 18.208
3. 15.25   8. 21.125   13. 125.21
4. 11.167   9. 15.042   14. 47.41
5. 22.708   10. 22.208   15. 444.645

XXIII. Decimals. Subtract:

1. 3.605   6. .564   11. .9
2. 2.33   7. 2.24   12. .32
3. .96   8. 25.503   13. 1.869
4. 1.171   9. .6   14. 7.375
5. .245   10. .767   15. 2.375

XXIV. Decimals. Multiply:

1. .625   6. 15.232   11. 11.4062
2. 1.955   7. 37.323   12. .4203
3. 13.104   8. 157.92   13. .399
4. 100.34   9. 33.125   14. .32759
5. 490.5   10. 3.94794   15. .942

XXV. Decimals. Multiply:

1. 1.0368   6. .14268   11. 1.5678
2. .00024   7. 6.734   12. 2.1056
3. .00063   8. .2159   13. 3.5697
4. .0043   9. 53.176   14. 1.93338
5. .6912   10. .3162   15. .030944

XXVI. Decimals. Divide:

1. .3   2. .6   3. 1.4
4. 11.4   5. .04   6. .08
7. .91   8. 3.23   9. .004

10. .040	11. .081	12. .498
13. 3.002	14. 1.409	15. 1.308
16. 2.120	17. 18.4	18. 56.54

XXVII. Decimals. Divide:

1. .25	2. .60	3. .50
4. .67	5. .74	6. .83
7. .25	8. .67	9. .80
10. .38	11. .67	12. .58
13. .75	14. .33	15. .41

XXVIII. Decimals. Divide:

1. .525	2. 8.8	3. 2.34
4. 2.415	5. 1.43	6. .37
7. .123	8. .365	9. .59
10. 1.38	11. 4.27	12. .31
13. .043	14. 9.95	15. 2.54

XXIX. Decimals. Divide:

1. 9.8	2. .096	3. 5895
4. .0142	5. 13250.	6. .091
7. .074	8. 230.	9. .091
10. 18.427	11. 88.3125	12. 89.526
13. 710	14. 830	15. 720

XXX. Change to decimals:

1. .1	7. 1.8	13. .38
2. .5	8. .0625	14. .6875
3. .25	9. .65	15. .36
4. .4	10. .96	16. .55
5. .75	11. .3125	17. .4375
6. .25	12. .8125	18. .14$\frac{2}{7}$

XXXI. Measures:

A.
1. 225 square feet	8. 3168 square yards
2. 324 square feet	9. 396 square feet
3. 112 square yards	10. 10 acres
4. 1008 square feet	11. 18$\frac{3}{4}$ acres
5. 4$\frac{1}{2}$ square feet	12. 37$\frac{47}{80}$ acres
6. 3888 square inches	13. 50$\frac{2}{3}$ acres
7. 48 square yards	14. 205$\frac{1}{2}$ acres
	15. 40,000 square feet

B.
1. 630 feet	6. 28 inches
2. 234 yards	7. 14 feet (4$\frac{2}{3}$ yards)
3. 80 inches (6$\frac{2}{3}$ feet)	8. 26 feet (8$\frac{2}{3}$ yards)
4. 44 feet	9. 80 feet
5. 30 inches (2$\frac{1}{2}$ feet)	10. 72 feet

C.
1. 24 cubic feet	7. 60 cubic feet
2. 210 cubic feet	or 48 bushels
3. 18,000 cubic feet	8. 39$\frac{7}{8}$ cubic feet
4. 144 cubic yards	9. 450,000 cubic feet
5. 1386 cubic inches	10. 2,527,200 cubic inches
or 6 gallons	1462$\frac{1}{2}$ cubic feet
6. 231$\frac{1}{4}$ cubic inches	54.166 cubic yards

D.
1. 8 ounces	14. 96 inches
2. $\frac{1}{2}$ bushel	15. 3$\frac{3}{4}$ pounds
3. 54 square feet	16. 5$\frac{1}{2}$ yards
4. 36 ounces	17. 30 quarts
5. 12 yards	18. 6$\frac{1}{4}$ bushels
6. 8 quarts	19. 38 days
7. 16 cups	20. 13 pints
8. 2 rods	21. 850 seconds
9. 3$\frac{1}{2}$ feet	22. 2$\frac{1}{12}$ hours
10. 3$\frac{3}{4}$ feet	23. 3$\frac{1}{6}$ dozen
11. 45 inches	24. 3$\frac{3}{4}$ gallons
12. 64 inches	25. 1$\frac{1}{3}$ hours
13. 200 minutes	26. 1$\frac{3}{4}$ feet

XXXII. Thought problems:

1. 128	9. 12 bags
2. $\frac{2}{3}$	10. 128 lengths
3. 280 pages	11. 6 days
4. $52.50	12. $\frac{3}{4}$ of them
5. 33$\frac{4}{7}$ miles per hr.	13. .525 in. ave
6. $2.00	14. $120.
7. $1.50	15. $340.05
8. 4$\frac{7}{8}$ pounds	16. $820.60

reading and english

I. **What do the underlined words and phrases mean? Instead of a dictionary, use the thoughts expressed by the sentences as clues to the meanings. (10 points)**

1. He <u>estimated</u> that temperatures on the desert were between 90 and 100 degrees.
2. The last <u>survivor</u> of the plane crash was rescued by air observers after two days of <u>intensive</u> search.
3. He was <u>whisked</u> to a hospital and his life was saved. The <u>extreme</u> exposure had <u>claimed</u> his two <u>companions</u>.
4. The three men had been on an <u>exploratory</u> trip to inspect a large piece of land which was said to be <u>ripe for development</u>.
5. In relating this <u>grim</u> experience, the survivor said it was all he could do to keep from <u>going berserk</u>.

II. **The list consists of words of motion. Select the one that best fits each sentence. You may use a dictionary. (10 points)**

1. The frightened little mouse _____ across the floor.
2. The injured football player _____ off the field.
3. Wearily the old man _____ up the hill.
4. In the last moment before the bell rang, she _____ to her locker for her books.
5. He _____ out of the room in anger.
6. In spite of the rain on Easter Sunday, the ladies _____ up and down the avenue.
7. She drove the car off the cliff and _____ into the ocean.
8. A large dog _____ at me as I walked through the gate.
9. She seemed as gay and carefree as a butterfly as she _____ through the field of daisies.
10. The airplane _____ over the steeple just in time.

dashed
tripped
trudged
limped
stamped
scurried
strutted
lunged
plunged
zoomed

III. **Underline the complete subject once and the complete predicate twice. (10 points)**
1. Jean doesn't live far from us.
2. Everyone laughed, giggled, or shouted.
3. The boys and girls wanted the rest of the story.
4. Bob laughed and finished it for them.
5. He went up to the North Woods last fall.

IV. **Name the kind of sentence each one is—declarative, interrogative, imperative, or exclamatory. (10 points)**
1. The children looked at the stars.
2. Tell us what they saw.
3. Did they look through telescopes?
4. What a big help telescopes would have been!
5. Could they see very much without telescopes?
6. Ask David what he saw.
7. The class expects to get a telescope.
8. Have you ever looked through a large telescope?
9. The view at night is breath-taking!
10. Visit a planetarium sometime.

V. **Underline the transitive verb once and its object twice. (10 points)**
1. Make a list of the nouns.
2. A dog should not attack a porcupine.
3. Porcupines do not actually shoot their quills.
4. The man questioned us for a long time.
5. I shall now tell my story.

VI. **Give the comparative and superlative degrees of the following adjectives and adverbs. (10 points)**
1. quick
2. quickly
3. many
4. well
5. often

VII. Give the second (past) and third (past with a helper) principal parts of these verbs. (10 points)

1. run
2. am
3. bring
4. do
5. give

VIII. Underline the prepositional phrases. (10 points)

1. The children ran to the store.
2. Only members of the club were admitted.
3. Stand between us.
4. Patty spoke to all the children in the class.
5. The boy with the red hair was elected president of the class.
6. Some stood on the sidelines and others walked out on the field.
7. We cheered for the winning team.

IX. Rewrite, correcting the one grammatical error in each sentence. (10 points)

1. I like those kind of shoes.
2. Alice wasn't no good at making speeches.
3. She hoped no one would notice nothing.
4. Her face it was certainly red.
5. "Of course," he said, "I once run a race with a tiger."
6. I wish we could have saw that.
7. They knew they had broke the record.
8. It learned me more than anything else.
9. What have you did recently that you have enjoyed very much?
10. Don't make no mistakes now.

X. Story telling. (10 points)

A. Check those sentences which you think would make good first sentences for stories.

_____ 1. A clam race isn't fast but it's lots of fun.
_____ 2. I laugh every time I think of this story.
_____ 3. Have you ever given a speech and noticed right in the middle of it that everyone is giggling?
_____ 4. Now I want to tell you about something that happened to my brother last summer.
_____ 5. Most of you have heard this story, but it's the only one I could think of.

B. Check those that you think would make good last sentences for stories.

_____ 1. And that's all I can remember about it.
_____ 2. Suddenly I knew that I had eaten the paper doily.
_____ 3. That was the last time my dog ever chased a skunk.
_____ 4. Some of the other boys were there, too.
_____ 5. Well, I guess that's about all.

arithmetic test

I. Add.
1. $6\frac{7}{16}$, $6\frac{5}{8}$, $3\frac{3}{4}$, $7\frac{1}{2}$
2. $5\frac{7}{8}$, $2\frac{1}{16}$, $5\frac{1}{2}$, $3\frac{1}{4}$
3. $4\frac{1}{6}$, $3\frac{3}{4}$, $2\frac{1}{12}$, $4\frac{2}{3}$
4. $7\frac{3}{4}$, $5\frac{4}{5}$, $4\frac{7}{10}$
5. $11\frac{1}{3}$, $2\frac{1}{2}$, $\frac{1}{6}$

II. Subtract.
1. $8\frac{7}{8} - 2\frac{2}{3}$
2. $10\frac{3}{4} - 6\frac{2}{5}$
3. $8\frac{4}{9} - 6\frac{1}{2}$
4. $20\frac{1}{12} - 10\frac{1}{3}$
5. $14 - 10\frac{2}{5}$

III. Multiply.
1. $\frac{3}{4} \times \frac{1}{6}$
2. $16 \times \frac{3}{8}$
3. $\frac{3}{4} \times 10$
4. $\frac{7}{8} \times \frac{2}{3}$
5. $12\frac{1}{2} \times \frac{4}{5}$

IV. Divide.
1. $6\frac{2}{3} \div 2\frac{2}{3}$
2. $6\frac{3}{7} \div 12\frac{1}{2}$
3. $3\frac{3}{5} \div 2\frac{1}{10}$
4. $8\frac{1}{4} \div 1\frac{3}{8}$
5. $9\frac{5}{8} \div 2\frac{3}{4}$

V. Multiply.
1. $12.5 \times .05$
2. $.85 \times 2.3$
3. $.0697 \times 4.7$
4. $.009 \times .07$
5. $.346 \times .58$

VI. Divide.
1. $220.8 \div 12$
2. $33 \div 55$
3. $7.245 \div 3$
4. $.7007 \div .7$
5. $460.8 \div .64$

VII. Change to decimals.
1. $\frac{3}{4}$
2. $\frac{3}{16}$
3. $\frac{13}{20}$
4. $\frac{2}{5}$
5. $\frac{1}{7}$

VIII. Find.
1. 25% of $2.50
2. 52% of $235.
3. 1% of $325.12
4. $66\frac{2}{3}$% of $.54
5. 5% of $100.

IX. Alice wants to buy a wrist watch for $17.25. If she can save $1.15 a week, in how many weeks will she have enough to buy the watch?

X. Mr. Dart drives a bus between towns 2.8 miles apart. He makes 18 round trips a day. He says he averages 6.3 miles on each gallon of gasoline. How many gallons of gasoline does he use a day?

XI. What does the diagram show?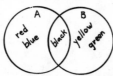

XII. Express in exponent form the place-value of each digit in a three-place numeral in
   a. the base four system:
   b. the base three system:
   c. the base five system:
   d. the base ten system:
   e. the base seven system:

final test answers   sixth grade

reading and english

I. (Allow for differences in expression.)
estimated—thought, or guessed
survivor—one who remained alive
intensive—very thorough
whisked—moved very quickly
extreme—very great
claimed—taken the lives of
exploratory—to look over closely
ripe for development—ready to be used
grim—harsh or terrible
going berserk—losing his senses

II.
1. scurried
2. limped
3. trudged
4. dashed
5. stamped
6. strutted
7. plunged
8. lunged
9. tripped
10. zoomed

III.
1. <u>Jean</u> <u>doesn't live far from us</u>.
2. <u>Everyone</u> <u>laughed, giggled, or shouted</u>.
3. <u>The boys and girls</u> <u>wanted the rest of the story</u>.
4. <u>Bob</u> <u>laughed and finished it for them</u>.
5. <u>He</u> <u>went up to the North Woods last fall</u>.

IV.
1. declarative
2. imperative
3. interrogative
4. exclamatory
5. interrogative
6. imperative
7. declarative
8. interrogative
9. exclamatory
10. imperative

V.
1. <u>Make</u>   <u>list</u>
2. <u>should attack</u>   <u>porcupine</u>
3. <u>do shoot</u>   <u>quills</u>
4. <u>questioned</u>   <u>us</u>
5. <u>shall tell</u>   <u>story</u>

VI.
1. quicker — quickest
2. more quickly — most quickly
3. more — most
4. better — best
5. more often — most often

VII.
1. ran — run
2. was — been
3. brought — brought
4. did — done
5. gave — given

VIII.
1. to the store
2. of the club
3. between us
4. to all the children
   in the class
5. with the red hair
   of the class
6. on the sidelines
   on the field
7. for the winning team

IX.
1. I like <u>that</u> kind of shoes.
2. Alice wasn't <u>any</u> good at making speeches.
3. She hoped no one would notice <u>anything</u>.
4. Her face ~~it~~ was certainly red.
5. "Of course," he said, "I once <u>ran</u> a race with a tiger."
6. I wish we could have <u>seen</u> that.
7. They knew they had <u>broken</u> the record.
8. It <u>taught</u> me more than anything else.
9. What have you <u>done</u> recently that you have enjoyed very much?
10. Don't make <u>any</u> mistakes now.

X.
A. 1, 3,
B. 2, 3.

arithmetic

I. Add.
1. $24\frac{5}{16}$
2. $16\frac{11}{16}$
3. $14\frac{2}{3}$
4. $18\frac{1}{4}$
5. 14

II. Subtract.
1. $6\frac{5}{24}$
2. $4\frac{7}{20}$
3. $1\frac{17}{18}$
4. $9\frac{3}{4}$
5. $3\frac{3}{5}$

III. Multiply.
1. $\frac{1}{8}$
2. 6
3. $7\frac{1}{2}$
4. $\frac{7}{12}$
5. 10

IV. Divide.
1. $2\frac{1}{2}$
2. $\frac{18}{35}$
3. $1\frac{5}{7}$
4. 6
5. $3\frac{1}{2}$

V. Multiply.
1. .625
2. 1.955
3. .32759
4. .00063
5. .20068

VI. Divide.
1. 18.4
2. .6
3. 2.415
4. 1.001
5. 720

VII. Change to decimals.
1. .75
2. $.18\frac{3}{4}$
3. .65
4. .4
5. $.14\frac{2}{7}$

VIII. Find.
1. $\$.62\frac{1}{2}$
2. \$122.20
3. \$3.2512
4. \$.36
5. \$5.

IX. 15 weeks

X. 16 gallons

XI. Set A = {red, blue, black}
Set B = {black, yellow, green}
A ∩ B = {black}

XII. a. base four
b. base three
c. base five
d. base ten
e. base seven

contents | seventh grade

helping your child in seventh grade

YOUR CHILD is about twelve years old. This can be a happy age for both you and your child. He can be a pleasant companion, co-operative, enthusiastic, and interested in everything. He has a great capacity to absorb details and a real eagerness to do so, a quality that is very helpful in his schoolwork.

The following sections give some idea of what your child will be taught in the seventh grade, and will enable you to help him with any special problems he may have.

reading | seventh grade

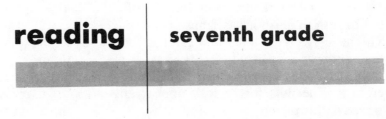

BY THE TIME your child is in the seventh grade he has learned the basic reading skills, but you can continue to help him by making good reading material available in your home. Encourage him also to go regularly to the library. Talk over with him the things he has read. Find out how well he understands what he is reading, because reading without comprehension is like not reading at all.

Refer to the basic list which follows. The books that are starred are the ones with which nearly everyone becomes familiar.

And remember: The best way for *anyone* to become a good reader, and to derive pleasure from reading, is to read, read, read.

books your seventh-grade child may enjoy

National Velvet—*Bagnold, Enid*
Wild Horse—*Balch, Glenn*
Understood Betsy—*Canfield, Dorothy*
William the Conqueror—*Costain, Thomas B.*
Two Years Before the Mast
   Dana, Richard Henry
Sign of the Seven Seas—*Dawson, Carley*
A Tale of Two Cities—*Dickens, Charles*
The Boys' Sherlock Holmes
   Doyle, Sir Arthur Conan
County Fair: A 4-H Romance—*Emery, Anne*
Pirates, Pirates, Pirates—*Fenner, Phyllis*

Hitty—*Field, Rachel L.*
Mr. Midshipman Hornblower—*Forester, C. S.*
All About the Atom—*Freeman, Ira*
Arctic Adventure—*Gilbert, Kenneth*
Adrift on an Ice-Pan—*Grenfell, Wilfred T.*
Alexander the Great—*Gunther, John*
Boys' Book of Great Detective Stories
   Haycraft, Howard
Will James' Book of Cowboy Stories
   James, Will
Captains Courageous—*Kipling, Rudyard*
Rebel Siege—*Kjelgaard, Jim*

writing | seventh grade

YOUR CHILD does so much writing in his schoolwork this year that he often has to rush to finish his assignments on time. This means he is apt to become careless about his handwriting. He will forget to cross his *t*'s or will not quite hit the *t* in his attempt to cross it. The dots for *i*'s may appear anywhere on his paper.

You can check his notebook work and homework papers and occasionally remind him not to let bad habits develop. If he remains relaxed and holds his pencil loosely, he will be able to write rapidly and at the same time legibly.

ENGLISH

You may have wondered why, in nearly all the grades, so much emphasis has been put on the importance of telling a good story. If your child can tell a good story, he can express himself effectively in other ways. He can communicate his wants and needs, and he can carry on an interesting conversation with his friends.

Up to now your child has related inci-dents real or imaginary, and has perhaps been able to create some interest in what he was saying. He is now able to see his own story-telling weaknesses and to do something about them.

He knows that every story must have a *situation,* and it must have *suspense,* and it must have a *plot.* He gets help and practice in school in telling stories, but the best help of all is for him to read good stories that other people have told. Ask for some good books of short stories at your library.

punctuation

Your child reviews rules for capital letters, punctuation, and proper usage. Look in earlier books to help him with this. Then attack the following sentences which have neither punctuation marks nor capital letters. Ask him to write them out correctly, without looking at the corrected sentences below. Check them against the correct sentences when he has finished. Refer back to the sixth grade ENGLISH section and review the rules first, if necessary.

1. one sunday evening before christmas dr and mrs knight and ann were sitting in the living room
2. was browny there too
3. yes browny was lying on a little rug in front of the radio
4. how carefully he listened to that song
5. then he seemed to say this is no good

6. look at browny exclaimed ann
7. he must dislike the singing said dr knight
8. well do you like it asked mrs knight
9. no said dr knight to his wife i never did like squeaky singers
10. here comes browny back again said ann laughing

Here are the same sentences correctly written.

1. One Sunday evening before Christmas, Dr. and Mrs. Knight and Ann were sitting in the living room.
2. Was Browny there too?
3. Yes, Browny was lying on a little rug in front of the radio.
4. How carefully he listened to that song!
5. Then he seemed to say, "This is no good."
6. "Look at Browny!" exclaimed Ann.
7. "He must dislike the singing," said Dr. Knight.
8. "Well, do you like it?" asked Mrs. Knight.
9. "No," said Dr. Knight to his wife, "I never did like squeaky singers."
10. "Here comes Browny back again," said Ann laughing.

Your child reviews what he has learned about good sentence structure. He reviews what he has learned in the sixth grade: the four kinds of sentences; subjects and predicates; parts of speech; common and proper nouns; plural and possessive nouns; principal parts of verbs; comparison of adjectives and adverbs; proper tenses of verbs.

He reviews synonyms, antonyms, homonyms, suffixes, and prefixes. It is a year for review and clearing up any trouble spots or weaknesses your child may have in his English work.

agreement of subject and verb

When speaking, some of us have trouble getting our subjects and verbs to agree. Rules to remember are:

▶ **A singular subject takes a singular verb.**

EXAMPLE:
The man waits.

▶ **A plural subject takes a plural verb.**
EXAMPLE:
The men wait.

▶ **A compound subject with *and* takes a plural verb.**

EXAMPLE:
The boy and girl wait.

Select the correct verb for these sentences (following the rules above):

1. Inside the city the parents (was, were) waiting.
2. Stories and poems (tell, tells) the result.
3. Soldiers and officers (was, were) watching.

Verbs and nouns form the backbone of our language. Have you ever tried to say something without using verbs and nouns? It can't be done. It takes much practice to be able to select the best verbs and nouns and to use them well. Use your dictionary.

reference work

Your child becomes familiar this year with additional ways to get information on topics that interest him. He uses a dictionary and encyclopedias, and he writes various sources, asking for information. When he discovers how pleased most organizations are to send information to schoolchildren, he will not hesitate to use these sources when he needs them.

pronouns

Much time is spent in reviewing all parts of speech, but extra time is spent on pronouns, because they have so many forms. These forms are taught a few at a time so your child will not become confused. (*See* the eighth grade ENGLISH section for still further development.)

Pronouns, like nouns, have three cases:

▶ **Pronouns used as subjects are in the nominative case.**

EXAMPLE:

Mother and I are coming home.

▶ **Object pronouns are in the objective case.**

EXAMPLE:

Please give it to me.

(*It* is the object of the verb *give*, and *me* is the object of the preposition *to*.)

▶ **Possessive forms of pronouns are in the possessive case.**

EXAMPLE:

This is my dress.

The words *who, whose, whom, which,* and *what* are called *interrogative pronouns* when they are used in asking questions.

EXAMPLE:

What is that in your hand?

The *indefinite pronouns both, several, few, some,* and *many* are always plural in number. *None* and *all* can be either singular or plural, depending on their use.

Pronouns must agree with their antecedents, the words to which they refer.

EXAMPLE: (referring to himself)

The boy said he would work.

Not:

The boy said they would work.

Some pronouns are indefinite pronouns because we cannot tell for whom or what they stand.

EXAMPLES:

Each wrote neatly.

Nobody was out of school.

diagraming sentences

In many schools, considerable time may be spent in diagraming sentences. A diagram is only a chart of a sentence, showing each part and its purpose in the sentence. If your child understands sentence structure, he can make better sentences of his own. Here is an explanation of the form used. Refer to it as you study the examples of the diagramed sentences.

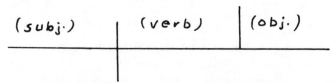

Long perpendicular line across the base line to separate the subject from the verb. Short perpendicular line to show an object.

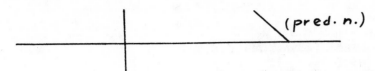

Line slanted toward the subject to show a predicate noun or predicate adjective.

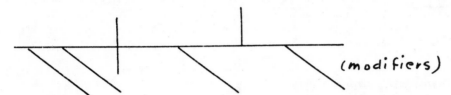

Modifiers are written on slanted lines under the words they modify.

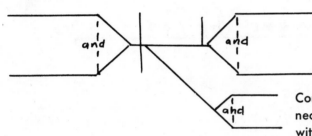

Compound subjects or objects, or even modifiers connected by *and*, are shown by parallel lines connected with a dotted line.

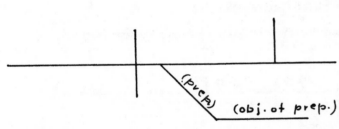

Prepositional phrases are written under the words they modify. The preposition is on the slanted line. The object of the preposition is on a line parallel to the base line.

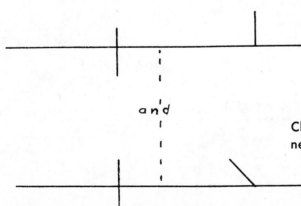

Clauses and parts of compound sentences are connected with dotted lines.

EXAMPLES of diagramed sentences:

1. New York was called New Amsterdam.

   (simple subject, intransitive verb, and predicate noun)

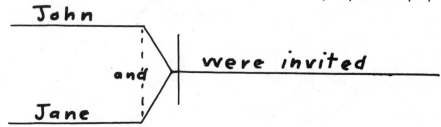

2. John and Jane were invited.

   (compound subject)

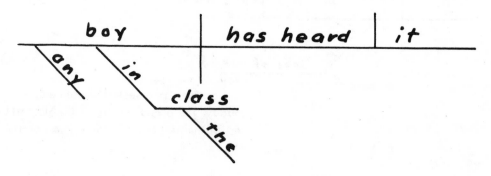

3. Has any boy in the class heard it?

   (a question must be turned into a statement first)

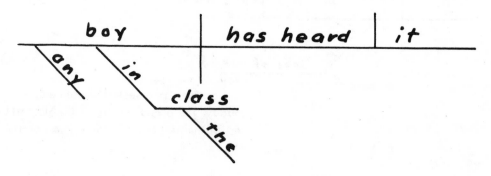

4. She sings well.

   (verb modifier)

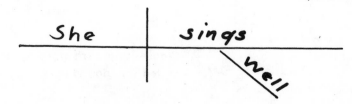

5. Livingstone was an explorer and doctor.

(double predicate nouns)

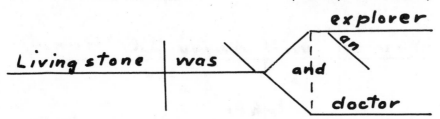

6. Stories about animals are popular.

(prepositional phrase)

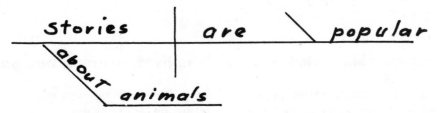

7. Sam sneezed and his sister giggled.

(compound or double sentence)

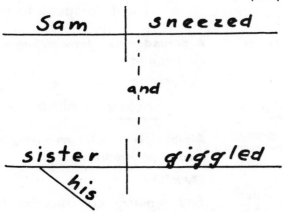

8. It was the coach that came at night.

(dependent adjective clause)

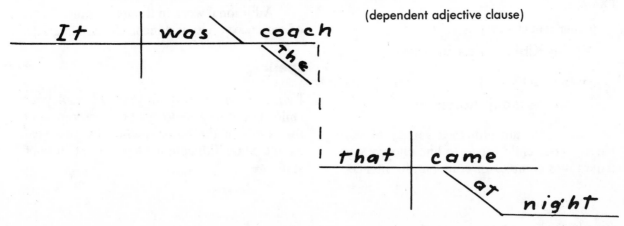

9. You will enjoy O. Henry when you read him.

(dependent adverbial clause)

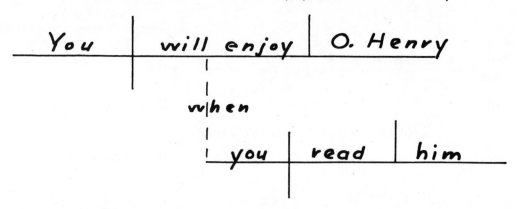

compound and complex sentences

A clause is a part of a sentence that has its own subject and predicate. Some clauses are independent and can stand alone as a complete sentence. Some are subordinate and depend upon an independent clause to give them meaning.

Compound sentences are made up of two or more independent clauses linked together.

EXAMPLE:

Kipling could write many stories about India because he spent many years there.

A **complex sentence** is made up of one independent, or principal, clause and one or more subordinate, or dependent, clauses.

EXAMPLE:

(dependent clause)

While Kipling was in India

(independent clause)

he wrote many stories.

Good writing utilizes a variety of sentences. Your child learns to link choppy sentences into complex or compound sentences.

infinitives, gerunds, and participles

To give his writing even more variety and interest, he learns to use:

An infinitive: to with a simple form of a verb.

EXAMPLE:

I wish to speak to you.

A gerund: a verb form ending in ing which is used as a noun.

EXAMPLE:

Looking at pictures is fun.

A participle: a verb form ending in ing which is used as an adjective.

EXAMPLE:

The moving car blurred the photograph.

Additional work in these and other forms of sentence variety is done in the eighth grade.

spelling

By the end of his seventh year in school, your child should be able to spell correctly most of the words in the basic spelling list prepared by the State Education Department in your state.

arithmetic | seventh grade

YOU AND YOUR child have, no doubt, discovered that "New Math" is only a new approach to old problems. It is more than simply working with figures. It is a way of thinking and a way of reasoning. This year your child applies mathematical concepts to problems in daily living.

numbers and numerals

Your child learns to use numbers in base systems other than the base ten system. The purpose of this work is to help him understand more clearly the same processes in the familiar base ten system.

There are three ways to add numbers in the base five system. Remember, the only digits in the base five system are 0, 1, 2, 3, 4. Use the base five grid (grade 6) to help you understand the following explanations.

EXAMPLES: Add: $32_{five} + 14_{five}$

1) By counting.

32_{five} is $30_{five} + 2_{five}$

14_{five} is $10_{five} + 4_{five}$

Step one: $2_{five} + 4_{five} = 11_{five}$ (See grade 6, counting in base five)

Step two: $30_{five} + 10_{five} = 40_{five}$

Step three: $40_{five} + 11_{five} = 101_{five}$ (The numbers 4 and 1 in second places equal 5. 5 fives are twenty-five, the value of 1 in the third place)

Finally: $32_{five} + 14_{five} = 101_{five}$ which means 1 twenty-five, 0 fives, 1 one.

2) By changing to base ten, then adding, then changing the sum back to base five.

32_{five} means 3 fives and 2 ones or   17

$+\ 14_{\text{five}}$ means 1 five and 4 ones or $\underline{+\ 9}$

                                              26

$26 = 25 + 1$ (One set of twenty-fives and one more)

$26 = 101_{\text{five}}$ (1 twenty-five, 0 five, 1 one)

3) By making a table for base five addition.

$$32_{\text{five}}$$
$$+\ 14_{\text{five}}$$
$$\overline{11_{\text{five}}}$$
$$\underline{4_{\text{five}}}$$
$$101_{\text{five}}$$

Multiplication in the base five system is made easier with the aid of the multiplication table for base five.

12_{five} means 1 five and 2 ones

$$\underline{\times 3}$$

3 fives and 6 ones

or

4 fives and 1 one

(6 ones is 11_{five} in the base five system)

or

41_{five}

The same methods are used in working with numbers in other base systems.

Base ten numerals can be changed to numerals in other base systems. One method is by successive divisions by the powers (place-values) of the base numbers.

EXAMPLES:

a) Change 177 to a base seven numeral.

   Powers of seven:

343	49	7	1
7^3	7^2	7^1	1

Step one:

$$49 \overline{)177} \; 3$$
$$\underline{147}$$
$$30$$

(177 < 343 and cannot be divided by 343. 177 > 49. Therefore, use 49 as the first divisor)

Step Two:

$$7 \overline{)30} \; 4$$
$$\underline{28}$$
$$2$$

(The next divisor is the value of the next place to the right in the grid)

Answer:

$$177 = 342_{\text{seven}}$$

(The quotients and the remainder compose the answer. They show 3 sets of forty-nine, 4 sets of seven, and 2 ones)

b) Change 247 to a base five numeral.

Powers of five:

125	25	5	1
5^3	5^2	5^1	1

Step one:

$$125\,\overline{)247}\,(\,1$$
$$\underline{125}$$
$$122$$

(247 > 125. Therefore, use 125 as the first divisor)

Step two:

$$25\,\overline{)122}\,(\,4$$
$$\underline{100}$$
$$22$$

(The next divisor, 25, is the value of the place to the right of the first divisor)

Step three:

$$5\,\overline{)22}\,(\,4$$
$$\underline{20}$$
$$2$$

(The next divisor, 5, is the value of the next place to the right of the second divisor)

Answer:

$$247 = 1442_{\text{five}}$$

(1 set of one hundred twenty-five,
4 sets of twenty-five,
4 sets of five,
2 ones)

Because more stress is placed on understanding than on method it is probable that your child may prefer an alternate method of changing a base ten numeral to another base. The following method involves repeated division by the base numeral.

EXAMPLE: Change 426 to a base five numeral.

Step one:	$5\overline{)426}$	1	(Record only the remainder in a column to the right of the division)
Step two:	$5\,\lfloor 85$	0	(Divide the next quotient by 5 and record the remainder)
Step three:	$5\,\lfloor 17$	2	(Divide the next quotient by 5 and record the remainder)
Step four:	$5\,\lfloor 3$	3	(Continue to divide by 5 until the quotient is 0)
	0		
Answer:	$426 = 3201_{\text{five}}$		(The numerals of the remainder from *bottom to top* are the digits of the base five numeral)

sets and subsets

Your child continues to work and to think in terms of sets. Use of sets helps him to understand and to explain mathematical ideas more accurately. Review with him the ideas of sub-sets, union and intersection of sets, empty sets, equal and equivalent sets.

addition, subtraction, multiplication, division

Daily practice on the basic skills is still necessary.

Review the specific properties of each of the basic processes with your child.

▶ **Addition.**

1. Addition is called a **binary operation,** which means that it is performed on only two elements. Only two numbers can be added at one time.

   EXAMPLE: $6 + 3 + 2 + 1 = 12$ (Add two numbers at a time in the most convenient way. One possibility: $2 + 1 = 3$, $3 + 3 = 6$, $6 + 6 = 12$)

2. Addition of natural numbers is **associative** (think of associative as *grouping*). Regrouping the addends does not change the sum.

   EXAMPLE: $(8 + 3) + 2 = 13$
   $8 + (3 + 2) = 13$
   $8 + 3 + 2 = 13$

3. Addition of natural numbers is **commutative** (think of commutative as *order*). The order of two numbers does not change the sum.

   EXAMPLE: $8 + 5 = 13$ and $5 + 8 = 13$

4. **Closure** is a special property of addition. When two numbers of a set are added and the sum is also within that set, it is said to be *closed under addition.*

   EXAMPLE: The set = all the whole numbers.
   $4 \quad + \quad 2 \quad = \quad 6$
   whole number   whole number   also a whole number

5. Zero is the *identity number* of addition. A number is not changed when zero is added to it.

   EXAMPLE: $6 + 0 = 6$

▶ **Subtraction.**

1. Subtraction is an inverse operation. It "undoes" addition.
   EXAMPLE: $4 + 7 = 11$ so $4 = 11 - 7$

2. Subtraction is not associative. Changing the grouping in subtraction usually changes the difference.
   EXAMPLE: $14 - (8 - 3) = 9$
   $(14 - 8) - 3 = 3$

3. Subtraction is not commutative. Reversing the order of the numbers used changes the difference.
   EXAMPLE: $7 - 4 = 3$
   $4 - 7 = -3$

4. The closure property cannot be applied to subtraction of positive whole numbers.
   EXAMPLE: The set = all of the whole numbers. $+ 4 - (+ 7) = - 3$

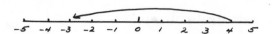

Start at 4 and move *left* 7 spaces. The answer is a negative number and not in the set of natural numbers. A natural number is a positive whole number.

5. Zero is the identity number in subtraction. Subtracting zero from any number does not change the number.
   EXAMPLE: $6 - 0 = 6$

▶ **Multiplication.**

1. Multiplication possesses the associative property. Regrouping the factors does not change the product.

EXAMPLE: $8 \times 3 \times 2 = 48$
$(8 \times 3) \times 2 = 48$
$8 \times (3 \times 2) = 48$

2. Multiplication is commutative. The order of multiplication of two numbers does not change the product.

EXAMPLE: $5 \times 7 = 35$ and $7 \times 5 = 35$

3. Closure is a special property of multiplication. When two elements of a set are multiplied and their product is again an element of the set, it is said to be *closed under multiplication.*

EXAMPLE: The set = all the whole numbers.
$4 \times 2 = 8$
whole number   whole number   also a whole number

4. 1 is the identity number of multiplication. When you multiply a number by 1 you do not change the value of that number.

EXAMPLE: $8 \times 1 = 8$ and $1 \times 8 = 8$

5. Multiplication has a distributive property over addition. The multiplier is "distributed" as it multiplies first the digit in ones place, then the digit in tens place, etc.

EXAMPLE: $27 \times 3 = 81$
$(20 + 7) \times 3 = 81$
(20×3) and $(7 \times 3) = 81$

▶ **Division.**

1. Division is the inverse operation of multiplication. Every division has a corresponding multiplication which shows the opposite relationship. Multiplication is used as a check for division. The product of the divisor and the quotient should equal the dividend.

EXAMPLE: $48 \div 6 = 8$ and $6 \times 8 = 48$

2. Division is not associative. The way in which numbers are grouped changes the quotient.

EXAMPLE: $(81 \div 9) \div 3 = 3$
$81 \div (9 \div 3) = 27$

3. Division is not commutative. The quotient is not the same when the dividend and divisor are reversed.

EXAMPLE: $27 \div 9 = 3$
$9 \div 27 = \frac{9}{27}$ or $\frac{1}{3}$

4. The closure property cannot be applied to division. The quotient may not necessarily be in the same set as the divisor and the dividend.

EXAMPLE: The set = all the whole numbers.
$27 \div 4 = 6\frac{3}{4}$
whole number   whole number   not a whole number

5. 1 is the identity number in division when 1 is the divisor. Dividing any whole number by 1 does not change the number.

EXAMPLE: $14 \div 1 = 14$

fractions

If your child seems to have trouble with fractions, it is advisable to turn back to the discussion of fractions in the fifth grade ARITHMETIC section.

Be sure he knows what a common fraction is. Work with him, go through the explanation and work pages of all the basic work in common fractions. By this time he should be able to add, subtract, multiply, and divide fractions whether their denominators are alike or different. He should be able to change fractions to lower or higher terms. He needs to know these things because work with fractions is extended in this grade. If he doesn't fully understand what has gone before, he will have trouble with what is ahead.

finding a whole when a part is known

Draw lines or diagrams to explain how to find a whole when a part is known.

EXAMPLE:

Joe was a salesman. He made $10 one week, which was ⅖ of what he sold. How much did he sell?

The whole line represents all he sold.

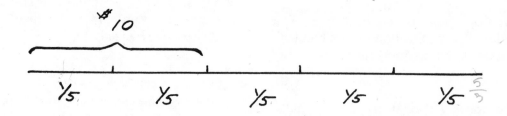

Divide it into fifths, since that is the fractional part we are using. There are 5 fifths in the whole. We know from the problem that ⅖ of this line are $10. First determine what one fifth is, then it will be easy to learn what the 5 fifths are.

One fifth is half of two fifths. Half of $10 is $5.00. Then one fifth is $5 and five fifths is 5 × $5 or $25.

REMEMBER: *Find out the value of one fractional part before finding out the whole.*

per cents

The meaning of *per cent* is taught again in this grade.

Remember, % or *per cent* means "per hundred." Use pictures or visual aids to help your child with this. Use the large square divided into 100 small squares to show that per cent and hundredths have the same meaning. (*See* the Sixth-Grade ARITHMETIC section.)

Parts of things can be written as common fractions, as decimal fractions, or as per cents. For example, if we are concerned with only 20 of the 100 squares, we can refer to them as $\frac{20}{100}$ (⅕), or .20 or 20%.

In a similar way we can show that 50% is .50 or $\frac{50}{100}$ is ½; that 100% is 1.00 or it is the whole; that 25% is .25 (25 of the hundred squares) or $\frac{25}{100}$ is ¼.

Example of a problem in per cent: Ruth spells 12 out of 15 words correctly. What per cent did she spell correctly?

Step one: $\frac{12}{15}$ (The ratio of 12 to 15 is shown as a common fraction)

Step two: ⅘ (Reduce the fraction to lowest terms)

Step three: $5\overline{)4.0}$ with quotient .8 (Change the common fraction to a decimal fraction)

Step four: .8 = .80 = 80% (Change the decimal to per cent)

A good time-saver is the table of common fractions and their decimal equivalents. Help your child memorize it.

½ is 50%	⅕ is 20%
⅔ is 66⅔%	⅖ is 40%
¼ is 25%	⅗ is 60%
⅛ is 12½%	⅙ is 16⅔%
⅓ is 33⅓%	¾ is 75%

⅘ is 80%

When comparisons are made they are often expressed in terms of per cent. Comparison is the same as ratio.

EXAMPLE:

The Lakeside team won 8 out of 11 of their games. Glenwood won 7 out of 10. Compare the winnings of both teams.

Lakeside won $\frac{8}{11}$ or $8 \div 11 = 72\frac{8}{11}\%$ of their games.

Glenwood won $\frac{7}{10}$ or $7 \div 10 = 70\%$ of their games.

Lakeside school had the higher standing.

business arithmetic

Your child's first acquaintance with business arithmetic comes in connection with per cent. Suppose he has something to sell. He learns that it is important to know the cost of the article as well as its selling price, and the relation of one price to the other.

Overhead, expenses, discounts, commissions, and interest are all touched upon in this grade.

discount

The amount of reduction in price is called the *discount*.

The *rate of discount* is the comparison of the *amount of discount* to the original price. It is expressed as a per cent.

EXAMPLE:

Don advertised a bicycle for sale for $25. He couldn't sell it, so the next week he advertised it for $20, and sold it. He reduced the price from $25 to $20. What was his rate of discount?

The original price was $25.
The amount of discount was $5.
($25 − $20 = $5).

$$\frac{\text{Discount}}{\text{Original price}} \quad \frac{\$5}{\$25} = \frac{1}{5} =$$

20% rate of discount.

EXAMPLE:

At a special sale Mary bought a $4 sweater for $3. What was the rate of discount?

The original price was $4.
The amount of discount was $1.
($4 − $3 = $1).

$$\frac{\text{Discount}}{\text{Original price}} \quad \frac{1}{4} = 25\%$$

The rate of discount was 25%.
Proof: 25% of $4.00 = $1.00.

The *net price* is the original price minus the amount of discount.

EXAMPLE:

The original price is $25.
The discount is $5.
The net price is $20.
($25 − $5).

EXAMPLE:

A $30 radio was sold at a 10% discount. What was the net price? First find out the amount of discount by taking 10% of $30.

$$10\% = \tfrac{1}{10}; \tfrac{1}{10} \text{ of } 30 = \$3.$$

Then subtract the amount of discount from the original price:

$$\$30 - \$3 = \$27, \text{ the net price.}$$

To find the *amount of discount*, multiply the *original price* by the rate of discount.

EXAMPLE:

The original price is $20. The rate of discount is 5%. Find the amount of discount:

$$5\% = \tfrac{1}{20}$$
$$\tfrac{1}{20} \text{ of } \$20 = \$1.$$

Change the per cent to the easiest form to use, then multiply.

$1 is the amount of discount.

To find the *original price*, find out what fractional part of the original price the sale price is. First, find what *one* fractional part is. Then find the whole.

EXAMPLE:

What was the original price of an article bought for $12, which has been discounted 25%? It was discounted 25% or ¼. The whole thing was 100% or $\frac{4}{4}$ to start with. Then the $12 sale price is only 75% or ¾ of the original price. If ¾ of the original price is $12, then each fourth is $4.

$$(\$12 \div 3 = \$4).$$

Four fourths or the original price is $16.

$$(4 \times \$4 = \$16).$$

EXAMPLE:

Sale price	Discount	Original price
$21	30%	?

If 30% is the discount, then the $21 is only 70% of the original price.

$$(100\% - 30\% = 70\%).$$
$$70\% = \frac{7}{10}.$$

The problem tells you $\frac{7}{10}$ is $21. Then $\frac{1}{10}$ is 21 ÷ 7 or $3. If $\frac{1}{10}$ is $3, then $\frac{10}{10}$ or 100% of it is $30 (10 × $3 = $30), the original price.

commission

Jane's father is a salesman. His salary is $75 a week, but he also gets a *commission* which is 12½% of the amount of his sales. That means that if he sold $400 worth of merchandise in a week, he would get 12½% of $400 in addition to his $75; 12½% (or $\frac{1}{8}$) of $400 is $50. His commission is $50.

$50
$\frac{75}{\$125}$

His commission added to his salary of $75 equals $125, which is his income for the week.

The $50 is called the commission. The 12½% is called the rate of commission.

If Jane's father sold $800 worth of merchandise the next week, his commission would be 12½% ($\frac{1}{8}$) of $800, or $100, and his income for that week would be $175.

Rate of commission is expressed in per cent. It is found by comparing the *amount of the commission* to the *amount of sales.*

EXAMPLE:

Bob sold $25 worth of seeds. His commission was $10. What was his rate of commission?

THINK:

What relation is $10 to $25? $10 is to $25 as $\frac{10}{25}$;

$$\frac{10}{25} \text{ or } \frac{2}{5}; \frac{2}{5} \text{ is } 40\%.$$

EXAMPLE:

Alice earned a commission of $6 for selling $24 worth of Christmas cards. Find her rate of commission.

$$\frac{\text{Amount of commission}}{\text{Amount of sales}} \quad \frac{6}{24} = \frac{1}{4} = 25\%$$

interest

Interest is money paid for the use of money.

EXAMPLE:

To buy a bicycle for his paper route, Bob had to borrow $50 from his uncle. He agreed to repay the $50 at the end of a year and also to pay his uncle 4% of $50 for the use of the money. The $50 that Bob borrowed from his uncle is called the *principal*. The length of time for which he borrowed the money is called the *time*. The 4% is called the *rate of interest*. 4% of $50 is 50 × .04 or $2.00, which is the *amount of interest*, or the amount Bob had to pay for the privilege of borrowing and using $50 for one year.

The principal ($50) plus the interest ($2) is called the *total amount* ($52). At the end of the year Bob will owe his uncle $52.

Interest rates are figured on the basis of a year. If Bob could have paid back all the money in a half year's time, the interest would have been cut in half or would have been $1.00. If he could not pay it back for 2 years, the interest would be 4% of the $50 for each year.

Try these problems before you look at the answers. Refer to the explanation if necessary.

1. The interest of $200 for 1 year at 6% is _____ .

   Answer: $200 × .06 = $12

2. Mr. Smith lends $400 for 3 months at 6%. How much interest should he get? _____
   What is the total amount he should get at the end of the 3 months? _____

   Answer: 400 × .06 = $24, interest for 1 year. 3 months is 1/12 or 1/4 of a year. Interest for 1/4 of a year is 1/4 of $24 or $6. $400 + $6 = $406, the total amount he would receive at the end of 3 months.

per cent of increase

To find the *per cent of increase* compare the *amount of increase* with the *original price*.

EXAMPLE:

The price of a quart of milk is increased from 20¢ to 25¢. Find the per cent of increase.

$$\frac{\text{Amount of increase}}{\text{Original price}} \quad \frac{5¢}{20¢} = \frac{1}{4} = 25\%$$

per cent of decrease

To find the *per cent of decrease*, compare the *amount of decrease* with the *original price*.

EXAMPLE:

Henry bought a book for $1.50. Later he sold it for .50. What was the per cent of decrease?

$$\frac{\text{Amount of decrease}}{\text{Original price}} \quad \frac{100¢}{150¢} = \frac{2}{3} =$$

$$66\tfrac{2}{3}\% \text{ of decrease.}$$

REMEMBER: It is the *original* number to which the increase or decrease is being compared.

margin, overhead, profit

Fred bought a second-hand bicycle for $15. He spent $7.50 to have it repaired. He then sold it for $25. The *cost* of Fred's bike was $15. The *selling price* was $25.

The *margin* was the difference between the selling price and the cost.

$$\$25 - \$15 = \$10.$$

The expense of fixing the bike was $7.50. This is called overhead expense or just *overhead*.

The *profit* is the difference between the margin and the overhead.

$$\$10 - \$7.50 = \$2.50 \text{ profit}$$

Expenses in a business, such as rent, heat, and wages, are called *overhead*. Mr. Smith, the grocer, may buy his corn for 18¢ a can and sell it to us for 28¢ a can. That margin of 10¢ a can has to help to cover all his expenses in running the store and leave him a few cents profit so he can clothe and protect and entertain his own family.

EXAMPLE:

Mr. Smith buys sneakers at $3.00 a pair and sells them for $4.50 a pair. Mr. Smith figures that he needs 33⅓% of the cost of each article he sells to cover his overhead. Is he making a profit on the sneakers? If so, how much? _____

$4.50 − $3.00 = $1.50, amount of margin.
33⅓% or ⅓ of $3.00 = $1.00, amount of overhead.
$1.50 − $1.00 = $.50, amount of profit on each pair of sneakers.

savings account

The money in a savings account is a sum the bank keeps safe for you.

Money put into a savings account in a bank draws interest.

EXAMPLE:

You have $100 in a savings account. The interest on it is paid at the rate of 2% semi-annually. (That means 1% every 6 months.)

If you leave $100 in the bank for a year, you would get back $100 plus 2% of $100, or $2. Total $102. If you leave the $100 for only 6 months, you would get back $100 plus 1% of $100, or $1. Total $101.

To put money into a bank it is necessary to make out a *deposit slip*. The deposit slip should show:

▶ **The name of the bank.**
▶ **Your name and address.**
▶ **The date of deposit.**
▶ **The number of your account in the bank.**
▶ **The total amount you are putting in.**
▶ **The form in which you brought it to the bank: checks, bills, or silver.**

You are the *depositor*. At the bank you give the deposit slip and the money to the *teller*. He makes a record of it in your *passbook*. He lets you keep your own passbook, and he keeps the deposit slip, from which he gets information for the permanent records of the bank.

Does your child have his own savings account? Any bank will open one for as little as $1.00.

checking account

Money is put into a checking account in the same way as it is put into a savings account. You are the depositor; you make out a deposit slip. You may or may not have a passbook in which the record of deposits is made.

The difference between a savings account and a checking account is this: A savings account does just what the name says; it *saves* your money. The bank takes care of it for you, and pays a little *interest* so that the total of your money grows.

A checking account is for your convenience only and *you* pay a service charge. It is an amount of money the bank is holding for you. It is a help in paying bills. It is safer to let the bank handle the money while you pay your bills with checks. It is safer to send money through the mail in the form of a check. Banks are fireproof, homes are not. Banks are better protected against robbery than homes are. Bank accounts are insured by the United States Government. It is more convenient to pay a large amount of money with one piece of paper than to use the many bills and silver pieces it would require otherwise.

Show your child how to make out a check correctly. Keep the checks and be sure you keep a record of them by keeping the stubs carefully filled in.

budgets

A budget is an account that we keep to find out where our money is going. Many times we spend our money and don't remember what we bought. A budget helps us keep track of these items. First we make an estimate of how much we can afford to spend for various things over a given period of time. Then we list how much we actually do spend. At the end of a week or a month we take totals to see if we are spending the amounts we think we ought to spend. If we are spending too much for something, we try to correct this in the next budget period.

EXAMPLE:

The weekly income is $75.00. Estimate the cost of items like rent, food, clothing, savings, recreation, other expenses. The best way is to estimate things by per cent. Then try your budget for a while and change it if you find you are wrong. Maybe you have allowed too much for one thing and not enough for another. A budget based on a $75.00 weekly income may look like this:

Rent	25% or $18.75		Savings	10% or $7.50
Food	35% or $26.25		Recreation	5% or $3.75
Clothing	15% or $11.25		Other	10% or $7.50

Help your child to budget his own income or allowance. He may or may not like to continue this, but even a short experience at budgeting will be helpful.

buying

Your experience in buying must have given you some valuable but sometimes costly lessons. Share these with your child so he doesn't have to make the same mistakes you did.

Keep some of these facts in mind:

▶ **Buying foods in season means a great savings to you. For example, strawberries in January can cost five or six times as much as they would in June.**

▶ **Buying in quantity can save you money.**

For example, dog food can cost 20¢ a pound, but cost 79¢ for a 5-pound bag—(a saving of 21¢). A company saves a lot on packaging and handling bigger packages. Of course, buying in large quantities is not a saving unless you can safely store what you buy!

▶ **Buy at sales if you can recognize value.**

▶ **When buying by mail, remember you have to add the postage for delivery to the cost of the articles purchased.**

▶ **Installment buying can be expensive. Carrying charges are added to the cost of the articles purchased.**

▶ **A bargain is not a "bargain" unless it is something you want and can use.**

measurements

Measurement of all kinds is stressed this year. Your child should be quite skilled in the use of a ruler, and now he will learn to use a protractor. This is an instrument for measuring angles. Your child was very probably given one to use in school or asked to buy one. It is made like a half-circle. The center is marked and the edge is divided into degrees. There are 360° in every complete circle, so there are 180° in the half-circle of a protractor.

In Fig. 1 I am measuring angle AOB. I place the point marked center on the vertex or point of the angle. Line OB is on the base of the protractor. The mark where line OA crosses the half circle tells you the size of the angle.

The protractor can be used to draw angles of a given size. To make a 90° angle, line OB is on the base of the angle and line OA of the angle must extend across the protractor at the point marked 90. It will look like Fig. 2:

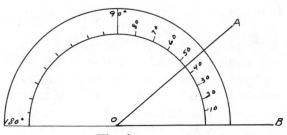
Fig. 1.

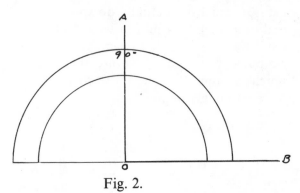
Fig. 2.

adding and subtracting
units of measurement

Your child adds and subtracts units of measurement of time and weight.

EXAMPLE:

Add	7 weeks	5 days
	4 weeks	6 days
	6 weeks	4 days
Total	17 weeks	15 days

Because there are 7 days in one week, he should change the 15 days to 2 weeks and 1 day. The 2 weeks is added to 17. The answer is written 19 weeks and 1 day.

EXAMPLE:

Add	6 lbs.	7 oz.
	2 lbs.	5 oz.
	1 lb.	4 oz.
Total	9 lbs.	16 oz.

or 10 lbs. (16 oz. equal 1 lb.)

EXAMPLE:

Subtract	8 weeks	2 days
	3 weeks	6 days

Before you can begin this problem you must borrow from the 8 weeks because you cannot subtract 6 from 2. When you do that you are really borrowing 7 days and adding it to the 2 in the day column. This problem now becomes:

7	9
8 weeks	2 days
3 weeks	6 days
4 weeks	3 days

planes

Your child reviews the geometric forms he has learned in earlier grades, and goes on to learn more.

A *square* has 4 equal sides.

A *triangle* has 3 sides.

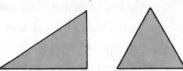

410

The sum of the angles of any triangle is 180°. (Angles are measured with a protractor.) An equilateral triangle has 3 equal sides.

A *hexagon* has 6 sides.

An *octagon* has 8 sides.

A *pentagon* has 5 sides.

These are all flat surfaces called *planes*. They have two dimensions—length and breadth.

solids

These figures can be drawn as *solids* by giving them a third dimension. Solids have length, breadth, and height.

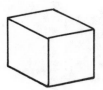

A cube has 3 equal dimensions.

Each side of a *rectangular solid* the shape of a rectangle.

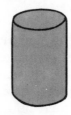

The ends of a *cylinder* are circles.

volume

To find the space a solid occupies is to find its volume. Solids are measured in cubic units such as cubic inches, cubic feet, cubic yards, etc. The volume is found by multiplying the height times the breadth times the width.

EXAMPLE:

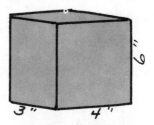

4 × 6 = 24 square inches
24 × 3 = 72 cubic inches.
Volume = length × width × height.
The formula is V = lwh.

A cube is a rectangular solid in which all dimensions are the same.

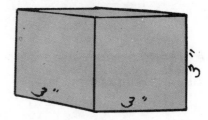

3 × 3 × 3 = 27 cubic inches.
This can be written 3^3, or 3 × 3 × 3.

area

The distance *around* any geometric figure is called the *perimeter*. Do not confuse perimeter with *area*. Area was studied in the fifth and sixth grades but is developed further here. Surface area is measured in square units (square inches or square feet, etc.). To find the area, multiply the number of the units in length by the number of units in the width. This rule can be written as a formula:

A (area) = lw (length × width).

This rule is used also in finding the area of a square, but since the sides of the square are all equal in length, the formula can be written $A = s^2$. This means Area = side × itself, or side squared. Any number times itself is the number squared.

EXAMPLE:

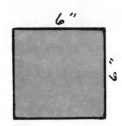

A = 6 × 6 = 36 square inches

If the area to be measured is irregular, as in this figure,

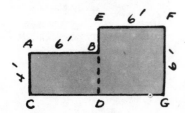

treat it as if it were two rectangular surfaces. ABDC is one surface. EFGD is another.

Add the areas of both rectangular surfaces to get the area of the over-all surface.

4′ × 6′ = 24 square feet.

6′ × 6′ = 36 square feet.

24 square feet + 36 square feet

= 60 square feet.

The *area of any triangle* is found by multiplying the base by the height and taking ½ the product. The height must be taken at right angles to the base.

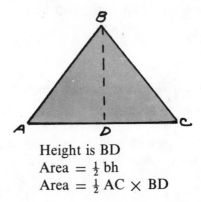

Height is BD
Area = ½ bh
Area = ½ AC × BD

Parallel lines are those that are everywhere the same distance apart, such as the lines on your paper.

A *parallelogram* is a four-sided figure whose opposite sides are parallel.

EXAMPLES:

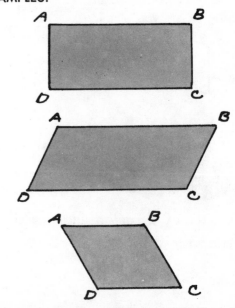

In each figure AD is parallel to BC.

EXAMPLE:

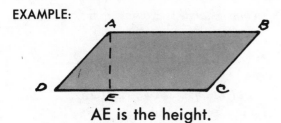

AE is the height.

The formula to find the *area of a parallelogram* is A = bh. However, the height of a parallelogram must be taken at a *right angle* to the base.

An acre is a unit of surface measure that contains 43,560 square feet. It can be in almost any shape—even circular.

circles

Perfect circles can be drawn with an instrument called a compass. Your child has no doubt been asked to buy one.

EXAMPLE:

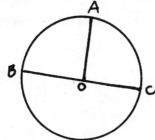

The point O is the center of the circle. The distance from the center to the edge is the *radius* (line OA). The *diameter* is the distance through the center of the circle (line BOC).

Any part of the curved line of a circle is an *arc*. BA and AC are both arcs.

A *semicircle* is half the circle (BAC).

The distance around a circle is its *circumference*. Mathematicians have found that the circumference is always a little more than 3 times the diameter. It is about 3.14 times, and people use the Greek letter π (pi) to represent this ratio. The formula for finding the circumference of a circle is C = πd (Circumference = pi times the diameter).

EXAMPLE:

Find the circumference of the circle if the radius is 3 inches.

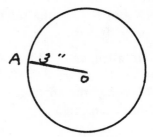

We know that the radius is 3″. The diameter is 2 times the radius, or 6″. The circumference is 3.14 × 6, or 18.84 inches.

EXAMPLE:

Find the circumference of a circle if the diameter is 9 inches.

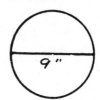

9 × 3.14 = 28.26

EXAMPLE:

Find the circumference of a circle if the diameter is 6 feet, 6 inches.

6 inches = ½ foot.
Then 6 feet, 6 inches = 6½ feet.
Change 6½ to 6.5 in order not to confuse multiplying decimals and common fractions.
6.5 × 3.14 = 20.41 feet.

The area of a circle is found by multiplying π (3.14) by the radius squared. The formula: A = πr^2.

angles

An angle is made by two straight lines meeting at a point, as in the figure shown here.

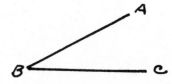

The lines AB and BC are the *sides* of the angle. The point B is the *vertex*.

The angle is called angle ABC, naming the letter of vertex between the letters of the sides. The size of the angle depends on the amount of the opening.

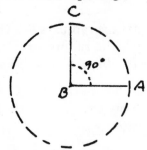

A *right angle* is a 90° angle. Or it can be considered ¼ of a circle.

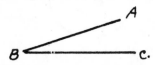

An *acute angle* is an angle smaller than a right angle.

An *obtuse angle* is greater than a right angle.

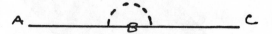

A *straight angle* is two right angles, or half of a complete circle.

thought problems

Your child will be given many arithmetic problems to solve this year.

In attacking a problem your child should:

▶ **Decide which facts are necessary and which can be discarded.**

▶ **Estimate an answer first.**

▶ **Find missing facts.**

▶ **Substitute easy numbers for hard ones until the method of work is established.**

▶ **Do as much mental arithmetic as possible.**

english exercises

I. Punctuate the following:

1. In recent years we have discussed many new phases
2. Will people always like stories about heroes
3. Yes therell always be lots of hero stories
4. How true this is
5. Our history teacher said Name three present-day heroes
6. Why are you so angry
7. Shakespeare wrote Twelfth Night
8. How many of Shakespeares plays have you read
9. Theyll have finished by the time we arrive
10. His address is 110 Main Street Amsterdam N Y
11. The childrens boots were all mixed up
12. Please check the following number of books titles of books and authors
13. George asked for five notebooks three pencils and a fountain pen
14. Lets sing America the Beautiful
15. Do you think practice makes perfect

II. Correct the grammar in these sentences.

1. Who would the class like? Correct: Whom would the class like? 2. To who do you think it was sent? 3. Each child was reading their own. 4. We would of gone if it hadn't rained. 5. They was all much too tired. 6. Have you ate it all already? 7. I think she begun it at nine. 8. "Where is the dog at?" he asked. 9. She learned us to weave place mats. 10. Leave me have my turn, please. 11. These kind of models are new. 12. It don't seem to fit very well. 13. I and John will go on the errand. 14. The balloons are different than planes. 15. She set on the freshly painted chair. 16. Us girls are making fudge. 17. She has already laid down for her nap. 18. Oh, lie it down on the bench. 19. I may have wrote that myself. 20. Have you got a raincoat? 21. Don't her story stick to the point? 22. I think I'll lay down for a while.

23. I seen fifty butterflies yesterday.   24. Let me alone, please.   25. They went and done it anyway!

III. Underline the simple subject (or subjects if compound) and simple predicate (or predicates if compound). Underline the helping verb also. Ex: have run.

1. Mary and Jane ran and jumped.

2. The children have worked a long time and have finished the whole job.

3. Some fish have a tongue covered with teeth.

4. Rows of fine teeth look like a little brush.

5. Strong sharp teeth of fish are used also for biting and fighting other fish.

6. I have a globe full of tiny fish.

7. Mr. Stickleback is a curious fellow and is well worth buying.

8. The stickleback is greedy, fearless, full of courage, and affectionate.

9. The colors of the stickleback brighten or fade according to his mood.

10. You can catch them without a hook.

IV. Pick out all the pronouns—tell whether they are in the nominative case, objects of verbs or prepositions, possessive pronouns, interrogative pronouns, relative pronouns, indefinite pronouns.

1. Who do you think you are? Who—inter., nom. case. You, nom. case. You, nom. case.

2. Which of you is going in my place? _____

3. It is getting late. _____

4. She lost her wallet. _____

5. Barye recovered it. _____

6. Your home is many miles away. _____

7. This is her first choice. _____

8. Several claimed it. _____

9. Nobody really wanted it. _____

10. The house that burned was an old one. _____

V. Fill in the blanks to show the other forms of these nouns.

Sing. Noun	Sing. Possessive	Plural	Plural Possessive
1. man	man's	men	men's
2. woman			
3. lady			
4. child			
5. banjo			
6. bison			
7. church			
8. melody			
9. key			
10. potato			
11. wolf			
12. salmon			
13. memory			
14. word			
15. director			
16. poem			
17. country			
18. shell			
19. fish			
20. model			
21. stone			
22. quotation			
23. phrase			
24. address			
25. life			

VI. What are the principal parts of these verbs?

Verb—Present	Past tense	Past participle (requires helper)
1. give	gave	given
2. sing		
3. is		
4. grow		
5. fly		
6. flow		
7. see		
8. speak		
9. run		
10. dive		
11. lie		
12. lay		
13. bring		
14. drink		
15. swing		
16. swim		
17. do		
18. set		
19. break		
20. come		
21. teach		
22. tear		
23. throw		
24. freeze		
25. am		

VII. Compare these adjectives and adverbs.

	Positive	Comparative	Superlative
1.	good	better	best
2.	little		
3.	fast		
4.	bad		
5.	fair		
6.	far		
7.	happy		
8.	slowly		
9.	fat		
10.	quietly		
11.	sure		
12.	real		
13.	lovely		
14.	large		
15.	securely		
16.	well		
17.	many		
18.	rare		
19.	interesting		
20.	clear		
21.	enjoyable		
22.	rough		
23.	old		
24.	new		
25.	beautiful		

VIII. Diagram these sentences.

1. Robert Fulton was an inventor.   2. Walter Damrosch was a conductor.
3. Gutzon Borglum was a sculptor.   4. The Rushmore Memorial is in
the Black Hills of South Dakota.   5. Newspapers and magazines will
furnish much material.   6. Ted walked across the logs and rescued the
puppy.   7. The audience cheered and clapped.   8. Bob raised the red
velvet curtain.   9. After the play Mrs. Jones gave a party for the cast.
10. How well can you read?   11. Did you bring the rabbit to school?
12. Begin your story with an interesting situation.   13. Attract the attention of the reader.   14. Write a plan for your story.   15. The kiln
was not too hot.   16. Mary and Alice labeled and exhibited the shells.
17. Jean and Nancy design and sew doll clothes.   18. Bob and Jim
collected old coins.   19. A stamp collector is called a philatelist.
20. The brilliant sunset inspired the artist.

**IX. Underline the prepositional phrases. Are they used as adjectives or adverbs? (Adjectives de-
scribe nouns or pronouns. Adverbs tell where, when, how, or why.)**

1. The dog was locked in the office.   2. The roof of the house blew off.
3. The history of our country makes a fascinating story.   4. The truth
was told by one boy.   5. This kind of story adds excitement.   6. They
moved to western Pennsylvania.   7. He liked living in a tent.   8. Cut
holes in it for your eyes.   9. The invention of the wheel has helped us
in many ways.   10. The fort at Mansfield was attacked.   11. Go to
the library on Saturday.   12. Miss Ford made a name for herself in the
theater.   13. The surface of the roof was ruined by the wind.   14. In
those days the cure was sugar water.   15. Children of all ages are invited.   16. Arthur was wounded in a battle.   17. In a little while a
gondola appeared.   18. We threw stones into the water.   19. The use
of each tool is carefully explained.   20. He brought his oboe to our
house.

X. Underline the infinitives (to plus a verb).

1. I like to eat.   2. She seems to be finished.   3. To write a play is a
noble accomplishment.   4. Her wish is to live in Florida.   5. It is a mistake to stop so often.   6. It is an experience to remember well.   7. I
went to Mother to get more suggestions.   8. Don't you like to see the

result?   9. It is well to look before you leap.   10. She was asked to write good sentences.

XI. Underline the gerunds (an <u>ing</u> form of verb used as a noun).

1. <u>Setting</u> the stage is fun.   2. Painting a house is not woman's work. 3. Calling the children together was my job.   4. Coaching a play is hard work.   5. Stepping into the limelight caused him to trip.   6. Singing well is a great joy.   7. Reading is easy for most people.   8. Writing has to be practiced.   9. Looking at pictures is always fun. 10. Finding the right picture isn't always fun.

XII. Underline the participle (<u>ing</u> form of the verb that is used as an adjective).

1. <u>Playing</u> in the water, he forgot about time.
2. The children, exchanging ideas, came up with a well planned program.
3. John, hearing his name called, immediately jumped to his feet.
4. A person reading a good story can forget everything around him.
5. List the words beginning with <u>ch</u>.
6. Seeing his master, the dog barked excitedly.
7. Stopping at the newsstand, Jerry bought a magazine.
8. Seeing the name of the feature film, we turned in at the "Drive-In."
9. Writing as fast as he could, the boy listed fifty names.
10. Meeting Mary in the street, I just handed her the letter.

arithmetic exercises

I. Number system. Write these numbers:

1. Five hundred three thousand, fifty-six. _____
2. Eight hundred thirteen thousand, two hundred four. _____
3. Eight million, seven hundred fifty-six thousand, one hundred. _____
4. Seven hundred billion. _____
5. One hundred eighty-six billion, three million, seventy-five thousand, twenty-five. _____
6. Nine million, one. _____
7. One hundred eleven billion. _____

8. Three million, three hundred forty-seven thousand, two hundred two.
_____

9. Seven billion, two hundred nineteen million, three hundred eighty-four thousand, one hundred twenty-four. _____

10. Nineteen million, seventeen. _____

II. Roman numerals. Write each numeral in the base ten number system:

1. I =	14. XI =	27. VII =	39. LXXIV =
2. V =	15. XVI =	28. XIII =	40. IX =
3. X =	16. LXI =	29. XXV =	41. DCXX =
4. L =	17. CLVI =	30. XLIX =	42. MDV =
5. C =	18. MDCX =	31. LXXV =	43. MCMLVI =
6. D =	19. DCV =	32. XCVI =	44. CCCXXV =
7. M =	20. MCVI =	33. XXXIX =	45. MCCXXXIII =
8. IV =	21. MDCLV =	34. LXVIII =	46. CDXIV =
9. IX =	22. XXIII =	35. XVIII =	47. XVII =
10. XL =	23. LXXXVIII =	36. XII =	48. XXII =
11. XC =	24. CCCLXXX =	37. XLI =	49. XXXIV =
12. CD =	25. MDCCCLXXXVII =	38. LXVI =	50. LXV =
13. CM =	26. III =		

III. Name two numerals in their natural order to fill the blanks.

Base two: ____ ____ ____ ____ ____ ____ ____ ____

Base three: ____ ____ ____ ____ ____ ____ ____ ____ ____

Base four: ____ ____ ____ ____ ____ ____ ____ ____ ____

Base five: ____ ____ ____ ____ ____ ____ ____ ____ ____ ____

Base six: ____ ____ ____ ____ ____ ____ ____ ____ ____ ____

Base seven: ____ ____ ____ ____ ____ ____ ____ ____ ____ ____

Base eight: ____ ____ ____ ____ ____ ____ ____ ____ ____ ____

Base nine: ____ ____ ____ ____ ____ ____ ____ ____ ____ ____

Base ten: ____ ____ ____ ____ ____ ____ ____ ____ ____ ____

IV. Add.

1. 23_{five}
   $\underline{21_{\text{five}}}$

2. 43_{five}
   $\underline{14_{\text{five}}}$

3. 132_{five}
   $\underline{43_{\text{five}}}$

4. 22_{five}
   $\underline{31_{\text{five}}}$

5. 33_{five}
   $\underline{24_{\text{five}}}$

6. 205_{five}
   $\underline{31_{\text{five}}}$

V. Change to base ten numerals.

1. 323_{four} _____
2. 323_{five} _____
3. 323_{six} _____
4. 432_{five} _____

5. 1011_{two} _____
6. 146_{seven} _____
7. 146_{nine} _____
8. 202_{three} _____

VI. Change to base five numerals.

1. 14 _____
2. 22 _____
3. 31 _____
4. 96 _____

5. 19 _____
6. 26 _____
7. 89 _____
8. 134 _____

VII. Multiply.

1. $3 \times 32_{\text{five}}$ _____
2. $2 \times 41_{\text{five}}$ _____
3. $3 \times 42_{\text{five}}$ _____
4. $4 \times 24_{\text{five}}$ _____

5. $3 \times 12_{\text{five}}$ _____
6. $4 \times 322_{\text{five}}$ _____
7. $24_{\text{five}} \times 413_{\text{five}}$ _____
8. $23_{\text{five}} \times 312_{\text{five}}$ _____

423

VIII. Fractions. Add:

1. $5\frac{1}{2}$
   $2\frac{1}{3}$
   $3\frac{3}{4}$

2. $2\frac{3}{8}$
   $5\frac{1}{2}$
   $7\frac{3}{5}$

3. $8\frac{1}{4}$
   $7\frac{3}{8}$
   $5\frac{7}{12}$

4. $\frac{5}{8}$
   $2\frac{3}{4}$
   $2\frac{1}{16}$

5. $13\frac{1}{2}$
   $5\frac{1}{6}$
   $4\frac{2}{3}$
   $2\frac{1}{4}$

6. $58\frac{7}{12}$
   $5\frac{2}{5}$
   $4\frac{1}{10}$
   $75\frac{1}{6}$

7. $27\frac{2}{3}$
   $4\frac{1}{9}$
   $2\frac{1}{36}$
   $4\frac{1}{2}$

8. $7\frac{1}{5}$
   $50\frac{2}{15}$
   $3\frac{1}{2}$
   $4\frac{2}{5}$

9. $18\frac{4}{5}$
   $2\frac{1}{3}$
   $5\frac{3}{10}$

10. $207\frac{1}{6}$
    $7\frac{2}{7}$
    $15\frac{1}{2}$

11. $4\frac{1}{9}$
    $2\frac{7}{8}$
    $4\frac{1}{2}$

12. $13\frac{1}{8}$
    $5\frac{3}{4}$
    $700\frac{1}{2}$

13. $4\frac{2}{5}$
    $7\frac{2}{3}$
    $15\frac{1}{6}$

14. $37\frac{1}{2}$
    $9\frac{5}{6}$
    $47\frac{1}{4}$

15. $38\frac{2}{7}$
    $4\frac{1}{2}$
    $15\frac{1}{5}$

IX. Fractions. Subtract:

1. $13\frac{1}{3}$
   $8\frac{3}{4}$

2. $\frac{4}{5}$
   $\frac{3}{8}$

3. $15\frac{3}{4}$
   $4\frac{1}{3}$

4. $8\frac{1}{2}$
   $4\frac{2}{3}$

5. $12\frac{1}{4}$
   $\frac{3}{5}$

6. $33\frac{1}{2}$
   $15\frac{5}{8}$

7. $27\frac{2}{3}$
   $19\frac{4}{5}$

8. 37
   $14\frac{5}{6}$

9. 3
   $2\frac{1}{2}$

10. 7
    $2\frac{2}{7}$

11. 80
    $7\frac{1}{3}$

12. 15
    $8\frac{1}{2}$

13. $58\frac{1}{3}$
    $7\frac{4}{5}$

14. $36\frac{1}{7}$
    $8\frac{5}{6}$

15. $17\frac{1}{9}$
    $8\frac{2}{7}$

X. Fractions. Multiply:

1. $\frac{1}{2} \times 2\frac{4}{5} =$
2. $\frac{1}{3} \times 3\frac{3}{4} =$
3. $\frac{1}{4} \times 8\frac{8}{10} =$
4. $\frac{1}{5} \times 15\frac{5}{6} =$
5. $\frac{1}{2} \times 4\frac{2}{10} =$
6. $\frac{1}{3} \times 6\frac{3}{10} =$

7. $\frac{1}{4} \times 12\frac{4}{6} =$
8. $\frac{1}{12} \times 12\frac{12}{16} =$
9. $\frac{1}{2} \times 6\frac{6}{8} =$
10. $\frac{1}{3} \times 12\frac{3}{8} =$
11. $\frac{1}{5} \times 5\frac{5}{8} =$
12. $\frac{1}{10} \times 20\frac{10}{12} =$

13. $\frac{1}{2} \times 10\frac{4}{8} =$
14. $\frac{1}{4} \times 4\frac{4}{5} =$
15. $\frac{1}{5} \times 10\frac{5}{10} =$
16. $\frac{1}{8} \times 16\frac{16}{32} =$
17. $2\frac{1}{5} \times 6\frac{1}{2} =$
18. $9\frac{2}{3} \times 6\frac{3}{4} =$

19. $8\frac{1}{8} \times 10\frac{4}{5} =$
20. $8\frac{9}{10} \times 7\frac{4}{5} =$
21. $9\frac{7}{10} \times 6\frac{3}{10} =$
22. $\frac{5}{8} \times 1\frac{1}{2} =$
23. $2\frac{1}{3} \times 3 =$
24. $\frac{3}{5} \times \frac{9}{10} =$

XI. Fractions. Divide:

1. $12 \div 12\frac{1}{2} =$
2. $\frac{1}{18} \div \frac{2}{9} =$
3. $5\frac{2}{3} \div \frac{2}{7} =$
4. $5 \div \frac{5}{7} =$
5. $\frac{4}{15} \div \frac{3}{7} =$
6. $6\frac{1}{12} \div \frac{3}{8} =$

7. $\frac{1}{9} \div 12 =$
8. $\frac{4}{17} \div \frac{15}{34} =$
9. $4\frac{7}{8} \div 1\frac{1}{9} =$
10. $\frac{4}{5} \div 2 =$
11. $\frac{3}{26} \div \frac{1}{13} =$
12. $2\frac{1}{5} \div 3\frac{1}{2} =$

13. $15 \div \frac{3}{5} =$
14. $3\frac{3}{4} \div 2\frac{5}{8} =$
15. $3\frac{3}{5} \div 4 =$
16. $4\frac{1}{6} \div 10 =$
17. $5\frac{5}{6} \div 5 =$
18. $8\frac{3}{4} \div 20 =$

19. $\frac{3}{4} \div \frac{1}{12} =$
20. $2\frac{1}{8} \div 2\frac{2}{3} =$
21. $10 \div 1\frac{3}{5} =$
22. $2\frac{3}{5} \div 4\frac{1}{5} =$
23. $6\frac{2}{5} \div 3 =$
24. $\frac{1}{5} \div 3\frac{2}{5} =$

XII. Decimals. Copy and add:

1. 3.86, 7.92, 5.60
2. 2.09, .36, 308.7
3. .70, 2.06, 31.99
4. 3.842, .57, 46, 4.06
5. 8.96, .401, 37.1, 805.61, 75.51

6. .96, .003, 87., 807.1, 476.035
7. .3, 4.05, .039, 400.1, 75.006
8. .64, 5.55, .0324, 6.5, 759.5
9. .36, 306.1, 36.01, 31.601, 3.
10. 3.9, 300, 32.4, .045, 3405.1

XIII. Decimals. Copy and subtract:

1. $35 - 17.45$
2. $239.75 - 15.28$
3. $67.375 - 2.788$
4. $389.621 - 295.7$
5. $85.3 - 1.7$

6. $625 - .20$
7. $67.52 - 1.381$
8. $196 - .56$
9. $75.501 - 1.79$
10. $400 - 7.5$

XIV. Decimals. Multiply:

1. 85.3
   $\underline{1.7}$
2. 625
   $\underline{.25}$
3. 67.52
   $\underline{1.38}$
4. 39.64
   $\underline{.502}$
5. 389.1
   $\underline{.003}$
6. 67.52
   $\underline{.7}$

7. 3.861
   $\underline{10}$
8. 3.892
   $\underline{.46}$
9. 423.7
   $\underline{.29}$
10. 7.563
    $\underline{.008}$
11. 96.42
    $\underline{.07}$
12. 83.9
    $\underline{2.7}$

XV. Decimals. Divide:

1. $3.8\overline{)9.12}$
2. $.52\overline{)7.80}$
3. $9.5\overline{)6.65}$
4. $.57\overline{).1653}$

5. $.078\overline{).429}$
6. $.386\overline{)13.51}$
7. $1.4\overline{).105}$
8. $1.64\overline{)4.1}$

9. $.0173\overline{)6.401}$
10. $2.05\overline{)8.815}$
11. $1.13\overline{).1356}$
12. $.63\overline{).1323}$

XVI. Measures. Add:

1. 3 ft. 8 in.
   5 ft. 6 in.
2. 3 wk. 5 da.
   4 wk. 3 da.
3. 3 wk. 5 da.
   1 wk. 6 da.
4. 2 ft. 3 in.
   4 ft. 9 in.

5. 5 ft. 8 in.
   7 ft. 10 in.

6. 4 gal. 1 qt.
   3 gal. 3 qt.

7. 3 pk. 6 qt.
   4 pk. 5 qt.

8. 3 lb. 14 oz.
   2 lb. 1 oz.

9. 8 ft. 9 in.
   6 ft. 7 in.

10. 6 yd. 2 ft.
    5 yd. 2 ft.

11. 2 ft. 8 in.
    4 ft. 2 in.

12. 5 ft. 10 in.
    3 ft. 6 in.

XVII. Measures. Subtract:

1. 6 ft. 4 in.
   3 ft. 10 in.

2. 6 wk. 5 da.
   2 wk. 3 da.

3. 3 lb. 8 oz.
   1 lb. 12 oz.

4. 8 hr. 20 min.
   3 hr. 30 min.

5. 8 ft. 7 in.
   3 ft. 4 in.

6. 8 ft. 6 in.
   3 ft. 9 in.

7. 5 yd. 1 ft.
   2 yd. 2 ft.

8. 10 lb. 12 oz.
    7 lb. 3 oz.

9. 6 lb. 4 oz.
   2 lb. 8 oz.

10. 5 wk. 3 da.
    2 wk. 4 da.

11. 5 hr. 50 min.
    2 hr. 30 min.

12. 6 hr. 20 min.
    4 hr. 45 min.

13.	Yr.	Mo.	Da.
	1952	10	17
	1949	3	15

14.	Yr.	Mo.	Da.
	1952	1	31
	1776	7	4

15.	Yr.	Mo.	Da.
	1845	6	8
	1767	3	15

XVIII. Measures. Multiply:

1. 5 ft. 4 in.
   ×4

2. 2 lb. 6 oz.
   ×5

3. 4 ft. 8 in.
   ×4

4. 3 wk. 5 da.
   ×5

5. 3 yd. 2 ft.	6. 2 bu. 3 pk.	7. 4 hr. 20 min.	8. 2 lb. 6 oz.
$\times 5$	$\times 6$	$\times 2$	$\times 4$

9. 4 qt. 1 pt.	10. 9 yd. 2 ft.	11. 9 gal. 3 qt.	12. 2 lb. 12 oz.
$\times 5$	$\times 4$	$\times 6$	$\times 8$

XIX. Measures. Divide:

1. $4\overline{\smash{)}9 \text{ yd. 2 ft.}}$ 2. $6\overline{\smash{)}9 \text{ gal. 3 qt.}}$ 3. $8\overline{\smash{)}54 \text{ lb. 12 oz.}}$ 4. $4\overline{\smash{)}9 \text{ ft. 3 in.}}$

5. $5\overline{\smash{)}8 \text{ wk. 4 da.}}$ 6. $4\overline{\smash{)}16 \text{ ft. 4 in.}}$ 7. $2\overline{\smash{)}7 \text{ bu. 2 pk.}}$ 8. $2\overline{\smash{)}6 \text{ bu. 6 pk.}}$

9. $2\overline{\smash{)}2 \text{ ft. 3 in.}}$ 10. $6\overline{\smash{)}40 \text{ min. 30 sec.}}$

XX. Measures. Equivalents:

1. $3\frac{3}{4}$ lb. = ___ oz.		13. 4 yd. 2 ft. = ___ ft.	
2. 3 ft. 10 in. = ___ in.		14. 86 yd. 1 ft. = ___ ft.	
3. 9 yd. 2 ft. = ___ ft.		15. 3 gal. 2 qt. = ___ qt.	
4. 51 in. = ___ ft. ___ in.		16. 54 gal. 3 qt. = ___ qt.	
5. 34 oz. = ___ lb. ___ oz.		17. 4 gal. 2 qt. 1 pt. = ___ pt.	
6. 42 qt. = ___ gal. ___ qt.		18. 15 gal. 1 qt. = ___ pt.	
7. 55 qt. = ___ gal. ___ qt.		19. 26 gal. 3 qt. = ___ qt.	
8. 73 in. = ___ ft. ___ in.		20. 2×8 oz. = ___ lb.	
9. 84 in. = ___ ft. ___ in.		21. 2 lb. 9 oz. = ___ oz.	
10. 7 ft. 4 in. = ___ in.		22. 15 lb. 11 oz. = ___ oz.	
11. 13 ft. = ___ yd. ___ ft.		23. 54 oz. = ___ lb. ___ oz.	
12. 220 ft. = ___ yd. ___ ft.		24. 6,270 lb. = ___ T ___ lb.	

25. $7\frac{1}{2}$ gal. = ___ pt.

XXI. Per cent. Change:

1. $\frac{1}{5} = \frac{}{100} = $ _____ %

2. $\frac{2}{5} = \frac{}{100} = $ _____ %

3. $\frac{6}{10} = \frac{}{100} = $ _____ %

4. $\frac{3}{20} = \frac{}{100} = $ _____ %

5. $\frac{3}{50} = \frac{}{100} = $ _____ %

6. $\frac{13}{50} = \frac{}{100} = $ _____ %

7. $\frac{7}{25} = \frac{}{100} = $ _____ %

8. $\frac{4}{25} = \frac{}{100} = $ _____ %

9. $\frac{1}{4} = \frac{}{100} = $ _____ %

10. $\frac{1}{2} = \frac{}{100} = $ _____ %

11. $\frac{5}{8} = $ _____ %

12. $\frac{4}{12} = $ _____ %

13. $\frac{3}{8} = $ _____ %

14. $\frac{9}{16} = $ _____ %

15. $\frac{7}{12} = $ _____ %

16. $\frac{7}{100} = $ _____ %

17. $\frac{7}{10} = $ _____ %

18. $\frac{1}{3} = $ _____ %

19. $\frac{3}{20} = $ _____ %

20. $\frac{1}{50} = $ _____ %

XXII. Per cent:

1. 5 is what per cent of 10? _____

2. 15 is 50% of _____ .

3. 12 is 25% of _____ .

4. 13 is 10% of _____ .

5. 6 is 1% of _____ .

6. 25 is what per cent of 75? _____

7. 14 is what per cent of 21? _____

8. 10 is what per cent of 50? _____

9. 40 is 20% of _____ .

10. 30 is $33\frac{1}{3}$% of _____ .

11. 24 is what per cent of 80? _____

12. 40 is what per cent of 120? _____

13. 18 is what per cent of 36? _____

14. 14 is what per cent of 56? _____

15. 9 is what per cent of 27? _____

16. 14 is what per cent of 32? _____

17. 18 is what per cent of 40? _____

18. 23 is what per cent of 54? _____

19. 38 is what per cent of 91? _____

20. 17 is what per cent of 29? _____

XXIII. Per cent. Find:

1. 84% of 425 =
2. 3.5% of 920 =
3. 48% of 91 =
4. 19% of 125 =
5. 5% of $350 =
6. $\frac{1}{2}$% of $5275 =
7. $1\frac{1}{2}$% of $7,930 =
8. 34% of 60 =
9. 52% of 84 =
10. 26% of 40 =
11. 21% of 35 =
12. 5% of 16 =

XXIV. Interest. Find the interest on:

1. $250.00 at $3\frac{1}{2}$% for 4 yrs. 3 mo.
2. $175.00 at 4% for 2 yrs. 6 mo.
3. $1050.00 at $4\frac{1}{2}$% for 5 yrs.
4. $756.00 at $2\frac{1}{2}$% for 3 yrs. 4 mo.
5. $840.00 at $4\frac{3}{4}$% for 2 yrs. 8 mo.
6. $970.00 at 5% for 4 yrs. 2 mo.

7. $1,650.00 at 6% for 3 yrs. 9 mo.
8. $1,375.00 at $5\frac{1}{2}$% for 5 yrs. 6 mo.
9. $2,060.00 at $5\frac{1}{4}$% for 4 yrs. 3 mo.
10. $920.00 at $4\frac{1}{2}$% for 3 yrs.
11. $250.00 at $4\frac{3}{4}$% for 6 mo.
12. $500.00 at $3\frac{1}{2}$% for 6 mo.

XXV. Thought problems:

1. 18 out of 36 students bought ice cream for dessert. What per cent bought ice cream? _____

2. Eric wanted to measure a distance to place a target. He could find only a broken yardstick that was $2\frac{1}{2}$ feet long. How many whole lengths of this broken stick would he need to get a distance of 25 feet? _____

3. A committee studying weather in Miss West's class recorded noon temperature last week as follows: Monday 72°, Tuesday 79°, Wednesday 65°, Thursday 60°, Friday 52°, Saturday 48°, Sunday 58°. What was the average daily temperature for the week?

_____

4. Paula is making a poster. She wants the ratio of width to height to be 4 to 3. If she makes it 16 inches wide its height must be _____ . If 9 inches high, its width must be _____ . If 24 inches wide, its height must be

_____ .

5. The ratio of a six-year-old child's dose of a certain medicine to an adult's dose is 1 to 3. If an adult should take 6 drops, how much should a six-year-old take? _____

6. How much did these flower plants cost Mrs. Smith?
$2\frac{1}{2}$ dozen zinnias @ $.80 a dozen _____
$1\frac{1}{4}$ dozen petunias @ $1.00 a dozen _____
5 dozen pansies @ $.10 each _____
Total _____

7. In Hank's home town the individual bus fare is 12 cents. He can buy tokens at four for 35 cents. If Hank rides the bus twice daily for 20 days a month, how much cheaper would it be for him to buy tokens than to pay individual fares? _____

8. During a measles epidemic 35% of the pupils were absent from Jill's school. How many were absent from the total enrollment of 740? _____

9. There are three seventh-grade rooms in Hank's school. Last semester 25% of the 24 pupils in Hank's room got A in mathematics, 12 of the 25 pupils in a second room got A, and 20% of the 30 pupils in the third room got A. How many seventh graders in all got A in mathematics? _____

10. A 15% discount on a $244.00 television set is $ _____ .

11. A 6% discount on a $95.00 radio is _____ .

12. Mr. Cove is a salesman for a large furniture manufacturer. His regular commission is 1% on the first $50,000 of sales in any month, and $1\frac{1}{2}$% on all sales above $50,000 a month. What was Mr. Cove's commission for a month when his sales were $64,000? _____

13. Paul sold programs at football games last fall. His commission rate was 10%. How much did he make on the 1000 programs he sold for the season at 50¢ each? _____

14. Last year there were 250 pupils who ate lunch in the cafeteria regularly at Crestwood School. This year the principal hopes to increase this by 16%. What would the total number of pupils be then? _____

15. In Mr. Barnes's business he figures his margin must be 25% of the cost of the goods. What then must he sell an article for that cost $3.60? _____

16. Joan's savings bank pays $2\frac{1}{2}$% interest every year. How much will Joan get in interest for a year when her savings account amounts to $150? _____

17. Find the area of a parallelogram whose base is 15 inches and height is 8 inches. _____

18. Find the area of a circle if the radius is 15 feet. _____

19. Find the area of:
    a. a triangle with altitude 12 inches and base 18 inches. _____
    b. a rectangle with length 16 inches and width 9 inches. _____
    c. a square with a side 3.5 inches _____
    d. a parallelogram with *a* 9 inches and *b* 13 inches _____

20. Find the volume of these cubes:
    a. side 7 inches; volume _____
    b. side 13 feet; volume _____
    c. side 12 inches; volume _____
    d. side 25 inches; volume _____

21. Draw:

a) cylinder	b) rectangle	c) triangle	d) square
e) parallel lines	f) cube	g) pentagon	h) hexagon

22. What part of a mile is the 440 yard dash? _____

23. Mrs. Simons, who owns a fabric shop, sold $2\frac{1}{2}$ yards of satin brocade the first week of last month, $1\frac{3}{4}$ yards the second week, $2\frac{3}{4}$ yards the third week, and $1\frac{1}{2}$ yards the fourth week. The four weeks this month, she sold $1\frac{5}{6}$ yards, $2\frac{5}{12}$ yards, $1\frac{2}{3}$ yards, and $2\frac{1}{2}$ yards. How many more yards did she sell last month than this month? _____

24. Write these numbers as decimals:
    a. Five hundred twenty-two thousandths _____
    b. Four and seven hundredths

    _____
    c. Sixteen and three hundred two thousandths _____
    d. Three hundred forty-six and one thousand ninety-five ten-thousandths _____
    e. Four hundred fifty-two thousand three hundred seven millionths

    _____

25. Bruce bought a pound can of weed killer. The directions say, "Use 1.5 ounces to 5 gallons of water." How much mixture can he get from the pound can? _____

26. Mrs. Newcomb's grocery bills for the past four weeks were: $18.75, $23.19, $26.92, and $20.40. What was the average cost of her groceries per week?

    _____

27. A recipe for peach jam calls for 2 pounds of sugar to 3 pounds of fruit. How much sugar would be needed for each of these quantities of fruit?
    a. 6 pounds of fruit _____ pounds of sugar
    b. 9 pounds of fruit _____ pounds of sugar
    c. 15 pounds of fruit _____ pounds of sugar

28. A telephone call from Lily's house to her sister in Denver costs $2.15 before 6 P.M. or $1.65 after 6 P.M. How much will Lily save by calling after 6 o'clock? _____

29. Mrs. Paulsen has 100 frying chickens for sale. They average $3\frac{1}{4}$ pounds apiece in weight. How much can she get for the flock at the market price of 46 cents a pound? _____

30. Last Christmas Sally Beale mailed 110 Christmas cards. She paid 5¢ each for 70 of them, 2 for 15¢ for 30 of them, and 10¢ each for the remainder. Stamps cost 3¢ for each card. How much did Sally spend to send her Christmas cards? _____

31. In one state, automobile licenses cost 30¢ per 100 pounds of car weight. (The weights are taken to the nearest 100 pounds.) What will the licenses cost for these cars?
    a. Car A   3,125 pounds _____
    b. Car B   3,470 pounds _____
    c. Car C   2,935 pounds _____

32. The baseball team at Hank's school played 12 games last year and won 75% of them. This year they played 15 games and won only $66\frac{2}{3}$%. How many games did the team win;
    a. Last year? _____   b. This year? _____

33. In a sale, a suit that had a regular price of $45.00 is priced at $36.00. a. What is the amount of the discount? _____
    b. What is the rate of discount? _____

34. If the original price of a bike is $45.00 and the discount is $8.00, what is the rate of discount? _____

35. Jess and Art decided to see if they could get more customers for their paper routes. The first afternoon Jess called at five houses and got one customer. Art called at eight houses and got two customers. Which boy had better luck considering the number of calls he made? _____

36. A sale of frozen food advertises asparagus at 40¢ reduced for sale to 30¢, and garden peas at 25¢ reduced for sale to 20¢. Which represents the greater per cent of reduction? _____

37. Mr. Smith owns these government bonds: three $100. bonds which cost $75.00 each, five $50. bonds which cost $37.50 each, twelve $25. bonds which cost $18.75 each.
    a. The twenty bonds cost him _____ .
    b. How much interest will Mr. Smith get if he holds them to maturity? _____

38. At Eastland School 108 boys participated in some major sport last season. This was 24% of all the boys in the school. How many boys were in Eastland School last year? _____

39. Write this number in Roman numerals: 5,683 _____

40. Make a suitable graph to show the growth in population in James County from 1951 to 1960.

    In 1951 the population was 48,000.
    In 1952 "   "   "   50.000.
    In 1953 "   "   "   50,000.
    In 1954 "   "   "   49,500.
    In 1955 "   "   "   49,000.
    In 1956 "   "   "   49,000.
    In 1957 "   "   "   51,000.
    In 1958 "   "   "   52,500.
    In 1959 "   "   "   53,000.
    In 1960 "   "   "   55,000.

I.
1. In recent years we have discussed many new phases.
2. Will people always like stories about heroes?
3. Yes, there'll always be lots of hero stories.
4. How true this is!
5. Our history teacher said, "Name three present-day heroes."
6. Why are you so angry?
7. Shakespeare wrote *Twelfth Night.*
8. How many of Shakespeare's plays have you read?
9. They'll have finished by the time we arrive.
10. His address is 110 Main Street, Amsterdam, N.Y.
11. The children's boots were all mixed up.
12. Please check the following: number of books, titles of books, and authors.
13. George asked for five notebooks, three pencils, and a fountain pen.
14. Let's sing "America the Beautiful."
15. Do you think practice makes perfect?

II.
1. Whom would the class like?
2. To whom do you think it was sent?
3. Each child was reading his own.
4. We would have gone if it hadn't rained.
5. They were all much too tired.
6. Have you eaten it all already?
7. I think she began it at nine.
8. "Where is the dog?" he asked.
9. She taught us to weave place mats.
10. Let me have my turn, please.
11. This kind of model is new.
12. It doesn't seem to fit very well.
13. John and I will go on the errand.
14. The balloons are different from planes.
15. She sat on the freshly painted chair.
16. We girls are making fudge.
17. She has already lain down for her nap.
18. Oh, lay it down on the bench.
19. I may have written that myself.
20. Have you a raincoat?
21. Doesn't her story stick to the point?
22. I think I'll lie down for a while.
23. I saw fifty butterflies yesterday.
24. Leave me alone, please.
25. They did it anyway!

III.

simple subject (or subjects)	verbs (simple predicates)
1. Mary, Jane	ran, jumped.
2. children	have worked, have finished.
3. fish	have
4. Rows	look
5. teeth	are used
6. I	have
7. Mr. Stickleback	is, is
8. stickleback	is

9. colors	brighten, fade
10. You	can catch

IV.

	Pro		Use
1.	Who	(interrog.)	nom. case, pred. nom. after "are."
	you		nom. case, subj. of "do think."
	you		nom. case, subj. of "are."
2.	Which	(interrog.)	nom. case, subj. of "is going."
	you		obj. case, obj. of prep. "of."
	my		poss. case, modifying "place."
3.	It		nom. case, subj. of "is getting."
4.	She		nom. case, subj. of "lost."
	her		poss. case, modifying "wallet."
5.	it		obj. case, obj. of "recovered."
6.	Your		poss. case, modifying "home."
7.	This		nom. case, subj. of "is."
	her		poss. case, modifying "choice."
8.	Several	(indef.)	nom. case. subj. of "claimed."
	it		obj. case, obj. of "claimed."
9.	Nobody	(indef.)	nom. case, subj. of "wanted."
	it		obj. case, obj. of "wanted."
10.	That	(rel.)	nom. case, subj. of "burned."
	one		nom. case, pred. pro. after "was."

V.

	Sing. poss.	Pl.	Pl. poss.
2.	woman's	women	women's
3.	lady's	ladies	ladies'
4.	child's	children	children's
5.	banjo's	banjos	banjos'
6.	bison's	bison	bison's
7.	church's	churches	churches'
8.	melody's	melodies	melodies'
9.	key's	keys	keys'
10.	potato's	potatoes	potatoes'
11.	wolf's	wolves	wolves'
12.	salmon's	salmon	salmon's
13.	memory's	memories	memories'
14.	word's	words	words'
15.	director's	directors	directors'
16.	poem's	poems	poems'
17.	country's	countries	countries'

	Sing. poss.	Pl.	Pl. poss.
18.	shell's	shells	shells'
19.	fish's	fishes	fishes'
20.	model's	models	models'
21.	stone's	stones	stones'
22.	quotation's	quotations	quotations'
23.	phrase's	phrases	phrases'
24.	address's	addresses	addresses'
25.	life's	lives	lives'

VI.

	Past Tense	Past Participle
2.	sang	sung
3.	was	been
4.	grew	grown
5.	flew	flown (as a bird)
6.	flowed	flowed (as a river)
7.	saw	seen
8.	spoke	spoken
9.	ran	run
10.	dived	dived
11.	lay	lain
12.	laid	laid
13.	brought	brought
14.	drank	drunk
15.	swung	swung
16.	swam	swum
17.	did	done
18.	set	set
19.	broke	broken
20.	came	come
21.	taught	taught
22.	tore	torn
23.	threw	thrown
24.	froze	frozen
25.	was	been

VII.

	Comp.	Super.
2.	less	least
3.	faster	fastest
4.	worse	worst
5.	fairer	fairest
6.	farther	farthest
7.	happier	happiest
8.	more slowly	most slowly (change sentence and use "slowest")
9.	fatter	fattest
10.	more quietly	most quietly
11.	surer	surest
12.	more real	most real
13.	lovelier	loveliest
14.	larger	largest
15.	more securely	most securely
16.	better	best
17.	more	most
18.	rarer	rarest
19.	more interesting	most interesting
20.	clearer	clearest
21.	more enjoyable	most enjoyable
22.	rougher	roughest
23.	older	oldest
24.	newer	newest
25.	more beautiful	most beautiful

VIII.

1. Robert Fulton | was \ inventor / an

2. Walter Damrosch | was \ conductor / a

3. Gutzon Borglum | was \ sculptor / a

4. The Rushmore Memorial | is \ in \ Black Hills / the / of South Dakota

5. Newspapers and magazines | will furnish | material \ much

6. Ted | walked \ across \ logs / the — and — rescued | puppy / the

7. The audience | cheered and clapped

8. Bob | raised | curtain / the \ red \ velvet

9. Mrs. Jones | gave | party / a \ After / for \ play / the \ cast / the

10. You | can read \ well \ how

11. You | did bring | rabbit / the \ to \ school

12. (You) | begin | story / your \ with \ situation / an \ interesting

13. (You) | attract | attention / the \ of \ reader / the

435

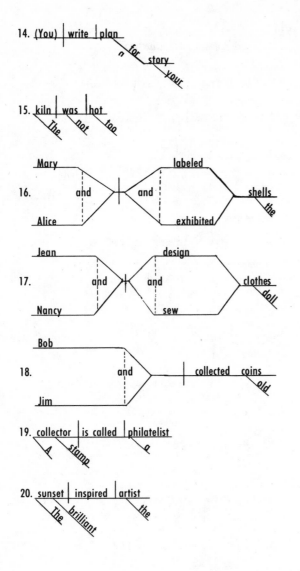

14. (You) | write | plan
    for story
    a / your

15. The kiln | was | hot
    too / not

16. Mary and Alice | labeled and exhibited | shells
    the

17. Jean and Nancy | design and sew | clothes
    doll

18. Bob and Jim | collected | coins
    old

19. A collector | is called | philatelist
    stamp / a

20. The brilliant sunset | inspired | artist
    the

1. in the office —adv.   2. of the house —adj.   3. of our country —adj.   4. by one boy —adv.   5. of story —adj.   6. to western Pennsylvania —adv.   7. in a tent —adj.   8. in it —adv.   for your eyes —adj.   9. of the wheel —adj.   in many ways —adv.   10. at Mansfield —adj.   11. to the library —adv.   on Saturday —adv.   12. for herself —adj.   in the theatre —adv.   13. of the roof —adj.   by the wind —adv.   14. In those days —adv.   15. of all ages —adj.   16. in a battle —adv.   17. In a little while —adv.   18. into the water —adv.   19. of each tool —adj.   20. to our house —adv.

X.

1. to eat	6. to remember
2. to be finished	7. to get
3. to write	8. to see
4. to live	9. to look
5. to stop	10. to write

XI.

1. setting	6. singing
2. painting	7. reading
3. calling	8. writing
4. coaching	9. looking
5. stepping	10. finding

XII.

1. playing	6. seeing
2. exchanging	7. stopping
3. hearing	8. seeing
4. reading	9. writing
5. beginning	10. meeting

ANSWERS   seventh grade arithmetic exercises

I. Number system:
1. 503,056
2. 813,204
3. 8,756,100
4. 700,000,000,000
5. 186,003,075,025
6. 9,000,001
7. 111,000,000,000
8. 3,347,202
9. 7,219,384,124
10. 19,000,017

II. Roman numerals:
1. 1
2. 5
3. 10
4. 50
5. 100
6. 500
7. 1000
8. 4
9. 9
10. 40
11. 90
12. 400
13. 900
14. 11
15. 16
16. 61
17. 156
18. 1610
19. 605
20. 1106
21. 1655
22. 23
23. 88
24. 380
25. 1887
26. 3
27. 7
28. 13
29. 25
30. 49
31. 75
32. 96
33. 39
34. 68
35. 18
36. 12
37. 41
38. 66
39. 74
40. 9
41. 620
42. 1505
43. 1956
44. 325
45. 1233
46. 414
47. 17
48. 22
49. 34
50. 65

III.
Base two: 0, 1, 10, 11, 100, 101, 110, 111.
Base three: 0, 1, 2, 10, 11, 12, 20, 21, 22.
Base four: 0, 1, 2, 3, 10, 11, 12, 13, 20, 21.
Base five: 0, 1, 2, 3, 4, 10, 11, 12, 13, 14, 20.
Base six: 0, 1, 2, 3, 4, 5, 10, 11, 12, 13, 14.
Base seven: 0, 1, 2, 3, 4, 5, 6, 10, 11, 12, 13.
Base eight: 0, 1, 2, 3, 4, 5, 6, 7, 10, 11, 12.
Base nine: 0, 1, 2, 3, 4, 5, 6, 7, 8, 10, 11.
Base ten: 0, 1, 2, 3, 4, 5, 6, 7, 8, 9, 10.

IV. Add.
1. 44_{five}
2. 112_{five}
3. 230_{five}
4. 103_{five}
5. 112_{five}
6. 240_{five}

V. Change to base ten.
1. 59
2. 88
3. 123
4. 117
5. 11
6. 83
7. 123
8. 20

VI. Change to base five.
1. 24_{five}
2. 42_{five}
3. 111_{five}
4. 341_{five}
5. 34_{five}
6. 101_{five}
7. 324_{five}
8. 1014_{five}

VII. Multiply.
1. 201_{five}
2. 132_{five}
3. 231_{five}
4. 211_{five}
5. 41_{five}
6. 2343_{five}
7. 22022_{five}
8. 13231_{five}

VIII. Fractions. Add:
1. $11\frac{7}{12}$
2. $15\frac{19}{40}$
3. $21\frac{5}{24}$
4. $5\frac{7}{16}$
5. $25\frac{7}{12}$
6. $143\frac{1}{4}$
7. $38\frac{11}{16}$
8. $65\frac{7}{30}$
9. $26\frac{13}{30}$
10. $229\frac{20}{21}$
11. $11\frac{35}{72}$
12. $719\frac{3}{8}$
13. $27\frac{7}{30}$
14. $94\frac{7}{12}$
15. $57\frac{69}{70}$

IX. Fractions. Subtract:
1. $4\frac{7}{12}$
2. $\frac{17}{40}$
3. $11\frac{5}{12}$
4. $3\frac{5}{6}$
5. $11\frac{13}{20}$
6. $17\frac{7}{8}$
7. $7\frac{13}{15}$
8. $22\frac{1}{6}$
9. $\frac{1}{2}$
10. $4\frac{5}{7}$
11. $72\frac{2}{3}$
12. $6\frac{1}{2}$
13. $50\frac{8}{15}$
14. $27\frac{13}{42}$
15. $8\frac{52}{63}$

X. Fractions. Multiply:
1. $1\frac{2}{5}$
2. $1\frac{1}{4}$
3. $2\frac{1}{5}$
4. $3\frac{1}{6}$
5. $2\frac{1}{10}$
6. $2\frac{1}{10}$
7. $3\frac{1}{6}$
8. $1\frac{1}{16}$
9. $3\frac{3}{8}$
10. $4\frac{1}{8}$
11. $1\frac{1}{8}$
12. $2\frac{1}{12}$
13. $5\frac{1}{4}$
14. $1\frac{1}{5}$
15. $2\frac{1}{10}$
16. $2\frac{1}{16}$
17. $14\frac{3}{10}$
18. $65\frac{1}{4}$
19. $87\frac{3}{4}$
20. $69\frac{21}{50}$
21. $61\frac{11}{100}$
22. $\frac{15}{16}$
23. 7
24. $\frac{27}{50}$

XI. Fractions. Divide:
1. $\frac{24}{25}$
2. $\frac{1}{4}$
3. $19\frac{5}{6}$
4. 7
5. $\frac{28}{45}$
6. $16\frac{2}{9}$
7. $\frac{1}{108}$
8. $\frac{8}{15}$
9. $4\frac{31}{80}$
10. $\frac{2}{3}$
11. $1\frac{1}{2}$
12. $\frac{22}{45}$
13. 25
14. $1\frac{3}{7}$
15. $\frac{9}{10}$
16. $\frac{5}{12}$
17. $1\frac{1}{6}$
18. $\frac{7}{16}$
19. 9
20. $\frac{51}{64}$
21. $6\frac{1}{4}$
22. $\frac{13}{21}$
23. $2\frac{2}{15}$
24. $\frac{1}{17}$

XII. Decimals. Add:
1. 17.38
2. 311.15
3. 34.75
4. 54.472
5. 927.581
6. 1371.098
7. 479.495
8. 772.2224
9. 377.071
10. 3741.445

XIII. Decimals. Subtract:
1. 17.55
2. 224.47
3. 64.587
4. 93.921
5. 83.6
6. 624.80
7. 66.139
8. 195.44
9. 73.711
10. 392.5

XIV. Decimals. Multiply:
1. 145.01
2. 156.25
3. 93.1776
4. 19.89928
5. 1.1673
6. 47.264
7. 38.61
8. 1.79032
9. 122.873
10. .060504
11. 6.7494
12. 226.53

XV. Decimals. Divide:

1. 2.4 2. 15 3. .7
4. .29 5. $5\frac{1}{2}$ (5.5) 6. 35
7. $.07\frac{1}{2}$ (.075) 8. $2\frac{1}{2}$ (2.5) 9. 370
10. 4.3 11. .12 12. .21

XVI. Measures. Add:

1. 9 feet 2 inches 2. 8 weeks 1 day 3. 5 weeks 4 days 4. 7 feet 5. 13 feet 6 inches ($13\frac{1}{2}$ feet) 6. 8 gallons 7. 8 pecks 3 quarts 8. 5 pounds 15 ounces 9. 15 feet 4 inches 10. 12 yards 1 foot 11. 6 feet 10 inches 12. 9 feet 4 inches

XVII. Measures. Subtract:

1. 2 feet 6 inches 2. 4 weeks 2 days 3. 1 pound 12 ounces 4. 4 hours 50 minutes 5. 5 feet 3 inches 6. 4 feet 9 inches 7. 2 yards 2 feet 8. 3 pounds 9 ounces 9. 3 pounds 12 ounces 10. 2 weeks 6 days 11. 3 hours 20 minutes 12. 1 hour 35 minutes 13. 3 years 7 months 2 days 14. 175 years 6 months 27 days 15. 78 years 2 months 23 days

XVIII. Measures. Multiply:

1. 21 feet 4 inches 2. 11 pounds 14 ounces 3. 18 feet 8 inches 4. 18 weeks 4 days 5. 18 yards 1 foot 6. 16 bushels 2 pecks 7. 8 hours 40 minutes 8. 9 pounds 8 ounces 9. 22 quarts 1 pint 10. 38 yards 2 feet 11. 58 gallons 2 quarts 12. 22 pounds

XIX. Measures. Divide:

1. $2\frac{5}{12}$ yards 2. $1\frac{5}{8}$ gallons 3. $6\frac{27}{32}$ pounds
4. $2\frac{5}{16}$ quarts 5. $1\frac{5}{7}$ weeks 6. $4\frac{1}{12}$ feet
7. $3\frac{3}{4}$ bushels 8. $3\frac{3}{4}$ bushels 9. $1\frac{1}{8}$ feet
10. $6\frac{3}{4}$ minutes

XX. Measures. Equivalents:

1. 60 ounces 2. 46 inches 3. 29 feet 4. 4 feet 3 inches 5. 2 pounds 2 ounces 6. 10 gallons 2 quarts 7. 13 gallons 3 quarts 8. 6 feet 1 inch 9. 7 feet 10. 88 inches 11. 4 yards 1 foot 12. 73 yards 1 foot 13. 14 feet 14. 259 feet 15. 14 quarts 16. 219 quarts 17. 37 pints 18. 122 pints 19. 107 quarts 20. 1 pound 21. 41 ounces 22. 251 ounces 23. 3 pounds 6 ounces 24. 3 tons 270 pounds 25. 60 pints

XXI. Per cent:

1. $\frac{20}{100}$, 20% 8. $\frac{16}{100}$, 16% 15. $58\frac{1}{3}$%
2. $\frac{40}{100}$, 40% 9. $\frac{25}{100}$, 25% 16. 7%
3. $\frac{60}{100}$, 60% 10. $\frac{50}{100}$, 50% 17. 70%
4. $\frac{15}{100}$, 15% 11. $62\frac{1}{2}$% 18. $33\frac{1}{3}$%
5. $\frac{6}{100}$, 6% 12. $33\frac{1}{3}$% 19. 15%
6. $\frac{26}{100}$, 26% 13. $37\frac{1}{2}$% 20. 2%
7. $\frac{28}{100}$, 28% 14. $56\frac{1}{4}$%

XXII. Per cent:

1. 50% 8. 20% 15. $33\frac{1}{3}$%
2. 30 9. 200 16. 44%
3. 48 10. 90 17. 45%
4. 130 11. 30% 18. 43%
5. 600 12. $33\frac{1}{3}$% 19. 42%
6. $33\frac{1}{3}$% 13. 50% 20. 59%
7. $66\frac{2}{3}$% 14. 25%

XXIII. Per cent:

1. 357 2. 32.2 3. 43.68
4. 23.75 5. $17.50 6. 26.37\frac{1}{2}$
7. $118.95 8. $20\frac{2}{5}$ 9. 43.68
10. $10\frac{2}{5}$ 11. 7.35 12. .8

XXIV. Interest:

1. 37.18\frac{3}{4}$ 5. $106.40 9. 459.63\frac{3}{4}$
2. $17.50 6. 202.08\frac{1}{3}$ 10. $124.20
3. $236.25 7. $371.25 11. 5.93\frac{3}{4}$
4. $63.00 8. 415.93\frac{3}{4}$ 12. $8.75

XXV. Thought problems:

1. 50% 2. 10 lengths 3. 62° 4. 12″, 12″, 18″ 5. 2 drops 6. $9.25 7. $1.30 8. 259 9. 24 10. $36.60 11. $5.70 12. $710 13. $50 14. 290 15. $4.50 16. $3.75 17. 120 sq. in. 18. $707\frac{1}{2}$ sq. ft. 19. (a) 108 sq. in. (b) 144 sq. in. (c) 12.25 sq. in. (d) 117 sq. in. 20. (a) 343 cu. in. (b) 2,197 cu. ft. (c) 1,728 cu. in. (d) 15,625 cu. in. 21.

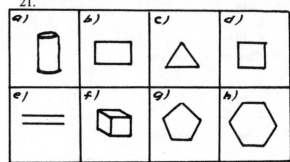

22. $\frac{1}{4}$ mile   23. $\frac{1}{12}$ yard   24. (a) .522   (b) 4.07   (c) 16.302   (d) 346.1095   (e) .452307 25. $53\frac{1}{3}$ gal. (ten 5-gal. cans and $\frac{2}{3}$ of the 11th) 26. $22.32 per week   27. (a) 4 pounds of sugar   (b) 6 pounds of sugar   (c) 10 pounds of sugar   28. 50 cents saved   29. $149.50

30. $10.05   31. (a) $9.30   (b) $10.40,   (c) $8.70   32. (a) 9 games   (b) 10 games   33. (a) $9.00   (b) 20%   34. $17\frac{7}{8}$%   35. Art had better luck.   36. Asparagus   37. (a) $637.50 (b) $212.50   38. 450   39. $\overline{\text{V}}$DCLXXXIII

40.

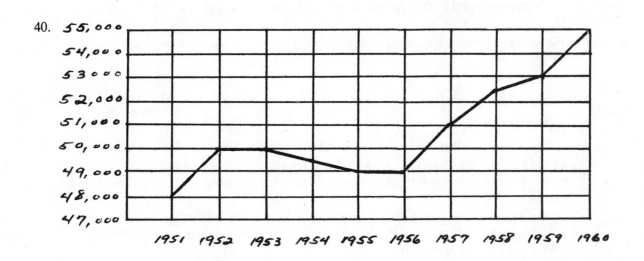

or

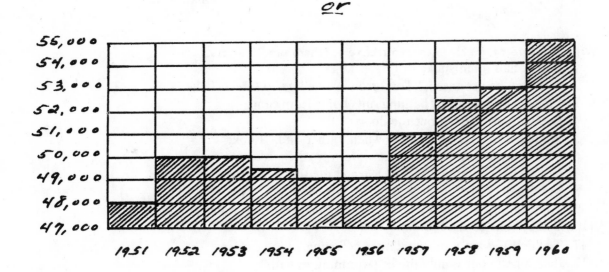

final english test   seventh grade

english

The sentences and words in this test are more difficult than those you have had before, but the rules you use are the same. Review the rules you have had earlier before you take the test. Do your work on separate paper in ink. Write as well as you can. Each question is worth 20 points.

A. Rewrite the following letter, punctuating and capitalizing where necessary. (There are 20 errors.)

20 West Street
Wichita Kansas
March 6 1960

Dear Uncle Tom

    Thank you for the stamps from Chile Egypt and France. I did not have any of them in my collection. Dr George B Knapp our neighbor saw them. He exclaimed Oh Dennis that green stamp from Chile is a beauty. I wish that I had one.

    My collection is growing fast. I find that I am learning a lot about Geography and History but my hobby doesn't help my english. During April I'll have to get better grades.

Affectionately Yours
Dennis

B. Write the correct form for each incorrect verb. (There are 20 errors.)
1. Father had often spoke of Green Lake.
2. Saturday he promised, "Tomorrow we will go to Green Lake."
3. I'm glad we brung our bathing suits home from camp.
4. Excitedly we busted out the door.
5. We had drove about ten miles when Father said, "Look."
6. Through the trees we seen the water.
7. We went swimming and Ted learned me the side stroke.
8. My friends come down to the lake last summer.
9. They didn't swim. They just throwed stones into the water and watched
10. as they sunk to the bottom.
11. Ted and I swam until the dinner bell rung.
12. Each one in our family prefer swimming to eating.
13. By six o'clock Mother had lain a white tablecloth on the ground and prepared our picnic.
14. After dinner Father laid back against a tree and fell asleep.
15. Ted and I done the dishes for Mother.
16. We was too excited to take a rest.
17. When Green Lake is froze, it's a good place to skate.
18. I like to lay down and dream about Green Lake.
19. When my dog sets down beside me, I tell him about our fun.
20. Neither the heat nor the cold prevent our outdoor fun.

C. Write the correct form for each incorrect pronoun. (There are 20 errors.)
1, 2—Since yourself and Richard are in the play, both you and him should come to the rehearsal tomorrow.

    3—In charge of the scenery are Sam, Marjorie, and me.

4, 5—The adviser loaned Helen and she there costumes.

6, 7—Mr. Smith says our's is a good play and everyone should be sure to see them.

    8—Will you lend Helen and myself that cape for the playe?

    9—The clerks in Flynn's store said he would help us.

10, 11—Why didn't I see yourself and he at the rehearsal last week?

    12—Hasn't anyone told you and she about the play?

    13—Acting is fun for most of we girls.

    14—Either Pat or Jane or me will sell tickets.

    15—Mr. Jones thinks us girls will do a good job.

    16—Everyone in the cast likes their particular role.

    17—Us girls want to put on a play next year, too.

    18—Roy said, boastingly, to Tom, "You're almost as good as me!"

    19—He didn't pay the compliment to we girls.

    20—Between you and I, I think we were as good as he was!

D. Copy the complete sentence, correcting the error in the use of an adjective or adverb. You may need your dictionary to help you. (20)

1. This was the worse of all our winter storms.
2. John's dog is the oldest of the pair.
3. Of the three rooms, this is the larger.
4. Her work is more easier than mine.
5. That quartet certainly sings good!
6. I'd like a apple pie.
7. She served a swell dessert.
8. We are sure glad to be here today.
9. We are having a real good time.
10. The hostess seems awfully nice.
11. Both of us worked the problem different.
12. Do you like algebra or geometry best?
13. Most everybody likes school.
14. Oh, put the book anywheres.
15. Less students attended this week's game.
16. This is certainly a healthy climate.
17. I am plenty annoyed by your actions.
18. Louise is the smartest one of the twins.
19. Ann plays tennis very bad.
20. You should learn to speak proper.

E. Diagram the following sentences. (20)

1. Miss Jones is my favorite teacher.
2. She is always cheerful.
3. She gave a candy Valentine to each child in her class.
4. We run errands for her.
5. She assigns lots of homework.
6. We don't mind that because we like her.
7. Miss Murphy and Miss Jones are good friends and roommates.
8. Miss Jones took Miss Duffy's place in the English Department in the Junior High School in January of last year.
9. Miss Murphy graduated from a large university in California.
10. You will like my teachers when you meet them.

arithmetic test
(Do your work on scratch paper.)

I. Add.

1. $23_{five} + 14_{five}$
2. $13_{five} + 21_{five}$
3. $24_{five} + 14_{five}$
4. $133_{five} + 204_{five}$
5. $10_{five} + 4_{five}$
6. $23_{five} + 22_{five}$
7. $34_{five} + 24_{five}$
8. $302_{five} + 123_{five}$
9. $14_{seven} + 16_{seven}$
10. $36_{seven} + 3_{seven}$

II. Find the whole when a part is known.

1. 8 is $\frac{1}{3}$ of what number? _____
2. 25 is $\frac{1}{5}$ of what number? _____
3. $\frac{1}{2}$ of what number is 4? _____
4. $\frac{1}{8}$ of what number is 8? _____
5. 18 is $\frac{2}{3}$ of what number? _____
6. 45 is $\frac{3}{4}$ of what number? _____
7. $\frac{3}{8}$ of what number is 27? _____
8. $\frac{5}{16}$ of what number is 30? _____
9. 21 is $\frac{7}{16}$ of what number? _____
10. 42 is $\frac{6}{7}$ of what number? _____

III. A. Change to per cent:

1. .1875 _____
2. .08 _____
3. .003/4 _____
4. 10 _____
5. .245 _____

B. Change to decimals:

1. 175% _____
2. $12\frac{1}{2}$% _____
3. 6% _____
4. $\frac{1}{4}$% _____
5. .1% _____

IV. Find the discount and the net price:

List price	Rate of discount	Discount	Net price
1. $140	15%	_____	_____
2. $265	18%	_____	_____
3. $856	$12\frac{1}{2}$%	_____	_____
4. $19.50	2%	_____	_____
5. $56.75	4%	_____	_____

V. Find the commission and net proceeds:

Sales	Rate of commission	Commission	Net proceeds
1. $628	2%	_____	_____
2. $124	20%	_____	_____
3. $732	5%	_____	_____
4. $5600	$2\frac{1}{4}$%	_____	_____
5. $258.40	$3\frac{3}{4}$%	_____	_____

VI. Find the interest and the total amount:

Principal	Rate	Time	Interest	Amount
1. $725	2%	3 years	_____	_____
2. $3200	5%	$\frac{3}{4}$ year	_____	_____
3. $4000	6%	3 years	_____	_____
4. $2400	2%	2 months	_____	_____
5. $6400	6%	6 months	_____	_____

VII. Per cent of increase or decrease:

1. A decrease in the price of a dozen oranges from 50¢ to 40¢ is a decrease of _____%.
2. An increase in pay from 80¢ to 90¢ an hour is an increase of _____ %.
3. The population of a small town increased from 800 to 900 in five years. What was the per cent of increase? _____
4. Mr. Pitt pays 45¢ a dozen for eggs and sells them for 60¢ a dozen. What per cent of increase is this? _____
5. Mr. Smith's truck was worth $900 last year. This year it is valued at $600. It has decreased about _____ %.

VIII. Change to base five numerals.

1. 10   6. 92
2. 42   7. 117
3. 59   8. 95
4. 132   9. 66
5. 250   10. 18

IX. A. Add:

1.
7 weeks 5 days
4 weeks 6 days
6 weeks 4 days

2.
6 pounds 7 ounces
2 pounds 5 ounces
1 pound 4 ounces

3.
3 gallons 3 quarts
2 gallons 1 quart
5 gallons 2 quarts

4.
2 hours 45 minutes
3 hours 30 minutes
4 hours 20 minutes

5.
2 feet 4 inches
8 feet 9 inches
7 feet 10 inches

B. Subtract:

1. 8 weeks 2 days − 3 weeks 6 days
2. 5 years 2 months − 4 years 9 months
3. 8 gallons 1 quart − 4 gallons 3 quarts
4. 6 yards 1 foot − 3 yards 2 feet
5. 8 weeks 1 day − 5 weeks 5 days

X. Find:

1. the circumference of a circle whose radius is 4 inches. _____
2. the circumference of a circle whose diameter is 10 inches. _____
3. the area of a triangle whose base measures 6 inches and whose height is 4 inches. _____
4. the area of an irregular surface as pictured;

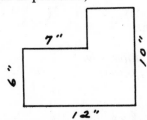

5. the area of a parallelogram that measures 7.5 inches at the base and is 10 inches high.

_____

443

english

A.

20 West Street
Wichita, Kansas
March 6, 1960

Dear Uncle Tom,

Thank you for the stamps from Chile, Egypt, and France. I did not have any of them in my collection. Dr. George B. Knapp, our neighbor, saw them. He exclaimed, "Oh, Dennis, that green stamp from Chile is a beauty! I wish I had one."

My collection is growing fast. I find that I am learning a lot about geography and history but my hobby doesn't help my English. During April I'll have to get better grades.

Affectionately yours,
Dennis

B.

1. had spoken
2. shall go
3. brought
4. burst
5. had driven
6. saw
7. taught
8. came
9. threw
10. sank
11. rang
12. prefers
13. had laid
14. lay
15. did
16. were
17. is frozen
18. to lie
19. sits
20. prevents

C.

1. *you* and Richard
2. you and *he*
3. Sam, Marjorie, and *I*
4. Helen and *her*
5. *their* costumes
6. *ours* is
7. to see *it*
8. Helen and *me*
9. said *they* would
10. *you*
11. and *him*
12. you and *her*
13. *us* girls
14. Jane or *I*
15. *we* girls
16. *his* particular role
17. *We* girls
18. as good as *I*
19. *us* girls
20. Between you and *me*

D.

1. This was the *worst* of all our winter storms.
2. John's dog is the *older* of the pair.
3. Of the three rooms, this is the *largest*.
4. Her work is *easier* than mine.
5. That quartet certainly sings *well!*
6. I'd like *an* apple pie.
7. She served a *delicious* dessert.
8. We are *surely* glad to be here today.
9. We are having a *really* good time.
10. The hostess seems *very* nice.
11. Both of us worked the problem *differently*.
12. Do you like algebra or geometry *better*?
13. *Almost* everybody likes school.
14. Oh, put the book *anywhere*.
15. *Fewer* students attended this week's game.
16. This is certainly a *healthful* climate.
17. I am *very* annoyed by your actions.
18. Louise is the *smarter* one of the twins.
19. Ann plays tennis very *badly*.
20. You should learn to speak *properly*.

E.

1.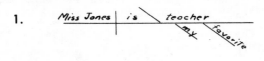
Miss Jones | is \ teacher
my favorite

2.
She | is \ cheerful
always

3.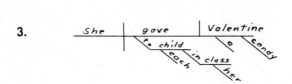
She | gave | Valentine
to each child in class her | a candy

4.
We | run | errands
for her

5.
She | assigns | lots
of homework

6.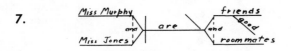
We | do mind | that
not because
we | like | her

7.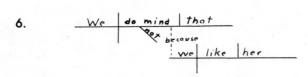
Miss Murphy
and | are | friends good
Miss Jones | and roommates

8.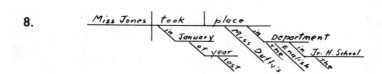
Miss Jones | took | place
in January of year last | Miss Duffy's in the English Department in Jr. H. School

9.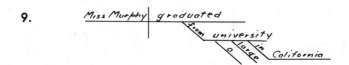
Miss Murphy | graduated
from university a large in California

10.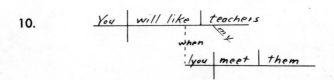
You | will like | teachers
when my
you | meet | them

arithmetic test answers

I. Add:
1. 42_{five}
2. 34_{five}
3. 43_{five}
4. 342_{five}
5. 14_{five}
6. 100_{five}
7. 113_{five}
8. 430_{five}
9. 33_{seven}
10. 42_{seven}

II. Find the whole:
1. 24
2. 125
3. 8
4. 64
5. 27
6. 60
7. 72
8. 96
9. 48
10. 49

III.
A.
1. $18\frac{3}{4}\%$
2. 8%
3. $\frac{3}{4}\%$
4. 1000%
5. 24.5%

B.
1. 1.75
2. $.12\frac{1}{2}$ or .125
3. .06
4. $.00\frac{1}{4}$ or .0025
5. .001

IV.
Discount	Net prices
1. $21	$119
2. $47.70	$217.30
3. $107	$749
4. $.39	$19.11
5. $2.27	$54.48

V.
Commission	Net proceeds
1. $12.56	$615.44
2. $24.80	$99.20
3. $36.60	$695.40
4. $126.	$5474.
5. $9.69	$248.71

VI.
Interest	Amount
1. $43.50	$768.50
2. $120	$3320
3. $720	$4720
4. $8	$2408
5. $192	$6592

VII. Per cent of increase or decrease
1. 20%
2. $12\frac{1}{2}\%$
3. $12\frac{1}{2}\%$
4. $33\frac{1}{3}\%$
5. $33\frac{1}{3}\%$

VIII. Change to base five.
1. 20_{five}
2. 132_{five}
3. 214_{five}
4. 1012_{five}
5. 2000_{five}
6. 332_{five}
7. 432_{five}
8. 340_{five}
9. 231_{five}
10. 33_{five}

IX.
A.
1. 19 weeks 1 day
2. 10 pounds
3. 11 gallons 2 quarts
4. 10 hours 35 minutes
5. 18 feet 11 inches

B.
1. 4 weeks 3 days
2. 5 months
3. 3 gallons 2 quarts
4. 2 yards 2 feet
5. 2 weeks 3 days

X. Find:
1. 25.12 inches
2. 31.40 inches
3. 12 square inches
4. 92 square inches
5. 75 square inches

contents | eighth grade

helping your child in eighth grade

YOUR CHILD is about thirteen years old. Next year he will be in high school! He is much more thoughtful and aware of himself. He still has last year's enthusiasm, but it is used more selectively. He also has greater powers of concentration.

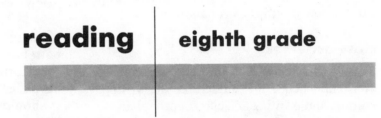

reading | eighth grade

AT THIS POINT everything your child does in school depends upon his ability to read and to understand what he reads. He uses his reading in his schoolwork in every class.

Encourage him to continue reading outside of school, to increase his speed and to broaden his fields of interest through reading. Do this by continuing to have a variety of magazines and books where he can get at them easily. (*See* the seventh-grade book.)

books your eighth-grade child may enjoy

White Falcon—*Arnold, Elliott*
Stampede for Gold—*Berton, Pierre*
Daughter of a Star—*Blizard, Marie*
The Leatherstocking Saga—*Cooper, James F.*
Hickory Hill
Sorority Girl
    Emery, Anne
Crash Club—*Felsen, Henry Gregor*
Fire-Fightin' Mose—*Felton, Harold W.*
Timber—*Fisher, Arleen*
The Little Shepherd of Kingdom Come
    Fox, John
Cruise of Danger—*Hammond, Ralph*
Hostess in the Sky—*Hill, Margaret*
Ring Neck—*Hinkle, Thomas C.*
Turquoise Horse—*Hull, Eleanor*
False Start—*Keating, Lawrence*
To Have and Not Hold—*Lyon, Jessica*
The Story of Albert Schweitzer—*Manton, Jo*

Struggle at Saddle Bow—*Meyers, Barlow*
Anne of Green Gables
    Montgomery, Lucy Maud
The Yearling—*Rawlings, Marjorie K.*
Purple Palomino—*Richard, James R.*
Three Stuffed Owls—*Robertson, Keith*
Bright Island—*Robinson, Mabel L.*
Black Falcon—*Sperry, Armstrong*
Girl Trouble
Prom Trouble
    Summers, James L.
Twenty Thousand Leagues Under the Sea
    Verne, Jules
Lost Worlds—*White, Anne Terry*
The Fire and the Gold—*Whitney, Phyllis*
Basketball Star—*Wilcox, Don*
Wild Winter—*Wood, Kerry*
Prudence Crandall: Woman of Courage
    Yates, Elizabeth

writing | eighth grade

IN WRITING, clarity and neatness are the main goals. If you cannot read your child's writing easily, tell him so. His teacher, too, will be having trouble with it. She may be checking some correct answers as wrong just because she cannot read them. Ask your child to help little brother or sister as he is learning to write. It is an indirect way of getting in a little practice on his own handwriting.

class activities

To put this knowledge into actual practice, your child's class may undertake the writing, editing, and printing of a class or school newspaper. It is excellent training. Your child will discover that he is better in one form of contribution than another. Encourage him to practice and develop what he likes best. It may be straight reporting of events, or it may be poetry, or writing editorials. He will appreciate your help—even if it is just to listen to his efforts.

His class will have some training in parliamentary procedure. He discovers that a businesslike procedure accomplishes more than a careless, unorganized meeting.

ENGLISH

Now that your child has a good background in the rules that make up good storytelling and conversation, he needs practice in using these rules. That is what he does this year.

He checks himself on his ability to make introductions, to carry on telephone conversations, to be a good listener as well as talker. He checks himself on his manners—and here are more suggestions for books that will help him:

If You Please
Allen, Betty, and Briggs, Mitchell P.
Let's Talk About You—Bro, Marguerite

Co-ediquette—Eldridge, Elizabeth
Teen-Age Manual—Heal, Edith
Good Manners for Girls—Irvin, Inez N.
It's More Fun When You Know the Rules
Pierce, Beatrice

letter writing

Your child gets practice in writing letters, both business and friendly.

Remind him that a friendly letter should have the "you" point of view, not all "I, I, I." It should sound as though it were an easy, lively conversation. It shouldn't be written unless there is something to say. Letters that are gloomy all through are not welcome. The reader should be made to feel happy whenever possible. Your child learns that there is a correct form to follow in writing a letter and that it is just as easy to be correct as it is to be incorrect.

There are many types of letters to be written. Some of them are: "I'll be glad to . . ." "So sorry . . ." "Thank you . . ." "Sorry you're ill . . ." and business letters.

poetry

In both the reading and the English classes some time is spent this year in learning to enjoy poetry. Some ideas and thoughts and feelings are communicated more effectively as poetry. Favorite poems will be read aloud for the pleasure they give, and then discussed as to rhyme, rhythm, imagery, and meaning.

Sometimes images and meanings have to be searched for, because in the poetic form so much is packed into so few lines. But when your child becomes accustomed to reading poetry, it will be easier for him to appreciate it fully.

verbs

Your child learns more ways to improve sentences. You might review him on these verb forms, which are sometimes forgotten.

▶ A *transitive verb* passes its action over to a receiver. (It takes an object.)

EXAMPLE:

Jim <u>wrote</u> a letter.

▶ An *intransitive* verb does not pass its action over to a receiver. (It does not take an object.)

EXAMPLE:

His family <u>laughed</u>.

▶ A verb ending in *ing* which is used as a noun is called a *gerund*. The noun or pronoun preceding the gerund must be in the possessive case.

EXAMPLES:

A. <u>Looking</u> at pictures is fun.

B. He approves of my <u>working</u> for money.

▶ When used as an adjective, a verb form that ends in *ing* is called a *participle*. Such a word must be related to another word in the sentence so it doesn't "dangle." It may have words closely related to it forming a participial phrase.

EXAMPLES:

A. The children, <u>talking</u> and <u>laughing</u>, formed a double line.

B. Henry, <u>listening</u> to his mother, turned and came back.

▶ The simple form of a verb preceded by the word *to* is called an *infinitive*. Infinitives should not be split or separated by other words. They are used as subjects of verbs, objects of verbs, predicate nouns, appositives, and even as adverbs.

EXAMPLES:

A. I like <u>to read</u>. (object of verb)

B. Harry went <u>to buy</u> a paper. (adverb)

tense of a verb

Verbs must show when the action is performed. This is called the *tense*.

EXAMPLES of the simple tenses:

Present tense is: "I know."

Past tense is: "I knew."

Future tense is: "I shall know."

Present tense tells what is happening now, and may be used with *am, is,* and *are* plus the *ing* form of the verb, or with *do* and *does* plus the simple form.

EXAMPLES:

I <u>am</u> singing.

I <u>do</u> sing.

Past tense shows what happened in the past. It may be conjugated with *was* or *were* plus the *ing* form of the verb, or with *did* plus the simple form of the verb.

EXAMPLES:

I <u>was</u> singing.

I <u>did</u> sing.

Future tense tells of what will happen in the future. *Shall* and *will* are used with the simple verb form. (*Shall* with *I* is a simple statement, but saying, "I will" shows determination. *Shall* with *you* or *he* shows determination.)

EXAMPLES:

I <u>shall</u> sing. (simple statement)

I <u>will</u> sing. (determination)

There are also three perfect tenses which are made up of the helping words *have, has, had, shall have,* and *will have* plus the third principal part of the verb. The three parts of a verb are the *present* (for example, *sing*); the *past* (for example, *sang*); the *past participle,* or the form used with a helper (for example, *sung*).

The *present perfect tense* tells of something that has just been completed. The helping words are *have* and *has.*

EXAMPLE:

I have sung.

The *past perfect tense* tells of something completed at some definite time in the past. The helper is *had.*

EXAMPLE:

I had sung.

The *future perfect tense* shows action that will have been completed some time in the future. *Shall have* and *will have* are the helping words.

EXAMPLE:

I shall have sung.

person of a verb

Verbs also show who is speaking. This is called the *person* of the verb. There are three persons.

First person means the one speaking.

Second person is the one spoken to.

Third person is the one spoken about.

When all the forms of a verb are given in order, we say the verb has been conjugated.

EXAMPLE:

The conjugation of the verb *know* in the simple tenses:

PRESENT TENSE

	SINGULAR	PLURAL
1st person	I know	we know
2nd person	you know	you know
3rd person	he, she, it knows	they know

PAST TENSE

	SINGULAR	PLURAL
1st person	I knew	we knew
2nd person	you knew	you knew
3rd person	he, she, it knew	they knew

FUTURE TENSE

	SINGULAR	PLURAL
1st person	I shall know	we shall know
2nd person	you will know	you will know
3rd person	he, she, it will know	they will know

EXAMPLE:

The conjugation of the verb *know* in the perfect tenses:

PRESENT PERFECT TENSE

	SINGULAR	PLURAL
1st person	I have known	we have known
2nd person	you have known	you have known
3rd person	he, she, it has known	they have known

PAST PERFECT TENSE

	SINGULAR	PLURAL
1st person	I had known	we had known
2nd person	you had known	you had known
3rd person	he, she, it had known	they had known

FUTURE PERFECT TENSE

	SINGULAR	PLURAL
1st person	I shall have known	we shall have known
2nd person	you will have known	you will have known
3rd person	he, she, it will have known	they will have known

voice of a verb

A change of form in transitive verbs is called *voice.* When the verb expresses action *performed* by the subject, it is in *active* voice. When the verb expresses action *received* by the subject, it is in *passive* voice.

EXAMPLES:

Active:

I called my puppy.

Passive:

I was called home.

Active:

Jack wrote a letter.

Passive:

A letter was written by Jack

correlatives

Correlatives are pairs of conjunctions, such as *either-or, neither-nor, both-and.* They should be used in correct pairs.

EXAMPLES:

Right:

I could use either the red or the blue one.

Wrong:

Neither Mary or Bob likes watermelon.

interjections

Interjections are simply words of great feeling such as *hurrah, heavens,* or *alas.* They are diagramed on a line apart from the main sentence. (*See* section on diagraming, pp. 9 to 12.)

nouns

Gender There are four genders: masculine, feminine, neuter, and common. The noun *man* is masculine, *woman* is feminine, *book* is neuter (neither masculine nor feminine). When a noun can be either masculine or feminine, such as *baby, parent,* or *teacher,* it is common gender.

The gender of the pronoun must be the same as the noun for which it stands.

EXAMPLE:

The manager turned in his reports.

(You now know that the manager is a man.)

An **appositive** (or noun in apposition) explains the noun or pronoun next to which it is placed.

EXAMPLE:

Miss Smith, our teacher, asked for our report.

A **collective noun** is a word meaning a group of persons or things. It is considered singular when the group is thought of as a whole. It is considered plural if the members of the group are thought of separately.

EXAMPLES:

The class was not ready to begin.

(singular)

The class were opening their books.

(plural)

Cases of nouns must be understood before going on to the diagraming of sentences. Nouns used as subjects of verbs and as predicate nouns are in the *nominative case.*

EXAMPLES:

Sam went away.

Sammy is a girl.

Nouns used as direct or indirect objects of verbs, or as objects of prepositions, are in the *objective case.*

EXAMPLES:

I like popcorn.   (object of verb)

He gave the popcorn to Joe.

(object of preposition)

He gave Joe the popcorn.

(indirect object showing to or for

whom the popcorn was given)

Nouns showing possession are in the *possessive case.*

EXAMPLE:

This is Sara's sweater.

pronouns

A pronoun must agree with the noun it stands for (its antecedent) in person, gender, and number.

EXAMPLES of how pronouns must agree with their antecedents:

Right:

John named his puppy Rosemary II after her mother.

Wrong:

All of us put their caps on.
(The right pronoun is our).

Pronouns have three persons: first person refers to the person speaking; second person refers to the person spoken to; and third person refers to the person or thing spoken about.

SINGULAR	NOMINATIVE CASE	OBJECTIVE CASE	POSSESSIVE CASE
1st person	I	me	my, mine
2nd person	you	you	your, yours
3rd person	he, she, it	him, her, it	his, her, hers, its
PLURAL			
1st person	we	us	our, ours
2nd person	you	you	your, yours
3rd person	they	them	their, theirs

An **intensive pronoun** is used only for emphasis.

EXAMPLE:

I myself have argued that with him.

A **reflexive pronoun** throws the action of the verb back to the subject. It means the same thing as the subject. It is always in the objective case.

EXAMPLE:

She made herself a dress.

A **relative pronoun** introduces an adjective clause subordinate to the principal clause. *Who, whose, whom, which,* and *that* are used as relative pronouns.

EXAMPLE:

It was the parrot that made all the

noise.

In using relative pronouns it is important to remember that *who* and *whom* refer only to persons; *whose* may refer to either persons or animals; *which* refers to animals and things; *that* may refer to persons, animals, or things.

Interrogative pronouns are those which ask questions, such as *who, whose, what, which.*

EXAMPLE:

Who is carrying the basket?

Demonstrative pronouns point out certain persons or objects, such as *this, that, these,* and *those.*

EXAMPLE:

That is my book.

(However, in "*That* book is mine," *that* is used as an adjective modifying *book.*)

Indefinite pronouns point out persons or objects without referring clearly to any noun.

EXAMPLE:

Neither of the boys looked happy.

Other indefinite pronouns are *anyone, each, everybody, somebody, anybody, nobody, nothing, no one, one, everyone, someone, either, neither.* They are singular in number.

The indefinite pronouns *both, some, many, several,* and *a few* are plural.

All and *none* may be either singular or plural.

diagraming sentences

More diagraming of sentences will be done, which strengthens your child's ability to construct good sentences, paragraphs, articles, and stories of his own. (For explanation and other diagramed examples, *see* the ENGLISH section in the seventh-grade book.)

▶ Indirect objects are put under the verb. Remember, indirect objects tell *to* or *for whom* the action was performed.

EXAMPLE:

He gave Joe the popcorn.

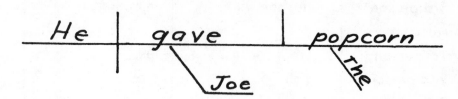

▶ A noun in apposition is placed beside the noun it explains.

EXAMPLE:

His cousin <u>John</u> became ill.

cousin (John) | became \ ill
His

▶ An adjective clause is connected to the noun it modifies.

EXAMPLE:

Mother is the lady <u>to whom we are indebted.</u>

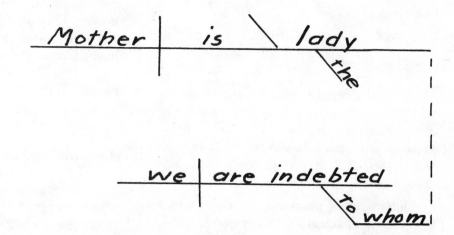

456

▶ **Adverbial clauses modify verbs.**

EXAMPLE:

Edison made a fortune <u>because his inventions were so valuable</u>.

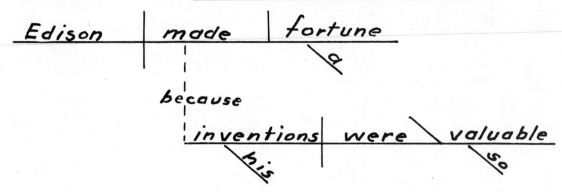

▶ **Noun clauses are diagramed as sentences and placed where they are used: (*a*) subject of sentence, (*b*) object of verb, (*c*) predicate noun.**

EXAMPLE:

<u>That the weather will be bad</u> is a sure thing.

(subject clause)

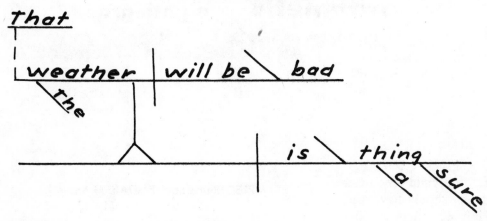

EXAMPLE:

We learned how <u>fudge is made</u>.

(object clause)

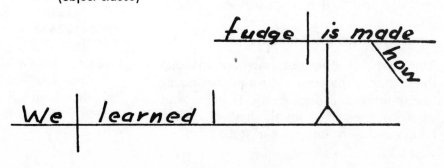

EXAMPLE:

Mary's excuse was <u>that she was ill</u>.

(predicate noun clause)

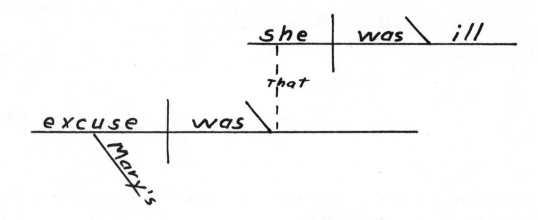

arithmetic | eighth grade

BY THE TIME your child has reached the eighth grade, he should have a good understanding of the basic structure of mathematics and the concepts of closure, commutativity, associativity, distributivity, inverse operations, and identity elements. These concepts are now used to introduce new concepts and to explain the old ones.

numbers and numerals

The study of numerical relationships that form unusual patterns cultivates the feeling of exploring and discovering. It helps your child learn much about the field of mathematics and gives him a lot of fun.

EXAMPLE: (Remember PMDAS, Grade 6.)

$$1 \times 9 + 2 = 11$$
$$12 \times 9 + 3 = 111$$
$$123 \times 9 + 4 = 1111$$
$$1234 \times 9 + 5 = 11111$$

From the pattern established so far, it can be assumed that:

$$12345 \times 9 + 6 = 111111$$
$$123456 \times 9 + 7 = 1111111$$

This is the way a mathematician studies problems to save himself a lot of work.

Can your child discover the patterns established in the following examples? Ask him to write at least one more step in each one.

EXAMPLES:

a) $1 \times 8 = 10 - 2$
       $2 \times 8 = 20 - 4$
       $3 \times 8 = 30 - 6$
       $4 \times 8 = 40 - 8$

(Next step:
$5 \times 8 = 50 - 10$)

b) $10 - 1 = 9$
       $100 - 1 = 99$
      $1000 - 1 = 999$
    $10,000 - 1 = 9999$

(Next step:
$100,000 - 1 = 99,999$)

c) $1 \times 8 - 1 = 7$
      $21 \times 8 - 1 = 167$
     $321 \times 8 - 1 = 2567$
    $4321 \times 8 - 1 = 34567$

(Next step:
$54321 \times 8 - 1 = 434567$)

"Magic squares" have always been valuable aids to mathematicians in their studies of number relationships, and they can be fun for your child. Can he discover why this square is "magic"?

8	1	6
3	5	7
4	9	2

(Ans. Every column, every row, and each of the two diagonals add up to the same sum.)

Your child continues to work in number systems other than the base ten system. The base two, or binary, system is used extensively in electronic computers. It is the simplest system because it has only two digits, 0 and 1. However, it becomes unwieldly because it requires so many digits to name the numbers.

EXAMPLES:

Addition in base two. (Refer to the base two grid and counting, Grade 6.)

a) 10110_{two}
 $+ \ 1001_{two}$
  11111_{two}

b) 1011_{two}
 $+ \ \ 111_{two}$
 10010_{two}

Multiplication in base two.

$$1101_{two}$$
$$\times \quad 101_{two}$$
$$\overline{1101_{two}}$$
$$\underline{110100_{two}}$$
$$1000001_{two}$$

Subtraction in base two.

$$11010_{two}$$
$$-\ 1101_{two}$$
$$\overline{1101_{two}}$$

(The borrowing:)
$$\overset{10\ 0}{11010}_{two}$$
$$-1101_{two}$$
$$\overline{1101_{two}}$$

Division in base two.

a)
$$\begin{array}{r} 110_{two}\ \text{R } 1 \\ 10_{two}\,\overline{)\,1101_{two}} \\ \underline{10} \\ 10 \\ \underline{10} \\ 10 \\ \underline{10} \\ 1 \end{array}$$

b)
$$\begin{array}{r} 111_{two} \\ 11_{two}\,\overline{)\,10101_{two}} \\ \underline{11} \\ 100 \\ \underline{11} \\ 11 \\ \underline{11} \end{array}$$

Changing base two to base ten.

1011_{two} means 1 eight, 0 fours, 1 two, 1 one, or 11.

11101_{two} means 1 sixteen, 1 eight, 1 four, 0 twos, 1 one, or 29.

Changing base ten to base two.

a) $14 = 1110_{two}$

$$\begin{array}{r} 2\,)\,\underline{14} \qquad 0 \text{ (remainders)} \\ 2\,)\,\underline{7} \qquad 1 \\ 2\,)\,\underline{3} \qquad 1 \\ 2\,)\,\underline{1} \qquad 1 \\ 0 \end{array}$$

b) $103 = 1100111_{two}$

$$\begin{array}{r} 2\,)\,\underline{103} \qquad 1 \\ 2\,)\,\underline{51} \qquad 1 \\ 2\,)\,\underline{25} \qquad 1 \\ 2\,)\,\underline{12} \qquad 0 \\ 2\,)\,\underline{6} \qquad 0 \\ 2\,)\,\underline{3} \qquad 1 \\ 2\,)\,\underline{1} \qquad 1 \\ 0 \end{array}$$

Your child uses a number line to clarify the meaning of negative numbers and to add and subtract them.

EXAMPLES:

a) $- 3 + (- 4) = - 7$ (Use parentheses when two symbols appear together)

(Begin at $- 3$. Move *left* to add a negative number)

b) $5 + (- 2) = 3$ (Start at positive 5. Move to the *left* 2 spaces to add negative 2)

c) $- 7 + (+ 4) = - 3$ (Start at $- 7$. Move *right* 4 spaces to add positive 4)

d) $3 + (- 5) = - 2$ (Start at positive 3. Move *left* 5 spaces to add negative 5)

e) $- 3 + (+ 3) = 0$ (Can you tell why?)

Your child also multiplies and divides negative numbers.

EXAMPLES:

a) $3 \times (- 2) = - 6$ (The product of a positive integer and a negative integer is always a negative integer)

(Move over two negative spaces three times)

b) $(- 24) \div 6 = n$ (The quotient of two integers, one positive and one negative, is a negative number)

Think: $6 \times n = - 24$ (Multiplication is the inverse operation of division)

$$n = - 4$$

Proof: $6 \times (- 4) = - 24$

The set of integers is frequently used in solving problems of profit and loss, temperatures above and below zero, gains and losses in altitude, upstream and downstream, etc.

EXAMPLE:

You are rowing a boat upstream at the rate of 5 miles per hour. The water is flowing at a rate of 3 miles per hour. How fast is the boat moving?

5 = the speed of the boat

− 3 = the flow of the water

5 + (− 3) = 2, the rate of the actual movement of the boat upstream.

Can you tell how fast the boat would be moving if you were rowing downstream?

(˙Ans. (− 5) + (− 3) = − 8, or 8 MPH)

Modular Arithmetic

Have you heard your child say that $2 + 2 \neq 4$? That $5 - 7 = 5$? That $11 + 3 = 2$? They are true equations but not until he first clearly defines the set of numbers he is working with. This different kind of arithmetic is called "modular" arithmetic, and the concepts of "larger" and "smaller" do not always apply.

EXAMPLES:

a) $2 + 2 \neq 4$ when, for example, the numbers are from the base three system. It must, in that case, be written correctly: $2_{\text{three}} + 2_{\text{three}} \neq 4$.

b) $5 - 7 = 5$ when the numbers are from the set of numerals representing the days of the week. Starting with Sunday as 1, Monday as 2, etc., then Thursday is 5. Going back (subtraction) 7 days from day number 5 brings you to Thursday of last week.

c) $11 + 3 = 2$ when the numbers are from the set of numerals on a clock face, each one representing an hour. Eleven o'clock and 3 more hours is two o'clock.

The Beginning of Algebra

Your child continues to work in mathematical sentences with symbols. A complete sentence either true or false is called a **closed sentence.**

EXAMPLES: $9 + 6 = 15$, $9 + 5 \neq 15$, $5 + 6 < 14$, $28 - 8 > 17$.

An incomplete sentence is called an **open sentence.** It may contain letters or symbols, called **variables,** to be replaced by numerals. Example: $7 + k = 11$.

The set of numbers whose names are to be used as replacements for variables is called the **replacement set.** The replacement set must be determined before solving the equation.

The distributive property is clearly shown with the use of letters.

EXAMPLE: $a (b + c) = ab + ac$

(A letter before the parenthesis or with another letter with no symbol indicates multiplication)

Proof: Replace the letters with numerals and solve the equation.

$a = 2$, $b = 3$, $c = 2$

$2(3 + 2) = (2 \times 3) + (2 \times 2)$

$2 \times 5 = 6 + 4$

$10 = 10$

This kind of work is your child's introduction to the study of algebra, which is based on the use of letters to express ideas in mathematical sentences.

Your child uses drawings to help him make his mathematical sentences, using a letter to represent the unknown quantity.

EXAMPLE:

A board is 40 inches long and is to be cut into three pieces so that the second piece is 3 times as long as the first piece and the third piece is twice as long as the second. How long will the first piece be?

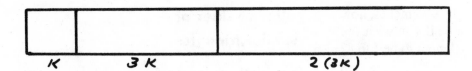

$$K \quad\quad 3K \quad\quad\quad\quad 2(3K)$$

Let k = the number of inches in the first piece.

$$k + 3k + 2(3k) = 40 \text{ inches}$$
$$10k = 40$$
$$k = 40 \div 10 \text{ (Division is the inverse operation of multiplication.)}$$
$$k = 4 \text{ inches}$$

Proof:

$$4 + (3 \times 4) + [2 \times (3 \times 4)] = 40$$
$$4 + 12 + 2 \times 12 = 40$$
$$4 + 12 + 24 = 40 \text{ Right!}$$

ratio

Probably the greatest stress in the eighth grade is put upon the various ways of showing relationships between numbers—one of the most important ideas in mathematics. This relationship is called ratio, and the study of ratio your child began last year is now extended.

One way to compare numbers is by subtraction.

EXAMPLE:

The total number of votes cast was 32. Bill received 24 votes. Sue received 8 votes. Bill received 16 more votes than Sue (24 − 8 = 16).

Another way to compare numbers is by division.

EXAMPLE:

Sue received 8 votes, Bill received 24. Think: Eight is what part of 24? Write it this way: $\frac{8}{24}$. Reduce $\frac{8}{24}$ to $\frac{1}{3}$. Sue received $\frac{1}{3}$ as many votes as Bill.

When you compare two numbers by division, you are finding a ratio. The ratio of 8 to 24 is $\frac{8}{24}$, or $\frac{1}{3}$. The ratio of 24 to 8 is $\frac{24}{8}$, or $\frac{3}{1}$ or 3. Ratios can also be expressed as decimals or per cents: $1\frac{1}{2}$ can be written 1.5 or 150%. The ratio $\frac{4}{5}$ can be expressed .80 or 80%.

Lines and distances can be compared by ratio.

EXAMPLE:

In which of the following rectangles is the ratio of the width (w) to the length (l)

about $\frac{1}{4}$? (first rectangle)
about $\frac{1}{2}$? (second rectangle)
about $\frac{1}{8}$? (third rectangle)

(Use your ruler.)

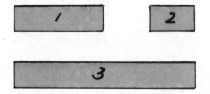

Try these problems of ratio with your child before you look at the answers.

1. What is the ratio of
   1 in. to 1 ft. (12 in.)? ($\frac{1}{12}$)
   1 in. to 1 yd. (36 in.)? ($\frac{1}{36}$)
   1 in. to 5 ft. (60 in.)? ($\frac{1}{60}$)
   $\frac{1}{2}$ in. to 1 in.? ($\frac{1}{2}$)

2. A recipe for punch calls for 3 cups of fruit juice to 5 cups of water.

   A. What is the ratio of fruit juice to water?
   Answer: A. $\frac{3}{5}$.

   B. What is the ratio of water to fruit juice?
   Answer: B. $\frac{5}{3}$ or $1\frac{2}{3}$.

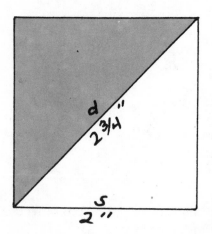

3. If the width of a rectangle is 20 inches, how long should the length be if you wish the ratio of the width to the length to be 5 to 8?

Answer: 20 is 4 times greater than 5. Then the length will be 4 times greater than 8, or 32. The ratio will be $\frac{20}{32}$. Reduced, this is $\frac{5}{8}$.

4. Ann weighs 98 pounds. Alan weighs 102 pounds. What is the ratio of Ann's weight to Alan's? Express the ratio as a decimal to hundredths.

Answer: Ann's weight is $96\frac{4}{51}\%$ of Alan's weight.

First reduce $\frac{98}{102}$ to $\frac{49}{51}$.

Then divide:

```
        .96
51/49.00
 45 9
 ────
  3 10
  3 06
  ────
     4
```

5. In the square above right, measure lines d and s accurately. Find the ratio of d to s. Express the ratio as a decimal to hundredths.

Answer:

d = $2\frac{3}{4}''$ or 2.75"
s = 2"
ratio d/s = $\frac{2.75}{2}$ = $1.37\frac{1}{2}$

```
 1.37½
2/2.75
```

ratios of sides of similar triangles

By using the ratios of sides of similar triangles, your child can find distances across rivers, heights of trees, or other lengths that cannot be measured directly. Remember: Similar triangles are triangles of different sizes but with the same angle measurements.

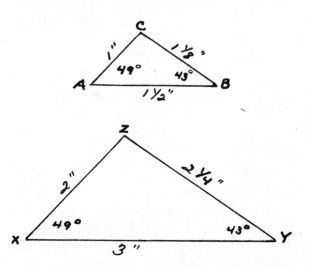

These triangles are similar because the angles in each are the same size as the corresponding angles in the other. The difference is in the length of the sides.

EXAMPLES using the triangles on preceding page:

To express the ratio of line AC to line XZ, write it this way: $\frac{AC}{XZ}$. The length of AC is 1″. The length of XZ is 2″. So $\frac{AC}{XZ} = \frac{1}{2}$. It is read: AC is to XZ as 1 is to 2.

What is the ratio of AB to XY? AB is 1½″, XY is 3″. Then the ratio is ½ because 1½″ is one half of 3″.

You will also find that the ratio of CB to ZY is ½, because in any two similar triangles the ratios of all corresponding sides are equal.

Problems of ratio of sides of similar triangles as your child may use them in his everyday experiences:

John found the height of the tree in front of his house by measuring its shadow and then measuring the shadow of a stake set upright in the ground.

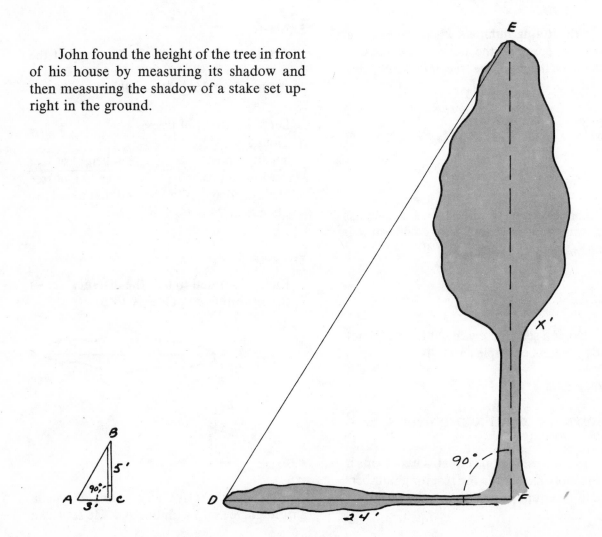

The two triangles are similar. The angles made by the shadows are the same size, that is, 90°. We learned that the ratios of corresponding sides in similar triangles are equal. We can see by measuring that the shadow of the tree is 8 times longer than the shadow of the pole. Then the height of the tree is 8 times longer than the height of the pole. If the pole is 5 feet long, the tree is 40 feet high ($5 \times 8 = 40$). That is what we think.

We write it:

$$\frac{AC}{DF} = \frac{BC}{EF}$$

We read it: AC is to DF as BC is to EF.

$$\frac{3}{24} = \frac{5}{x}$$

Substituting numbers where we can, and letting x represent the number we want to find, or the height of the tree, it looks like this. Reduce $\frac{3}{24}$.

$$\frac{3}{24} = \frac{1}{8}$$

$$\text{Then } \frac{1}{8} = \frac{5}{x}$$

The value on both sides of the equals sign must be the same. An equal ratio is $\frac{1}{8} = \frac{5}{40}$, so the unknown x is 40.

$$\frac{1}{8} = \frac{5}{40}$$

Do you see where you got the 40? If not, study the next example carefully.

EXAMPLE:

Solve for x in the problem $\frac{3}{4} = \frac{6}{x}$.

The ratios must be equal. That means if we multiply *diagonally* the resulting numbers should be equal. With this in mind multiply $\frac{3}{4} \times \frac{6}{x}$ diagonally.

$$\frac{3}{4} \diagup \!\!\!\! \diagdown \frac{6}{x}$$

The result is $3x = 24$. Then think: 3 times *what* equals 24? $3 \times 8 = 24$, so x is 8. Check it by substituting 8 for x. Does $\frac{3}{4} = \frac{6}{8}$? Did you discover that you could divide 24 by 3 to find x?

EXAMPLE:

Find what number the letter stands for:

$$\frac{x}{4} = \frac{7}{2}$$

Think: $2x = 28$ when multiplying diagonally. Then $x = 14$. Have you discovered that you could divide 28 by 2 to find x?

EXAMPLE:

A tree casts a shadow 36 feet long at the same time that a post 4 feet tall casts a shadow 6 feet long. How tall is the tree?

Let x = height of tree
Then $\frac{4}{6} = \frac{x}{36}$
$$\frac{\text{height of post}}{\text{shadow of post}} = \frac{\text{height of tree}}{\text{shadow of tree}}$$
Multiply diagonally and find that $6x = 144$
Then $x = 24$ ($144 \div 6 = 24$)

EXAMPLE:

Richard wanted to find the distance across the swamp from points A to B.

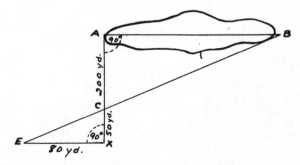

He set a stake at C so that line AC made a right angle (90°) with line AB. He set stake

466

C 200 yards from A. He needed a similar triangle now to help him figure AB. He just continued line AC for 50 yards and set a stake at X. He made a 90° angle at X and walked until he was in line with CB. This made two similar triangles. He measured XE and found it to be 80 yards. Line CX corresponds to line AC and line XE corresponds to line AB.

This is the way the ratio reads.

$$\frac{CX}{AC} = \frac{XE}{AB}$$

Substitute numbers where they are known; let x equal the unknown.

$$\frac{50}{200} = \frac{80}{x}$$

Multiply diagonally.

$$16,000 = 50x$$
$$16,000 \div 50 = 320$$

Then $x = 320$ yards, the distance across the swamp. (You have discovered by this time that to find x you divide the complete number on one side of the equals sign by the number on the other side before the x.)

Fractions

Your child continues to rename rational numbers (fractions) as decimals. Some rational numbers become **terminating decimals.**

EXAMPLE: $\frac{1}{2} = .5$ because $2\overline{)1.0}\;\;.5$

A terminating decimal can be changed back to a rational number by simply writing it as it is read, and reducing it.

EXAMPLE:

.5 (Read it)

$\frac{5}{10}$ (Write it)

$\frac{1}{2}$ (Reduce it)

Some rational numbers become **repeating decimals.**

EXAMPLE:

$\frac{1}{3} = .3333\frac{1}{3}$ because

$$3\overline{)1.000}\quad .333\ldots\ldots$$

A bar over the repeating digit or block of digits shows repetition of those digits.

EXAMPLE: $\frac{1}{3} = .3333\ldots$ or $\frac{1}{3} = .3\overline{3}$

$\frac{4}{11} = .363636\ldots$ or $\frac{4}{11} = .36\overline{36}$

$\frac{23}{27} = .621621621\ldots$ or $\frac{23}{27} = .621\overline{621}$

It is more difficult to change a repeating decimal to an exact rational number. An approximate rational number can be arrived at by first rounding out the decimal, and then proceeding as with terminating decimals.

To round out a decimal: Take note of the digit which is one place to the right of the place to which you are rounding. If that digit is 5 or more, increase the preceding digit by 1. If this digit is less than 5, drop it.

EXAMPLE:

Round to nearest hundredth: $.3333\frac{1}{3}$.
It becomes .33
Round to nearest thousandths: .621621.
It becomes .622.

per cent

The meaning of per cent is reviewed (*see* the seventh grade ARITHMETIC section) and studied further.

the following are good rules to remember

▶ **To change a per cent to a decimal, omit the % sign and move the decimal point two places to the *left*. (When no decimal point is shown, it is assumed to be to the right of the number.)**

EXAMPLE:

5%   .05

▶ To change a decimal to a per cent, move the decimal point two places to the *right* and write the % sign after the number.

EXAMPLE:

$$.06 = 6\%$$
$$.075 = 7.5\%$$

($7\frac{1}{2}\%$, because .5 is $\frac{5}{10}$ or $\frac{1}{2}$.)

▶ To change a per cent to a fraction, write the number without the per cent sign over 100. Then reduce the fraction to lowest terms.

EXAMPLE:

$$25\% = \frac{25}{100} = \frac{1}{4}$$

▶ To change a fraction to a per cent, first change the fraction to a decimal (numerator divided by the denominator) and then change the decimal to a per cent.

EXAMPLES:

$$\frac{1}{2} = 2\overline{)1.00} \quad \frac{.50}{} = 50\%$$

$$\frac{2}{7} = 7\overline{)2.00} \quad \frac{.28}{} = 28\frac{4}{7}\%$$
$$\frac{1\ 4}{60}$$
$$\frac{56}{4}$$

▶ To find a per cent of a number, do either of the following: (a) Change the per cent to a decimal and then multiply the number by the decimal.

EXAMPLE:

$$25\% \text{ of } \$450 = \$112.50$$
$$\$450$$
$$\times .25$$
$$\overline{2250}$$
$$900$$
$$\overline{\$112.50}$$

(b) Change the per cent to a fraction and then multiply the number by the fraction.

EXAMPLE:

$$25\% \text{ of } \$450$$
$$\tfrac{1}{4} \text{ of } 450 = 112\tfrac{1}{2} \text{ or } \$112.50$$

Sometimes we work with less than 1% or more than 100%.

The diagram is again valuable in explaining this concept. (*See* diagram in the ARITHMETIC section of the sixth-grade book.)

The large square is the whole, or 100%. It is divided into 100 small squares. Each small square is one part of the 100 squares, or $\frac{1}{100}$, or 1%. But if one of those small squares is divided into even smaller parts, those smaller parts will be only fractions of the 1%. Half of a little square will be $\frac{1}{2}$ of 1%, or $\frac{1}{2}$ of $\frac{1}{100}$ which is $\frac{1}{200}$. Changed to a decimal it is

$$200\overline{)1.000} \quad .005$$

.005 changed to per cent is .5% (*see above*, the second rule to remember).

If the small square (1%) is divided into 3 parts, then $\frac{1}{3}$ of it is $\frac{1}{3}$ of 1%.

FIRST THINK:

$$\tfrac{1}{3} \text{ of } \tfrac{1}{100} = \tfrac{1}{300}$$

THEN WORK:

$$300\overline{)1.0000} \quad .0033\tfrac{1}{3}$$
$$\frac{900}{1000}$$
$$\frac{900}{}$$

THE ANSWER:

$$.0033\tfrac{1}{3} = .33\tfrac{1}{3}\%$$

On the other hand, if two of the large squares are used, there are two 100%s, or 200%. 100% is the whole; twice the whole is 200%, three times the whole is 300%. Never forget that *per cent means hundredths,* so 200% is $\frac{200}{100}$.

metric system

The metric system is a system of measurement used in all countries of South America and in all European countries except Great Britain. It is used a little here and in Great Britain, but not commonly. However, in scientific work it is used almost exclusively. It is simple to use because it is based on the number ten, as is our number system.

The inch, foot, yard, and mile are units of length in the English system of measure. Units of length having similar uses in the metric system are centimeter, decimeter, meter, and kilometer. It is not easy to change back and forth from metric units to English units.

A meter stick is a little more than 39 inches long (39.37"). A 100-meter dash is over 9 yards longer than the 100-yard dash.

Centi means one hundred or one hundredth part, so a **centimeter** is $\frac{1}{100}$ of a meter. There are 100 centimeters in a meter.

Milli means one thousand or one thousandth part. There are 1000 **millimeters** in a meter.

Deci is one tenth, so a **decimeter** is one tenth of a meter.

Kilo is a thousand, so a **kilometer** is 1000 meters.

table of metric measures

10 millimeters (mm.)	=	1 centimeter (cm.)
10 centimeters	=	1 decimeter (dm.)
10 decimeters	=	1 meter (*or* 100 centimeters)
1000 meters	=	1 kilometer (km.)

Using the table, can you see that:

5 dm.	=	50 cm.
20 dm.	=	200 cm.
3.5 km.	=	3500 m. or 350,000 cm.

problems using metric measures

Read the problem, study the explanations and read the answers. Then go back and try to work them again, without looking at the explanations.

In recent Olympic Games, the 800-meter race was won by an American in 1 min. 49.2 sec. How many yards are 800 meters?

(If 1 meter is 39.37 inches, then one meter is also 1.09 yards [39.37 ÷ 36 because there are 36 inches in one yard]. 800 meters then is 800 × 1.09, or 872 yards.)

What part of a mile is a kilometer?

THINK:

1 meter is 39.37 inches.
A kilometer is 1000 meters, so a kilometer is 1000 × 39.37 inches or 39,370 inches. To change these inches to feet divide by 12 (12" = 1') 39,370 inches ÷ 12 is about 3280 feet.

There are 5280 feet in a mile. Then what part of a mile is 3280 feet? It is $\frac{3280}{5280}$ miles. Reduced this is about $\frac{5}{8}$ or .62 mile.

We have discovered that 1 kilometer is about .62 mi. For ordinary purposes the approximate solution is satisfactory.

469

The distance from Paris to Brussels is 310 kilometers. How many miles is it? Because each kilometer is .62 miles, multiply 310 × .62 = 192 miles.

What speed in kilometers per hour is equivalent to a speed of 250 miles per hour?

$$62\overline{)25000.0}$$
$$403.2$$

As long as kilometers are smaller than miles, there will be more than 250 of them to equal the rate of 250 miles per hour. Therefore, to change 250 miles to kilometers, divide 250 by .62. (Dividing by a fraction always increases the number, for example, 10 wholes make 20 halves.)

You may have a map of an area (for example, Cuba) where distances are shown on a scale of miles and a scale of kilometers. Approximations are all that are asked in changing miles to kilometers and kilometers to miles.

Your child should know, however, that *it takes about* $2\frac{1}{2}$ *centimeters to make an inch, that a meter is about 39 inches,* and that *a kilometer is about* $\frac{5}{8}$ *of a mile.*

metric units of area and volume

Metric units of *length* go by 10s. Metric units of *area* go by 100s. Metric units of *volume* go by 1000s.

The formula is the same. A cubic centimeter is a cube that measures 1 centimeter on each surface.

In place of our quart, the metric system has the *liter* (lee-ter). In France gasoline is sold by the liter. A liter is equal in volume to 1000 cubic centimeters and is a little more than a quart, about 1.1 quart.

EXAMPLE:

If you put twelve gallons of gas in your car, about how many liters did you put in? (There will be fewer liters than there are quarts, because a liter is equivalent to more than a quart).

THINK:

1 gallon = 4 quarts.
12 gallons = 48 quarts.
48 divided by 1.1 = 43.6 $\frac{4}{11}$ liters.

metric units of weight

The standard metric unit of weight is the *gram.* A gram is the weight of one cubic centimeter of water at 39.2° Fahrenheit. (Water has different weights at different temperatures because it expands as it gets warm and contracts and becomes more solid at cooler temperatures.)

A **gram** is only about .035 ounce.
A **kilogram** (1000 grams) is more useful for weighing ordinary things. It is about 2.2 pounds.

EXAMPLE:

John weighs 140 pounds. If he were a student in France, he would say he weighed ____ kilograms (to the nearest kilogram).

THINK:

Because we know that a kilogram is more than twice as much as a pound, the number expressing John's weight in kilograms will be a smaller number than it is in pounds. Therefore divide 140 by 2.2.

$$\text{Work: } 2.2\overline{)140.0.0}$$

$$
\begin{array}{r}
63.6 \\
\underline{132} \\
80 \\
\underline{66} \\
140 \\
\underline{132} \\
8
\end{array}
$$

Ans.: 140 pounds is over 63¾ kilograms.

470

board feet

Lumber is sold by a special unit of measure called a board foot. A board foot (bd. ft.) is a foot square, but only an inch thick. A board 1' long, 1' wide, and 1" (or less) thick contains 1 board foot. The number of board feet in a piece of lumber is the number of square feet of the top surface times the thickness in inches. When it is written, put the thickness first (in inches), then the width (if it is in inches it must be changed to feet), and then the length (in feet).

EXAMPLES:

A. A board is 1" × 4" × 5'. To figure the board feet, it must be written:

$$1 \times \tfrac{1}{3}' \times 5' = \tfrac{5}{3} = 1\tfrac{2}{3} \text{ bd. ft.}$$

B. Thickness less than an inch is counted as 1 inch. Find how many board feet there are in a board $\tfrac{3}{4}" \times 8" \times 24'$.

THINK:

$$1 \times \tfrac{2}{3}' \times 24'.$$

$$\frac{1}{1} \times \frac{2}{\cancel{3}} \times \frac{\overset{8}{\cancel{24}}}{1} = 16 \text{ board feet.}$$

Plywood and veneer are sold by the square foot, and priced according to the number of layers or plies.

area of a circle

The formula for finding the area of a circle is $A = \pi r^2$.

Do you remember what π means? $\pi = 3.14$. The radius is r, the point from the center of the circle to the outer edge; r^2 is the radius squared, or the radius times itself.

EXAMPLE:

Find the area of a circle if the radius is 5 inches.

If $r = 5$ inches, to find πr^2 you would first square 5 (5 × 5) and then find 3.14 times 5^2. Thus the area becomes $3.14 \times 25 = 78.5$ square inches.

EXAMPLE:

Find the area of a circle with a 20" diameter.

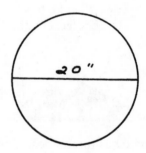

$A = \pi r^2.$
$A = 3.14 \times 10^2.$
(If the diameter is 20", then the radius is 10", because $r = \tfrac{1}{2} d$.)
$A = 314$ square inches.

If r is a mixed number, then use π as a mixed number. It is about $3\tfrac{1}{7}$.

EXAMPLE:

Find the area of a circle with a diameter of 7 inches.

471

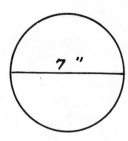

$A = \pi r^2.$

$A = 3\frac{1}{7} \times (3\frac{1}{2} \times 3\frac{1}{2}).$

$A = \dfrac{\overset{11}{\cancel{22}}}{\underset{1}{\cancel{7}}} \times \dfrac{\overset{7}{\cancel{49}}}{\underset{2}{\cancel{4}}} = \dfrac{77}{2} = 38\frac{1}{2}$ square
inches

geometric figures

Your child reviews what he has learned about squares, triangles, circles, etc., and continues this study.

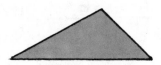

A triangle has three sides. If no two sides are equal, it is a *scalene* triangle.

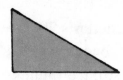

A *right triangle* has one right angle.

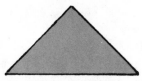

An *isosceles triangle* has two equal sides.

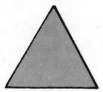

An *equilateral triangle* has three equal sides.

An *obtuse triangle* is a triangle having one angle that is larger than 90°.

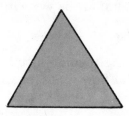

An *acute triangle* is one having all its angles smaller than 90°. An *acute triangle* with three equal sides is called an *equiangular triangle*.

Parallel lines are straight lines that have the same direction. They will never meet. The symbol ‖ means parallel.

A four-sided figure with opposite sides parallel is a *parallelogram*. The opposite sides are also equal.

If a parallelogram has right angles, it is a *rectangle*.

A *square* is a rectangle with four equal sides. It has four right angles and four equal sides.

A *circle* is a closed curve in which all the radii are equal. (*Radii* is the plural of *radius*.)

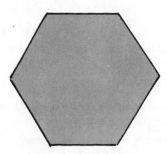

A *hexagon* has six sides.

A *regular pentagon* has five equal sides and five equal angles.

Your child finds a knowledge of geometric forms helpful in making all sorts of designs in art work, in sewing class, in woodworking and decorating. Many geometric designs are patterned after things in nature, such as leaves of plants and trees, snowflakes, rock crystals, and flowers.

An iris seems to be based on a triangle. A poppy has four petals which form a square.

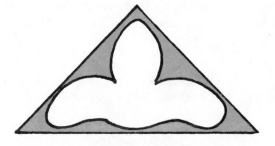

symmetry

A design or figure is *symmetrical* when one half is just like the other half.

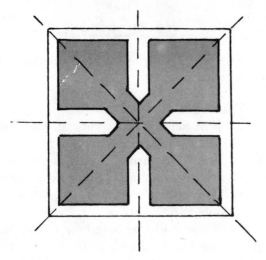

EXAMPLE:

No matter where you cut this design in half —in other words, no matter which *axis of symmetry* you use—one half is just like the other half.

Most designs have only one axis of symmetry. For example a heart design:

The left is like the right half, but the top is not like the bottom.

bisecting angles

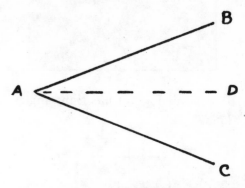

To bisect an angle means to divide it into two equal parts. Work with angles has many practical applications. Surveyors and builders, for instance, do much work with angles, and their work must be accurate, as they lay out roads and property lines, measure for foundations, build bridges and tunnels, etc.

Before thinking about how to bisect an angle accurately, ask your child to draw any angle (BAC) and then draw by estimate a line (AD) to bisect the angle.

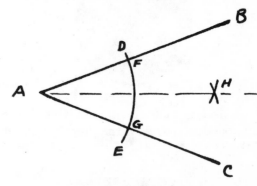

Then, using a protractor (*see* the seventh grade ARITHMETIC section), let him check his accuracy. He must follow four steps to bisect an angle accurately.

▶ **Place the point of a compass on the vertex of the angle (A).**

▶ **Draw an arc that intersects both sides of the angle (see DE above).**

▶ **Using each point where the arc crosses the sides as a center (F and G), and using the same radius each time, draw intersecting arcs *within* the angle (H).**

▶ **Draw a line from the vertex through this intersection (AH). This line bisects the angle.**

474

To divide a circle into equal parts, first divide it into halves by drawing a diameter; then, using a protractor, construct a 90° angle on the diameter line at the center and draw another diameter at right angles to the first one; then bisect these four angles.

EXAMPLE:

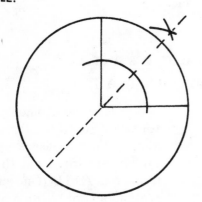

When a surveyor measures angles he uses an instrument called a *transit*. Your child must have seen surveyors many times standing beside roads peering through their transits. A transit is actually made of a telescope and two protractor scales. One protractor is horizontal and is used to measure horizontal angles. The other is vertical.

To measure a horizontal angle the surveyor stations himself as the vertex (A) of the angle and sets his protractor at 0°. He looks through the telescope and locates a certain post or tree (B). Then he moves the telescope until he sights his second post or tree (C). Then he reads his protractor. If he moved the telescope 35°, then the protractor will read 35°.

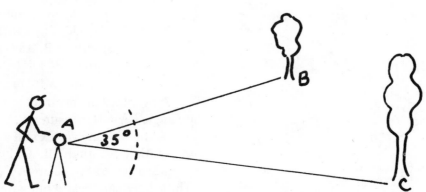

Angle BAC is a 35° angle.

It is necessary to make an accurate map of an area, locating hills, rivers, etc., before roads can be laid out. It is the surveyor's job to locate these spots for the mapmaker.

congruent triangles

Congruent triangles are those that are exactly alike in size and shape. To make them, it is necessary to make first one side of the triangle to specified length, then the angle as required, then the other side as specified. The third side will naturally fall into place. It is not possible to make congruent triangles by making the sides first and then the angle.

EXAMPLE:

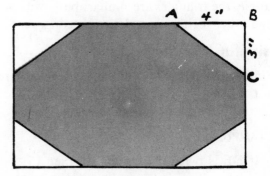

Your child may want to make four cardboard triangles for the corners of the blotter pad on his desk. He wants each triangle to have a 3-inch side and a 4-inch side with a right angle between them.

First he will draw line AB 4 inches long. Next he will make a 90° angle at B with his protractor. Then he will draw line BC 3 inches long and connect points A and C.

Builders frequently need to make congruent triangles. Being accurate is important to good construction.

Here is a use for congruent triangles in measuring distances:

EXAMPLE:

A is your house. P is Peter's house across a creek. Find the distance from A to P.

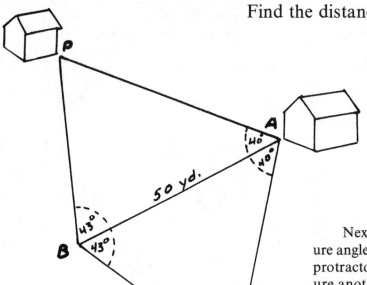

A large homemade protractor can be used to measure the angles. First measure approximately 50 yards along the bank from point A to B. (One long step is about a yard.) With a protractor at B, the angle ABP is found to be 43°. Then with the protractor still at B, it is turned to find another 43° angle, ABD. Place a stake at D to mark this angle.

Next place the protractor at A and measure angle BAP. It measures 40°. Then turn the protractor with the vertex still at A and measure another 40° angle, BAC. Place a stake at C. Place a stake at S, where AC and BD cross. (These lines can be laid out with string or just by pacing them.)

Triangles ABS and ABP are congruent because two angles and the side AB of both are the same.

By measuring AS you know the distance of A to P. It may be about 35 yards.

With your child select a distance to be measured in your own yard. Find it by making congruent triangles. Remember: If two angles of one triangle are equal to two angles of another triangle, the triangles are similar; but a side of one also has to be equal to the corresponding side of the other for the triangles to be congruent.

similar triangles

Similar triangles have the same *shape* but are not necessarily the same *size*. The ratios of corresponding sides must be equal.

EXAMPLE:

If DE is twice as long as AB, then EF has

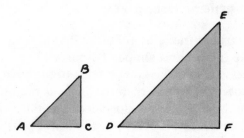

to be twice as long as BC and DF twice as long as AC.

See similar triangles under the section on ratio to find practical uses for this knowledge.

law of Pythagoras

Pythagoras was a Greek mathematician who lived in the sixth century B.C. He found the following statement to be true: "In any right triangle the square of the hypotenuse (longest side) equals the sum of the squares of the other two sides."

By the same law a triangle in which the sum of the squares of the two shorter sides equals the square of the longest side is a right triangle. The hypotenuse is the longest side and is opposite the right angle.

The law written as a formula is

$c^2 = a^2 + b^2$.

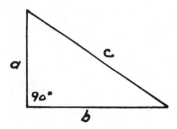

Proof of the statement can be seen in this figure:

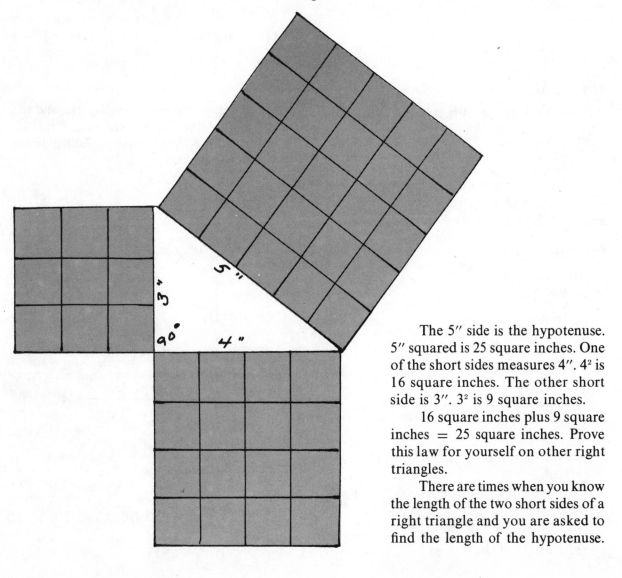

The 5″ side is the hypotenuse. 5″ squared is 25 square inches. One of the short sides measures 4″. 4^2 is 16 square inches. The other short side is 3″. 3^2 is 9 square inches.

16 square inches plus 9 square inches = 25 square inches. Prove this law for yourself on other right triangles.

There are times when you know the length of the two short sides of a right triangle and you are asked to find the length of the hypotenuse.

477

For example: ABCD represents a rectangular lot measuring 6 rods across and 8 rods deep. A path has been worn from D to B. How long is the path marked O?

The rule of Pythagoras can be used again.

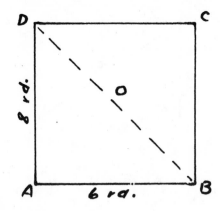

$O^2 = 8^2 + 6^2$

$O^2 = 64 + 36$

$O^2 = 100$

$O = $ (what $\times$ what $= 100$?) 10 rods.

There are other times when you know the length of the hypotenuse and of one of the short sides and you are asked to find the length of the other short side.

EXAMPLE:

How long is AC?

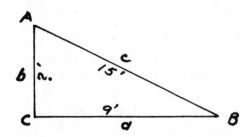

Use the same formula you have been using: $c^2 = a^2 + b^2$.

Substitute numbers where you have them: (15×15) 225 $= (9 \times 9)$ 81 $+$?

It is simple subtraction to find b^2:

$225 - 81 = 144$.

If b^2 is 144, then the length of AC is the square root of 144, or 12 ($12 \times 12 = 144$).

square root

In addition to knowing the rule of Pythagoras, it is necessary to know how to find the square root of a number. When two equal numbers are multiplied ($5 \times 5 = 25$), either one of these equal numbers is called the square root.

It is written like this $\overset{5}{\sqrt{25}}$ and read, "The square root of 25 is 5."

Can you tell $\sqrt{36}$?
(It is 6, because $6 \times 6 = 36$.)

What is $\sqrt{100}$?
(It is 10, because $10 \times 10 = 100$.)

EXAMPLE:

Using both the rule of Pythagoras and the method of finding square root, find the length of the hypotenuse in the following right triangle.

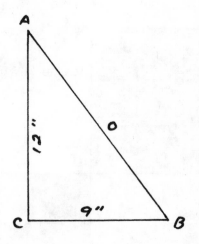

$O^2 = 9^2 + 12^2$.

$O^2 = 81 + 144$.

$O^2 = 225$.

$O = \sqrt{225}$ (15″ because $15 \times 15 = 225$).

It must be realized that the square roots of most numbers are approximate.

EXAMPLE:

$$\sqrt{42}$$

THINK:

6×6 are only 36, so the square root of 42 must be more than 6. 7×7 are 49, so the square root of 42 is less than 7. 42 is about halfway between 36 and 49, so the square root of 42 is about halfway between 6 and 7; it is about $6\frac{1}{2}$. Prove it. Take $6\frac{1}{2} \times 6\frac{1}{2}$. The answer is $42\frac{1}{4}$. A square root of $6\frac{1}{2}$ would be accepted as correct.

EXAMPLE:

The square root of 18 feet is not a whole number. 4^2 is 16, and 5^2 is 25. However, 4^2 is nearer to 18 than 5^2 is, so the square root of 18' to the nearest foot is 4 feet.

People like surveyors, engineers, and builders, who need to do much of this kind of arithmetic, have prepared tables of squares and square roots; this saves them much time.

To find square roots of larger numbers, use division.

EXAMPLE:

Find the square root of 9,216.

$$\sqrt{9216}$$

A First divide the number, using little check marks, into groups of two figures beginning at the decimal point. Remember when there is no decimal point written, it is assumed to be to the right of the number.

B Beginning with the numbers up to the first check mark judge approximately what times what gives 92 or less. Think: 9×9 are 81 and 10×10 are 100; but 100 is larger than 92, so 10 is too much.

$$\begin{array}{r} 9\checkmark \\ \sqrt{92\,16} \\ \underline{81} \\ 11 \end{array}$$

C Write the 9 above as in a division problem. Write the 81 under the 92 and subtract as you do in a long division problem.

$$\begin{array}{r} 9\checkmark \\ \sqrt{92\,16} \\ \underline{81} \\ 1116 \end{array}$$

D The next step is to draw a line in front of the 11 and bring down the next *group* of numbers, those up to the second check mark or to the end of the number.

$$\begin{array}{r} 9\checkmark \\ \sqrt{92\,16} \\ \underline{81} \\ 1116 \end{array}$$

E Now we continue by division. We need a trial divisor. *The trial divisor is the number above* $\sqrt{}$ *times 20,* a number arrived at by mathematicians and which we must accept. In this problem the trial divisor (t.d.) is 180. Think: How many times does 180 go into 1116? It will probably go about 7 times.

$$\begin{array}{rl} \text{t.d.} & 180 \\ & \quad\underline{7} \\ \text{r.d.} & 187 \end{array}$$

F But the *real divisor* (r.d.) is the trial 180 plus the trial 7, which makes the real divisor 187. Try 7×187. It equals 1309. That is much too large. Let us try 6 instead of 7. Add 6 to the trial 180, making the real divisor 186. $6 \times 186 = 1116$. That is exactly right. Write the 6 above the $\sqrt{}$. Now you have found the square root of 9216 to be 96.

$$\begin{array}{r} 9\checkmark 6 \\ \sqrt{92\,16} \\ \underline{81} \\ 1116 \\ \underline{1116} \end{array}$$

t.d.   180
         6
r.d.   186

$$\begin{array}{r} 32 \\ \times 32 \\ \hline 64 \\ 96 \\ \hline 1024 \end{array}$$

My problem was right!

Prove your answer. 96 × 96 should be 9216.

$$\begin{array}{r} 96 \\ \times 96 \\ \hline 576 \\ 864 \\ \hline 9216 \end{array}$$

Study these examples following the steps exactly as listed above.

EXAMPLE:

Find the square root of 1024.

Step a. $\sqrt{10\overset{\vee}{2}4}$

Steps b. & c. $\begin{array}{r} 3^{\vee} \\ \sqrt{1024} \\ 9 \\ \hline 1 \end{array}$

Step d. $\begin{array}{r} 3^{\vee} \\ \sqrt{1024} \\ 9 \\ \hline 124 \end{array}$

Steps e. & f. $\begin{array}{r} 3\ 2 \\ \sqrt{1024} \\ 9 \end{array}$

$\begin{array}{l} 124 \quad \text{t.d.} \quad 60 \\ 124 \qquad\qquad\ 2 \\ \qquad\quad \text{r.d.} \quad 62 \end{array}$

The answer is 32. To prove it, multiply 32 by 32: The answer should be 1024.

EXAMPLE:

Find the square root of 12,321.

$$\overset{1\ 1\ 1}{\sqrt{12321}}$$

$\begin{array}{lll} & & 1 \\ \text{t.d.} & 20 & \mid\ 23 \\ & \underline{\ 1} & \mid\ 21 \\ \text{r.d.} & 21 & \mid\ 221 \\ \text{t.d.} & 220 & \mid\ \underline{221} \\ & \underline{\ 1} & \\ \text{r.d.} & 221 & \end{array}$

EXAMPLE:

Find the square root of 14,641.

$$\overset{1\ 2\ 1}{\sqrt{14641}}$$

$\begin{array}{lll} & & 1 \\ \text{t.d.} & 20 & \mid\ 46 \\ & \underline{\ 2} & \mid\ 44 \\ \text{r.d.} & 22 & \mid\ 241 \\ \text{t.d.} & 240 & \mid\ \underline{241} \\ & \underline{\ 1} & \\ \text{r.d.} & 241 & \end{array}$

EXAMPLE:

Find the square root of 7225.

$$\overset{8\ 5}{\sqrt{7225}}$$

$\begin{array}{lll} & & 64 \\ \text{t.d.} & 160 & \mid\ 825 \\ & \underline{\ 5} & \mid\ 825 \\ \text{r.d.} & 165 & \end{array}$

Now let me give you the correct square roots of a few numbers. You try to do the work and see if you get the same root.

1. The square root of 8281 is 91.
2. The square root of 5776 is 76.
3. The square root of 17,161 is 131.
4. The square root of 14,161 is 119.
5. The square root of 15,625 is 125.

thought problems

The ability to solve problems is not taught as a single process. It is a skill that grows as your child's power to reason is developed. This development takes place as he learns the many other skills in arithmetic.

Encourage him to translate given facts into mathematical sentences whenever possible.

EXAMPLE:
  Roger is 7 pounds heavier than David. David weighs 75 pounds. How much does Roger weigh?
  Let r = Roger's weight
      75 = David's weight
  Then $r = 75 - 7$
       $r = 82$

Your child will find key words to help him decide which operation is necessary to solve a problem.

EXAMPLES:
  a) 36 less than 75 .... (subtraction)
  b) one-third of n .... (division)
  c) 5 feet longer than .... (addition)
  d) triple amounts .... (multiplication)

GLOSSARY OF TERMS COMMONLY USED IN "NEW MATH" AS PRESENTED IN THIS SERIES

ASSOCIATIVITY — The manner of grouping numbers under addition does not affect their sum. The manner of grouping numbers under multiplication does not affect the product.

CLOSURE — The sum and product of any two whole numbers is also a whole number.

COMMUTATIVITY — The order in which numbers are added does not affect their sum. The order in which two numbers are multiplied does not affect their product.

DISTRIBUTIVITY — The product of a number and the sum of two numbers is the same as the sum of the products obtained by multiplying each of the other numbers by the first number. $3(4 + 5) = (3 \times 4) + (3 \times 5)$.

ELEMENT — A member of a set.

EQUATION — A number sentence that contains the phrase "is equal to" or =.

EXPONENT — The small number indicating how many times the base number is used as a factor.

FRACTION — A rational number may be represented by a numeral called a fraction.

INTEGER — The set of integers is composed of all the positive and all the negative whole numbers and zero.

INVERSE OPERATION — An operation that does the opposite of another operation. Subtraction "undoes" addition; division "undoes" multiplication.

LINE — A set of points without limit in two directions.

NUMBER LINE — Numbers may be assigned to the points in a line to be used in interpreting mathematical ideas.

LINE SEGMENT — A line segment is a subset of a line and has two end points.

RAY	A line segment that has one end point.
MODULAR ARITHMETIC	An arithmetic based upon a limited set of numbers.
NUMBER BASE	The number upon which a numeration system is constructed.
NUMERAL	A symbol used to name numbers.
NUMBER	A mathematical idea of "how many."
CARDINAL NUMBER	The number of elements in a set.
COMPOSITE NUMBER	Any natural number which is not prime.
NATURAL NUMBERS	The numbers we commonly use for counting.
ORDINAL NUMBERS	The number that identifies the place of an element in a set (first, second, etc.).
PRIME NUMBER	A number whose only factors are 1 and itself.
RATIONAL NUMBER	A number that shows the ratio of two whole numbers. It is written as a fraction.
IRRATIONAL NUMBER	A number that is not rational. It cannot be written as a fraction.
REAL NUMBERS	The set of numbers of both rational and irrational numbers.
RECIPROCAL	If the product of two numbers is 1, the numbers are reciprocals. 2 and ½ are reciprocals.
SETS	A set is a collection of objects.
DISJOINT SET	Two sets that have no elements in common.
EMPTY SET	A set having no elements.
EQUAL SETS	If two sets contain precisely the same elements, they are equal.
EQUIVALENT SETS	If the cardinal number of two sets is the same, they are equivalent.
INTERSECTION OF SETS	The elements of two sets that are common to both sets.
SUBSETS	A set which is a part of another set.
UNION OF SETS	The elements of two sets are united to make one set.
SYMBOL	An arbitrary mark representing a number, operation, or relationship.
	{ } enclose the elements in a set; ∪ union of sets; ∩ intersection of sets; ⊂ is a subset of; ~ is equivalent to; +, −, ×, ÷ show operations; = is equal to; ≠ is not equal to; < is less than; > is greater than; 1, 2, 3 . . . names of numbers.

english exercises

I. Can you find all the mistakes in these sentences?

1. That boy he could of been hurt.   2. I seen Jim at the ball game.   3. We asked them to set with us.   4. The picture it sure was pretty.   5. Them men begun to shoot at us.   6. I haven't got any of them things.   7. It don't seem possible that the whole year is over.   8. Me and the girls was tired after that long swim.   9. They busted their balloons right of way. 10. Please open the door. I want in!   11. Oh, leave me help you!   12. It's good to meet up with you again.   13. He had ran in the wrong direction. 14. He ought to of did something about it.   15. I had wrote Tom all the directions.   16. Them three kids are Boy Scouts.   17. They should of helped the old lady.   18. These here are a wonderful collection.   19. Between you and I, John is the best player.   20. Most everybody are glad to quit.

II. Are the underlined verbs in these sentences transitive (with an object) or intransitive (without an object)?

1. We drove to the city last night.   2. The moths ate holes in our blankets. 3. Gretchen is preparing dinner.   4. Study your handwriting   5. Do you think you are improving?   6. You can learn the tricks if you practice. 7. Can you hear the music?   8. We can listen to it from here.   9. The choir has sung the opening song.   10. Bob consulted several books. 11. They rise twenty feet into the air.   12. Someone told the story about Darius Green.   13. He used his mother's umbrella.   14. Each paragraph should develop a single topic.   15. Everyone ate heartily.

III. Pick out the gerunds and participles.

1. Spelling is my hardest subject. (gerund)   2. I got sleepy lying in the sun. 3. My sister gets good marks in spelling.   4. The short boy carrying the beach ball is Tommy.   5. Carrying a heavy load of books, the child walked carefully.   6. Do you like skating?   7. Bobby began asking questions.

8. Bob likes fishing and rowing.   9. Driving carefully, she arrived home in plenty of time.   10. The moon, coming from behind the cloud, lighted our camp brightly.   11. My motor, coughing and wheezing, sounded sick. 12. The turkeys, frightened by the noise, ran for shelter.   13. Rowing a boat develops muscles.   14. Speaking clearly is necessary in business. 15. I hope to learn typing.

IV. Underline the infinitives.

1. To skate is fun.   2. He was about to jump off the cliff.   3. We all like to sing.   4. His plan was to meet us at nine.   5. This is a very good book to read.   6. He worked hard to pay for his board.   7. He tried to win. 8. I want to congratulate you.   9. I hurried to catch the bus.   10. Our aim is to complete it.   11. To play the piano well requires much practice. 12. We expect to spend a week there.   13. We all want to see that movie. 14. It took us an hour to get out.   15. Mary tried to learn the melody.

V. What is the tense of the underlined verbs?

1. The bat flew over my head.   2. I know him well.   3. I shall think it over. 4. I'm sure you have finished it.   5. I had never done this work before. 6. By that time he will have finished it.   7. You do like the taste, don't you?   8. We were hiding all the time.   9. He has grown so tall.   10. We shall sing "America."

VI. What are the principal parts of these verbs? A dictionary will help you.

Present	Past	Past participle (the form used with a helping word)	Present	Past	Past participle (the form used with a helping word)
1. am			13. leave		
2. beat			14. let		
3. bring			15. lie		
4. fall			16. rise		
5. go			17. run		
6. choose			18. see		
7. do			19. set		
8. burst			20. shake		
9. begin			21. sink		
10. drink			22. sit		
11. hide			23. spring		
12. lay			24. teach		

VII. **Are the underlined verbs in the active or passive voice?**

1. Mother <u>made</u> some pies.   2. The president is <u>elected</u> by the people.
3. The house was <u>built</u> by my uncle.   4. I <u>ate</u> two eggs for breakfast.
5. Gretchen <u>baked</u> these cookies.   6. The cookies were <u>eaten</u> by a hungry boy known as Bob!   7. A long, exciting story was <u>told</u> by the visiting missionary.   8. Did you ever <u>shoot</u> a bear?   9. A large black bear was <u>shot</u> by a friend of mine.   10. This picture was <u>painted</u> especially for her.
11. He certainly <u>made</u> a good speech.   12. Miss Smith <u>gave</u> them some stiff assignments.   13. Many songs were <u>composed</u> by the group.
14. Mary <u>will protect</u> Gretchen.   15. The lights <u>went</u> out immediately.

VIII. **Select the correct verb. Don't hesitate to use the dictionary.**

1. Please (take, bring) me the vase from the cupboard.
2. You know I (can, may) do the work.
3. Where did you (lie, lay) the book?
4. When will the concrete be (laid, lain)?
5. Mother (laid, lay) awake and made plans.
6. She always (sets, sits) there and waits for us.
7. Please (set, sit) the cake on the table.
8. His job each day is to (rise, raise) the flag.
9. I had just (raised, rose) the window.
10. I promised Dad that I (shall, will) never do it again.

IX. **These sentences are awkwardly constructed or are not complete. Can you improve them?**

1. Many good stories about manners.
2. The old lady she hadn't wanted to cross the street.
3. Here is a story which it proves the point.
4. There isn't but one good road home from here.
5. I will not go without you going too.
6. He couldn't play no more.
7. To at all times write well is important.
8. The boys climbed the trees and they were maples.
9. Neither one or the other are hard to read.
10. Running down the street, a lamppost stopped me.
11. Walking on a slippery street, a car hit me.
12. The girl leading the dog wearing the red dress is Mary.
13. Coming out of the dark, the light hurt my eyes.
14. I seen him sitting back of me.

X. Change the verb to agree with the subject in person and number.

1. A box of oranges were sent from Florida.   2. Two girls, besides my own, is here.   3. There was two men at the door.   4. Neither of the girls are home now.   5. Every man, woman, and child are welcome.   6. Frank don't swim well yet.   7. Why don't he come now?   8. The news were good.   9. Your trousers is too long.   10. There was a dog and a cat in the chair.   11. It just don't seem possible!   12. A magazine and a paper was lying on the floor.   13. There was three hundred persons at the concert.   14. Are each of the boys working now?   15. Wasn't you here last year? (Always use were with you.)

XI. What is the gender of each of these nouns?

1. girl
2. Sam
3. princess
4. school

5. doctor
6. relative
7. king
8. buck

9. cow
10. mother
11. paper
12. nurse

XII. Name the case of each noun—nominative, objective, or possessive.

1. The sun rose over Lake Como.   2. A horde of bandits attacked the camp.   3. Detroit's streets are wide and long.   4. Spring is the season I like best.   5. My sister will start school this fall.   6. In August we will visit Uncle Harry who lives in Wichita.   7. Last Sunday Erick came to our house.   8. Gregory has the measles.   9. A large pack of coyotes frightened the travelers.   10. Mimi's pony escaped from the barn.

XIII. Change the incorrect pronouns so they will agree with their antecedents. When the gender is not known, use masculine.

1. Everyone brought their lunch.   2. Won't somebody please let me borrow their pencil?   3. If anyone wishes to go, they may do so now.   4. The girls prepared her little speeches.   5. Has everyone done their theme?   6. Will each student leave their paper on my desk?   7. Both John and Bob are using his own canoe today.   8. Everyone is expected to pay their share.   9. Will everyone please help themselves?   10. Not one of the dogs hurt their feet.   11. All guests must leave his check stub at the desk.   12. Each one must prepare their own work carefully.   13. Neither Gretchen nor Mary cleaned their rooms.   14. Many a college student has to work their way through.   15. Someone offered the use of their car.

XIV. Diagram these sentences.

1. Edison invented the phonograph.
2. He worked long and hard.
3. Do you know what a radiometer is?
4. For many years scientists have tried to use energy from the sun.
5. In 1870 a scientist invented a machine that worked by sun power.
6. Mirrors reflected the heat of the sun.
7. The engine was not very successful.
8. This is the boy who is studying electricity.
9. The flies which buzz around us are man's enemy.
10. Jane wrote a letter to the company ordering a new sweater.
11. The sweater arrived but it was not the right color.
12. Wearing it would spoil the effect of her outfit.

XV. What part of speech is each word in the sentence?

1. The dog poked the young man gently with his nose.
2. Whew! That was a close call.
3. The child said something to his mother about the taste of the drinking water.
4. Bob wrote a long letter to his family.
5. An interesting story was told about the school party.
6. Quickly she slipped into the coatroom to hide.
7. "Of course," said Bob, "I want to get in practice."
8. It was too bad but it was time to go home.
9. Finally they asked everybody to sit down.
10. Probably you are overusing some words.

XVI. Which sentences are simple, which ones are compound, which are complex?

1. England has many ships, but France has few.
2. France sold some land to the United States.
3. In many American homes the father and children prepare the meals to-gether.
4. A bowl which contained fruit was placed in the center of the table.
5. As soon as the meal was finished, the children were excused.
6. The boy who sang is from Chicago.
7. You cannot be excused until your work is finished.
8. When we last saw him he was with Bill.

9. They saw land and shouted for joy.

10. The boys whom you saw are visitors from the city.

XVII. **Underline the topic sentence in each paragraph, the sentence that tells you what the paragraph is about.**

1. The mouth of the grasshopper is wide, and has strong jaws. However, they are not so strong as those of his cousin, the cricket.

2. It you could look inside a grasshopper's body, you would see that he has a gizzard, much like that of a chicken. It is made of little bands set with fine teeth. These teeth chew up into a pulp the leaves which the grasshopper has eaten.

3. Many years ago, a great poet wrote a song to the grasshopper. In this song he said that the grasshopper was the happiest of living things. It did nothing but dance and sing; it ate fresh leaves, and drank cool dew. When the glad summer of its life was done, it died, it did not live to be sick, or hungry, or cold.

XVIII. **What are the plurals of the following words? (Use a dictionary.)**

1. boy _____
10. news _____

2. birch _____
11. A _____

3. baby _____
12. and _____

4. monkey _____
13. self _____

5. life _____
14. echo _____

6. tomato _____
15. piano _____

7. mother-in-law _____
16. buffalo _____

8. tooth _____
17. loaf _____

9. deer _____
18. pants _____

XIX. **Write one word with each prefix. (Use your dictionary.)**

1. ad — adverb
9. in _____

2. ex _____
10. inter _____

3. dis _____
11. mis _____

4. fore _____
12. pre _____

5. re _____
13. pro _____

6. anti _____
14. sub _____

7. com _____
15. trans _____

8. de _____
16. un _____

XX. Write one word with each suffix. (Use your dictionary.)

1. ance—maintenance or remem-
    brance
2. ate _____
3. ation _____
4. ative _____
5. en _____
6. er _____
7. ent _____
8. fy _____
9. hood _____
10. ing _____
11. ish _____

12. ive _____
13. ize _____
14. ly _____
15. ment _____
16. ness _____
17. ship _____
18. tion _____
19. ty _____
20. ward _____
21. able _____
22. ful _____
23. less _____

XXI. What are three synonyms you could use instead of the overworked words on the left?

1. nice _____
2. dumb _____
3. pleasant _____
4. unpleasant _____
5. big _____
6. pretty _____
7. awful _____
8. swell _____
9. fine _____
10. wonderful _____

XXII. Put <u>who</u> or <u>whom</u> in each blank. ("Who" is nominative, "whom" is objective.)

1. Can you guess _____ it is?   2. I don't know _____ is to act in my place.   3. _____ can it be?   4. Can it be he _____ they mean?   5. _____ shall I call for tonight?   6. Of _____ are you thinking, Mary?   7. For _____ are you knitting that?   8. _____ did he mean?   9. I saw the girl to _____ you sent the package.   10. Guess _____ it was.   11. These are the boys _____ are called The Top-notchers.   12. I don't know to _____ they are talking.   13. To _____ did you refer as the tallest one in the group?   14. _____ did you think it was?   15. _____ was it?

XXIII. Punctuate the following sentences.

1. Who can help asked Mother
2. Mary who was one of the fastest runners came in second
3. What a thrill we get from Beethovens music
4. We practice for an hour on Saturdays Sundays and holidays
5. Did you know that Beethoven was deaf
6. Will you get a months vacation
7. I dont want it she cried
8. Hurrah There he is now
9. The short chubby man inquired where is the City Hall
10. Why dont you cross your ts
11. They live at 15 Melrose Avenue Miami Florida
12. What do you want James inquired
13. When Pat called I was busy in the kitchen
14. Where he asked did you find this
15. Whos at the door Frank

XXIV. Select the proper pronoun.

1. The mailman had letters for (he, him) and (I, me).
2. One of the girls lost (her, their) books.
3. Each of the men did (his, their) duty.
4. Will somebody share (his, their) book with me?
5. Some of the guests brought (his, their) musical instruments.
6. They met Peter and (I, me) at the door.
7. Nobody wants to do (his, their) work.
8. (Him, He) and (me, I) are friends.
9. Mother didn't like (me, my) being out late.
10. Between you and (I, me) I don't like this coat.
11. He spoke to (we, us) boys.
12. He sent my brother and (me, I) a gift.
13. If I were (her, she) I'd be ashamed.
14. It looks like (her, she).
15. The girl is shorter than (he, him).

490

arithmetic exercises

I. Arrange in columns and add:

1. 372 + 1056 + 2375 + 6892 + 5765 + 10632.
2. 8762 + 9325 + 5789 + 3599 + 42563 + 67897.
3. 106 + 20785 + 3547 + 87695 + 100910 + 46.
4. 7875 + 492 + 187449 + 691 + 56332.
5. 10563 + 2753 + 306549 + 387 + 16542.
6. 356432 + 205699 + 1338250 + 1467.
7. 64895 + 3270 + 107999 + 65688 + 29.
8. 678500 + 354605 + 738967 + 78924.
9. 66 + 95 + 7 + 987 + 402 + 1703.
10. 25 + 1032 + 647 + 2945 + 387 + 555.

II. Subtract:

1. 63249	2. 98675	3. 48111	4. 888848	5. 107654
27507	34907	23677	78927	105342

6. 654321	7. 797254	8. 266403	9. 705792	10. 7335
239585	321607	198965	405293	1097

11. 6953	12. 75632	13. 4627	14. 5648620	15. 10276490
4004	30754	2859	4352897	8753364

III. Multiply:

1. 162	2. 653	3. 347	4. 236	5. 8765
83	20	45	79	130

6. 9867	7. 6758	8. 5939	9. 26543
709	4539	1876	2486

IV. Divide:

1. $32\overline{)6752}$ 2. $48\overline{)3648}$ 3. $38\overline{)2926}$ 4. $29\overline{)1305}$

5. $18\overline{)486}$ 6. $79\overline{)18844}$

V. Fractions. Add:

1. $6\frac{1}{4}$ 2. $3\frac{1}{4}$ 3. $17\frac{1}{8}$ 4. $\frac{3}{4}$
   $5\frac{1}{2}$ $2\frac{1}{4}$ $23\frac{3}{4}$ $\frac{7}{8}$

5. $3\frac{3}{4}$ 6. $\frac{2}{3}$ 7. $1\frac{7}{8}$ 8. $3\frac{2}{3}$
   $2\frac{1}{2}$ $\frac{3}{4}$ $3\frac{1}{4}$ $2\frac{1}{4}$
                                          $2\frac{1}{2}$ $5\frac{1}{2}$

9. $4\frac{7}{8}$ 10. $2\frac{5}{12}$ 11. $3\frac{5}{6}$ 12. $3\frac{11}{16}$
   $5\frac{1}{4}$ $3\frac{7}{12}$ 2 $4\frac{5}{16}$
   $3\frac{1}{2}$ $1\frac{11}{12}$ $1\frac{1}{2}$ $2\frac{9}{16}$

VI. Fractions. Subtract:

1. $\frac{11}{12}$ 2. $2\frac{1}{12}$ 3. $4\frac{1}{4}$ 4. $3\frac{5}{16}$ 5. $10\frac{1}{8}$
   $\frac{1}{2}$ $\frac{1}{2}$ $1\frac{3}{4}$ $1\frac{7}{8}$ $3\frac{1}{4}$

6. $8\frac{2}{3}$ 7. $3\frac{1}{8}$ 8. 10 9. $8\frac{2}{3}$ 10. $8\frac{1}{5}$
   $2\frac{3}{4}$ $\frac{15}{16}$ $3\frac{9}{16}$ $5\frac{7}{12}$ $2\frac{1}{4}$

11. $3\frac{5}{16}$ 12. $8\frac{5}{12}$ 13. $4\frac{3}{16}$ 14. 12 15. $4\frac{3}{8}$
    $2\frac{7}{8}$ $3\frac{3}{4}$ $1\frac{3}{8}$ $11\frac{11}{12}$ $1\frac{13}{16}$

VII. Fractions. Multiply:

1. $10 \times 3\frac{2}{5} =$
2. $2\frac{3}{4} \times 12 =$
3. $\frac{4}{5} \times \frac{1}{3} =$
4. $\frac{2}{3} \times 3\frac{2}{3} =$
5. $\frac{4}{5} \times 10\frac{1}{2} =$
6. $\frac{4}{5} \times \frac{2}{3} =$
7. $12 \times 5\frac{2}{3} =$
8. $8\frac{2}{3} \times 3 =$

9. $\frac{2}{3} \times \frac{1}{8} =$
10. $\frac{3}{4} \times 8\frac{1}{2} =$
11. $\frac{4}{5} \times 3\frac{1}{3} =$
12. $\frac{2}{3} \times 4\frac{1}{2} =$
13. $2\frac{3}{4} \times 5\frac{1}{3} =$
14. $12\frac{1}{2} \times 3\frac{3}{4} =$
15. $3\frac{2}{3} \times 4\frac{3}{5} =$
16. $8\frac{1}{4} \times 6\frac{2}{3} =$

VIII. Fractions. Multiply:

1.	2.	3.	4.	5.	6.
$12\frac{3}{4}$	57	$12\frac{3}{16}$	306	$27\frac{1}{6}$	1000
$\underline{\quad 5 \quad}$	$\underline{\quad 2\frac{1}{2} \quad}$	$\underline{\quad 8 \quad}$	$\underline{\quad 5\frac{5}{8} \quad}$	$\underline{\quad 8 \quad}$	$\underline{\quad 263\frac{2}{3} \quad}$

7.	8.	9.	10.	11.	12.
106	34	937	$97\frac{3}{5}$	$1351\frac{1}{5}$	308
$\underline{\quad 3\frac{2}{3} \quad}$	$\underline{\quad 8\frac{1}{7} \quad}$	$\underline{\quad 18\frac{1}{9} \quad}$	$\underline{\quad 30 \quad}$	$\underline{\quad 17 \quad}$	$\underline{\quad 15\frac{1}{4} \quad}$

IX. Fractions. Divide:

1. $3\frac{1}{2} \div \frac{1}{2} =$
2. $5\frac{1}{2} \div \frac{1}{2} =$
3. $4 \div \frac{1}{8} =$
4. $3\frac{1}{8} \div \frac{1}{8} =$
5. $2\frac{1}{2} \div \frac{3}{4} =$
6. $1\frac{3}{5} \div 2\frac{1}{2} =$
7. $4\frac{1}{3} \div \frac{1}{6} =$
8. $\frac{3}{4} \div 8 =$

9. $\frac{5}{6} \div \frac{2}{3} =$
10. $8 \div \frac{3}{4} =$
11. $\frac{2}{3} \div \frac{5}{6} =$
12. $18 \div 1\frac{1}{2} =$
13. $9\frac{3}{8} \div 18\frac{1}{2} =$
14. $12\frac{2}{3} \div 6\frac{3}{4} =$
15. $18\frac{1}{2} \div 9\frac{3}{8} =$
16. $3\frac{1}{4} \div 1\frac{1}{2} =$

X. Decimals. Change to decimals (nearest hundredth):

1. $\frac{1}{2} =$

2. $\frac{1}{4} =$

3. $\frac{4}{5} =$

4. $\frac{1}{3} =$

5. $\frac{1}{16} =$

6. $\frac{7}{12} =$

7. $\frac{1}{8} =$

8. $\frac{3}{4} =$

9. $\frac{1}{5} =$

10. $\frac{23}{25} =$

11. $\frac{1}{7} =$

12. $\frac{2}{3} =$

13. $\frac{11}{12} =$

14. $\frac{1}{10} =$

15. $\frac{2}{5} =$

16. $\frac{3}{5} =$

17. $\frac{1}{6} =$

18. $\frac{1}{12} =$

19. $\frac{5}{6} =$

20. $\frac{11}{16} =$

21. $\frac{1}{9} =$

XI. Decimals. Multiply:

1. 34.2
     .12

2. 30.45
     .25

3. 6.48
     .12

4. 5286
     .25

5. .03
     .2

6. 32.5
     1000

XII. Decimals. Divide:

1. $1.7\overline{)2.89}$

2. $1.7\overline{)28.9}$

3. $.17\overline{).289}$

4. $1.7\overline{).289}$

5. $1.3\overline{)15.6}$

6. $.13\overline{)15.6}$

7. $.65\overline{).325}$

8. $4.7\overline{)60.}$

9. $6.5\overline{)29.}$

10. $2.3\overline{)6.5}$

11. $3.4\overline{)8.7}$

12. $8.7\overline{)34.}$

XIII. Decimals. Watch the signs:

1. $.2\overline{)1}$

2. $3.0 + .8 =$ _____

3. $1 \div .001 =$ _____

4. $.3$ of $\frac{1}{2} =$ _____

5. $1.2 \times .12 =$ _____

6. $1.2 \div .2 =$ _____

7. $1.02 \times 1000 =$ _____

8. $102 \div .1 =$ _____

9. $5.32 \times 6.3 =$ _____

10. $.4 \times .25 =$ _____

11. $.1 \div .001 =$ _____

12. $.07 \times .8 =$ _____

13. $.07 \times .08 =$ _____

14. $21 \div .21 =$ _____

15. $.3 \times .4 =$ _____

16. $\frac{1}{2}$ of $.1 =$ _____

17. $\frac{1}{2}$ of $.3 =$ _____

18. $1.2 - .3 =$ _____

19. $1.2 \div .02 =$ _____

20. $10.2 \div .1 =$ _____

21. $24.3 \times 2.6 =$ _____

22. $.02 \div .2 =$ _____

23. $.1 \times 4 =$ _____

24. $\frac{1}{10}$ of $.01 =$ _____

XIV. Ratio. Express in fractions:

1. The ratio of a nickel to a dime is _____
2. The ratio of a nickel to a quarter is _____
3. The ratio of an ounce to a pound is _____
4. The ratio of an inch to a foot is _____
5. The ratio of a pint to a gallon is _____
6. The ratio of 60 lb. to 50 lb. is _____

7. The ratio of $\frac{1}{8}$ to $\frac{3}{8}$ is _____
8. The ratio of $\frac{1}{4}$ in. to 6 in. is _____
9. The ratio of 7.98 to 2.01 is about _____
10. The ratio of 7 to 9 is _____
11. The ratio of 15 to 74 is about _____
12. The ratio of 4 to 3 is _____

XV. Ratio. Express in per cent. Find the ratio of:

1. $.50 to $1.00
2. 1 to 2
3. 3 to 6
4. 3 to 4
5. 3 to 5

6. 4 in. to 2 ft.
7. 10 cents to 5 cents
8. 60 min. to 90 min.
9. 8 oz. to 16 oz.
10. 3 in. to 12 in.

XVI. Metric system:

1. To change miles to kilometers, divide the number of miles by _____

2. To change kilometers to miles, multiply the number of kilometers by _____

3. Since 1 qt. is about .91 of a liter, 1 gal. is about _____ liters.

4. One kilogram (kg.) is about 2.2 lb.; 10 kg. are about _____ lb.

5. One liter is 1.1 qt. Then 10 liters are _____ qt.

6. A truck that weighs a ton weighs about _____ kg.

7. Which is cheaper: butter at $1.50 per kg. or at $.70 per lb.?

8. Which is cheaper: gasoline at 25 cents a gal. or at 8 cents per liter?

9. If 1 inch equals 2.54 centimeters, then 1 yard equals _____ centimeters.

10. The distance between Los Angeles and New York is about 3,000 miles or _____ km.

11. If a pound of butter is worth 80 cents, a kilogram of butter would be worth about _____

12. If 1 kg. equals 2.2 lb., then 1 lb. equals _____ kg.
   (Ratio of 1 to 2.2; 1 ÷ 2.2)

13. A tree grew about 90 cm. in 5 years; therefore it grew on the average of about _____ cm. per yr.

14. One foot is about _____ cm.

15. One foot is about _____ meters.

XVII. Per cent. Write the fractional equivalents of:

1. $50\% =$
2. $20\% =$
3. $66\frac{2}{3}\% =$
4. $12\frac{1}{2}\% =$
5. $8\frac{1}{3}\% =$
6. $150\% =$

7. $25\% =$
8. $30\% =$
9. $70\% =$
10. $37\frac{1}{2}\% =$
11. $6\frac{1}{4}\% =$
12. $110\% =$

13. $75\% =$
14. $40\% =$
15. $10\% =$
16. $62\frac{1}{2}\% =$
17. $16\frac{2}{3}\% =$
18. $125\% =$

19. $33\frac{1}{3}\% =$
20. $60\% =$
21. $80\% =$
22. $87\frac{1}{2}\% =$
23. $30\% =$
24. $100\% =$

XVIII. Write as decimals:

1. $\frac{1}{2}\% =$
2. $\frac{2}{5}\% =$
3. $225\% =$
4. $4\frac{1}{2}\% =$

5. $\frac{1}{4}\% =$
6. $2\frac{1}{2}\% =$
7. $350\% =$
8. $3\frac{3}{4}\% =$

9. $\frac{3}{4}\% =$
10. $.2\% =$
11. $160\% =$
12. $2\frac{1}{3}\% =$

13. $2\frac{3}{4}\% =$
14. $2\frac{7}{8}\% =$
15. $325\% =$
16. $8\frac{1}{2}\% =$

XIX. Find:

1. 225% of 60 =
2. 350% of 80 =
3. 210% of 1000 =

4. 240% of $5000 =
5. $\frac{2}{5}$% of 1504 =
6. $2\frac{1}{2}$% of $9980 =

7. $2\frac{7}{8}$% of $3000 =
8. $\frac{1}{2}$% of 1984 =
9. 2% of $1294 =
10. .2% of 987 =

XX. Interest:

PRINCIPAL	YEARLY INTEREST RATE	TIME	INTEREST
1. $250.	$3\frac{1}{2}$%	4 yr. 3 mo.	_____
2. $175.	4%	2 yr. 6 mo.	_____
3. $1,050.	$4\frac{1}{2}$%	5 yr.	_____
4. $756.	$2\frac{1}{2}$%	3 yr. 4 mo.	_____
5. $840.	$4\frac{3}{4}$%	2 yr. 8 mo.	_____
6. $970.	5%	4 yr. 2 mo.	_____
7. $1,650.	6%	3 yr. 9 mo.	_____
8. $1,375.	$5\frac{1}{2}$%	5 yr. 6 mo.	_____
9. $2,060.	$5\frac{1}{4}$%	4 yr. 3 mo.	_____
10. $920.	$4\frac{1}{2}$%	3 yr.	_____

XXI. Find the total amount:

PRINCIPAL	INTEREST RATE (compounded annually)	TIME	TOTAL AMOUNT
1. $150.	4%	3 yrs.	_____
2. $225.	6%	2 yrs.	_____
3. $290.	$4\frac{1}{2}$%	3 yrs.	_____
4. $350.	5%	4 yrs.	_____
5. $430.	$5\frac{1}{2}$%	2 yrs.	_____
6. $560.	6%	4 yrs.	_____
7. $725.	$3\frac{1}{2}$%	3 yrs.	_____

8. $980.	4%	4 yrs.	_____
9. $870.	$6\frac{1}{2}$%	2 yrs.	_____
10. $650.	5%	4 yrs.	_____

XXII. Using a letter to stand for a number.

Find what N is in each problem:

1. If $N + 5$ is 11, then $N = 11 - 5 =$ _____

2. If $3N = 27$, then $N = \frac{27}{3}$ (or $27 \div 3$) = _____

3. If $N - 7 = 15$, then $N = 15 + 7 =$ _____

4. If $\frac{N}{7} = 3$, then $N = 3 \times 7 =$ _____

5. $\frac{N}{8} = 6$; $N =$ _____   9. $9N = 63$; $N =$ _____

6. $N + 9 = 13$; $N =$ _____   10. $8N = 56$; $N =$ _____

7. $N - 23 = 7$; $N =$ _____   11. $\frac{N}{49} = 7$; $N =$ _____

8. $N - 15 = 15$; $N =$ _____   12. $N - 18 = 7$; $N =$ _____

XXIII. Geometric facts:

1. There are _____ degrees in a complete circle

2. There are _____ degrees in a half circle

3. There are _____ degrees in a quarter circle

4. An angle less than 90° is called an _____ angle

5. An angle that has between 90° and 180° is called an _____ angle

6. A 90° angle is called a _____ angle

7. Lines that do not intersect are called _____ lines

8. Perpendicular lines form _____ angles

9. A square is a rectangle whose four sides are _____

10. A rectangle is a parallelogram whose angles are _____ angles

11. An equilateral triangle is a triangle having _____ _____ _____

12. An isosceles triangle is one having _____ _____ _____

13. The sum of the angles of a triangle is _____ °

14. A right triangle is a triangle one of whose angles is _____ °

498

XXIV. Area:

A. Rectangles. Fill in the missing number:

	AREA	LENGTH	WIDTH
1.	?	1"	1"
2.	?	2'	2'
3.	?	3'	3'
4.	?	1 yd.	6 yd.
5.	?	2"	$2\frac{1}{2}$"
6.	10 sq. in.	?	5"
7.	16 sq. in.	2"	?
8.	?	1.6'	2.5'
9.	?	$1\frac{1}{3}$ yd.	$\frac{3}{4}$ yd.
10.	?	12 in.	12 in.

B. Triangles. Fill in the missing number:

	AREA	HEIGHT	BASE
1.	?	1"	1"
2.	?	1"	2"
3.	?	2'	1'
4.	?	2 ft.	1 yd.
5.	20 sq. in.	?	10 in.
6.	?	5.0'	3.6'
7.	?	2 cm.	4 cm.
8.	1 sq. ft.	?	1 ft.
9.	?	$1\frac{7}{8}$ ft.	$2\frac{1}{2}$ ft.
10.	?	10 in.	12 in.

C. Circles. If the

1. radius is 10", the area is _____
2. radius is 5", the area is _____
3. radius is 20", the area is _____
4. radius is 1", the area is _____

5. radius is $8\frac{1}{2}''$, the area is _____   8. radius is 6.4', the area is _____

6. radius is 2.4'', the area is _____   9. radius is $1\frac{1}{2}'$, the area is _____

7. radius is 3.6', the area is _____   10. radius is $2\frac{7}{10}'$, the area is _____

XXV. Volume of rectangular solids. (V = lwh):

1. 1 in. × 1 ft. × 1 yd. = _____ cu. in.   6. 4 in. × 4 in. × 12 ft. = _____ cu. in.
2. 3 ft. × 3 ft. × 3 ft. = _____ cu. ft.   7. $3\frac{1}{2}$ in. × 2 in. × $1\frac{1}{2}$ in. = _____ cu. in.
3. 12 in. × 12 in. × 12 in. = _____ cu. in.   8. 150 ft. × 8 ft. × 45 ft. = _____ cu. ft.
4. 1 yd. × 2 ft. × 1 ft. = _____ cu. ft.   9. 21 ft. × $1\frac{1}{2}$ ft. × 18 ft. = _____ cu. ft.
5. 1 ft. × 8 in. × 4 in. = _____ cu. in.   10. $37\frac{1}{2}$ in. × $\frac{1}{2}$ in. × 3 in. = _____ cu. in.

XXVI. Cost, overhead, profit, loss:

A. Fill blanks. (Overhead is 30% of selling price.)

	COST	SELL. PRICE	OVERHEAD	PROFIT	LOSS
1.	$ 1.50	$ 2.50	_____	_____	_____
2.	_____	$ 1.50	$ .50	$ .25	_____
3.	$ .75	$ 1.00	_____	_____	$.05
4.	_____	$ 10.00	_____	$2.00	_____
5.	$12.00	$ 12.00	_____	_____	_____
6.	_____	$150.00	$45.00	$5.00	_____

B. Find:

	COST	OVERHEAD	PROFIT	SELLING PRICE
1.	$100.	30% of sell. price	15% of sell. price	_____
2.	$250.	25% of sell. price	10% of sell. price	_____
3.	_____	20% of sell. price	10% of sell. price	$200.
4.	$ 60.	40% of sell. price	_____	$150.
5.	$ 80.	_____	40% of sell. price	$200.

ANSWERS

I.

1. That boy could have been hurt.
2. I saw Jim at the ball game.
3. We asked them to sit with us.
4. The picture was very pretty.
5. The men began to shoot at us.
6. I haven't any of those things.
7. It doesn't seem possible that a whole year is over.
8. The girls and I were tired after that long swim.
9. They broke their balloons right away.
10. Please open the door. I want to come in.
11. Oh, let me help you!
12. It's good to meet you again.
13. He had run in the wrong direction.
14. He ought to have done something about it.
15. I had written Tom all the directions.
16. Those three boys are Boy Scouts.
17. They should have helped the old lady.
18. This is a wonderful collection.
19. Between you and me, John is the best player.
20. Most everybody is glad to quit.

II.

1. intrans.
2. trans.
3. trans.
4. trans.
5. trans.
6. trans.
7. trans.
8. intrans.
9. trans.
10. trans.
11. intrans.
12. trans.
13. trans.
14. trans.
15. intrans. (a clause is the obj.)

III.

1. Spelling — gerund
2. lying — participle
3. spelling — gerund
4. carrying — participle
5. carrying — participle
6. skating — gerund
7. asking — gerund
8. fishing, rowing — gerunds
9. Driving — participle
10. coming — participle
11. coughing, wheezing — participles
12. (no gerund or participle)
13. Rowing — gerund
14. Speaking — gerund
15. typing — gerund

IV.

1. to skate
2. to jump
3. to sing
4. to meet
5. to read
6. to pay
7. to win
8. to congratulate
9. to catch
10. to complete
11. to play
12. to spend
13. to see
14. to get
15. to learn

V.

1. past
2. present
3. future
4. present perfect
5. past perfect
6. future perfect
7. present
8. past
9. present perfect
10. future

VI.

	Past	Past Participle
1.	was	been
2.	beat	beaten
3.	brought	brought
4.	fell	fallen
5.	went	gone
6.	chose	chosen
7.	did	done
8.	burst	burst
9.	began	begun
10.	drank	drunk
11.	hid	hidden
12.	laid	laid
13.	left	left
14.	let	let
15.	lay	lain
16.	rose	risen
17.	ran	run
18.	saw	seen
19.	set	set
20.	shook	shaken
21.	sank	sunk
22.	sat	sat
23.	sprang	sprung
24.	taught	taught

VII.

1. active
2. passive
3. passive
4. active
5. active
6. passive
7. passive
8. active
9. passive
10. passive
11. active
12. active
13. passive
14. active
15. active

VIII.

1. bring
2. can
3. lay
4. laid
5. lay
6. sits
7. set
8. raise
9. raised
10. will

IX.

1. There are many good stories about manners.
2. The old lady had not wanted to cross the street.
3. Here is a story which proves the point.
4. There is only one good road home from here.
5. I will not go unless you go too.
6. He could not play any more.
7. To write well at all times is important.
8. The boys climbed the maple trees.
9. Neither of them is hard to read.
10. When running down the street, I was stopped by a lamppost.
11. A car hit me as I was walking on a slippery street.
12. The girl wearing a red dress and leading a dog is Mary.
13. The sudden light hurt my eyes as I came out of the dark.
14. I saw him sitting back of me.

X.

1. was sent	6. doesn't swim	11. doesn't
2. are	7. doesn't	12. were lying
3. were	8. was	13. were
4. is	9. are	14. Is
5. is	10. were	15. Weren't

XI.

1. fem.	5. common	9. fem.
2. masc.	6. common	10. fem.
3. fem.	7. masc.	11. neuter
4. neuter	8. masc.	12. common

XII.

1. sun—nom.; Lake Como—obj.
2. horde—nom.; bandits—obj.; camp—obj.
3. Detroit's—poss.; streets—nom.
4. Spring—nom.; season—nom.
5. sister—nom.; school—obj. (*fall* is an adverb, it tells *when*).
6. August—obj.; Uncle Harry—obj.; Wichita—obj.
7. (Sunday—used as an adv.—tells *when*) Erick —nom.; house—obj.
8. Gregory—nom.; measles—obj.
9. pack—nom.; coyotes—obj.; travelers—obj.
10. Mimi's—poss.; pony—nom.; barn—obj.

XIII.

1. *their to his.*	9. *themselves to himself.*
2. *their to his.*	10. *their to his.*
3. *they to he.*	11. *his to their*
4. *her to their.*	*(check to checks)*
5. *their to his.*	12. *their to his.*
6. *their to his.*	13. *their to her.*
7. *his to their.*	*(rooms to room)*
(canoe to canoes)	14. *their to his.*
8. *their to his.*	15. *their to his.*

XIV.

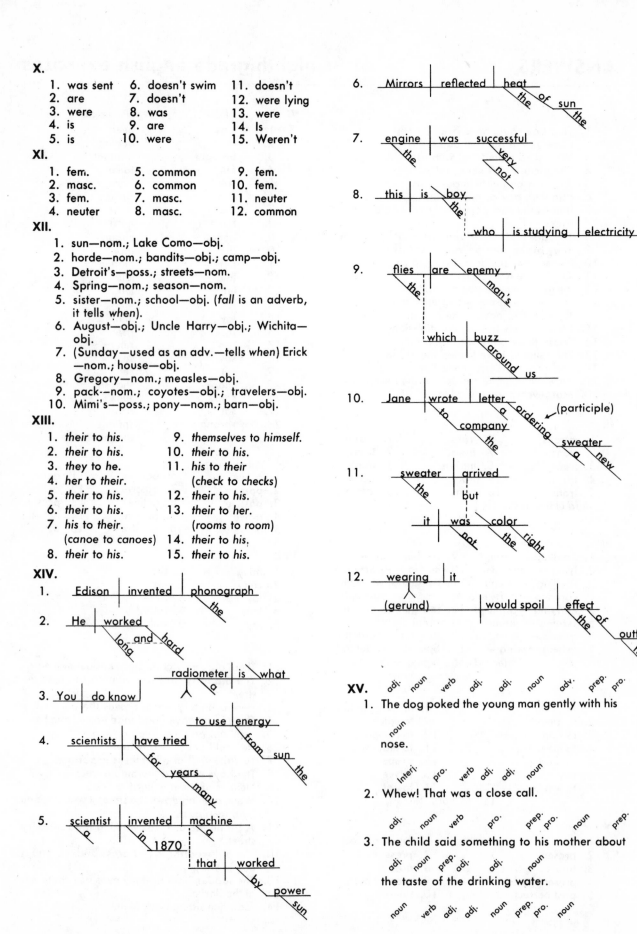

XV.

1. The dog poked the young man gently with his nose.
   (adj. noun verb adj. adj. noun adv. prep. pro. noun)

2. Whew! That was a close call.
   (Interj. pro. verb adj. adj. noun)

3. The child said something to his mother about the taste of the drinking water.
   (adj. noun verb pro. prep. pro. noun prep. noun verb adj. adj. noun prep. pro. noun)

4. Bob wrote a long letter to his family.

   adj.   *adj.*   *noun*   *verb*   *prep.*   *adj.*   *adj.*

5. An interesting story was told about the school

   noun

party.

   adv.   *pro.*   *verb*   *prep.* *adj.*   *noun*   *infin.* *adv.*

6. Quickly she slipped into the coatroom to hide.

       adv.   *verb*   *noun* *pro.* *verb*   *inf. noun* *prep.*
                                            (obj.)

7. "Of course," said Bob, "I want to get in

   noun

practice."

   pro. *verb* *adv.* *adj.* *conj.* *pro.* *verb* *noun* *inf. noun* *noun*
                                             (app.)

8. It was too bad but it was time to go home.

   adv.   *pro.*   *verb*   *pro.*   *inf. noun*   *adv.*
                                    (obj.)

9. Finally they asked everybody to sit down.

   adv.   *pro.*   *verb*   *adj.*   *noun*

10. Probably you are overusing some words.

XVI.

1. compound
2. simple
3. simple
4. complex
5. complex
6. complex
7. complex
8. complex
9. compound
10. complex

XVII.

1. The mouth of the grasshopper is wide, and has strong jaws.
2. If you could look inside a grasshopper's body, you would see that he has a gizzard, much like that of a chicken.
3. Many years ago, a great poet wrote a song to the grasshopper.

XVIII.

1. boys
2. birches
3. babies
4. monkeys
5. lives
6. tomatoes
7. mothers-in-law
8. teeth
9. deer
10. news
11. A's
12. ands
13. selves
14. echoes
15. pianoes
16. buffaloes
17. loaves
18. pants

XIX.

2. extract
3. disinterest
4. foreground
5. renew
6. antidote
7. compel
8. decrease
9. incite
10. intermediate
11. misjudge
12. predetermine
13. produce
14. subsoil
15. transport
16. undecided

XX.

2. numerate
3. publication
4. relative
5. enliven
6. safer
7. antecedent
8. magnify
9. brotherhood
10. singing
11. foolish
12. prohibitive
13. magnetize
14. manly
15. argument
16. awareness
17. friendship
18. recognition
19. unity
20. onward
21. valuable
22. useful
23. useless

XXI.

1. agreeable, pleasant, attractive
2. stupid, moronic, silent
3. merry, gay, agreeable
4. disagreeable, offensive, revolting
5. huge, expansive, massive
6. beautiful, attractive, becoming
7. terrifying, appalling, unpleasant
8. stylish, protrude, bulge
9. excellent, superior, handsome
10. marvelous, excellent, delightful

XXII.

1. who
2. who
3. Who
4. whom
5. Whom
6. whom
7. whom
8. Whom
9. whom
10. who
11. who
12. whom
13. whom
14. Who
15. Who

XXIII.

1. "Who can help?" asked Mother.
2. Mary, who was one of the fastest runners, came in second.
3. What a thrill we get from Beethoven's music!
4. We practice for an hour on Saturdays, Sundays, and holidays.
5. Did you know that Beethoven was deaf?
6. Will you get a month's vacation?
7. "I don't want it!" she cried.
8. Hurrah! There he is now.
9. The short chubby man inquired, "Where is the City Hall?"
10. Why don't you cross your t's?
11. They live at 15 Melrose Avenue, Miami, Florida.
12. "What do you want?" James inquired.
13. When Pat called I was busy in the kitchen.
14. "Where," he asked, "did you find this?"
15. Who's at the door, Frank?

XXIV.

1. him, me
2. her
3. his
4. his
5. their
6. me
7. his
8. He, I
9. my
10. me
11. us
12. me
13. she
14. her
15. he

I. Add:
1. 27,092
2. 137,935
3. 213,089
4. 252,839
5. 336,794
6. 1,901,848
7. 241,881
8. 1,850,996
9. 3,260
10. 5,591

II. Subtract:
1. 35,742	2. 63,768	3. 24,434
4. 809,921	5. 2,312	6. 414,736
7. 475,647	8. 67,438	9. 300,499
10. 6,238	11. 2,949	12. 44,878
13. 1,768	14. 1,295,723	15. 1,523,126

III. Multiply:
1. 13,446	2. 13,060	3. 15,615
4. 18,644	5. 1,139,450	6. 6,995,703
7. 30,674,562	8. 11,141,564	9. 65,985,898

IV. Divide:
1. 211	2. 76
3. 77	4. 45
5. 27	6. 238 R 42

V. Fractions. Add:
1. $11\frac{3}{4}$	2. $5\frac{1}{2}$	3. $40\frac{7}{8}$
4. $1\frac{5}{8}$	5. $6\frac{1}{4}$	6. $1\frac{5}{12}$
7. $7\frac{5}{8}$	8. $11\frac{5}{12}$	9. $13\frac{5}{8}$
10. $7\frac{11}{12}$	11. $7\frac{1}{3}$	12. $10\frac{9}{16}$

VI. Fractions. Subtract:
1. $\frac{5}{12}$	2. $1\frac{7}{12}$	3. $2\frac{1}{2}$
4. $1\frac{7}{16}$	5. $6\frac{7}{8}$	6. $5\frac{11}{12}$
7. $2\frac{3}{16}$	8. $6\frac{7}{16}$	9. $3\frac{1}{12}$
10. $5\frac{19}{20}$	11. $\frac{7}{16}$	12. $4\frac{2}{3}$
13. $2\frac{13}{16}$	14. $\frac{1}{12}$	15. $2\frac{9}{16}$

VII. Fractions. Multiply:
1. 34	2. 33	3. $\frac{4}{15}$
4. $2\frac{4}{9}$	5. $8\frac{2}{5}$	6. $\frac{8}{15}$
7. 68	8. 26	9. $\frac{1}{12}$
10. $6\frac{3}{8}$	11. $2\frac{2}{3}$	12. 3
13. $14\frac{2}{3}$	14. $46\frac{7}{8}$	15. $16\frac{13}{15}$
	16. 55	

VIII. Fractions. Multiply:
1. $63\frac{3}{4}$	2. $142\frac{1}{2}$	3. $97\frac{1}{2}$
4. $1,721\frac{1}{4}$	5. $217\frac{1}{3}$	6. $263,666\frac{2}{3}$
7. $388\frac{2}{3}$	8. $276\frac{5}{6}$	9. $16,970\frac{1}{9}$
10. 2,928	11. $22,970\frac{2}{5}$	12. 4697

IX. Fractions. Divide:
1. 7	2. 11	3. 32
4. 25	5. $3\frac{1}{3}$	6. $\frac{16}{25}$
7. 26	8. $\frac{3}{32}$	9. $1\frac{1}{4}$
10. $10\frac{2}{3}$	11. $\frac{4}{5}$	12. 12
13. $\frac{75}{148}$	14. $1\frac{71}{81}$	15. $1\frac{73}{75}$
	16. $2\frac{1}{6}$	

X. Decimals. Change to decimals from common fractions:
1. .50	8. .75	15. .40
2. .25	9. .20	16. .60
3. .80	10. .92	17. .167
4. .333	11. .143	18. .083
5. .0625	12. .666	19. .833
6. .583	13. .917	20. .6875
7. .125	14. .10	21. .111

XI. Decimals. Multiply:
1. 4.104	2. 7.6125	3. .7776
4. 1321.50	5. .006	6. 32,500

XII. Decimals. Divide:
1. 1.7	2. 17	3. 1.7
4. .17	5. 12	6. 120
7. .5	8. $12\frac{36}{47}$	9. $4\frac{6}{13}$
10. $2\frac{9}{23}$	11. $2\frac{19}{34}$	12. $3\frac{79}{87}$

XIII. Decimals. Watch the signs:
1. 5.	9. 33.516	17. .15
2. 3.8	10. .1	18. .9
3. 1000	11. 100	19. 60
4. $\frac{3}{20}$	12. .056	20. 102
5. .144	13. .0056	21. 63.18
6. 6.	14. 100	22. .1
7. 1,020	15. .12	23. .4
8. 1,020	16. .05	24. .001

XIV. Ratio. Express in fractions:
1. $\frac{1}{2}$	5. $\frac{1}{8}$	9. 4
2. $\frac{1}{3}$	6. $1\frac{1}{5}$	10. $\frac{7}{9}$
3. $\frac{1}{16}$	7. $\frac{1}{3}$	11. $\frac{1}{5}$
4. $\frac{1}{12}$	8. $\frac{1}{24}$	12. $1\frac{1}{3}$

XV. Ratio. Express in per cent:
1. 50%	4. 75%	7. 200%
2. 50%	5. 60%	8. $66\frac{2}{3}$%
3. 50%	6. $16\frac{2}{3}$%	9. 50%
	10. 25%	

XVI. Metric system:
1. .62	8. .25 per gal.
2. .62	9. 91.44 cm.
3. 3.64 liters	10. 4830 km.
4. 22 lb.	11. $1.76
5. 11 qt.	12. .45 kg.
6. 900 kg.	13. 18 cm.
7. at $1.50 per kg.	14. 30.5 cm.
	15. .3 m.

XVII. Per cent. Equivalents:

1. $\frac{1}{2}$	7. $\frac{1}{4}$	13. $\frac{3}{4}$	19. $\frac{1}{3}$
2. $\frac{1}{5}$	8. $\frac{3}{10}$	14. $\frac{2}{5}$	20. $\frac{3}{5}$
3. $\frac{2}{3}$	9. $\frac{7}{10}$	15. $\frac{1}{10}$	21. $\frac{4}{5}$
4. $\frac{1}{8}$	10. $\frac{3}{8}$	16. $\frac{5}{8}$	22. $\frac{7}{8}$
5. $\frac{1}{12}$	11. $\frac{1}{16}$	17. $\frac{1}{6}$	23. $\frac{3}{10}$
6. $1\frac{1}{2}$	12. $1\frac{1}{10}$	18. $1\frac{1}{4}$	24. 1

XVIII. Per cent to decimals:

1. .005	5. .0025	9. .0075	13. .0275
2. .004	6. .025	10. .002	14. .02875
3. 2.25	7. 3.50	11. 1.60	15. 3.25
4. .045	8. .0375	12. .0233	16. .085

XIX. Find per cent of:

1. 135	4. $12,000	7. $86.25
2. 280	5. 6.016	8. 9.92
3. 2100	6. $249.50	9. $25.88
	10. 1.974	

XX. Interest:

1. $37.19	6. $202.08
2. $17.50	7. $371.25
3. $236.25	8. $415.94
4. $63.00	9. $459.64
5. $106.40	10. $124.20

XXI. Find the total amount (if int. comp. annually):

1. $168.73	6. $706.99
2. $252.81	7. $803.82
3. $330.94	8. $1146.46
4. $425.42	9. $986.78
5. $478.60	10. $790.08

XXII. Find the value of N:

1. 6	5. 48	9. 7
2. 9	6. 4	10. 7
3. 22	7. 30	11. 343
4. 21	8. 30	12. 25

XXIII. Geometric facts:

1. 360	8. right
2. 180	9. equal
3. 90	10. right
4. acute	11. three equal sides
5. obtuse	12. two equal sides
6. right	13. 180°
7. parallel	14. 90°

XXIV. Area. A—Rectangles:

	Area	L	W
1.	1 square inch		
2.	4 square feet		
3.	9 square feet		
4.	6 square yards		
5.	5 square inches		
6.		2 inches	
7.			8 inches
8.	4 square feet		
9.	1 square yard		
10.	144 square inches		

B—Triangles:

	A	Height	Base
1.	$\frac{1}{2}$ square inch		
2.	1 square inch		
3.	1 square foot		
4.	3 square feet		
5.		4 inches	
6.	9 square feet		
7.	4 square centimeters		
8.			2 feet
9.	$2\frac{11}{32}$ square feet		
10.	60 square inches		

C—Circles:

1. 314 square inches	6. 18.086 square inches
2. 78.5 square inches	7. 40.69 square feet
3. 1256 square inches	8. 128.614 square feet
4. 3.14 square inches	9. 7.065 square feet
5. 226.865 square inches	10. 22.91 square feet

XXV. Volume:

1. 432 cubic inches	6. 2,304 cubic inches
2. 27 cubic feet	7. $10\frac{1}{2}$ cubic inches
3. 1,728 cubic inches	8. 54,000 cubic feet
4. 6 cubic feet	9. 567 cubic feet
5. 384 cubic inches	10. $56\frac{1}{4}$ cubic inches

XXVI. Business arithmetic:

A.

	Cost	Sell. Price	Overhead	Profit	Loss
1.			$ .75	$.25	
2.	$ .75				
3.			$ .30		
4.	$ 5.00		$3.00		
5.			$3.60		$3.60
6.	$100.				

B.

	Cost	Overhead	Profit	Sell. Price
1.				$181.82
2.				$384.62
3.	$140			
4.			20%	
5.		20%		

final arithmetic test | eighth grade

Write only your answers on this paper.

1. Subtract $28\frac{3}{4}$ from 50. _____

2. Change $\frac{4}{15}$ to a decimal correct to the *nearest hundredth*. _____

3. A steak weighed 2 pounds, 4 ounces. How much did it cost at $.92 per pound? _____

4. During his summer vacation a boy earned $4.50 per day and saved 60% of his earnings. If he worked 45 days, how much did he save during the vacation? _____

5. At an annual rate of $.40 per $100, what is the fire insurance premium for one year on a house that is insured for $8000? _____

6. A meter equals approximately 1.09 yards. How much longer, in *yards*, is a 100-meter dash than a 100-yard dash? _____

7. A train leaves New York City at 8:10 a.m. and arrives in Buffalo at 4:45 p.m. on the same day. How long, in hours and minutes, does it take the train to make the trip? _____

8. A jacket that was marked at $12.50 was sold for $10. What was the rate of discount on the marked price? _____

9. In the formula $S = 6e^2$, find the value of S when $e = 5$. _____

10. The area of a rectangular room is 1000 square feet. If the width of this room is 25 feet, what is the length of the room in feet? _____

11. Find the simple interest on $600 for one year at a yearly rate of 3½%. _____

12. A circular flower garden has a diameter of 21 feet. How many feet of fencing will be required to enclose this garden? _____

13. In a small community the town tax rate during a recent year was $27.80 per $1000 of the assessed valuation. The school tax rate was $20.30 per $1000 of the assessed valuation. A man's house, valued at $15,000, was assessed for 30% of its value.
    a What is the assessed valuation of the house? _____
    b What was the total amount the man paid that year in town and school taxes? _____

14. A girl works in a dress shop where her salary is $25 a week. In addition, she receives a commission of 4% on all sales she makes each week over $250. Her sales for one week amounted to $635 and for the next week, $850. What were her total earnings for this two-week period? _____

15. A boy had some hens as a project in his 4-H club. The expenses of caring for the hens, including food, averaged $4.20 a week. He collected an average of 24 eggs per day.
    a Find the cost of caring for the hens for 18 weeks _____
    b If the boy sold the eggs at an average price of $.50 a dozen, find his total profit during the 18-week period. _____

16. A farmer harvested potatoes from a rectangular field that was 32 rods long and 45 rods wide. This field produced an average of 360 bushels to the acre, and the potatoes were sold for $1.20 a bushel.
    a How many acres were there in this field? [Use 160 sq. rd. = 1 acre.] _____
    b How much did the farmer receive for the potatoes harvested from this field? _____
    c What was the average income *per acre* from this field? _____

These questions appeared on a New York State Regents examination.

17. Name each of the figures below.

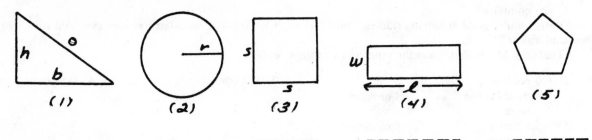

(1)   (2)   (3)   (4)   (5)

— — — —   — — — —   — — — —   — — — — —   — — — —

18. Referring to the figures above, write the formula needed to find the
a area of figure 2
b perimeter of figure 3
c area of figure 4
d ratio of h to b in figure 1
e length of o in figure 1

19. The graphs below were published by the federal government to show where the tax dollar comes from and where it goes. (1956)

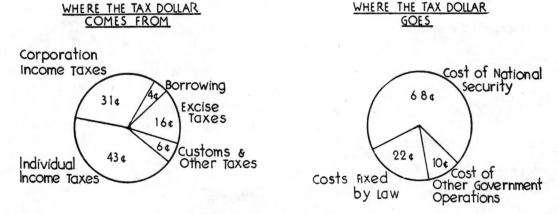

WHERE THE TAX DOLLAR COMES FROM

Corporation Income Taxes
31¢
Borrowing 4¢
Excise Taxes 16¢
Customs & Other Taxes 6¢
Individual Income Taxes 43¢

WHERE THE TAX DOLLAR GOES

Cost of National Security 68¢
Costs Fixed by Law 22¢
Cost of Other Government Operations 10¢

Use the graphs above to answer the following questions:
a What per cent of the federal tax dollar was spent on national security?
b What per cent *more* money was obtained from individual income taxes than from corporation income taxes?
c How many dollars, of every million dollars collected in taxes, were obtained from excise taxes?
d List the *four* sources of income whose total approximately equals the amount spent for national security.

20. Jim deposited $200 in a savings account. The bank paid interest at the rate of 4%. How much did he have in his account at the end of the third year? (Interest in savings banks is compounded semi-annually.)

1. (20 points)

"Betty, you're good at solving riddles," said Susan. "Can you tell me what has four eyes and runs two thousand miles?"

"Thats the Mississippi," was the other girl's prompt reply.

2. (20 points)

Word Underlined	Correction
were	was
frequent	frequently
became	become
wore	worn
was	were
them	those
day's	days
went	gone
⎰wouldn't	would
or	
⎱never	ever
took	taken

3. (20 points)

a 2
b 3
c 3
d 2
e 1
f 2
g 2
h 1
i 2
j 1

4. (15 points)

a 1
b 2
c 4
d 1
e 3
f 2
g 1
h 3
i 2
j 3
k 5
l 4
m 2
n 3
o 5

5. Diagrams (25 points)

1.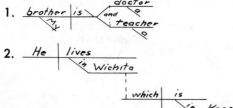

2.

3.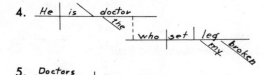

4.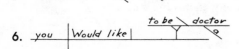

5.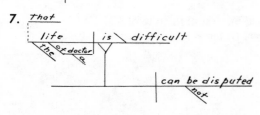

6.

7.

8.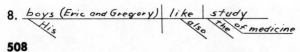

9.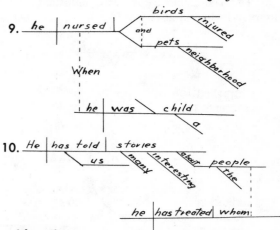

10.

arithmetic

(5 points for each complete answer)

1. $21\frac{1}{4}$
2. .27
3. $2.07
4. $121.50
5. $32
6. 9 (or 9 yds.)
7. 8 hr. 35 min.
8. 20%
9. 150
10. 40 (or 40 ft.)
11. $21
12. 66 (or 66 ft.)
13. a $4500
   b $216.45
14. $89.40
15. a $75.60
   b $50.40
16. a 9
   b $3888
   c $432

17. (1) triangle
   (2) circle
   (3) square
   (4) rectangle
   (5) pentagon
18. a $A = \pi r^2$
   b $P = 4s$
   c $A = lw$
   d $n/b = r$
   e $0 = \sqrt{h^2 + b^2}$
19. a 68%
   b 12%
   c $160,000
   d borrowing,
     excise taxes,
     customs and other taxes,
     individual income taxes
20. $225.23

FINAL TEST ON "NEW MATH."

Choose the correct answer and write it on the blank space provided.

(400, 4000, 400,000)   1. $10 \times 10 \times 10 \times 10 \times 10 \times 4 = $ _____

($=$, $<$)   2. {A, B, C} _____ {A, B, C}

($\neq$, $=$)   3. {4, 5, 6} _____ {6, 5, 4}

($=$, $\sim$)   4. {A, B} _____ {C, D}

($>$, $<$)   5. 2^3 _____ 3^2

($\cup$, $\subset$, $\cap$)   6. {A, B, C, D} = {A, B} _____ {C, D}

($\cup$, $\subset$, $\cap$)   7. {A, C} _____ {A, B, C, D}

({A}, {A, B}, {A, C})   8. {A, B, C} $\cap$ {A, D, C} = _____

($\cup$, $\subset$)   9. {vowels} _____ {letters of the alphabet}

(empty, disjoint)   10. Sets with no common elements are _____ .

(symbol, idea)   11. A number is a/an _____ .

(ratio, difference)   12. A rational number shows _____ .

(sum, grouping, order)   13. Associativity means _____ .

(prime, composite)   14. 7 is a _____ number.

(prime, composite)   15. 23 is a _____ number.

(prime, composite)   16. 81 is a _____ number.

(five, four)   17. There are _____ digits in the base five number system.

(47_{five}, 102_{five}, 51_{five})   18. $44_{five} + 3_{five} = $ _____ .

(322_{five}, 332_{five})   19. $43_{five} \times 4_{five} = $ _____ .

(21_{five}, 201_{five})   20. $11 = $ _____ $_{five}$.

(1, 2, 3, 4, 5, 6, 7, 8, 9)   21. __, __, __, __, __ are prime numbers.

(associative, commutative)   22. $4 \times 2 = 2 \times 4$ shows the _____ principle of multiplication.

(distributive, closure)   23. $6 + 4 = 10$ shows the _____ principle.

(addition, multiplication)   24. shows _____ .

(division, multiplication)   25. shows _____ .

answers to test on "new math."

1. 400,000
2. $=$
3. $\doteq$
4. $\sim$
5. $<$
6. $\cup$
7. $\subset$
8. A, C
9. $\subset$
10. disjoint
11. an idea
12. ratio
13. grouping
14. prime
15. prime
16. composite
17. five
18. 102_{five}
19. 332_{five}
20. 21_{five}
21. 1, 2, 3, 5, 7
22. commutative
23. closure
24. addition
25. multiplication

TABLE OF MEASUREMENTS

LINEAR MEASURE
12 inches (in.) = 1 foot (ft.)
3 feet = 36 inches = 1 yard (yd.)
5½ yards = 16½ feet = 1 rod (rd.)
320 rods = 5,280 feet = 1 mile (mi.)

SQUARE MEASURE
144 square inches (sq. in.) = 1 square foot (sq. ft.)
9 square feet = 1 square yard (sq. yd.)
30¼ square yards = 1 square rod (sq. rd.)
160 square rods = 1 acre (A.)
640 acres = 1 square mile (sq. mi.)
An acre = 4,840 square yards = 43,560 square feet

CUBIC MEASURE (volume)
1,728 cubic inches (cu. in.) = 1 cubic foot (cu. ft.)
27 cubic feet = 1 cubic yard (cu. yd.)
128 cubic feet = 1 cord of wood (at 4 ft. lengths)

TIME
60 seconds (sec.) = 1 minute (min.)
60 minutes = 1 hour (hr.)
24 hours = 1 day (da.)
7 days = 1 week (wk.)
30 days = 1 month (mo.)
12 months = 1 year (yr.)
365 days = 1 year
366 days = 1 leap year
10 years = 1 decade
100 years = 1 century

DRY MEASURE
2 pints (pt.) = 1 quart (qt.)
8 quarts = 1 peck (pk.)
4 pecks = 1 bushel (bu.)

LIQUID MEASURE
2 cups = 1 pint
2 pints = 1 quart
4 quarts = 1 gallon (gal.)

WEIGHT MEASURE
16 ounces (oz.) = 1 pound (lb.)
100 pounds = 1 hundredweight (cwt.)
2,000 pounds = 1 ton (T.)
2,240 pounds = 1 long ton

COUNTING MEASURE
12 things = 1 dozen (doz.)
20 things = 1 score
12 dozen = 1 gross
12 gross = 1 great gross

METRIC UNITS of LENGTH
10 millimeters (mm.) = 1 centimeter (cm.)
10 centimeters = 1 decimeter (dm.)
10 decimeters = 1 meter (m.)

CONVENIENT METRIC EQUIVALENTS
A kilometer is about ⅝ of a mile (.62)
A meter is about 39.37 inches
A kilogram is about 2.2 pounds
A liter is about 1.1 quarts

MEASURES of ANGLES and ARCS
60 seconds = 1 minute
60 minutes = 1 degree (1°)
360 degrees (of an arc) = a circumference
360 degrees (of an angle) = a complete rotation
90 degrees = a right angle
180 degrees = a straight angle
An acute angle is *less* than a right angle
An obtuse angle is greater than 90 degrees but less than 180 degrees